Ox[ford University Pre]ss

De[...]vice

By [...] *ifornia, Berkeley*

How[...]ral control, be made to
opera[...]ner addresses the question [...]round of the American
publi[...]the domination of the
publi[...]public service. This is
the f[...]Democracy, edited by
Rosc[...]

1968[...] paper $2.25

Th[...]
STA[...]

Edi[...] WALTER DEAN
BU[...]
1967[...] paper $2.50

Fr[...]
CIV[...]ATES

By [...]*lvania*
1967[...] paper $2.50

British Cabinet Government

By KARL LOEWENSTEIN, *Amherst College. Translated from the German by* ROGER EVANS

1967   224 pp.   paper $2.50

The Politics of Science:
READINGS IN SCIENCE, TECHNOLOGY, AND GOVERNMENT

Edited by WILLIAM R. NELSON, *United States Air Force Academy*

1968   500 pp.   paper $3.95

Basic Documents In International Law

Edited by IAN BROWNLIE, *Wadham College, Oxford*

1967   168 pp.   cloth $4.00   paper $2.50

♔ OXFORD ♔ UNIVERSITY ♔ PRESS
200 Madison Avenue, New York, N.Y. 10016

Kindly mention THE ANNALS *when writing to advertisers*

Kindly mention THE ANNALS *when writing to advertisers*

VOLUME 376

MARCH 1968

THE ANNALS

of The American Academy *of* Political
and Social Science

THORSTEN SELLIN, *Editor*
RICHARD D. LAMBERT, *Associate Editor*

SEX AND THE CONTEMPORARY
AMERICAN SCENE

Special Editor of this Volume

EDWARD SAGARIN
Assistant Professor of Sociology
City College of New York

PHILADELPHIA

© 1968, by THE AMERICAN ACADEMY OF POLITICAL AND SOCIAL SCIENCE
All rights reserved

Library of Congress Catalog Card Number: 68-21995

24833

Issued bimonthly by The American Academy of Political and Social Science at Prince and Lemon Sts., Lancaster, Pennsylvania 17604. Cost per year $10.00 paper-bound; $14.00 clothbound. Second-class postage paid at Lancaster and at additional mailing offices.

Editorial and Business Office, 3937 Chestnut Street, Philadelphia, Pennsylvania 19104.

CONTENTS

iii

BOOK DEPARTMENT

EUROPEAN GOVERNMENT AND HISTORY

ASIA AND AFRICA

SOCIOLOGY

PHILOSOPHY AND EDUCATION

The articles appearing in THE ANNALS are indexed in the *Reader's Guide to Periodical Literature*, the *Book Review Index*, and the *Public Affairs Information Service Bulletin*.

Taking Stock of Studies of Sex

By Edward Sagarin

ABSTRACT: Scientific studies of sexual behavior have proliferated during recent decades. One period of research was ushered in by Freud; a second, by Kinsey; and perhaps a third is being innovated by Masters and Johnson. Four major problems, that demand solutions at this stage of research, are cited. They include the ethical problem of the effect of research on the subject, the ideological one of researchers' biases, the social one of the effects of the sexual revolution on behavior and on human fulfillment, and the normative one of the establishment of guideposts for sexual activity in a world in which sex and procreation are but slightly related.

Edward Sagarin, Ph.D., New York City, Assistant Professor of Sociology, City College of New York, has previously taught at Brooklyn College, New York University, and Pratt Institute. Dr. Sagarin is contributor to and book review editor of Salmagundi, author of The Anatomy of Dirty Words (1962), and coauthor (with Albert Ellis) of Nymphomania (1964) and The Liberal Parent's Guide to Sex Education (1968). He is presently engaged in a study of voluntary associations of stigmatized and deviant people.

THE scientific investigation into any field of human activity proceeds by spurts and then slows to a leisurely pace —goes forward with sudden proliferation of research and publications, followed by a seeming lag in interest, while the main efforts of scholars are focused elsewhere. Science has its fads and its vogues, its seminal figures who produce followers as well as imitators, its ideological motivations which cause a concentration of attention in one area while leaving another untouched by research, and its political associations which bring money, prestige, and personnel to a field that had hitherto been left to a lonely and struggling researcher.

Before Freud and some of his contemporaries (particularly Havelock Ellis, Hirschfeld, Forel, Bloch, and even, one might add, Bertrand Russell), the literature on sex was meager. It was primarily confined to the theologians and moralists, with their antisexual biases, and to the belletrists, the poets and romancers whose literary forms, save for the most outspoken and pornographic, concealed but slightly their prosexual predilections. Before Freud, here and there, a medical man would discover sex: such a person was Richard von Krafft-Ebing; and until only recently, "all the best parts" were still in Latin.

Before Kinsey, the scientific study of things sexual was largely the domain of the investigators of the mind, a term meant to encompass psychiatrists, psychoanalysts, and psychologists. As clinicians, these people studied primarily the aberrant, the abnormal, the sick; and although Freud had warned that one looks at the abnormal the better to understand the normal, his warning could be ignored so long as the fundamental dichotomy between the perverse and the rest of humanity remained unquestioned.

Kinsey ushered in at least three new phases of sex research. First, he counted; he talked to the average Joe Smith who works on Main Street, to the normal and decent everyday person who lives next door (or in our own home?), to determine who, what, when, where, and how often. This did not exhaust the questions, for he seldom asked why. Then, he discovered for sexuality what was known in almost all other fields of investigation, namely, that phenomena can frequently be better understood as existing on a continuum, rather than as mutually exclusive polarities. Finally, as is now obvious in retrospect, Kinsey ushered in the era of respectability in sex research. Now one could ask who, what, and when, and one could even obtain government funds and foundation grants. Suddenly, scientific journals offered to print reports, and university departments consented to accept the material for doctoral dissertations.

The growing respectability was accompanied by moments of doubt. Frightened principals and even university deans often vetoed questionnaires and demanded that work not be done in their schools. "Not that *we* object," they hastened to add, "for we know it's research, but parents are so narrow-minded, and what would the alumni say!" Furthermore, scholars beginning to specialize in the field would find that colleagues looked on them a little peculiarly. "He's only interested in sex!" they began to say. To which one might reply, "Do you make the same objections when a man has been devoting all his research to race relations, or organization theory, or even alcoholism?"

So sex research was given a great new impetus. An untapped (shall we say virgin?) field opened up, and scholars could feel that their work in this area was respectable as well as useful. From 1948, when the first Kinsey report appeared, to the present, there has been a proliferation of research and publications on sexual behavior—its many pathways and byways, all so rich from a quantitative viewpoint—that it far outstrips rival fields of investigation in this age of research and the information explosion. After Kinsey, everything could be investigated, everything could be counted and analyzed, and almost nothing was unprintable. The ultimate seemed to have been reached when a colleague (here unnamed) informed me that he was preparing to do a participant-observation study of "wife-swapping."

Perhaps we are at the beginning of a third era, also to be innovated by one or two dynamic figures. It is too early to predict, but it is not unlikely that writers a few years hence will see a difference in kind between the work initiated before the mid-1960's and that initiated after and, when describing the various phases of sex research, will start one of their sections: "Before Masters and Johnson. . . ." Are we arriving at the terminus of the period when we determine the percentage of men from various socioeconomic groups and various religions and educational levels who have premarital experiences with prostitutes, just as once before we put aside, without entirely abandoning, the preoccupation with unconscious symbols that these men may have brought to such experiences? Are we now about to synthesize the psychic meanings, the sociocultural ones, and the biological capacities into a more generalized frame of reference for the understanding of human sexuality? If the key word, after Kinsey, was *behavior*, is it now to become *response*?

More research into sexuality is taking place at this moment in America than ever before in the history of this country, and the impact of that statement is not seriously lessened when we realize that the same is true of research into many other kinds of human activity.

Today, the work proceeds with such rapidity that specialists are developing within the specialty: there are those whose chief interests are in illegitimacy, pornography, or abortion, for example.

It might, then, be a propitious moment to take inventory, to decide what is in stock and what is required; but it is an inventory being taken, to prolong the metaphor, while the store is filled with customers and the counters and displays are being rapidly rearranged. In presenting this issue of THE ANNALS, the first in its history devoted to the theme of sexuality in the contemporary American setting, we are offering an abbreviated summary of a few highlights, as viewed by a small number of scholars, authorities, and specialists in this field. If their orientations are frequently divergent, this is a reflection of the state of the art; and if there are lacunae herein, this is a reflection of the large number of areas involved in a study of sex behavior, of which we could touch but a few. These are, we hope, the highlights.

PROBLEMS TO BE SOLVED

At the present moment, it would seem to this writer that there are some problems fundamental to further research into sex behavior which should be met by those engaged in this research. Some of these are methodological, some ethical, some conceptual. I suggest:

First, attention should be focused on the effect of research on the subjects of that research. In reviewing a book by John Seeley, Bennett Berger writes:

Research necessarily intervenes in the social processes it attempts to study, and it irrevocably alters both the student and his subjects. Moreover, sociological research and analysis inevitably damage the objects of their study, both in the general Wordsworthian sense that dissection kills, and in the more specific sense that fragile things, used to the dark, can only be injured by exposure to the bright glare of research.[1]

Perhaps some readers would challenge the words *damage* and *injure*, and insist on retaining the already employed *alter*. Many would claim that research into the lives of ghetto-educated children does not, or at least need not, damage and injure them. But researchers into sexuality have hitherto avoided this delicate subject, and have been content to dismiss with a scoff any suggestion that either the people directly interrogated, or others who identify with their problems, might have been hurt by Kinsey and the many who came after him. Milton Rokeach, whose work went far beyond questioning and came closer to manipulation, answered the ethical problem for himself by deciding that his patients (all long-term inmates of a mental institution, suffering from schizophrenic-paranoiac delusions) could only benefit, and not be further harmed, by his research activities.[2]

Sexuality, already in so delicate a balance for so many people, cannot be analogous to a condition where the subjects were considered to have "little to lose and, hopefully, a good deal to gain."

Nevertheless, the social scientist who faces this problem is caught in a bind. How can he answer the question of whether or not some investigations into human sexuality are injurious to the subjects (as well as to others), unless he researches the problem? And, if he researches the problem and arrives at the affirmative conclusion that such

studies can and do bring about damage, has he not compounded this damage by performing such research on the problem?

THE QUESTION OF IDEOLOGY

Second, researchers should study the question of the ideological bias that seems to enter into a great deal of research on human sexuality. There is evidence that much of the research is being undertaken by people who have answers before they arrive at the data, and who either arrange the data to provide the desired answers or interpret the material in such a manner that the expected answers will be forthcoming.

The sources of ideological bias in human sexual research are many, and they can be isolated without even entering into the recesses of the unconscious. Religious and other antisexual prejudices may hamper the researcher, imposing on his work a value system based on the acceptance of monogamous heterosexual relations, or, at the least, sex-love relations. Underdog ideological bias may push the researcher toward seeing something healthy and normal, natural and self-fulfilling, in many types of deviant acts, because they are performed by people who are unfairly oppressed by the society. Those imbued with antireligious and antipuritanical biases may find personal and social harm in all restrictive moral codes that act to limit the freedom of two or more individuals to act sexually without fear of social sanction. The researcher may have a personal-psychological bias toward finding certain pursuits socially harmless and personally fulfilling, because he is himself driven toward such acts, and is looking toward his studies for self-justification and for the bolstering of his own ego needs. On the other hand, there may be a reverse type of bias, that motivates another researcher

---

[1] Bennett M. Berger, Review of *The Americanization of the Unconscious,* by John Seeley, *American Sociological Review,* Vol. 32 (October 1967), p. 823. The quotation is from Berger, not Seeley, but in content it seems to express the viewpoint of both.

[2] Milton Rokeach: *The Three Christs of Ypsilanti: A Psychological Study* (London: Arthur Barker, 1964). See particularly pp. 198–199.

to condemn activities toward which he is driven, because of self-hate or because of the cleansing and cathartic effects of self-castigation.

How can biases of this type be located, and how can they be overcome? Are they present in sex research to a greater extent than in other types of social-psychological studies? What forms do they take? The task of investigating research bias is formidable, and has thus far been almost totally ignored.

Third, what can be done to discover the effects of the sex revolution (and surely there is agreement that there has been a revolution, at least in communication about sex) on behavior and on fulfillment of human needs? Is there, for example, more masturbation today among adolescents than a generation ago, or is this activity merely more readily admitted? And, whatever the answer to these questions, is such masturbation less frequently accompanied by shame, guilt, and remorse? Has the open discussion of homosexuality resulted in an increase of this type of activity? Has such increase resulted from other aspects of the social system (family structure, urbanism, geographic mobility) or is the increase purely illusory, resulting from a little more of the iceberg coming above the water level? These are but a few questions for which answers have not been forthcoming, and which center around a more basic problem, namely, the effect of the sex revolution on changes in the character, quantity, and quality of behavior.

Fourth, what normative frames of reference can be expected, believed in by large masses of people, and followed, in a society which no longer requires that people be fruitful and multiply, in which the people have adequate methods for the control of pregnancy, and in which the possibility of injury to voluntary participants in a sexual encounter (in the form of venereal disease) can be diminished to the vanishing point? Will monogamy, fidelity, and the union of sex with love become anachronisms? Will the prohibition on adult-child sexuality and on incestuous relationships be thrown overboard as part of a heritage that is no longer meaningful in a not-too-brave but very new world?

In other words, what are the philosophical-ethical-moral-psychological precepts that will emerge and be meaningful in a world that re-examines sexuality after some two thousand or more years of fears and inhibitions, of rituals and myths? Without procreation, with its fears and desires and its human and social needs, where is sex? What is it?

Thus, one could continue. The problems are many, they are difficult, but they are not insoluble. The contributions in this book are a beginning of the process of taking stock. Sex will, no doubt, survive in the fast-changing society; we hope that research will, as well.

The Decline and Fall of the Double Standard

By Erwin O. Smigel and Rita Seiden *

ABSTRACT: The limited available information on premarital, heterosexual behavior of young people in the United States reveals that the changes in sexual behavior which took place in the 1920's have changed only slightly in the 1960's, and that this slow change is continuing. The belief that a gradual transformation is taking place (except in overtness) rests on a comparison of the early studies on sexual behavior, the data from attitudinal studies, researched from 1940 to 1963, and observations of the current scene. Conclusion: the double standard is declining but has not yet fallen.

Erwin O. Smigel, Ph.D., is Professor of Sociology and Head of the Department of Sociology at New York University. He is author of The Wall Street Lawyer (1964), editor of Work And Leisure (1963), and a former editor of the sociological journal, Social Problems.

Rita Seiden, New York City, is a graduate assistant in the Department of Sociology at New York University.

* The authors wish to acknowledge gratefully the criticisms and suggestions of Martha Crossen Gillmor, Irwin Goffman, and Edward Sagarin.

TO find meaningful correlations,[1] especially in a pluralistic society, between the multitude of social forces and sexual behavior is difficult; to determine these correlations accurately, when appropriate data on sexual behavior are not available, is impossible. Nonetheless, it is our assignment to examine these social forces in order to see what effect they have had on sexual behavior and attitudes—specifically on sexual behavior and attitudes of unmarried heterosexuals of college age and younger in the United States.

Most recent examinations of sexual behavior still cite Kinsey's data[2] (1938–1949) and/or Terman's[3] (1934–1935). No one has published a Kinsey-type study for the United States in the 1960's. However, a few limited studies[4]

on premarital sexual behavior have been completed since Kinsey published *The Human Male* in 1948. The various studies of college students show percentages of premarital coitus for males and females which range from 54:35 in 1929;[5] 51:25 in 1938;[6] to 56:25 in 1951;[7] and, in 1953, 68:47, 41:9, or 63:14, depending on whose figures are accepted.[8] The most recent examination of sexual behavior puts the rate of college female premarital experience at 22 per cent.[9] This is consistent with Kinsey's findings that 20 per cent of all college women had had premarital intercourse.[10]

Most of the studies of sex completed after Kinsey's main works appeared have been limited to collecting statistics on attitudes. The most extensive of these studies, for which data was collected through 1963, was conducted by Ira Reiss, on sexual permissiveness.[11] Reiss's findings point to a coming together of sexual practices, and, for the young at least, of attitudes about sex. He found definite movement away from the orthodox double standard toward a standard of permissiveness with affec-

---

[1] It is understood that even if it were possible to determine these correlations accurately, we would not have an explanation of causation.

[2] Alfred C. Kinsey, Wardell B. Pomeroy, Clyde E. Martin, Paul Gebhard *et al.*, *Sexual Behavior in the Human Female* (Philadelphia: W. B. Saunders, 1953). The data on the female subjects were collected from 1938 through 1949. Alfred C. Kinsey, Wardell B. Pomeroy, and Clyde E. Martin, *Sexual Behavior in the Human Male* (Philadelphia: W. B. Saunders, 1948). Data on the male subjects were collected from 1938 to 1947.

[3] Lewis M. Terman *et al.*, *Psychological Factors in Marital Happiness* (New York: McGraw-Hill, 1938).

[4] Gilbert Youth Research, "How Wild Are College Students?," *Pageant*, Vol. 7 (1951), pp. 10–21, Ernest W. Burgess and Paul Wallin, *Engagement and Marriage* (Chicago: J. P. Lippincott, 1953); Judson T. Landis and Mary Landis, *Building a Successful Marriage* (3rd ed. rev.; Englewood Cliffs, N.J.: Prentice-Hall, 1957); Winston Ehrmann, *Premarital Dating Behavior* (New York: Henry Holt, 1959); Mervin B. Freedman, "The Sexual Behavior of American College Women: An Empirical Study and an Historical Study," *Merrill-Palmer Quarterly*, Vol. 2 (1965), pp. 33–48; Ira L. Reiss, *The Social Context of Premarital Sexual Permissiveness* (New York: Holt, Rinehart and Winston, 1967), chap. vii. Reiss's primary purpose was not to examine behavior (at least not in this latest presentation); he

was interested in attitudes. He asked 268 students (42 of them males) in an Iowa college about their behavior. What he did was to correlate expressed feelings of guilt with behavior, and found relationships with age and behavior and relationships between expressed standards and behavior. The Institute for Sex Research at Indiana University conducted a 1967 study of sex behavior among college students, but the final results have not as yet been published.

[5] Gilbert V. Hamilton, *A Research in Marriage* (1st ed., New York: Albert and Charles Boni, 1929; 2nd ed., New York: Lear, 1948), p. 348.

[6] D. D. Bromley and F. H. Britten, *Youth and Sex* (New York: Harper, 1938), p. 36.

[7] Gilbert Youth Research, *op. cit.*, p. 15.

[8] Burgess and Wallin, *op. cit.*, p. 330; Landis and Landis, *op. cit.*, pp. 216 and 212; Ehrmann, *op. cit.*, pp. 33–34 and p. 46.

[9] Freedman, *op. cit.*, p. 47.

[10] Kinsey, *The Human Female*, p. 288.

[11] Reiss, *op. cit.*

tion (shorthand for "premarital sex is acceptable when there is mutual affection between the partners").

The earlier statistics of Kinsey and Terman point up important differences in sexual behavior between the generation of women born before 1900 and the generation born in the following decade. Kinsey found that 73.4 per cent of women born before 1900 had had no premarital intercourse, but among those born between 1900 and 1909, only 48.7 per cent had been virgins at marriage. The figures for those born in the 1920–1929 generation are the same—48.8 per cent.[12] Terman's findings are essentially in agreement. The statistics for both the Kinsey and Terman studies referred to here are for women of all ages, and not just for college women.[13] Terman found that 74 per cent of the females born between 1890 and 1899 had had no premarital intercourse, whereas among those born between 1900 and 1909, the percentage of virgin brides had dropped to 51.2. His figures reveal that this trend also held for men: of those interviewees born between 1890 and 1899, 41.9 per cent had had no premarital coitus,

whereas of the interviewees born in the next generation, 32.6 per cent had had no such premarital experience.[14] Clearly, the major change in sex practices occurred in the generation born in the decade 1900–1909, which came to sexual age during or immediately after World War I, a period characterized by marked social change and innovation.

It may well be true that changes in sexual behavior and attitudes are related to the social changes which began in the late nineteenth century and accelerated rapidly over the past 67 years. It is not as clear, except perhaps for the post-World War I years, exactly what the effects of these social changes have been on sexual behavior. Reiss argues that, despite popular belief to the contrary, "the sexual revolution [is] a myth and the only basic change [is] a trend toward more equality between the sexes. . . . There has been less change than [is] popularly believed between modern American males and their Victorian grandfathers."[15]

It is generally thought, however, that

[12] Ira L. Reiss, "Standards of Sexual Behavior," in Albert Ellis and Albert Abarbanel (eds.), Encyclopedia of Sex (New York: Hawthorne Books, 1961), p. 999. "These data were based on Kinsey (1953), but were especially prepared for [Reiss's] paper . . . [by] Drs. Gebhard and Martin of the Institute of Sex Research. These were based on 2,479 women who either were or had been married by the time of the interview."

[13] Confirming this change are data reported by K. B. Davis, Factors in the Sex Life of Twenty-two Hundred Women (New York: Harper, 1929), p. 232. Of those women who attended college in the early 1900's (that is, were born before 1900), only 7 per cent had premarital intercourse. According to Bromley and Britten, loc. cit., 25 per cent of the college women of the 1930's had premarital intercourse. And according to Freedman, op. cit., p. 45: "The rate of premarital nonvirginity tripled from 1900 to 1930."

[14] Terman, op. cit., p. 321; Kinsey, The Human Male, p. 395. Kinsey noted generational differences within his male sample; but the "generations" were formed by dividing his subjects into "younger" (under 33 years of age at the time of the interview) and "older" (over 33 years of age at the time interviewed) groups. He did not compare them by decade of birth as he did the women. The median age of the younger group was 21.2 years, that is, born approximately between 1917 and 1926. The median age of the older group was 43.1 years, that is, born approximately between 1895 and 1904 (Kinsey, The Human Female, chap. vii). Information is provided here that premarital petting had increased with each generation since 1920 even though incidence of premarital coitus had not. One of the possible explanations for the continued relatively high number of virgins is that heavy petting is now very common, so that there are a large number of "technical" virgins who engage in almost everything except coitus.

[15] "Iowa Sociologist Calls Sex Revolution A Myth," New York Times, October 22, 1967, Section I, p. 80.

the late-nineteenth-century break with Victorian morality was a tangential result of the Industrial Revolution, urban migration, war, the feminist movement, and the scientific study of once-taboo topics. Wilbert Moore, a leading authority on social change, credited industrialization with certain effects on the social structure;[16] and it is our opinion that industrialization affected sex attitudes and behavior as well. He specified increased social and geographic mobility; growth of industrial centers with concomitant concentration of population in urban areas; emphasis on rationality as a necessary part of an industrialized society (for example, a lessening of the influence of religion); transition from extended (rurally located) families to nuclear (urban) families; emphasis on individualism resulting from the breakdown[17] of the extended kinship system; decreased family size accompanied by a decline in the economic significance of the family unit as the unit of survival; and, finally, increased education.

Each of these general effects of social change can be shown, at least theoretically, to have potential impact on sexual behavior and attitudes. As the population moves from small towns and intimate personal relationships to urban centers, old forms of social control break down. This disintegration and the accompanying anonymity is speeded by new and faster forms of transportation which further increase the possibilities of anonymity and independence. A rational society affects the individual's world view, and he tends to see his own life in terms of more rational standards. As the extended kinship system dissolves or loses its importance, mate-selection processes become a more personal responsibility, and increase the importance of peer group norms, which take precedence over family norms. In the evolving industrial society, women take a new and larger part in the working world, thereby securing greater independence for themselves and increased equality in male-female relationships. The general increase in education has made possible widespread dissemination of sex information to the public.

In sum, the family has declined in importance as the unit upon which or around which society is organized, and individualism, in relationship to the family, is in the ascendency. As individualism has grown, sexual behavior has become more a personal matter and is less exclusively influenced by family and procreational considerations.

The complex social changes discussed have been gradual, but the impact of war can be immediate and abrupt. This is clearly indicated in the data on sexual behavior during and immediately after World War I. In any war, the mores governing family life tend to decay. Removed from some of the responsibilities, restrictions, and supports of the family, removed from the all-seeing eye of the small town or the neighborhood, soldiers are suddenly subject only to the mostly approving observations of their fellow soldiers. In the face of death or the possibility of being severely wounded, hedonism becomes the prevailing attitude. This attitude appears to be contagious and spreads to the civilian population. In World War I, it particularly affected the young women who were working in factories, taking on

[16] Wilbert E. Moore, *Social Change* (Englewood Cliffs, N.J.: Prentice-Hall, 1963), pp. 100–103.

[17] In a recent article, Thomas K. Burch casts doubt on whether there has indeed been a breakdown of the extended family or a decline in the size of the family because of urbanization. See Thomas K. Burch, "The Size and Structure of Families: A Comparative Analysis of Census Data," *American Sociological Review*, Vol. 32 (1967), pp. 347–363. We feel, however, that there can be little doubt about the relation between urbanization and changes in function and meaning of the family.

roles and responsibilities that had once belonged exclusively to men, often for the first time living alone in relative anonymity, and in many instances emotionally involved with men who were scheduled to be sent overseas. (This same hedonistic philosophy may be held by contemporary young people who are faced with the dangers of limited wars and the always present possibility of extinction by nuclear explosion.)

Many soldiers had contact with prostitutes and contracted venereal diseases. The United States Interdepartmental Social Hygiene Board reports: "Between September, 1917, and February 14, 1919, there were over 222,000 cases of venereal disease in the army and there were over 60,000 in the navy." [18] Venereal disease and the prostitute taught the soldier more about sex in his relatively short career in the armed services than he might normally have learned. The incidence of venereal disease was so high that it became a matter of both private and official army talk. The consequence was that most soldiers left the service knowing not only the protective effects but also the birth control uses of prophylactic sheaths. This kind of sex education became a standard part of the army curriculum.

The soldier who went abroad had new sexual experiences and came in contact with women whose behavior derived from different and more permissive sex norms; the returned veteran brought back with him sexual attitudes shaped by these new norms. Although they were not consciously intended for his mother, sister, wife, or wife-to-be, they tended to affect them as well.

War also tends to spread industrialization and to extend the need for women in industry, and, in turn, to increase their economic independence. The war and wartime experiences intensified the gradual way in which industrialization was changing the social structure.

War, industrialization, and an increase in political democracy seem to have led to the struggle for equal rights for women. The nineteenth-century feminists, who fought for financial and social rights and by 1920 had been enfranchised, were now also demanding more sexual freedom. Margaret Sanger, an American housewife, was a leader in this war. She waged a courageous battle for the control of pregnancy, and she was brought to trial for making birth control information available to interested persons. It was the trial, the wide publicity she received, and her persistence which helped to acquaint the public with the possibilities of birth control. She and other fighters for female sexual freedom were supported by a backdrop of the new norms of the returning soldiers, the effects of economic gains for women, and an increase in the scientific study of sex.

Although Krafft-Ebing,[19] Havelock Ellis,[20] and others were writing about sex pathology and sexuality, Freud's writings about the unconscious and the effect of sex on personality had the most influence upon American behavior and attitudes. Although *Studies in Hysteria,* written by Freud and Breuer, which made these ideas available to the public, was published in 1895, "it was not until after the war that the Freudian gospel began to circulate to a marked extent

[18] T. A. Storey, "The Work of the United States Interdepartmental Social Hygiene Board" (New York: United States Interdepartmental Social Hygiene Board, 1920), p. 6.

[19] *Psychopathia Sexualis,* the best known work of Krafft-Ebing, was originally published in German in 1886. The first English translation was published shortly thereafter.

[20] *The Psychology of Sex,* which represents Ellis' main body of work, was published in English in six separate volumes from 1900 to 1910 by F. A. Davis, Philadelphia. Volumes I and II had appeared in French (1897) before they appeared in English.

among the American reading public." [21] No one can estimate what popularization of psychoanalytic theory has done to free individuals—particularly women —from the puritan anxieties about sex. The fact of its influence, however, cannot be doubted. These studies by the sexologists and those by the sociologists, anthropologists, and psychologists studying and writing in the late 1920's and early 1930's provided the setting for the public acceptance of Kinsey's impressive work—which may in turn have had great influence on a society already impatient with Victorian sex mores. In any event, studies of sex were being undertaken, and they provided information about taboo topics which helped to free the average individual from the restraint against serious discussion of sexual behavior. Each generation of sex researchers has extended the study and broadened the understanding of sex, from Kinsey's counting of sexual outlets in the 1940's to Masters and Johnson's detailed study of human sexual response[22] in the early 1960's.

In addition to those factors already described, which have affected so many aspects of the social structure, other elements, although less powerful forces for general change, have also contributed to the alteration of sexual mores in a more immediate sense. Cultural interchange resulting from wartime contact since World War I and from the great increase in travel has led to a broadened participation with other societies. Furthermore, the disappearance of the chaperon undoubtedly created opportunities for sexual freedom which are not subject to the social sanctions of one's own society. The availability

of the automobile, the affluent society which permits young people to live apart from their parents, and the growth of community size made privacy much more accessible. There has been a virtual removal of "fear-evoking" deterrents with the development of effective contraceptive devices.

All of these factors seem to be related to the change in sexual practices and to the apparent liberalization of sexual standards reflected in Reiss's data.[23] Since these social forces are still operating in the same direction, we should also expect to see changes in the direction of permissive sexual attitudes and behavior to continue.

The data we have on sexual behavior are limited; but more data are available on attitudes.

The research statistics are analyzed in Tables 1, 2, 3, and 4.[24]

Reiss's later data, collected in 1959 and 1963,[25] confirm the trends evidenced

[21] Frederick Lewis Allen, *Only Yesterday: An Informal History of the Nineteen-Twenties* (New York: Blue Ribbon Books, 1932), p. 98.

[22] William H. Masters and Virginia E. Johnson, *Human Sexual Response* (Boston: Little, Brown, 1966).

[23] Ira L. Reiss, *Premarital Sexual Standards in America* (New York: Free Press of Glencoe, 1960), pp. 219–221.

[24] These tables are rearranged in chronological order and condensed for our purposes from the ones appearing in Reiss, *The Social Context of Premarital Sexual Permissiveness*, pp. 16–18. The categories used by L. Rockwood and M. Ford in their (1940) study of Cornell students, *Youth, Marriage, and Parenthood* (New York: John Wiley and Sons, 1945), p. 40, were used for classifying the data of the other studies. The 1947 and 1952–1955 studies were made by J. T. Landis and M. Landis and reported in *Building a Successful Marriage*, p. 215. Their categories were: "Sexual Relations: For both, None for either, For men only, Between engaged only." The 1958 study by Ehrmann, *op. cit.*, p. 189, used the standards: "Double (comparable to Sex Relations for men only), Conservative single (Abstinence), General liberal single (Sex Relations for both), and Lover liberal single (Sex Relations for those engaged or in love)" as categories.

[25] Reiss, *The Social Context of Premarital Sexual Permissiveness*, pp. 25–27, Tables 2.5, 2.6, and 2.7. The reverse double standard category has been omitted, for Reiss says that

TABLE 1—ATTITUDES TOWARD PREMARITAL INTERCOURSE (IN PERCENTAGES)

APPROVE OF	1940 Cornell[a]			1947 Michigan State University[b]			1952–1955 11 Colleges[b]			1958 University of Florida[c]		
	M	F	Total	M	F	Total	M	F	Total	M	F	Total
1. Sex Relations for both	15	6	9	16	2		20	5		42	7	25
2. Abstinence	49	76	65	59	76		52	65		20	86	52
3. Sex relations for men only	23	11	16	10	15		12	23		33	0	17
4. Sex relations for engaged/in love	11	6	8	15	7		16	7		5	7	6
(N)	(73)	(100)	(173)			(2000)			(3000)	(45)	(42)	(87)

[a] Percentages are based on N of 173, but 3 per cent (1 per cent male, 2 per cent female) did not answer the question. The total per cent appearing in Reiss is 101; therefore, ours totals 98.

[b] Separate N's for the male and female samples were not given; therefore, it was not possible to compute total percentage advocating each standard.

[c] Total percentages were not shown by Reiss and were computed by the authors of this article.

in the findings of the earlier studies (see Table 2).

We can probably safely conclude from these data:

(1) Abstinence and permissiveness with affection are the favored standards for both males and females.

(2) There has been a rise in female approval of permissiveness with affection and a decline in approval of the abstinence standard.

(3) Permissiveness without affection, if we consider it comparable to a blanket endorsement of casual sex relations for both, is apparently on the decline—even more sharply for men than for women.

(4) The orthodox double standard is

this "response is almost certainly an error." For his discussion of this point, see *ibid.*, p. 24. Reverse double standard adherents are understood to believe that women should have greater sexual freedom than men. Percentage accepting this standard were: 1959—9 per cent male, 6 per cent female, 7 per cent total; 1963—0 per cent male, 5 per cent female, 4 per cent total.

also on the decline if we compare the Table 1 data (sex relations for men only) with the Table 2 data (orthodox double standard).

(5) The percentage of men who favor permissiveness with affection has increased markedly while the female endorsement remains about the same. The redistribution of women's attitudes seems to be away from abstinence and the orthodox double standard toward greater endorsement of the transitional double standard—coitus is all right for men under any condition, but is acceptable for women only if they are in love. Therefore, while women still endorse abstinence more highly than other standards, they are coming to favor sexual relations in the context of affection. Reiss's 1963 data support the 1959 evidence which indicates an increasingly favorable attitude on the part of females[26] toward sex with affection.

[26] *Ibid.*, p. 128. The data for males have not been utilized because the men represent only a small percentage of the total number of cases in the sample.

TABLE 2—PERCENTAGE[a] ACCEPTING
EACH STANDARD

STANDARD	1959[c]		
	Male	Female	Total
Permissiveness with affection	24	15	19
Permissiveness without affection	13	2	7
Abstinence	28	55	42
Orthodox double standard	9	13	11
Transitional double standard[b]	18	10	14
N =	(386)	(435)	(821)

[a] Percentages of adherents to the reversed double standard have been omitted. Therefore, totals do not equal 100 per cent.

[b] Transitional double standard means that sex relations are considered all right for men under any condition, but are acceptable for women only if they are in love.

[c] The 1959 sample was drawn from the student populations of five schools: two Virginia colleges (one Negro, one white); two Virginia high schools (one Negro, one white); and one New York college.

Eighteen per cent favor permissiveness with affection; one per cent endorse permissiveness without affection; 56 per cent support abstinence. The percentage endorsing the transitional double standard was not given.[27]

(6) Succinctly: The percentage of

[27] Reiss reported 20 per cent of the females endorsing the double standard, but did not break down the figure to show the percentage accepting the orthodox standard nor the percentage accepting the traditional standard.

both men and women who accept increased permissiveness with affection as their standard has increased (see Table 3).

Since the 1947, 1952–1955, and 1959 studies used the largest number of subjects and employed somewhat more rigorous sampling techniques, they are probably more reliable indicators of the trend in these attitudes. They strongly support the assumption that there has been an important change in attitudes toward sex in the direction of permissiveness.

In explaining the differences between statistics on sexual behavior and statistics on attitudes (namely, that behavior seems to have changed little since the 1920's, but attitudes have become more liberal), Reiss suggests that we are seeing a "consolidation process" taking place, that is, "a change in attitudes to match the change in behavior" is occurring.[28] Nelson Foote cites a variety of evidence which, he claims, indicates the decline of the double standard: decline in prostitution, increasingly equal sexual opportunities and experiences for women, increase in orgasm in marital sex relations, "the steady approach to equivalence of male and female premarital petting and marital sex play techniques," the increase of extramarital coitus, decreasing insistence on virginity in females at marriage, and "some decline in frequency of marital

[28] Reiss, *Premarital Sexual Permissiveness in America*, p. 233.

TABLE 3—PERCENTAGE ACCEPTING THE STANDARD

SEX RELATIONS FOR ENGAGED/IN LOVE	1940		1947		1952–1955		1958		1959[a]		1963[a]	
	M	F	M	F	M	F	M	F	M	F	M	F
	11	6	15	7	16	7	5	7	24	15	[b]	18

[a] We are considering Reiss's "permissiveness with affection" as equivalent to "sex relations for engaged/in love."

[b] Figure for men has been omitted as total number of male interviews is a small proportion of the total sample.

coitus implying more mutual consent and less unilateral demand." [29]

Finally, in line with both Reiss's and Foote's arguments that there is a trend toward a new single standard of permissiveness with affection, Robert Bell suggests that for young adults, sex becomes acceptable today when the couple feels they are in love. Peer group members accept and approve of sex without marriage, but not of sex without love.[30]

For the unmarried, there is an increasing tendency to reject marriage as the arbitrary dividing line between "socially approved and socially disapproved sexual intimacy." [31] And in the same way that male and female roles have become more equal in other areas of life, greater equality has come to the area of sexual relations: "fair play has been replacing chastity as the badge of honor in the interpersonal relations of the sexes." [32]

The results of the various studies of attitudes show two particularly interesting and possibly related findings:

First, there has been an increase in permissive attitudes toward sex since the 1940's. This may be due to the accumulating reforming influence of those social factors which was operating in the twentieth century. Certainly, the changed attitude shows itself sharply in the increase in sexual content of movies, the candid use of sexual lures in advertising, an increasing social sanctioning (if not precisely approval) of sexual material in popular literature, and a generally freer atmosphere which permits open talk about sex. But the new standard for coital involvement insists on permissiveness with affection.

[29] Nelson N. Foote, "Sex As Play," *Social Problems,* Vol. 1 (1964), p. 161.
[30] Robert Bell, "Parent-Child Conflict in Sexual Values," *Journal of Social Issues,* Vol. 22 (1966), pp. 38–39.
[31] *Ibid.,* p. 43.
[32] Foote, *op. cit.,* p. 161.

Second, the parent generation (sampled in 1963 by Reiss) is far more conservative than the younger generation —and is apparently more conservative than it was when it was the younger generation. In Reiss's 1963 adult sample, only 17 per cent endorsed permissiveness with affection for males and only 5 per cent endorsed this standard for females.[33]

Apparently, the conservative parent generation refuse to endorse for their children standards of behavior in which members of their generation, and perhaps they themselves, engaged. What appears to be a "generation gap," however, is probably a manifestation of a change in role.[34] Reiss's data on his adult sample give a concise picture of the relationship between role position and attitudes.

TABLE 4—"MARITAL AND FAMILY STATUS AND PERMISSIVENESS IN THE ADULT SAMPLE"[a]

MARITAL AND FAMILY STATUS	PER CENT PERMISSIVE	N
Single	44	(108)
Married		
No Children	23	(124)
All Preteen	22	(384)
Preteen and Older	17	(218)
All Teen and Older	13	(376)

[a] Reiss, *The Social Context of Premarital Sexual Permissiveness,* p. 142, Table 9.2 (some data omitted).

Permissiveness evidently reaches its highest point on one curve (for the college student) while it reaches its lowest point on another curve (for the parents of the college student). What the data describe, then, are changes which occur as individuals come to occupy parental role positions, and they are not descriptive of differences between individuals of the post-World

[33] Reiss, *The Social Context of Premarital Sexual Permissiveness,* p. 142. From Table 2.7.
[34] *Ibid.,* pp. 140–143, and Bell, *op. cit.,* pp. 38–39.

War II generation and their parents' generation.

In part, this information suggests that parents try to modify behavior in their children in which they themselves participated as young adults. This reaction may portend how the current young adult generation will feel when they are parents themselves. However, the qualification to be noted here is that the generation which came to maturity in the 1920's broke with previous generations in terms of behavior. The following generations continued in the same kind of practices but gradually came to express more liberal attitudes. The new liberalism of the younger generation may very well contribute to a shift in expressed adult values for the parent generations of the late 1960's and 1970's.

We know that sexual attitudes have changed and that sexual standards appear to be in a period of transition. "What was done by a female in 1925 acting as a rebel and a deviant can be done by a female in 1965 as a conformist." [35]

Data based on a large sample are available on sex behavior up to 1949 and on attitudes up to 1963. We do not know what has happened during the last five years or what is happening now. The general public impression is that there has been a very recent sexual revolution and that it is still going on. Most researchers do not believe that this is the case. The authors of this article, as social observers and recent reviewers of the literature on sexual behavior and attitudes toward sex, will attempt to "crystal ball" what has occurred during the last five years and what is occurring now. What follows, then, is not fact, but guess.

Past trends in social change, in behavior, and in attitudes toward sex are continuing. What seems to be taking place (except for pockets of our society) is a growing tendency toward more sexual permissiveness among the young unmarried. Sex with affection appears to be increasingly accepted. More and more this norm is based on personal choice, and it manifests itself for middle-class college youth in the form of trial marriage, for the girl, and for the boy at least as a stable, monogamous relationship, to the point of setting up housekeeping. Increasingly, this happens with parental knowledge though not necessarily with parental approval. If Kinsey repeated his study today, he would probably find premarital virginity slightly lower and figures for those who have had premarital intercourse only with their spouse, a circumstance which was already on the increase in 1947 (born before 1900, 10.4 per cent; born 1920–1929, 27.3 per cent),[36] somewhat higher.

Promiscuity, a word objected to by many young people, probably has lessened. Certainly the use of prostitutes has diminished. If we are correct in believing that more young people are living monogamously together, and if marriage for both men and women (the figures are: median age of first marriages in 1890 for brides was 22.0 and for grooms was 26.1;[37] for 1966, the median age for brides was 20.5 and for grooms 22.8[38]) is occurring at earlier

[35] Reiss, "The Sexual Renaissance: A Summary and Analysis," *Journal of Social Issues,* Vol. 22 (1966), p. 126.

[36] Reiss, "Standards of Sexual Behavior," *loc. cit.*

[37] U.S., Department of Health, Education, and Welfare, *Vital Statistics: National Summaries,* Vol. 50, 28 (November 1959). Source: U.S., Department of Commerce, Bureau of the Census, "Population Characteristics," *Current Population Reports,* Series P–20, 105–3.

[38] U.S., Bureau of the Census, *Statistical Abstracts of the United States, 1967* (88th ed.; Washington, D.C.: U.S. Government Printing Office, 1967), Table 75: "Median Age at First Marriage, by Sex: 1920–1966." Source: U.S., Department of Commerce,

ages, then the statistical probabilities of premarital promiscuity have lessened, except when it is a reflection of mental illness. Today, except for the "hippies," who, according to the press, indulge in group sex, promiscuity as a form of rebellion is significantly on the decline.

We are living in a much more permissive society, and we are much more vocal about sex. As Walter Lippman put it, even as early as 1929: "It was impossible to know whether increased openness about sex reflected more promiscuity or less hypocrisy." [39] While we do not have much new evidence concerning sexual behavior, we do have nonsystematic overt indications about attitudes. It is seen in advertisements which are much more suggestive than they used to be. At one time, an advertiser would indicate to a male reader that, if he used a certain product, a pretty girl would kiss him. Now the ads suggest that she will have intercourse with him: "When an Avis girl winks at you she means business," and as Chateau Martin asks, leering only slightly, "Had any lately? " Movies have become less suggestive and more obvious; nudity as well as intercourse have become not uncommon sights. The Scandinavian picture, *I, A Woman,* for example, consists of a number of seductions with a number of different men. Perhaps what is more significant is that censorship boards, the courts, and power groups in this country have sharply amended their definitions of obscenity. The theater has, for some time, been more open about sex and its various ramifications, and four-letter words are becoming a theatrical cliché.

Bureau of the Census, *Current Population Reports,* Series P–20, No. 159.

[39] Walter Lippman, *A Preface to Morals* (New York: The Macmillan Company, 1939; originally published in 1929; Beacon edition, 1960), p. 228.

Another indicator of this generation's expressed attitudes toward sex are the omnipresent buttons, which express not only political, but also sexual opinions. The buttons are designed for fun and shock, and for public declaration for sexual freedom. Sold in large cities all over this country, they range from simple position-statements such as "Make Love Not War," "I'm For Sexual Freedom," or "Equality for Homosexuals," to inviations which read "Roommate Wanted," "Join the Sexual Revolution—Come Home With Me Tonight," to such shock jokes as "Phallic Symbols Arise," "Stand Up For S-X," and "Come Together."

More sophisticated young people feel that the dirty-word movements or the shock words no longer have any impact. In the October 26, 1967, *Washington Square Journal,* a New York University publication, the student reviewer of an off-Broadway production, *The Beard,* which freely uses four-letter words and ends with an act of cunnilingus on stage, says: "Unfortunately the force of the play rests on the anticipated violation of social taboo, and violating social taboos just isn't what it used to be."

Except for the rediscovered poor, the United States is a society of unprecedented abundance. Upper- and middle-class white Americans pamper their children, give them cars and money, send them to college and abroad, and set them up in their own apartments while they are going to school. These young people have leisure and the wherewithal to use it in amusing themselves—only the war is real, which gives a special significance to college as a way of avoiding the war. This abundance means that college-age men and women can travel together, live together, and have a sex life encouraged by their peers, whose opinions they have now come to value more than those of their elders.

Abundance for the young unmarrieds in the city has made it possible to meet other young unmarrieds in new ways. Apartment houses are being built for them; clubs are formed for them, but perhaps the most significant of all the developments is the use of bars, now often called pubs, which serve as meeting places where singles can meet without prejudice. A girl who visits the pub is under no obligation to "go to bed" with the man whom she meets and with whom she may leave. These pubs (and they begin to specialize in different kinds of singles), in a sense, institutionalize a system of bringing together like-minded people; they speed the dating and the trial-and-error process, for they offer this particular group of affluent young people a wide variety of partners to choose from, and they can choose quickly, independently, and frequently.[40]

Many observers of the current scene consider the "pill" the most significant single force for increased sexual freedom. A count of the articles listed in the Reader's Guide to Periodical Literature reveals that more articles were published about birth control in the period March 1965 to February 1966 than were listed in a ten-year sampling starting with 1925 and ending with 1957. The sampling yielded 89 titles. But we doubt that the pill has added materially to the increase in the numbers of young adults or adolescents who have had premarital sex. Effective techniques of birth control existed, and were used, before the pill. True, the pill makes birth control easier to manage (except for the memory requirement), but romantic love is still im-portant; it makes taking the pill, when no definite partner is available, undesirable. What the pill does is to give sexual freedom to those who are having steady sexual relationships, for then the use of the pill adds to romantic love by making elaborate preparations unnecessary.

According to our crystal ball, which, of course, may be clouded, we have not had a recent or current sexual revolution in terms of behavior. However, there probably has been some increase in the proportion of women who have had premarital intercourse. It is our guess that the increase has occurred largely among women who have had premarital sex only with their spouses-to-be. If there has been a sexual revolution (similar to the 1920's but ideologically different[41]), it is in terms of frankness about sex and the freedom to discuss it. Women have demanded and have achieved more education, more independence, and more social rights; one of these is the right to choose a partner for sex. Men are accepting many of these changes in the status of women and are tempering their insistence on what have generally been considered male prerogatives, for example, the right to demand that a bride be a virgin. Young men today are probably less promiscuous and more monogamous, and their relationships tend to be more stable. Both sexes are approaching a single standard based on sex with affection. We are still in a stage of transition. Despite the title of this article, the only indisputable conclusion which we can draw from the current scene is that we are witnessing the decline, but not yet the fall, of the double standard.

---

[40] For an interesting comment on this phenomenon see "The Pleasures and Pain of the Single Life," Time, September 15, 1967, pp. 26–27.

[41] See Bennett M. Berger, "The New Morality," Unpublished paper, read at the Plenary Session of the Society for the Study of Social Problems, August 27, 1967.

The Beige Epoch: Depolarization of Sex Roles in America

By CHARLES WINICK

ABSTRACT: One of the most pervasive features of our cultural landscape is the depolarization of sex roles and a concomitant blurring of many other differences. The appearance, given names, and play of boys and girls have become less gender-specific since World War II. Young girls appear to be demonstrating the sexual precocity and aggressiveness once associated with boys. Clothing and appearance are steadily becoming increasingly ambisexual, along with recreational activities, work, and family roles. Extremes of taste in food and drink are less common. Blandness also characterizes the color and shape of home interiors and the exteriors of many buildings. Opera, theatre, musical theatre, and movies have been dominated by women in recent decades although male stars once were the major audience attractions. Our rapid industrialization and World War II are among the contributors to depolarization, and the trend may have some ominous implications for the future.

Charles Winick, Ph.D., New York City, is Professor of Sociology at the City University of New York. He has been Director of Research of the New York State Joint Legislative Commission on Narcotics and of the Anti-Defamation League and has conducted many studies of factors which are modifying social and sex roles. He has also taught at the Massachusetts Institute of Technology, Columbia University, and the University of Rochester.

PERHAPS the most significant and visible aspect of the contemporary American sexual scene is the tremendous decline, since World War II, in sexual dimorphism. Sex roles have become substantially neutered and environmental differences, increasingly blurred.

Our Age of the Neuter begins to leave its mark on young people in their very tender years. Gender-linked colors like pink and blue for children's clothing are yielding to green, yellow, and other colors which can be used for either Dick or Jane. Such names, however, are less likely nowadays. A study of a large sample of given names reported in birth announcements in the *New York Times* from 1948 to 1963 concluded that almost one-fifth of them were not gender-specific, for example, Leslie, Robin, Tracy, Dana, Lynn, although the 1923–1938 period had few such names.[1] Since the name helps to position a person in his culture, many young people are starting out with an ambisexual given name.

The hair of little girls is shorter and that of little boys is longer, and such blurring is given fashionable designations, that is, the Oliver or Beatle haircut. Other kinds of his-hers appearances are chic for young people. Boys and girls may have similar toys, and the last few years have witnessed the popularity of dolls for boys (G.I. Joe and his many imitators).

Reading habits of young people are less related to gender than they were a generation ago. Both sexes are likely to enjoy the same books, for example, *The Moon Spinners* and *Island of the Blue Dolphins,* and there is less interest in books which are clearly sex-linked, like the *Nancy Drew* series for girls or the *Hardy Boys* for boys. School curricula are offering fewer subjects which

[1] Charles Winick, *The New People: Desexualization in American Life* (New York: Pegasus, 1968), chap. vi.

are unique to each sex, and both sexes learn some subjects, for example, typing.

THE TEEN-AGER

Dating behavior of teen-agers reflects the crossing over of sex roles which pervades so much of the preadolescent years. The teen-age girl increasingly is looking for her own satisfaction and may want to be even more equal than her date. Such tendencies have become more important since the 1950's, which experienced the first movie about a sexually aggressive teenager (*Susan Slept Here*, 1954), an extraordinarily successful novel about a sexually sophisticated girl (*Lolita*, 1958), and, perhaps most important, a series of very popular mannequin dolls, beginning with Betsy McCall in 1954 and culminating in Barbie in 1959. Barbie is a sexy teen-ager, and playing with her involves changing costumes and thereby preparing for dates. During the last decade, an average of more than 6,000,000 mannequin dolls was sold each year.

The rehearsal for dating provided by Barbie and her imitators may even further accelerate the social development of their owners. By the time an owner is ready to engage in actual dating, she could be much more forward than her male companion. Studies of teen dating suggest that, not too long ago, the aggressiveness displayed by many contemporary teen-age girls was once found primarily in young men.[2]

So much time separated the nine-year-old with an old-fashioned baby doll from her role as mother that she could enjoy fantasies about motherhood and not be concerned about doing something about them. But the distance in years that separates a Barbie fan from

[2] Ira L. Reiss, "Sexual Codes in Teen-Age Culture," THE ANNALS, *American Academy of Political and Social Science*, Vol. 338 (November 1961), pp. 53–62.

a socially active ten- or eleven-year-old girl is slight, and she can easily translate doll-play fantasies into real social life. Barbie owners may be more ready than any previous generation to take the traditional male role in teen-age courtship behavior.

CLOTHING AND APPEARANCE

The most conspicuous example of sexual crisscrossing is provided by clothing and appearance, which are important, because the costume we wear reflects the customs by which we live. When World War II provided an urgent occasion for a re-evaluation of social roles, Rosie the Riveter, in slacks, became a national heroine. At the same time, many of the 14,000,000 men in uniform, who had a limited number of outlets for their money, began to buy fragrance-containing colognes, hair preparations, and after-shave lotion. Wearing the uniform probably helped to allay any fears that the products' users might be unmanly or were indulging themselves.

The most recent postwar impetus for men's fragrance products was the great success of Canoe in 1959. College men traveling abroad began to bring back the sweet and citrus-scented French cologne, used it for themselves—and gave it to their girl friends. The appetite of college students and teen-agers for strongly scented products in turn influenced their fathers, uncles, and older brothers.

Scent is a method of adornment by which a man of any age can unbutton his emotional self and attract attention, in frank recognition of women's growing freedom to pick and choose.[3] Very strong fragrances may have special appeal to men who are suffering from feel-

[3] Charles Winick, "Dear Sir or Madam, As the Case May Be," *Antioch Review,* Vol. 23 (Spring 1963), pp. 35–49.

ings of depersonalization. Just as anointing and incense helped to extend the body's boundaries and reach toward God, a man using a strong fragrance transcends his body's boundaries and creates a unified atmosphere that projects him toward people. Other men who are confused about their body-image may use zesty essences as one way of reassuring themselves, in our deodorized age, that their body is recognizable and has exudations. For these and other reasons, men in the Scented Sixties spend three times as much money on fragrance-containing preparations as women do.

With men smelling so sweet, it is small wonder that the constitutionality of the New York State statute prohibiting a man from wearing a woman's clothes was challenged in 1964 for the first time. Apparel may oft proclaim the man, but many bells are jangling out of tune in the current proclamation. Men are wearing colorful and rakishly epauleted sports jackets, iridescent fabrics, dickies, and bibbed and pleated shirts of fabrics like batiste and voile.

Men's trousers are slimmer and in many instances are worn over girdles of rubber and nylon. Ties are slender and often feminine. The old reliable gray fedora has given way to softer shapes and shades, sometimes topped by gay feathers. Sweaters are less likely to have the traditional V-neck than a boat neck adopted from women's fashions. Padded shoulders on a suit are as out of date as wide lapels and a tucked-in waist. The new look is the soft, slender, straight-line silhouette that also characterizes the shift, which has been the major woman's dress style of the 1960's. Men accessorize their clothes with cuff links, tie bars and tacks, bracelets, rings, and watch bands.

Loss of gender is especially conspicuous in shoes, with women wearing boots or low-heeled, squat, square-toed, and heavy shoes at the same time that men's footwear has become more pointed, slender, colorful, and high-heeled. Men have adopted low-cut and laceless models from women's styles.

A modishly dressed couple might be walking along with the woman in hip-length boots, "basic black" leather coat, a helmet, and a pants suit or straight-line dress of heavy fabric. Her male companion might be wearing a soft pastel sack suit, mauve hat, and a frilled and cuff-linked pink shirt. He could sport a delicate tie and jewelry, exude fragrance, and wear tapered shoes with stacked heels. Both could have shoulder-length hair, and their silhouettes would be quite indistinguishable.

RECREATION AND LEISURE

The couple might be on the way to visit a family billiard center or bowling alley, now that both recreations have become somewhat feminized and have abandoned their connotations of the spittoon. Women are participating in many other previously male recreational activities, especially outdoor sports and competitive athletics. They accounted for 30 per cent of our tennis players in 1946 but today represent 45 per cent. The proportion of women golfers has risen from one-tenth to more than one-third in the same period. The pre-World War II golf club, which did not permit women, has become the family-centered country club. Men's city clubs have also substantially abandoned their formerly exclusionist attitudes toward women.

Social dancing has become almost a misnomer for the self-centered, nonrelational dances which have succeeded the Twist since 1961 and have largely replaced traditional steps like the waltz and fox trot, in which the man led and the woman followed. In the Frug and Boogaloo and other current favorites, there is no leading or following. The man and woman do not even have to look at each other or start or finish together.

WORK AND THE HOME

We are so familiar with decreased resistance to the employment of women and their continually improving preparation for work that we may sometimes forget some implications of the trend. Well over one-third of our workers are women, and, every year, proportionately more married women enter the labor market. Over 2,300,000 women earn more than their husbands. Now that the United States is the first country in which the majority of jobs are in service industries, it has also become the first country where men may soon be competing for what were previously women's jobs.

Men are less and less likely to require physical strength on the job. They are also hardly likely to assume a traditional male role in the home. The husband must often take over household tasks that were once assigned to the wife. Over three-fifths assist in cooking. In many ways, the husband has become a part-time wife. As one result of this trend, initiative and aggressiveness may become less common in boys, who may have less opportunity to see their fathers functioning in either a traditional or masterful manner.

FOOD AND DRINK

As Talcott Parsons has so eloquently reminded us, the social structure constitutes a subtly interrelated and almost homeostatic series of interrelationships. At a time when the most basic difference in a society—between men and women—is dwindling, we might expect to find other differences becoming less significant. Extremes of taste sensation in food and drink have diminished as part of our culture's larger homogenization.

Blended whiskey's comparative lack of bouquet and flavor is probably the chief reason for its now accounting for over two-thirds of all domestic whiskey production. The most successful Scotches of the last fifteen years have all been brands which are light amber in color and possess a minimum of maltiness, smokiness, and body.

The dilution of distinguishing characteristics that is represented by "soft" whiskey and Scotch can be seen most dramatically in vodka, which jumped from one per cent of the 1952 domestic liquor market to 10 per cent in 1967. United States government regulations specify that it must be "without distinctive character, aroma or taste," so that its major appeal is a lack of the very qualities that traditionally make liquor attractive. Beer is also becoming "lighter" every year.

It would be logical to expect our great technological proficiency to have produced foods with an enormous range of taste, texture, and aroma. Yet our marriage of technology and convenience has led to wide acceptance of many foods with a blander and less explicit taste than in previous generations. Although access to more than 7,000 quick-preparation convenience items has exposed Americans to many new foods, the taste, aroma, and texture of such products tend to be more homogenized and less sharp than the fresh foods of earlier decades, as nonchemically treated fruits, home- or bakery-made bread, ethnic cooking, and many other contributors to strong taste experiences become less common.

INNER AND OUTER SPACE

In the Beige Epoch, color extremes are less welcome than they used to be.

Even cosmetics stress paleness. The muted appearance of no-color color makes an ideal of "the suddenly, startlingly candid new beauties" whose makeup "turns on the immensely touching *au courant* look of the untouched, nude complexion." [14]

Beige has become the single most popular color for home interiors, carpeting, telephones, draperies. At the same time, interiors are less likely to have the heavy furniture, dark colors, and coarsely grained dark woods generally linked with men or the delicate furniture, light colors, and finely grained light woods that are associated with women.

Rooms with gender may soon be subjects for archaeologists, as a result of the continuing displacement of rooms by areas that merge into one another. And with the near-disappearance of masculine (for example, the leather club model) or feminine (for example, the chaise longue) chairs, foam rubber has become the Space Age's upholstering of choice. It is neutral and has no "give," in contrast to traditional upholstering's indentations after someone has been sitting on it.

Our manipulation of outer space, via architecture, reflects the blurring of gender which also characterizes how we use furniture in the organization of inner space. Few clearly feminine (for example, the Taj Mahal) or masculine (for example, the Empire State Building) structures have been built during the last generation. When men and women wear the same straight-line silhouette and are surrounded by furniture which avoids protuberances or padding, it is hardly surprising that their buildings so literally resemble "filing cases for people," although Frank Lloyd Wright intended his famous description to be only a metaphor.

[4] *Harper's Bazaar,* No. 3041 (April 1965), p. 214.

Function is almost as difficult to identify as gender in many new buildings. Hotel, bank, air terminal, lobby, store, office, and restaurant may look alike and play the same monotonous canned music, which provides a seamless wallpaper of sound.

THE PERFORMING ARTS

Men began to lose their dominant chairs at the head of the formerly rectangular dinner table at just about the time that they were yielding the center spotlight in each of the major performing arts to women. Caruso was the dominant figure of the Golden Age of Opera, but Birgit Nilsson, Joan Sutherland, Renata Tebaldi, Leontyne Price, and Maria Callas are typical of the divas who completely overshadow the male singers opposite whom they appear.

When Actors Equity celebrated its fiftieth birthday in 1963 by enacting some representative episodes from the recent past, not one actor did a major scene.[5] Lillian Gish, Helen Hayes, and Beatrice Lillie were the stars of the evening, performing excerpts from *Our Town, Victoria Regina,* and *Charlot's Review,* respectively. The male matinee idol (E. H. Sothern, John Barrymore, Richard Mansfield, John Drew, Joseph Schildkraut) took his final bow some decades ago. It would be nearly impossible to make up a list of "first men" of the contemporary theatre, but women have dominated our stage for about forty years. Anne Bancroft, Geraldine Page, Kim Stanley, and Julie Harris are only a few younger current Broadway actresses who project characters with valid juices. Aggressive performers like Ethel Merman, Mary Martin, Barbra Streisand, Carol

Channing, and Julie Andrews star in musicals which feature male leads who are either innocuous or nonsingers and are puny successors to the male singers, dancers, and comedians who made the American musical our happiest export.

The interrelationships and mutual reinforcement among the mass media are so pronounced that we might expect women to have assumed much greater importance in movie roles since World War II. Death or retirement claimed Humphrey Bogart, Clark Gable, Spencer Tracy, William Powell, and other actors who shouldered through the "movie movies" of the 1930's. Actresses are now more important than ever before, and Doris Day has played more consecutive starring roles than any performer since talkies began forty years ago. Marilyn Monroe became an unforgettable symbol of the child-woman, and Elizabeth Taylor is not only the highest paid performer in history ($2 million plus for *Cleopatra*) but also the prototype of the devouring Medusa in her private life. As in the earlier case of Ingrid Bergman, Miss Taylor made the key decision to leave one man for another, and both men acquiesced.

One of the most significant changes in the post-World War II performing arts was the emergence in the 1950's of the pianist Liberace as television's first and only superstar who had the qualities of a matinee idol. Liberace was not a particularly distinguished pianist, and much of his appeal seems to lie in his ability to communicate many characteristics of a five- or six-year-old child, of either gender.[6] His extraordinary rise to fame as America's biggest single concert attraction, barely thirty years after the disappearance of the virile stage idol in form-fitting doublet and dashing skin-tight breeches,

[5] Paul Gardner, "3 of Stage's First Ladies Salute Actors Equity on 50th Birthday," *New York Times,* May 6, 1963.

[6] Charles Winick, "Fan Mail to Liberace," *Journal of Broadcasting,* Vol. 6 (Spring 1962), pp. 129–142.

is a striking commentary on changes in American fantasy needs.

WHY DEPOLARIZATION?

It would be possible to identify many other areas in which our society is manifesting a depolarization and bleaching of differences. Such neutering and role-blurring represent only one dimension in the dynamics of social change. It is possible that these trends necessarily develop in any society which becomes as highly industrialized as ours. There is reason to suspect that our acceptance of androgyny is, to some extent, one outcome of World War II. Studies of chidren from homes in which the father was absent during the war have suggested that many such children later exhibited considerable sex-role confusion.[7] Large numbers of such children could have been so affected by their fathers' absence and might be significantly represented in the ranks of today's young adults.

A fuller consideration of the conditions and factors producing neutering would include political, economic, technological, cultural, and demographic dimensions as well as rates of invention, acculturation, cultural diffusion, and resistance to change. Our no-war, no-peace situation also contributes to the situation, along with the blurring of categories in other fields.

The unique capacities of each sex are especially significant these days, when at least some quantitative aspects of a Great Society seem within reach. The emancipation of women and their greater equality and participation in the affairs of society were long overdue. But equality does not mean equivalence, and a difference is not a deficiency.

Multivalent, amorphous, and depolarized roles might theoretically lead to increased flexibility and options in behavior, but in actuality may tend to invoke uncertainty. Some tolerance of ambiguity is desirable for a healthy personality, but today's environment and culture are ambiguous enough to tax the adaptability of even the healthiest personalities.[8] The other extreme is represented by the completely polarized sex roles that we associate with the reactionary ideology of totalitarianism.

There is no evidence that any one kind of family structure is inherently healthier than any other, and history seems to suggest that almost any male-female role structure is viable, so long as there is clear division of labor and responsibilities. An equally important lesson of the past is that overly explicit roles can be pathogenic, because they do not permit the expression of individual differences or of a personal style. It is most disquieting to contemplate the possibility that the ambiguity of sex roles in our open society might ultimately prove to be almost as hazardous as the rigidities of authoritarianism.

---

[7] Lois M. Stolz, *Father Relations of War-born Children* (Palo Alto: Stanford University Press, 1951).

[8] T. W. Adorno, E. Frenkel-Brunswik, D. J. Levinson, and R. Nevitt Sanford, *The Authoritarian Personality* (New York: Harper, 1950), pp. 480–481.

Sex and Family Life*

By J. Richard Udry

ABSTRACT: Sex plays a fundamentally different role in the lives of women than it does in the lives of men. A partial explanation of this may be that men are sexually more conditionable by their environment. Men and women also attach different meanings to sex. Not only is sex a more important determinant in a man's decision to marry, but also it is a more important factor in his evaluation of his marriage. Sexual behavior and sexual values are derivative for women. Emotional factors are more responsible for a woman's satisfaction with her marriage. These factors are irrelevant, however, for the highly segregated marriages of the lower class. The role of parents in shaping the adult sexual behavior of their children is not clear. The only apparent, important considerations are their provision of the socioeconomic and religious backgrounds for the development of sexual attitudes and behavior.

J. Richard Udry, Ph.D., Chapel Hill, North Carolina, is Associate Professor of Sociology, and Associate Professor of Maternal and Child Health, at the University of North Carolina at Chapel Hill. He is the author of The Social Context of Marriage (1966), and a frequent contributor to sociological journals. He is presently engaged in research into the sociological aspects of human reproduction.

* The author has profited from comments by Hallowell Pope on an earlier draft of this paper.

SEX is not equally important in all cultures. Among the Gilyak, a Siberian hunting tribe, for example, the pursuit of erotic adventure was elaborated into a major activity of the group,[1] while among the Shakers, an American utopian religious group, separate living and eating quarters were provided for men and women, and sex as an activity (although not perhaps as a mental preoccupation) was virtually eliminated.[2] Likewise, the role which sex plays in marriage and family formation needs to be thought of as variable from one society to another and one time to another, depending on the structure and functions of the family in a particular setting.

In the United States in the twentieth century, the functions of the nuclear family (husband, wife, and children) have become more and more specialized to the realm of the emotional, with the family providing the major source of emotional security for adults and children during most of life. As other institutions in the community become more impersonal, the nuclear family has become almost emotionally explosive. Especially in the middle class, satisfaction of the basic subsistence needs are no longer problematical, and men and women have turned their concern to the emotional adjustment of their offspring and to the nuances of the marital relationship. There is both opportunity and competence for a man to be concerned about how he feels about the way his wife feels about the way he feels about her. This produces conditions for the "emotionalization" of sex in the marriage. As the sexual relationship becomes freighted with emotional

significance for the total marriage, it becomes a more complicated factor with greater potential for both the enhancement and the destruction of the marriage. Someone has said that Americans think sex is the most important thing in the world because they have never been hungry.

While these conditions prevail among the educated middle class, marriage in the lower-class and working-class American population does not fit this description. Here, kin and same-sex peers play a much more important role in the emotional lives of adults.[3] Nuclear family members expect less emotional involvement with one another, and at the same time are, by inclination and training, less competent to support one another emotionally. Subsistence needs in the lower class and economic security in the working class are significant concerns. This is not to say that lower-class Americans have fewer emotional needs, but only that the structure of the marriage does not make emotional gratification the focus of family functions.[4] Particularly in the lower-class, sex, rather than becoming an intimate part of the emotional structure of the marriage, tends to remain on the sensual level only.[5] The primary emotional significance of sex in the lower-class setting is oriented *away* from the marital relationship.[6] For the man, sexual conquest remains a way of validating one's masculinity to one's male friends. This serves to weaken the

[1] Chester S. Chard (trans. and ed.), "Sternberg's Materials on the Sexual Life of the Gilyak," *Anthropological Papers of the University of Alaska*, Vol. 10 (1961), pp. 13–23.

[2] Edward D. Andrews, *The People Called Shakers* (New York: Dover Publications, 1963).

[3] Joel I. Nelson, "Clique Contacts and Family Orientations," *American Sociological Review*, Vol. 31 (October 1966), pp. 663–672.

[4] Mirra Komarovsky, *Blue Collar Marriage* (New York: Random House, 1964).

[5] Lee Rainwater, "Some Aspects of Lower-Class Sexual Behavior, *Journal of Social Issues*, Vol. 22 (April 1966), pp. 96–108.

[6] William Simon and John H. Gagnon, "Heterosexuality and Homosociality: A Dilemma of the Lower-Class Family," (Bloomington: Institute for Sex Research, Indiana University, 1966). (Mimeographed.)

orientation of sex within marriage, since, as Simon and Gagnon point out, a man can only seduce his wife once.[7] For the lower-class woman, the emotional significance of sex is a source of "trouble." Sex tends to estrange rather than unite husband and wife.

EQUALITY OF THE SEXES

Americans are now in the process of integrating a tradition which legitimates the authority of men over women and adults over children with the newer values which emphasize the equality of men and women and the rights of children to be free from arbitrary authority. Since different rights are not commensurable (it is hard to measure career rights with the same yardstick as child-rearing rights), there is a general tendency for equality of the rights of the sexes to be transformed into similarity of rights and then to justify this similarity of rights in terms of similarity of needs. This has fostered the development of a belief that men and women are basically similar in their intellectual capacities and in their emotional and sexual needs. As might be expected, this belief system is far more prevalent in the middle class, and is not the prevailing belief among the less educated and the lower class.

In the middle class, then, men and women are believed to have equal rights to the enjoyment of marital sex. The operation of this norm can be seen in the results of research showing couples' preferred frequency of intercourse. In the Burgess-Wallin sample, for one couple in six, the wife reported a desired frequency which was higher than the husband reported for himself. In these couples, the wives reported a desired frequency averaging about twelve per month, and also reported about the same desired frequency for their husbands. These husbands reported a de-

[7] *Ibid.*

sired frequency averaging about six per month, and reported about the *same* desired frequency for their wives.[8] Evidently, the norm of equality works to prevent the couples from recognizing the wife's higher desire. In the case of those where the wife's desired frequency was lower than her husband's, both men and women correctly perceived this, but underestimated the difference in desired frequency.

The norm of sexual equality seems to require that the enjoyment should be not only equal, but of the same kind, and that therefore the sexual response patterns of the sexes should be similar. "Marriage manuals" (really books of instruction in sex techniques) directed toward couples teach that women should initiate intercourse as often as their husbands, that their passions should be equally intense, and that each should reach orgasm, preferably simultaneously. Many couples have come to believe that failure to experience this similarity is equally frustrating for each sex. Inability to carry out this pattern, it is generally believed, can be accounted for by the repressive socialization of the wife during childhood, or by the husband's ineptness at technique. Many couples seek professional assistance in their attempts to come up to the ideal of mutual sexual reciprocity. Many husbands feel guilty when they do not provide their wives with a full flowering of sexual passion. One husband commented:

I have a sense of guilt when I have relations with her and feel she doesn't enjoy

[8] Paul Wallin and Alexander Clark, "Cultural Norms and Husbands' and Wives' Reports of Their Marital Partners' Preferred Frequency of Coitus," *Sociometry*, Vol. 21 (September, 1958), pp. 247–254. Essentially the same findings were replicated by George Levinger, "Systematic Distortion in Spouses' Reports of Preferred and Actual Sexual Behavior," *Sociometry*, Vol. 29 (September 1966), pp. 291–299.

them as much as I do. The fact that she's not getting orgasm takes the pleasure of intercourse from me.[9]

Some wives in this situation develop practical techniques for dealing with the problem, as in the following report:

I have never had an orgasm. Of course my husband thinks I do. . . . I try to be as active in intercourse as I can. I fool him so I guess I am all right.[10]

Sexual relations in lower-class couples create different problems. The lower-class husband is likely to look upon sexiness in his wife as a drive which will make her untrustworthy, and lead her outside the marriage for her sex. Lower-class women, on the other hand, are much more likely to feel "used" in marital sex, think of sex as primarily "something men want." [11]

Careful scholars of human sexual behavior have come to recognize the behavior prescriptions above as a *belief* system rather than a description of actual sexual behavior. But belief systems affect the behavior of those who believe them because they become a standard against which to evaluate one's own experience. Actual marital sex, as revealed in a growing number of studies, shows considerable discrepancy from the beliefs of the middle class and the marriage manual. Men and women are really quite different in their sexuality, and this has been recognized by most societies.[12] Sex has different meanings for men and women. These differences in meaning probably derive from the different contexts in which men and women experience sexual learning.

THE CONTEXT OF MALE SEXUALITY

For most males, sex is a matter of considerable interest and involvement before they have any heterosexual experience. Sex is a big topic of conversation among boys, even before puberty. By age fifteen, 80 per cent of boys (compared to 20 per cent of girls) have already masturbated, and during adolescence it is an almost universal experience for boys.[13] In the context of the male youth group, sex has two general meanings. First, sex is fun—pleasure—pure visceral pleasure, not necessarily connected with females in any way. Second, sex is masculinity: masculine status is achieved through the sexual conquest of women. These orientations continue to be basic to the sexuality of males even after they have married. In later adolescence, middle-class males and some working-class males come to experience sex in the context of romantic love, and may come to see sex as one way of expressing love. But, for males, love arrives primarily in a sexual context.[14] In marriage as well as out, therefore, most men tend to think of sex as play, as a favorite form of recreation. It is surprising to note that serious researchers have rarely conceptualized sex as a form of play, to be engaged in for its own sake. Perhaps we have feared that if we admit sex as a legitimate form of play, it will lose its moral restraints and slip away from social control. Nelson Foote comments:

If so, the thinker does not understand the nature of play. For play—any kind of

[9] Ernest W. Burgess and Paul Wallin, *Engagement and Marriage* (Philadelphia: J. B. Lippincott, 1953), p. 671.

[10] Burgess and Wallin, *op. cit.*, p. 672.

[11] Lee Rainwater, "Marital Sexuality in Four Cultures of Poverty," *Journal of Marriage and the Family*, Vol. 26 (November 1964), pp. 457–466.

[12] Alfred C. Kinsey, Wardell B. Pomeroy, Clyde E. Martin, and Paul H. Gebhard, *Sexual Behavior in the Human Female* (Philadelphia: W. B. Saunders, 1953), pp. 642–689.

[13] Kinsey *et al., op. cit.*, p. 141; Alfred C. Kinsey, Wardell B. Pomeroy, and Clyde E. Martin, *Sexual Behavior in the Human Male* (Philadelphia: W. B. Saunders, 1948), p. 500.

[14] For an elaboration of this conceptualization, see J. Richard Udry, *The Social Context of Marriage* (Philadelphia: J. B. Lippincott, 1966), chap. iv.

play—generates its own morality and values. And the enforcement of the rules of play becomes the concern of every player, because without their observance, the play cannot continue; the spoilsport is sternly rejected.[15]

Sex games in marriage appeal to men, and they are always inventing new variations. (In this sense, the "marriage manual" may be more profitably thought of as a manual for games of sex, rather than as scientific writing.) "Seduction" is a favorite marital game because it tunes in on the "conquest" values men have associated with sex. Some prefer gymnastic games, while others enjoy the stimulation of "playing" on a different "court" for variety.

Few girls have any experience with deliberate sexual stimulation until puberty, and masturbatory behavior is infrequent and sporadic among adolescent girls.[16] The context of sexuality in the young female group associates sex first with having babies and later with being in love. Girls tend first to think of men as love objects, and of sex as an expression of that love.

SEXUAL DIFFERENCES IN THE SEXES

Other differences in sexuality add to the differences built into the socialization process. It now seems clear that the basic difference in biology which causes differences in sexual behavior of males and females is that males' sexual responses are more easily conditionable than those of females. This means that each sexual experience of the male tends to affect his subsequent sexual behavior more than is the case for females. By this sexual conditioning, males come to live in an environment which is sexually stimulating, and are therefore propelled

to seek sexual activities.[17] Females, being less stimulated by the environment, do not usually seek sexual activities, but rather respond sexually to the approaches of males. Thus, the initiation of sexual encounters by males needs to be seen as more than a culture pattern.

The foregoing explanation of differences should in no way be interpreted to mean that females do not enjoy sexual encounters. Kephart has captured the meaning:

But enjoyment or responsiveness during coitus is not necessarily an index of sex drive. A woman who has been sexually responsive during coitus may have no specific afterthoughts of sex or desires for sexual intercourse for a period of weeks, or months, or even longer. Extended periods without coitus may well have no adverse effects. In short, although she actively enjoys coitus *when it occurs,* her sexual needs remain low as compared with most men.[18]

THE PLACE OF SEX IN HUMAN RELATIONSHIPS

Prevailing values in America today require that sex take place only within love relationships, between partners who are emotionally attached and interpersonally committed to one another. Adults and young people disagree somewhat as to whether it is necessary for that commitment to take the form of marriage,[19] but the young are even

[15] Nelson Foote, "Sex as Play," *Social Problems,* Vol. 1 (April 1954), pp. 159–163.

[16] Kinsey *et al., Sexual Behavior in the Human Female,* p. 141.

[17] *Ibid.,* p. 642–689; Clelland S. Ford and Frank A. Beach, *Patterns of Sexual Behavior* (New York: Hoeber Medical Division, Harper and Brothers, 1951), p. 241.

[18] William M. Kephart, *The Family, Society, and the Individual* (2nd ed.; Boston: Houghton Mifflin, 1966), p. 438.

[19] Ira L. Reiss, "The Scaling of Premarital Sexual Permissiveness," *Journal of Marriage and the Family,* Vol. 26 (May 1964), pp. 188–198; Robert R. Bell and Jack V. Buerkle, "Mother and Daughter Attitudes to Premarital Sexual Behavior," *Marriage and Family Living,* Vol. 23 (November 1961), pp. 390–392.

more nearly unanimous than the adults that emotional attachment is a precondition for sexual involvement. In studies of several samples of American youth and adults, Reiss has found that those with the most "permissive" sex codes indicate more approval of full sexual relations before marriage in the presence of strong affection than of kissing not motivated by affection. Generally, adult groups are less interested in the presence of affection in the relationship and more concerned with preventing the more intimate levels of sexual involvement, affection or no affection.[20]

There can also be no mistaking that women are more committed than are men to the necessity of emotional commitment preceding sexual involvement.[21] In fact, the feigning of emotional commitment has been a basic part of the seduction repertoire of males for generations. In this sense, masculine attitudes toward the meaning and place of sex in human relationships still carry a fundamentally amoral component which contradicts the morally supported values of sexuality. The polemical point of view taken by Albert Ellis[22] on the one hand, and by *Playboy* on the other, is an attempt to legitimize the "underworld" values of the male subculture by defining these values as "healthy," and by describing the prevailing values (which are closely patterned from female values) as "sick," and as evidence of an emotionally disordered society.

SEX AS A FACTOR IN MARRIAGE FORMATION

From our understanding of the differences in the context of male and female

[20] Reiss, *op. cit.*
[21] Winston Ehrmann, *Premarital Dating Behavior* (New York: Henry Holt, 1959), p. 189.
[22] Albert Ellis, *Sex Without Guilt* (New York: Lyle Stuart, 1958).

sexuality, it can easily be seen that sex is a much more basic motivating force in the behavior of men than in the behavior of women. Furthermore, all man-woman relationships are much more fundamentally sexualized for men than for women, whether we think of marriage, courtship, dating, or the relationships between men and women in other than heterosexual roles. In such diverse role relationships as repairman-housewife, vendor-buyer, employer-employee, psychiatrist-patient, and even gynecologist-patient relationships, when one of the pair is a man, he is much more aware of and motivated by sexual considerations.

The role of sex in the formation of marriages, then, is clearly a more important consideration for men than for women. One of the most important motivations of men for marriage is the promise it holds out of the regular availability of a sexual partner whenever he wants her, without the uncertainties and irregularities of nonmarital sex life. To the average woman anticipating marriage, mature and unfettered by sexual neuroses, the sexual life of marriage may be pleasantly anticipated, but it does not constitute a fundamental part of the motivation propelling her into marriage. The fact that neither men nor women appear to be aware of these differences in motivation attests to the opaqueness of each sex to the other.

THE RELATIONSHIP BETWEEN SEXUAL BEHAVIOR AND MARITAL SATISFACTION

In the past forty years, much research has been done on the relationship between sexual behavior and marital satisfaction. Most of these studies have used middle-class respondents, and the results of all of them are more or less consistent. Two specific sexual factors have repeatedly been shown to be related to general marital satisfaction: the frequency of orgasm in the wife and the relative equality of sexual desire.[23] Those men who report that they and their spouses are equal or nearly equal in enjoyment or preferred frequency of coitus are generally more satisfied with their marriages than those who report disparity in enjoyment or desired frequency. This is less consistently true for women.[24] Likewise, those couples who report that the wife always or nearly always experiences orgasm in sexual relations are more satisfied with their marriages than those who report that the wife has orgasm only in a small proportion of their coitus. Finally, those couples who report being highly satisfied with their sexual relationship are more satisfied with the remainder of their relationship than those couples who report dissatisfaction with their sexual relationship.[25] Researchers have repeatedly asked, but never definitively answered, the question: Does marital satisfaction cause sexual satisfaction, or does sexual satisfaction cause marital satisfaction? Or is the relationship reciprocal, that is, each contributing to the satisfaction of

the other? The definitive research in this area is yet to be done, but we are now able to set forth a reasonably satisfactory answer, which is also consistent with the known differences in male and female sexuality.

The significance of orgasm and equality of sex desire for marital adjustment can probably best be interpreted in the light of the norms of equality and reciprocity discussed earlier. Wallin and Clark have shown that husbands and wives who report themselves satisfied with their marriages tend to *perceive* equality of desired sex frequency, even when this is not the case,[26] suggesting that people who are satisfied with their marriages tend to distort perceptions of aspects of their marriages in such a way as to make them congruent with reciprocity norms.[27]

For those couples who are not able to see their sex interests as equal, the difference registers as dissatisfaction with the marriage. The case of orgasm frequency serves as a specific norm for demonstrating this point. Husbands and wives who have internalized the reciprocity norm strongly will react with strong disappointment to their inability to achieve it by the wife's "achievement" of orgasm to match her husband's. We can reasonably hypothesize that where this norm is not held strongly (as in the lower class), lack of orgasm will not be a disturbing influence on the marital relationship.

Taking a more global look at sexual satisfaction and its effect on marriage, from the differences in the context of male and female sexuality, we should expect to find male sexual satisfaction a basic determinant of marital satis-

[23] Burgess and Wallin, *op. cit.;* Harvey J. Locke, *Predicting Adjustment in Marriage: A Comparison of a Divorced and a Happily Married Group* (New York: Henry Holt, 1951); Lewis M. Terman, *Psychological Factors in Marital Happiness* (New York: McGraw-Hill, 1938); Bruce Thomason, "Marital Sexual Behavior and Total Marital Adjustment: A Research Report," in J. Himelhoch and S. L. Fava (eds.), *Sexual Behavior in American Society* (New York: W. W. Norton, 1955); G. V. Hamilton, *A Research in Marriage* (New York: Albert and Charles Boni, 1929).

[24] Paul Wallin and Alexander Clark, "Marital Satisfaction and Husbands' and Wives' Perception of Similarity in their Preferred Frequency of Coitus," *Journal of Abnormal and Social Psychology,* Vol. 57 (November 1958), pp. 370–373; Levinger, *op. cit.*

[25] Thomason, *op. cit.;* Terman, *op. cit.;* Burgess and Wallin, *op. cit.*

[26] Wallin and Clark, "Marital Satisfaction and Husbands' and Wives' Perception of Similarity in Their Preferred Frequency of Coitus," pp. 370–373. 370–373.

[27] Levinger, *op. cit.*

faction. And we should expect to find the basic determinant of sexual satisfaction in men to be the congruence of their marital sexual experience with the reciprocity norms. If a man is dissatisfied with the marital sexual relationship, it is likely to disturb the whole marriage and, in the process, make his wife unhappy. The wife who does not regularly achieve orgasm, for example, makes her husband dissatisfied with his sex life, which both disturbs their enjoyment of sex and makes him unhappy with the marriage. Cutright has recently reanalyzed the Burgess-Wallin data and shown that the data may reasonably be interpreted to show that sexual adjustment causes marital adjustment for men, rather than the reverse.[28] There does not seem to be much reason to postulate a reciprocal effect of general marital adjustment on the sex adjustment of men.[29] There is nothing in the male value system which says that in order to enjoy sex with a woman you must have a satisfying affectional relationship with her.

For women, on the other hand, the association between emotional involvement and sexual involvement is so basic to the value system that we would expect quite the reverse of the relationship found for men between marital and sexual satisfaction. A woman with otherwise high marital satisfaction should not be made generally unsatisfied with her marriage solely on account of low sexual satisfaction. Burgess and Wallin remark,

. . . wives are less disposed than their husbands to be critical of, or dissatisfied with their sexual relationship. The explanation for this may be that women do not expect as much as men from the sexual sphere of their marriage. . . . These wives

are apparently not greatly disturbed by being deprived of sexual satisfaction.[30]

Given high marital satisfaction, on the other hand, we should expect to see the quality of a woman's sex life improve, and, given low marital satisfaction, we should expect to see her sex appreciation deteriorate. Within limits, this seems to be exactly what happens. Clark and Wallin, looking at data for couples married eighteen to twenty years, report as follows.

. . . wives whose marriages are consistently positive in quality are increasingly likely to be sexually responsive *up to the time they have been married about five years*. If by then they do not usually or always have orgasm in intercourse with their husbands, they will probably not do so in the years that follow. Similarly it appears that a shift from negative to positive in the quality of marriages from the early to middle years is not accompanied by any increase in the responsiveness of wives who are party to these marriages. On the other hand, the findings indicate that a deterioration in the quality of marriages after the early years often is accompanied by a decrease in responsiveness and that this may also occur in marriages which are consistently of negative quality. This decrease in responsiveness is almost certainly in most instances a consequence of the cultural norm which proscribes a woman "giving herself" in a relationship which has been designated as negative in quality. The negative quality of a marriage thus can inhibit women's responsiveness even where a pattern of responsiveness has already been established.[31]

Other evidence produced by Wallin and Clark tends to support the idea that sexual satisfaction is derivative from general marital satisfaction for women but not for men. From data on the

[28] Phillips Cutright, Unpublished research proposal, Vanderbilt University, May 1967. (Mimeographed.)

[29] Levinger, *op. cit.*

[30] Burgess and Wallin, *op. cit.*, p. 697.

[31] Alexander L. Clark and Paul Wallin, "Women's Sexual Responsiveness and the Duration and Quality of Their Marriages," *American Journal of Sociology*, Vol. 71 (September 1965), pp. 187–196.

same group of couples, they learned that among women with low sexual satisfaction, those who were highly involved in religious activity showed no reflection of this low sex satisfaction in their general satisfaction with the marriage. For men, this was not true. Men with low sexual satisfaction were unhappy with their marriages whether they had high religious involvement or not.[32] This suggests that, given other sources of satisfaction and involvement, women can do without sexual satisfaction and still enjoy their marriages. This is apparently not true for men. The causal relationships between marital and sexual satisfaction are diagrammed here in the Figure below. (Arrows indicate direction of major effect.)

SEX AND THE SOCIAL CONTEXT OF THE MARRIAGE

In the lower-class setting, much that has been said above is either untrue or irrelevant. Most lower-class and some working-class couples enter marriage with no expectation that it is to be a relationship of great emotional significance. It is more or less taken for granted by them that the man will live in a man's world and the woman in a world of women.[33] The marriage provides the convenience of a division of labor, the comfort of regular sex, and the security of a home. (Among the lower-class Negro group, marital expectations appear to be much more pessimistic than this.)[34] In couples whose marital lives are thus segregated, with most of their emotional investments outside the marriage, the emotional significance of sex as an integral part of a general emotional involvement is greatly reduced.[35] In this way, sex is simplified, and, for the woman, the level of satisfaction she receives from sex may be rather irrelevant for her satisfaction from the marriage. In any case, her expectations of emotional gratification from any part of the marital relationship are probably quite modest. In Rainwater's sample of lower-class respondents, the de-emphasis of the interpersonal rewards of sex in favor of the simple physical pleasure stands out sharply in those couples with highly segregated marital relationships. Only one-third of the women in highly segregated relationships stressed the interpersonal rewards from sex, while nearly three-fourths of those in less segregated relationships saw the rewards of sex in

[32] Paul Wallin, "Religiosity, Sexual Gratification, and Marital Satisfaction," *American Sociological Review,* Vol. 22 (June 1957), pp. 300–305; Paul Wallin and Alexander L. Clark, "Religiosity, Sexual Gratification, and Marital Satisfaction in the Middle Years of Marriage," *Social Forces,* Vol. 42 (March 1964), pp. 303–309.

[33] Komarovsky, *op. cit.*

[34] Lee Rainwater, "Crucible of Identity: The Negro Lower-Class Family," *Daedalus* Vol. 95 (Winter 1966), pp. 172–216.

[35] Lee Rainwater, "Marital Sexuality in Four Cultures of Poverty," *Journal of Marriage and the Family,* Vol. 26 (November 1964), pp. 457–466.

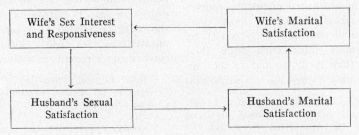

FIGURE—THE RELATIONSHIP BETWEEN SEXUAL SATISFACTION AND MARITAL SATISFACTION

interpersonal terms. Similar sharp differences were found for lower-class men.[36]

Given this restricted meaning of sex for those in highly segregated relationships, it is not surprising to find that men and women living in highly segregated marriages do not appear to be as interested in, or to derive as much enjoyment from, sex as those in less segregated marriages. Among Rainwater's subjects, 64 per cent of the women in less segregated marriages reported great interest and enjoyment in sex, while fewer than one in five of the women in highly segregated marriages reported this high level of interest and enjoyment. Similar findings hold for men.[37]

It can be concluded that when marriages are highly segregated, there is little emotional content to the marital relationship. Under these circumstances, sex is stripped of its interpersonal significance, and does not become the important source of satisfaction that it is in more emotionally intimate marriages.

THE FAMILY AS AN AGENT FOR SEXUAL SOCIALIZATION

It is taken for granted by most students of the American family that the sexual behavior of adults is shaped by their experiences during childhood in the family. And, in general terms, no doubt, this is true. On the other hand, in terms of specific factors of socialization and their effect on adult sex life, it is surprising how few relationships can be demonstrated. When Americans are asked about the sources of their sexual information, most report extrafamilial sources. Girls report receiving more information from their mothers than do boys, and fathers apparently play almost no role in providing sexual information.[38] Most writers consider the lack of sex education in the family setting to be deplorable, but it is difficult to determine that family sex education is superior to education received outside the family in terms of producing adults who enjoy sex in a socially responsible way. Most parents are so uncomfortable talking about sex that they are probably poor teachers of sex anyway. Gagnon suggests:

In addition to the parents' incapacity to deal with the indirect elements which affect sexuality, they are also unable to deal with the problem of the supply of specifically sexual information. Since the parents persist in patterns of information control that are mostly composed of negative sanctions and nonlabeling and mislabeling of behavior, the child must search for information in the meager resources of his equally misinformed friends. . . . Given, then, the troubled quality of adults when they deal with sexuality, it may be better for the children to learn through the informal channels of other children, since material from parents that might be overloaded with anxiety is reduced in significance and impact.[39]

Perhaps the deliberate imparting of sexual information is not the way in which the parents affect the subsequent sexual behavior of their children. In research which has sought background factors associated with adult sexual functioning, so far, only nonsexual factors have been shown to be significant. Strong religious training in the family has been shown to be associated with conforming sexual behavior in women, and to a far lesser degree in men,[40] but it has not been shown to be related to a satisfying or unsatisfying sex life. Socioeconomic class of one's parents is a strong deter-

[36] Lee Rainwater, "Some Aspects of Lower-Class Sexual Behavior," *Journal of Social Issues,* Vol. 22 (April 1966), pp. 96–108.
[37] *Ibid.*

[38] John Gagnon, "Sexuality and Sexual Learning in the Child," *Psychiatry,* Vol. 28 (August 1965), pp. 212–228.
[39] *Ibid.*
[40] Kinsey, Pomeroy, Martin, and Gebhard, *op. cit.;* Kinsey, Pomeroy, and Martin, *op. cit.*

minant of the kind of sexual behavior in which adults engage,[41] but it is not clear that this has anything to do with the behavior of the parents as compared, for example, to the behavior and attitudes of one's peers. In the most extensive search for childhood-experience items from family life which predicted sexual satisfaction in adult women, Terman could find no sign that particular types of sexual socialization were important predictors.[42] Yet psychiatric practice and common sense tells us that what children learn at home must have some more specific effects on their later sex life. We simply do not know what these effects are at this time.

There are good reasons for suggesting that research is not likely to turn up important relationships between sexual socialization within the family and adult sexual behavior. The general desexualized nature of parent-child relationships tends to make any specific sexual socialization by parents awkward and out of character with the rest of the relationship with their children, and this itself is going to minimize the amount of sexual learning that takes place. Sexual socialization in our society has become firmly institutionalized in the adolescent peer groups and the mass media, and there is now a strong push to make sexual instruction a part of the formal educational curriculum. Family socialization may provide certain predispositions, but these are likely to be general orientations characteristic of certain socioeconomic positions and religious affiliations. The impact of the extrafamilial sources may well obliterate the differences developed within the family. This does not mean that really bizarre family experiences will not produce sexual cripples or criminals, but only that when this small fringe is removed, re-

maining differences in sexual behavior in the population are not likely to be associated with particular family socialization experiences.

SUMMARY — excellent.

Contrary to prevailing middle-class values, sex plays a fundamentally different role in the lives of women from its role in the lives of men. The difference is probably due in part to the greater sexual conditionability of men and in part to the different meanings which men and women learn to give to sex. In the marital relationship as well as outside of it, sex is a more important motivator of men than of women. Both in feminine values and in the behavior of women, sex is a derivative behavior. Sex plays a more important role in motivating men for marriage than in motivating women. Sexual satisfaction plays a determining role in a man's evaluation of his marriage, and in the middle-class group, a husband's sexual satisfaction is primarily a function of his wife's level of sexual interest and responsiveness. A woman's evaluation of her marriage in emotional terms is an important determinant of her interest in and responsiveness to sex. This is not true in the segregated marriages of the lower class, where the emotional shallowness of the marriage reduces the interpersonal emotional significance of sex, and therefore the importance of sex in the marital relationship. The role of parents in shaping the future sexual behavior of their children is poorly understood, but probably important. The greatest known effect of parents is simply in providing the religious and socioeconomic-class environment from which children will absorb their sexual orientations, rather than in specific sexual attitudes and information imparted to the children.

[41] *Ibid.*
[42] Terman, *op. cit.*

Attitudes toward Sex in American "High Culture"

By Robert Boyers

ABSTRACT: An analysis is presented of particular themes and attitudes in several works of fiction published in the United States in the last decade. There is a special emphasis on varieties of apocalyptic sexuality, with an attempt to relate this focus to broader questions of a political and social nature. Problems of literary style and characterization connected with the presentation of sexual styles and orientations are also discussed, and there is comparison of typical American and European literary customs with regard to the presentation of sex.

Robert Boyers, M.A., New York City, is a member of the English Department at the Baruch School of the City College of New York, and a lecturer at the New School for Social Research. He is the author of a variety of articles for such publications as the New Leader, Kenyon Review, and Dissent; the editor-in-chief of Salmagundi, a quarterly of the arts and social sciences; and editor of a collection of essays on the poetry of Robert Lowell, to be published by October House this year.

THIRTY-FIVE years ago, in his remarkable novel *Towards a Better Life*, Kenneth Burke admonished us to remember "that as the corrective of wrong thinking is right thinking, the corrective of all thinking is the body." Set as it is in the context of an elegant and extremely high-toned fiction, Burke's sentence could not have meant for his original readers what it says for us. More perhaps than he knew, Burke anticipated an inclination which has become almost a formalized convention of the serious literature at present being written and discussed in this country. The body has become for our writers that oracle wherein lie value and truth, and balm for the pains of consciousness. Our literature is created under the same star which has guided the fantasies of pornographers since the origins of that frequently black, yet somehow sacred profession. If our more serious writers are more than pious pornographers, there is at the same time no doubt that they represent experience largely "as seen through the eye of a penis." Steven Marcus' sniggering, even condescending, indictment of pornography on this ground, as on others (in his book *The Other Victorians*), serves as well to describe manifestations rampant in contemporary high culture, though it is possible that we disagree on what is "high" and on what is "culture."

So that there shall be no mistaking what we are observing here, it may be necessary to mention that for our purposes the word "culture" is to be taken in its narrowest sense, signifying the collected presence and impact of all works of the creative imagination in every medium, as well as that body of criticism and philosophy which seeks perpetually to alter or encourage or simply to explain the work with which it deals. It is not as easy to locate what we mean by "high" culture, and

any definition will inevitably seem exclusivist to those more or less serious practitioners of an art, or their defenders, who cannot comfortably be placed within the magic circle, as it were. Acquiescently to extend the circumference of such a circle is no answer, however, for this would constitute an evasion of standards, and a sacrifice of that taste which it is the duty of every critic vainly to parade before his readers, as the badge both of his conviction and his fallibility. The serious literature to which I shall refer, then, will indicate my impressions of what is significant in contemporary culture. So that our focus will not be overly dispersed, we shall concentrate primarily on a few recent books of fiction which readily illustrate particular attitudes toward sex that I should like to explore.

To return, then, to the body—we having successfully, one would hope, mastered that inclination to be content with mere sex in the head which a no less renowned sexual reactionary than D. H. Lawrence could propose as a viable possibility for mature men and women—to that body which beckons to us, no longer sinful, nor even dirty, nor yet beautiful, but brimming nonetheless with promise, the promise of deliverance from all that is inauthentic or smugly innocent. What courses through our literature is this promise, rarely if ever kept, yet never wholly abandoned, as if all other frontiers had been reached, all other modes of knowing explored, and nothing left to do but plug on in search of that ultimate body which we plunder in our dreams, or that apocalyptic orgasm in which all barriers are magically removed, all connections passionately restored.

It is curious that a countertendency may be discerned in the literature of our high culture, though a tendency which similarly exalts the importance of the body. Among the writers of this second group, there is a conviction of the body as a limitation, a limitation which must be pursued. Here involvement with the body represents not a path to vitality nor a means to making contact with what is most real and complex in oneself. Instead, the body is seen as a mode of escape from painful realities, a mode of forgetfulness, in a sense a mode of a blessed nonbeing. In both tendencies, the body is cultivated as a means of redirecting energy and attention—in the one case, away from what is lying, hypocritical, convenient, inauthentic; in the other case, away from what may, in fact, be too utterly authentic, too much a pattern of experience in which one has been rendered the passive spectator of one's own inglorious dissolution.

SEX AS MAGIC

Probably the most talented, serious, and proclaimed champion of apocalyptic sexuality in this country is Norman Mailer, whose recent works of fiction have been received with howls of dismay and disbelief. *An American Dream* is a pop-art caricature of ideas which Mailer has held for some time, but which somehow never seemed quite so banal and ludicrous as they now largely appear. This is not at all to suggest what so many critics have insisted upon: that the novel is simply bad. Mailer can do more with a line of English prose than any man currently writing fiction. His imagination is teeming with invention, and his metaphors have the reach of genius. But Mailer's great gifts cannot conceal the fact that Mailer is a rather corny romantic who has been posing for years as a kind of big bad boy, obsessed by visions of brutality and voracious sexuality. As Elizabeth Hardwick has observed, "no heat arises from [the novel's] many brutal couplings." Through everything, one sees Mailer himself,

sweating to make us feel something he himself cannot feel. His characters have no real lives of their own to which we can respond. They are plastic creatures, whom Mailer consistently fails to motivate adequately. Mailer is pathetically anxious for us to believe in his vision, and his earnest entreaties are frequently embarrassing.

Mailer's protagonist Stephen Richards Rojack is a war-hero, a former congressman, a one-time friend of Jack Kennedy, and an intellectual who compares the pain of a shrapnel wound to the "delicious pain clean as a mistress' sharp teeth going 'Yummy' in your rump." Clearly, an extraordinary character! In every way, he appears to be a libertarian type, but in the first pages of the novel he gives himself away. His wife Deborah has committed five confessed adulteries during the eight years of their marriage, and Rojack recognizes each of these adulteries, with its subsequent revelation, as "an accent, a transition, a concrete step in the descent of our marriage." Rojack values fidelity as an index of love, in the most conventional way possible. For all his brutal frankness, Rojack is as puritanical as one might expect him to be, given his swagger and his panting insecurities. He speaks of the sexuality implicit in the act of murder, with its thrill of violent release, and Rojack indeed does murder his wife. But there is nothing erotic in the actual murder. The woman's neck is broken, and her corpse thrown out of a window, without any voluptuous emotions attendant upon the scene. In fact, the whole thing is not even titillating in the way one expects of a good horror story. Rojack is practically unconscious throughout the proceedings, moving from step to step almost in a trance. Nowhere is there a trace of passion or conviction.

Inevitably, he rushes to climb into bed with the German maid, whom he surprises, "all five fingers fingering like a team of maggots at her open heat. She was off in that bower of the libido where she was queen." They make violent love, Mailer permitting us to imagine for ourselves just how Rojack managed to pry those fingers from that "open heat." Rojack's bout with Ruta may best be described as a hysterico-comic exercise in advanced gymnastics. Back and forth Rojack springs, from orifice to orifice, fore and aft, "a raid on the Devil and a trip back to the Lord." Ultimately, full of guilt, Rojack drops his load at the door of the Devil.

It is appropriate that a book espousing apocalyptic sexuality should employ a reasonably flexible religious terminology. What is important for Rojack is making the correct connections during and as a result of his sexual transports. He views the sexual act as a kind of test in which he is gravely judged, not for his virility or endurance, but for his courage and profundity. Rojack's very soul is somehow at stake even in the most casual encounters. He worries over his commitment to life, and sees in each sexual lapse or crudity an acquiescence in that death-wish which laps at our very heels.

Rojack wants to be a Faustian type, but he is too much a victim of conventions that he thinks he has passed beyond. He wants to fly in the face of a civilization for which he would like to have righteous contempt. In identifying his stubborn reluctance to abandon anal intercourse with an attraction to the Devil, Rojack is passing a severe judgment on himself. For him, there is something sinful in following his own instinct or whim, for such indulgence denies man's fundamental responsibility to subject himself to a will more general and embracing than his own. In denying Ruta her orgasm, when she had every right to expect that Rojack would "think of her," he calls down a judgment

upon his head. Rojack's happiness, or his right to experiment with human life, whether on a purely physical or emotional level, cannot be positive values in themselves, but must subserve the more basic requirement of preserving respect for the feelings and even for the gratification of others. In the light of Rojack's bowing before such an ethic, it is rather appalling to think how little he suffers over the murder of his wife. One can only conclude that, for Rojack, the taking of a life is a minor matter compared with the integrity of one's performance between the sheets.

There is something faintly touching and not a little bit absurd in attributing to poor coitus a burden of such momentous gravity. Indeed, Mailer's characters display the sort of elaborate, one might almost say literary, awareness of themselves and the symbolic significance of their every genital thrust which renders the possibility of their experiencing true passion or release highly unlikely. At its most intense, Mailer's characters seem to feel, sexual activity has the capacity of conferring on both participants an awareness of grace, of that still point in the midst of flux in which the sorrows of the world wash by, are lamented, but cannot really disturb the fundamental equilibrium so tenuously achieved. In *An American Dream,* predictably, Rojack falls in love, with a girl named Cherry, no less. Naturally, the full magnitude and depth of their feeling for one another is understood during intercourse. Rojack and Cherry barely know each other as people, but there is something bittersweet in Cherry's juices which tells Rojack he has found the thing he has needed. Cherry is for Rojack a symbol of the eternal victim, a perpetual child in a world that plunders and corrupts and uses those who cling to their innocence. When Cherry spreads her mournful legs, it is consolation she seeks, not an electric charge. For Rojack and Cherry, sex is an activity which ideally takes one out of the body, and enables a communion with the diverse and determinedly unresponsive elements in the universe.

A reader must ask himself whether such projections can be valid. What the question really comes down to, of course, is whether Mailer has been able to make them appear, if not reasonable, then at least conceivable for us. It is difficult to consider Mailer's vision of human sexuality other than as symptomatic of a kind of pathological attempt to impose will on an experience which ought to be less a matter of will than of untrammeled emotion. Undoubtedly, there is something unpleasantly expedient, if not crude, in attempting to draw a distinction between aspects of human behavior which never function wholly independently of one another, and yet I think it is a distinction which must be drawn if we are to see what Mailer and other writers have done.

Rojack experiences a sexual gratification in which his partner is appreciated to the degree that she fits conveniently into a symbolic pattern which confers peculiar value wholly apart from any actual human qualities the partner may have. We are here in the presence of a phenomenon which is more than familiar, which may, in fact, be a predominating characteristic of Western sexuality. Moreover, it involves a mechanism which is intrinsic to an understanding of the Western love ethic that exalts marriage and fidelity as keys to fulfillment. In his deservedly classic work *Love in the Western World*, Denis de Rougemont argues that marital fidelity is based upon a construct which has no particular merit of its own that should recommend it to lovers, aside from the fact that it is a construct which *they* have decided upon and de-

termined to respect. In de Rougemont's own words:

I propose to speak only of a troth that is observed *by virtue of the absurd*—that is to say, simply because it has been pledged—and by virtue of being an absolute which will uphold husband and wife as persons. Fidelity . . . contradicts the general belief in the revelatory value of both spontaneity and manifold experiences. . . . It denies that its own goal is happiness. It offensively asserts first, that its aim is obedience to a truth that is believed in, and secondly, that it is the expression of a wish to be constructive.

In de Rougemont's view, then, the love ethic by which most men in the Western world have measured themselves, and according to which they have structured their lives, has not been supportive of untrammeled emotion, but has worked as a counterforce to passion. Marital fidelity is profoundly unnatural for any normal human being. Its capacity to gratify lies precisely in the opportunity it affords the individual of transcending the demands of his own ego, the demand, for example, to be happy on the most instinctual level. In marriage, there is a pride in renouncing what one would desire if permitted to do so, and a commitment to an alternative object which is viewed as more important—the willed making of a relationship, despite contingency, despite desires which would thwart one's project. The marital partners are permitted to grow only through obedience to the particular laws and requirements of the relationship that binds them, in a subjection to which they actively consent.

Rojack's view of human sexuality is closely related to and, one would suppose, derivative from this Western love ethic. To the degree that sexual pleasure is purely or even largely physical, he considers it base and dehumanizing. He can have little affection for Deborah because "making love she left you with no uncertain memory of having passed through a carnal transaction with a caged animal." Rojack rejects carnal transactions in which he is unable to attach symbolic, even transcendent importance to his partner, and to their shared roles as part of some vast, if arbitrary, scheme. In his earliest sexual encounter with Cherry, Rojack is again disappointed: "We paid our devotions in some church no larger than ourselves." It is the prison of the self from which Rojack wishes to escape. He is embarrassed by the insistent demands, frequently perverse or sadistic, of his ego. For Rojack, sex is a means of replenishing the universe, of infusing the universe with the vitality of original creation. In its most authentic form, sex, like love itself, transcends particular personalities, just as there is a devaluation of particular sexual organs. All that matters is the vow to believe in the value of something which is, at its root, arbitrary and absurd. Rojack makes what one might properly term an extreme statement of this view, after discovering the authenticity of his love for Cherry: "Love was love, one could find it with anyone, one could find it anywhere. It was just that you could never keep it. Not unless you were ready to die for it, dear friend."

The nature of Mailer's apocalyptism has never been clearer. For Mailer, it is not sex itself which opens the gates to Paradise, nor is it the monumental orgasm which shatters forever one's allegiance to the shoddy and banal and mundane. He sees nothing liberating *per se* in the sexual act. In fact, there is almost nothing in Mailer's view of sex that one would expect of a sexual apocalyptist. For Mailer, authentic sexuality is a task, a difficult commitment, for it imposes a terrible burden upon both participants. It is the burden of perpetually mythologizing the nature of

an experience which could so easily represent nothing more than sheer forgetfulness and release. The apocalyptic element in Mailer's vision has to do with the liberating potential of any act of the creative imagination, the imagination which perceives the ostensibly crucial obstacles to harmony among men and things as basically superficial and capable of being transcended. As an activity which enlists the total energies and attention of participants, sex has the capacity to tap man's deepest resources of feeling and thought, which, as an artist of considerable distinction, Mailer identifies with the imagination. Far from being an end in itself, sex is merely a kind of catalyst which releases a unique degree of zeal and energy that, in their turn, may alter man's pattern of existence. Moreover, not all or even most sexual activity can make such rewards available. Only sex in which the burden of consciousness is unrelentingly pursued, and in which the full weight of the beloved as an object of, in many ways, impenetrable density is accepted for himself, can promise the fulfillment which Mailer admires. As in de Rougemont's notions of marriage, what is important for Mailer is not happiness, nor the immediate gratification of instincts. Sex, like marriage, is a means to realizing qualities of the human personality which are resolutely unnatural, though qualities which the processes of civilization, and the refinements of culture, have conditioned responsible men to value.

RHETORIC AND WISH-FULFILLMENT

How utterly sophisticated all of this is, despite so much that is ludicrous and crude in Mailer's novel, when one compares it to the fiction of several other talented people who work from a related orientation. Jeremy Larner is a younger writer, whose first novel *Drive,*

He Said contains passages of singular virtuosity and extraordinary humor. It fails, however, to give one a clear sense of what Larner really feels on various subjects, not least among these the question of human sexuality. The alternation of heavy-handed satire and an almost hysterical sincerity is handled rather sloppily, so that one cannot quite be certain as to what Larner wishes us to take seriously, and what satirically. Parts of the novel even strike one as patent adolescent wish-fulfillment, as mature, beautiful women permit themselves to be regularly ravished by young students who really have little to recommend them but their ardent desires and, one assumes, healthy erections.

There is considerable attention devoted in this novel to the possibilities of apocalyptic orgasm. The actor Tony Valentine, for example, is known as an orgasm man, who has "fuzzy intimations of how the orgasm might be just one feature of a hitherto unthought of psychic politics that could swing our desperate world into a new wild millennium of pleasure." Unfortunately, Valentine is a preposterous figure, whose intimations are deservedly bestowed with the epithet "fuzzy." Even more unfortunate, though, is that Larner never really tries to come to grips with Valentine's ideas, to which he is inexorably attracted, despite the satirical detachment he manages to affect. Larner's protagonist Hector Bloom takes his sexual transports very seriously indeed, and his friend Gabriel Reuben is driven insane by his inability to combine sexual passion with what he considers true feeling, something apparently distinct from passion in his view. Both Hector and Gabriel view sex in terms of instant revelation, though neither of them are clear on what it is they expect to have revealed. Proper orgasm is supposed to effect all kinds of remarkable transformations not only on a personal level,

but in the social and political spheres as well, with attendant metaphysical vibrations. But it is all so much a matter of rhetorical indulgence that one is unable to discuss the ideas in Larner's novel seriously.

In a way, this should not be surprising, either with regard to *Drive, He Said* in particular, or to American writing in general. We have a great tradition of writers who have been consistently unable to deal seriously with sex, particularly with mature sexual relations between fully developed male and female characters. Leslie Fiedler contributed the definitive demonstration of this thesis in *Love and Death in the American Novel,* a book of criticism which perhaps says as much about the American psyche as any book of recent years. Even in the fiction of the 1960's, there is little or no evidence that Fiedler's thesis could not be easily extended. And it is not that we simply lack serious writers. Saul Bellow is a novelist of undeniable genius, but, as V. S. Pritchett has pointed out, his women characters fail to impress as real people. We cannot approach them as we are able to approach Bellow's male protagonists. There is in Bellow's entire fictional output no convincing illumination of the nature of normal sexual relations in American society. In *Herzog,* Bellow makes a valiant effort, but his sexual encounters are bathed in a kind of pathos, or a kind of dreary if occasionally quaint sentimentality which renders them almost ineffably idyllic. On the other hand, the female character who has most to do with the direction taken by the novel's protagonist is in the tradition of the all-American bitch-goddess, a figure whom we need never consider too closely, for we know she is a mere creature of those dire fantasies which we maintain to justify our inexplicable terrors.

To be sure, then, the rhetorical extravagance we have come to associate with most treatments of sex by American writers is understandable as an evasion of fundamental issues which they are still unable or unwilling to treat. It is almost impossible to conceive of an American novelist treating sex with the sort of spare, relentlessly analytic style of certain French masters who can philosophize about sex without wallowing in sentimentality or yielding to grandiloquence. The one American writer of distinction who, in her criticism at least, has managed to discuss erotics as a fundamental element in the consideration of any art form is Susan Sontag. Perhaps Miss Sontag's distinction in this area is partially attributable to her profound absorption in European, and especially French, literature. In a recent article entitled "On Pornography," Miss Sontag dealt at length with several pornographic novels, including one entitled *Story of O* by a pseudonymous author who is conveniently called Pauline Reage. This French novel has had a wide distribution in this country, and has evoked rather sober discussion in the more prestigious intellectual and literary publications— perhaps a sign of a new receptivity to the notion of pornography as potentially serious literature.

There is no need at this point to go into *Story of O,* nor into its predecessors in the distinguished tradition of European pornography, in any great detail; but it might prove instructive to suggest possible affinities with works of American fiction which have been popularly characterized as lewd, if not deliberately pornographic. According to Miss Sontag, what one may justifiably respond to and appreciate in a work like *Story of O* is the integrity with which the author consistently pursues a largely diabolical vision. There is no inclination on the part of the author to justify

his vision, or the fantasies of characters, as in some way representative of a widely held position. The author is not primarily interested in impressing us with the universal implications of his work, but is more concerned with impressing upon us the passion and singularity of his absorption in a vision which may be uniquely his. Nor is the author worried lest we should think him deranged. What is important is "the originality, thoroughness, authenticity and power of that 'deranged consciousness' itself, as it is incarnated in a work."

What the more creative and original writers in the European tradition have understood and accepted is that sex is not a normal activity. Miss Sontag, as we have learned to expect of her, makes the statement in the most extreme and yet most cogent way: "Even on the level of simple physical sensation and mood, making love surely resembles having an epileptic fit at least as much, if not more, than it does eating a meal or conversing with someone." In American literature, even when sex is described in patently brutal or perverse terms, one is almost always conscious of an attempt to mediate the extremity of the vision, to assure us that only very rare (if not actually deranged) people are capable of a sexual response of inordinate violence. Even Mailer's Rojack, whom one would not ordinarily expect to make explicit confessions of inhibition, is driven to cry out in the extremity of physical and emotional passion, when his involvement with Cherry has become consuming: "Let me love her some way not altogether deranged and doomed. . . . Let me love her and be sensible as well." Unlike the author of a work like *Story of O,* Mailer is not possessed by a vision, but is instead the extremely self-conscious writer balancing several visions of possibility at once. Whatever

Mailer says about the demoniacal energies inherent in sexual activity, his own understanding of these energies is mainly literary, and consequently limited in conviction.

PORNO-POLITICS

There is no lack of conviction in Ken Kesey's *One Flew over the Cuckoo's Nest,* but neither is there an attempt to deal with human sexuality as a complex phenomenon. Kesey's novel is wholly successful as an indictment of modern society, and as an exploration into the kind of subtly repressive mechanisms we help to build into the fabric of our daily lives. Kesey's solution to our common problem is the opening of floodgates, the releasing of energies which have too long lain unused or forgotten. Chief among these are the twin resources of laughter and uninhibited sexuality, the linkage between which Kesey manages to clarify in the course of his novel.

The novel is set in a mental institution which is, in many respects, a microcosm of the society-at-large. It is to Kesey's credit that he never strains to maintain the parallel at any cost—it is a suggested parallel at most, and, where it suits his novelistic purposes, Kesey lets it go completely. His protagonist is one Patrick Randall McMurphy, pronounced psychopathic by virtue of being "overzealous in [his] sexual relations." His purpose in the institution, as in life apparently, is both to have a hell of a good time, and to defy "ball cutters," defined by McMurphy himself as "people who try to make you weak so they can get you to toe the line, to follow their rules, to live like they want you to." McMurphy is a truly monumental character—a gambler, a braggart, a fantastic lover, and a gadfly who insults and goads those who resist his charismatic injunctions. While he is something of a sensualist who dwells reg-

ularly on the ecstasies of sexual transport, and even goes so far as to bring his whores into the hospital to restore the vitality of his moribund fellow-psychopaths, McMurphy feels himself and his comrades the victims of women, not their lords and masters as his rhetoric would have it. His techniques of resistance and defiance are mostly pathetic, as they can achieve what are at best pyrrhic victories. One is never tempted to question the validity, the nobility, or even the necessity of McMurphy's defiance, but no mature reader will be convinced that his techniques can realistically accomplish what Kesey claims for them at the novel's end—the reclamation of numerous human beings who had grown passive and torpid before McMurphy's arrival.

At one point, McMurphy characterizes the inmates of the hospital as "victims of a matriarchy." In Kesey's view, modern society is a reflection of womanish values—archetypically responsible, cautious, repressive, deceitful, and solemn. One must look to the spirit of the whore if one would know what is best in women, and what can best bring out what is vital in men. There is no doubt that Kesey labors under a most reactionary myth, involving the mystique of male sexuality, which sees men as intrinsically better than women in terms of the dynamism and strength they can impart to the universe. Unable rationally to account for the disparity between such a projection and the puny reality of our male lives, Kesey waxes fatalistic, though never submissive, and sees "ball cutters" everywhere. It is a kind of paranoid, conspiratorial view of things, not without its measure of accuracy, but it somehow evades the crucial issues which Kesey and others have raised.

At the heart of Kesey's notion of what is possible for modern liberated man is a phenomenon which one may call porno-politics. It is a phenomenon which resides primarily in the imagination of a few thousand people, most of them young and bright, and which is occasionally manifested in the hysterical behavior of certain radical partisans of unpopular causes, a behavior which, by the way, many would call resolutely antipolitical, for all its pretensions to the contrary. Advocates of porno-politics are usually utopian socialists who lack the vision and patience to realize their goals politically: that is, they are youthful dreamers who are frustrated by the customary routines through which men achieve power or influence in order to alter the political relations which obtain in their society. Frequently, the retreat into varieties of porno-politics results from people relying too heavily on the flexibility of a given political system, and on the sheer magnetism of their own sincerity, which they and their associates had always considered irresistible. When the erstwhile utopian realizes how restrictive and closed the political structure of his society is, despite its aggressive disclaimers, and when he is made aware of the basic indifference to his ideals and to his attractiveness among the masses of people, he is suffused by a kind of anger and dread. As the society affords him virtually no outlet for these feelings, which rarely become specific enough to fix legitimate targets anyway, the befuddled utopian permits his vision of the possible to undergo a remarkable transformation. Unable to affect masses of men or to move political and social institutions, he transfers the burden of realizing a perfectly harmonious society to sex.

In Kesey's novel, we have what seemingly amounts to a *reductio ad absurdum* of familiar Freudian propositions. It is repressed sexuality which ostensibly lies behind every psychosis, and which is responsible for the acquiescence of all men in the confining conventions of Western society. It is in the spirit of random and thoroughly abandoned sexuality that Kesey's McMurphy would remake men, and subsequently the world. What is a little frightening in a novel like this, though, is that such a projection does not at all operate on a metaphorical level. Sex is not here a mere metaphor for passion, nor for any positive engagement with one's fellow human beings. There is a literalism in Kesey's suggestions of sexual apocalypse, with its unavoidable ramifications into a political and social context, which cannot be lightly taken. Other talented people are caught up in such projections, and are delivering gospels of sexual salvation with a hysterical dogmatism that is, for many of us, laughable and pathetic. This is so particularly for those who have observed the failure of libertarian sexual experimentation and random coupling to affect substantially the pettiness and self-absorption even of those who are most easily committed to libertarian modes and who have no need perpetually to justify such commitments ideologically. How futile it is for intelligent people seriously to expect their sexual programs and practices to have a liberating effect on masses of men, when what these people want is to be left alone to enjoy what they have. What porno-politics essentially amounts to is a form of entertainment for a middle-class audience, which alternatively writhes and applauds before the late-night news, and welcomes the opportunity to indulge and express postures it considers intrinsic to its worth as modern men: tolerance and righteous indignation.

Kesey's brilliance is evidenced by his ability to be seduced by porno-political utopianism, and yet not to yield to it entirely. What save him are his sense of the ridiculous and his understanding of men as fundamentally dishonest and irresolute. Kesey wants to believe that the source of all terror and passivity is somehow sexual, that the liberation of sexual energies in the form of primal fantasies will enable men to conceive of themselves as more passionate and autonomous individuals. But his intelligence forces him, as it were, against his will, to tell a truth which is more complex and disheartening. He recounts a group therapy session which had taken place in the institution some years before McMurphy's arrival. Unlike the usual dispirited proceedings, this particular session stood out for the violent release of confessions that it evoked from the habitually desultory and tight-lipped inmates. Once the momentum is established, the inmates begin shouting confessions: "I lied about trying. I did take my sister!"/ "So did I! So did I!"/ "And me! And me!"

At first, all of this seems satisfying, at least from a conventionally clinical point of view: repressed memories are rising to the surface, where they can be handled therapeutically. But, almost immediately, we are shown that not only did such events never occur in the lives of these men; they do not even represent their fantasy lives. Such "confessions" have nothing at all to do with the wish-fulfillment that is a strong component of compulsive fantasies. What the inmates have done is simply to exploit certain readily available clichés issuing from standard interpretations of modern man as the perennial victim of sexual repression. The inmates are victims of something much more embracing and diversified than simple sexual guilt or repression, though the sexual element may be particularly significant in the case of two or three inmates among many. What is sickening is their desire to please the therapists by revealing what they are supposed to, rather than what is really inside them. Finally, they are shamed by the resounding

announcement of hopeless old Pete: "I'm tired," he shouts—a confession so simple and true that it puts an abrupt end to the rampant dishonesty of the others. Kesey loves McMurphy, and identifies with his aspirations—he wants men to be free, to laugh the authorities down, to refuse to be manipulated. He wants, moreover, to go along with McMurphy's sexual orientation, and to be as optimistic as McMurphy about the effects of sexual liberation on the reigning political and social atmosphere. But McMurphy is not a mask for Kesey, nor is any single character in the novel. In fact, as much as Kesey admires McMurphy's stratagems for outwitting the matriarch *par excellence* who goes under the title Big Nurse, we are never quite certain whether to laugh at McMurphy as well as with him. Big Nurse, as the personification of "the system" at its most callow, repressive, yet ostensibly enlightened, represents a tendency toward antiseptic desexualization which is abhorrent. We want McMurphy to bewilder her, to kill her with his charming nonchalance and boyish exuberance, and to parade his own aggressive sexuality before her. We want her to be teased and tempted so that she will be provoked to try to castrate McMurphy, if not actually, then symbolically, as she has successfully whipped the other inmates. We want to see McMurphy put to the test of the vitality and resilience he proudly proclaims, as if he could redeem us from any misgivings we might have about our own potency.

And yet, throughout this novel, we know that nothing McMurphy does, or encourages his comrades to do, will make any substantive difference to the system that we all despise. McMurphy, through an ideological predisposition, which in his case is more instinctive than learned, attributes to sex what even he knows it cannot accomplish.

His is a heroic endeavor in every way, but McMurphy is at bottom a little lost boy who gets into the big muddy way up over his head. The picture of him, in bed with his whore at last, almost at the end of the novel, is utterly revealing: ". . . more like two tired little kids than a grown man and a grown woman in bed together to make love." McMurphy can behave as brashly as he likes, and speak with utter abandon of sex, but for him it has still an element of mystery, of vows exchanged, even if only for a brief duration. His libertarian apocalypticism is sincere, but in McMurphy's own character we can see that a libertarian sexual orientation ultimately has little to do with making men free as political and social beings. McMurphy needs no sexual swagger to be free, though, in his case, it is a believable accouterment of his personality. What is indispensable in McMurphy's character is his propensity to laugh, in his lucid moments to see himself as something of a spectacle, not wholly detached nor different from the other inmates who have failed to retain their resilience. When he loses his laugh, he grows desperate, and places upon sex that burden of hope for transcendence which the reality of sexual experience must frustrate. When, at the very conclusion of the book, McMurphy rips open Big Nurse's hospital uniform, revealing, for all to see, her prodigious breasts, we see where McMurphy's porno-political vision has led him. Unable to affect a world that victimizes him, a civilization which, in the words of the British psychoanalyst R. D. Laing ". . . represses not only 'the instincts,' not only sexuality, but any form of transcendence," McMurphy is driven to rape the reality incarnated in Big Nurse. In his fear and frustration, he does not see what, of all things, should be most obvious to him: that he cannot make another human being

aware of his humanity by destroying or suppressing those elements of his own humanity that have made McMurphy a beautiful person. By his action, he demonstrates the original futility of his project, the necessary brutalization of his sexual ethic, and the dehumanization implicit in the act of invoking an *Eros* which is imperfectly understood and crudely employed.

SEX AS EVASION

Among writers who treat sex as a means of relief from painful reality, though not as a means of transforming that reality, several contrasting approaches are discernible. These approaches are largely a function of the individual writer's temperament, rather than a reflection of any ideological point of view. All of these writers are concerned with that crisis of identity which Western writers have been engaging for forty years or more; all of them are cynical of the solemnity with which educated people customarily bow before conventions of thought and concern that they ought to have outgrown; and all of them view sexuality as a necessary evasion of issues which civilization has unfortunately encouraged us to confront.

John Barth is one of the most cynical, serious, and accomplished writers of this inclination. While his recent, extremely ambitious fiction has been given a great deal of attention, his earlier work is equally interesting, and especially rewarding for our present purposes. In particular, his 1958 novel *End of the Road* is a superb exploration of attitudes that we cannot overlook. Barth's protagonist is Jacob Horner, who fears he has no identity as a man, that he is, in fact, nothing more substantial than his moods, which are many and various. He adopts postures or roles, and holds on to them as long as they satisfy his requirements in given situations. A quack doctor who helps him in time of need strengthens his predilections toward what is an extreme relativism. All that is important for both the doctor and Horner is that man retain his ability to make choices, to act. There is only one wrong choice—the choice which leads to immobilization, an unresolved tension.

Such an orientation, of course, will lead a man to value noninvolvement, unless his character becomes so strong over an extended period of time that he learns to identify himself with a particular course of action which implicates every aspect of his being. Where Horner is concerned, the doctor advises against both marriage and love affairs, which are too complicated and might involve a man in painful tensions. Masturbation is recommended as a wise choice.

In the course of the novel, Horner pursues and goes to bed with two women, with whom we become familiar. In his sexual relations, the true ugliness of Horner's inclinations and aversions becomes gruesomely manifest. He is an inveterate son of a bitch, though he says some brilliantly witty things, and does manage even to suffer a bit. In his relations with poor Peg, who, in early middle-age, is desperate for a man, Horner's behavior is disgusting. He has always been uncomfortable, he confides, "with women who took their sexual transports too seriously." Moreover, he sincerely exalts sexual relations in which he is not thought of as a human being, so that it does not become incumbent upon him to consider his partner as human.

Barth is not Jacob Horner, but Barth's attitudes toward sex and toward human involvement in general emerge rather clearly in *End of the Road*. These attitudes emerge in the form of a tension established between Horner and his opposite number, a fellow named Joe Morgan. Joe takes himself very seriously. He is a brilliant young professor, hard at work on a book. His relations with his wife Rennie are terribly self-conscious and absorbing. They are, in a sense, each other's project, and their pride in what they accomplish in their relationship spills out into their communications with others, and, in fact, dominates their secondary relationships.

At first, Horner can do no more than sneer at Morgan, but his aversion quickly turns to admiration, then to jealousy, and finally into a compelling desire to expose Morgan's integrity and discipline as essentially dishonest. Convinced that no one can be genuinely decent, or devoted to another human being as he is devoted to the gratification of his own needs, Horner has an affair with Joe's guilt-ridden wife, and grows curious as to how the inordinately generous and open-minded Joe Morgan will respond to the revelation of his cuckoldry. But before they have a chance to apprise him, Joe is caught literally with his pants down, or at least with his zipper opened. What Barth gives us is an unforgettable tableau which can stand as an image, complete unto itself, of what Barth thinks of high-mindedness, total commitments, and pretensions of having transcended the demands of the diabolical self. Joe Morgan is observed by wife and friend executing military commands, mugging ridiculous faces at himself in the mirror, then, finally, simultaneously picking his nose while masturbating. It is one of the funniest scenes in all of literature, heightened as it is by Barth's sheer stylistic virtuosity, but it is not at all poignant. We are not shattered by this revelation of Joe, for we knew all along somehow that Horner, and even Barth, would have it this way. Morgan was too good to be true, too much an obstacle in the ready flow of cynicism that pours like syrup over Barth's fictions, and sticks to everything it touches.

Barth's attitude toward sex, then, as one might suppose, is very much bound up with his total view of things. A line of Horner's says it rather succinctly: "Maybe the guy who fools himself least is the one who admits that we're all just kidding." One requires a great deal of irony and a great deal of courage to feel this way about oneself, as about men in general, it seems to me. But perhaps when one grows sick enough of man's pervasive hypocrisy, and tired enough of one's own inability to commit one's self to anything beyond one's own pleasures, perhaps then the defensive irony and detachment come easily, and the cynicism grows into a mask not readily removed. What we are left with is the image of man as masturbator, mechanically satisfying his needs, unwilling to romanticize those needs in terms of suggesting that they might be more profound or consuming than, in fact, they are. And Barth, to be sure, sees nothing demonic or even obscene in the various expressions of sexuality. Nothing in his universe is sacred or taboo: it is a landscape with which we have suddenly become all too familiar.

Varieties of Evasion

In the hands of lesser writers than Barth, such materials and attitudes are worked on more casually, and more superficially. Barth's fiction has an energy and a relentless logic which is truly remarkable, given the bizarre creations that are the very texture of his work. In a writer like James Purdy, one cannot but feel that we are dealing with a man who has attitudes at second hand, and who writes novels with the express purpose of having a platform from which he can crudely denounce the popular deities. The attitudes are not all that different from Barth's, but their expression is puerile and lax by comparison with Barth's presentation.

Cabot Wright Begins, to select but one example, is a novel about a rapist, and incidentally about everything in the modern world—everything, that is, that Purdy can think of, which are usually the most apparent things. I mention him at all only because his reputation is very high among some responsible critics, and because he has managed to treat the problems of human sexuality with some maturity, if not with precision.

The crux of Purdy's "message" is that, for all the abandoned talk of sex, for all that liberalism has accomplished, "there isn't a stiff pecker or a warm box in the house." Of course, Purdy may be right, but I doubt it—I doubt even the sense of his character's assertion. What is more important, though, is that it really does not matter very much, for, in Purdy's view, sex is an experience which suggests an extreme impoverishment of other faculties that might instill vigor into the personality. Characters in Purdy frequently resort to sex almost as a last resort, and the novel challenges the very notion of sex as closely related to passion. Cabot Wright is a prodigious rapist not because he is in thrall to his passion, but because he has tried everything else and has been bored to distraction. Finally, of course, the sex fails adequately to satisfy, and Purdy can attribute to it nothing more than minimal significance, which is perhaps as much as it deserves. As one of Purdy's main characters engages in a casual homosexual affair, he is politely set straight by his partner: "A little pressure here, a little pressure there lifts the weight of the world from the heart, but no need to celebrate it by way of explanation." It is difficult to argue with so temperate a statement.

It is not at all surprising that the point of view with which we have here been dealing tends to consider both masturbation and homosexuality as not in any way deviant, nor especially different in the satisfaction they can afford, from "normal" heterosexuality. Some of our better writers, of course, retain a more traditionalist position, though this, too, has its complexities. In a recent story entitled "Whacking Off," Philip Roth recounts an adolescence and a young adulthood tainted by the spectral presence of masturbation and the fear of exposure. For Roth's character, who speaks in the first person, "My wang was all I really had that I could call my own!" Beset by a world which has destroyed his confidence in his ability to make choices for himself, which has instilled in him a fear of life itself, he escapes into the privacy and sanctity of his room to work variations on his monomaniacal obsession. What is unfortunate in the story is Roth's need to explain the bleak and cowardly world view with which he has been impressed as a peculiarly Jewish phenomenon. How frayed and worn the "Jewish mother" gambit has become, with its images of the perennial nag, neurotically concerned to prevent diseases and see to it that the members of her family eat appropriately. One wonders whether Jewish writers like Roth do not believe that Irish mothers frequently express such concerns, and that Irish sons sometimes resort to masturbation as a means of evading a depressing environment.

In any case, what is important for us is that Roth's character implicitly harbors a view of "normal" sexuality as potentially satisfying to the degree that it represents adjustment to the world, engagement with its realities, and the ability to overcome a heritage of petty fears. Masturbation he views as a necessary mode of disengagement in which the masturbator ceases to recognize the unreality of the fantasy that grips him. Roth's character is compelled to reside in the realm of the imagination, but he is fundamentally dissatisfied because he cannot stave off the encroaching reality that surrounds him. The dream of omnipotence is shattered by his social instincts, which advise him to join the world and to consider his evasion immoral and cowardly.

THE OUTER LIMITS

It is perhaps difficult to conceive that there is anything new left to say on the subject of sex. To be sure, our avant-garde writers, including artists as well as social scientists, have more or less exhausted considerations of the possible varieties of sexual experience. What is remarkable, though, is the degree to which emphases have been shifted and primary allegiances re-examined. This is largely the work of a few influential neo-Freudians, including Herbert Marcuse and Norman O. Brown, though it would be misleading to suggest that such men work from a common orientation or proceed in similar directions. What Brown is especially responsible for is a criticism of sexuality as essentially a matter of genital organization. In *Life Against Death* and the more recent *Love's Body*, Brown has articulated an elaborate, if largely fragmented and incoherent, theory of the body as the proper medium for mystical experience, and has tried to move beyond our notions of the genital orgasm either as central or indispensable to human sexuality. To reach his conclusions, Brown has exploited and extended familiar Freudian concepts, particularly Freud's observations of polymorphous perversity identified in the behavior of infants.

Brown has been widely read and discussed in recent years, and his work has been praised in all quarters of our high culture. Even where Brown's proposals have been questioned or vilified, he has been taken seriously, and ideas which we associate with him and with other influential people have become part of our circulating intellectual currency.

This influence is reflected in the way that many of these ideas arise in the creative work of some of our best young writers, who cannot ignore their fascination even though they may be repelled or dubious. One example is the novel *Beautiful Losers* by a Canadian writer named Leonard Cohen. The book has been so popular in the literary community as well as among generally literate readers in the United States, and it is so pervaded by a tone which is undeniably American, that we need not apologize for treating it as a product of American culture. Cohen speaks as one of us, alternately bemused, bewildered, and appalled by the dimensions of experience which our writers and artists have tempted us to explore.

Cohen's is not a balanced vision. The tone of *Beautiful Losers* is shrill and hysterical, reflecting Cohen's conviction that we have become inured to so much that we have almost lost the capacity to feel the numbness that creeps over us. Cohen's pessimism is so embracing as to leave almost no loophole for the soul. He is driven, as it were, to extreme positions, but these do not seem tenable once they are considered in real terms, rather than as abstractions. Cohen's characters exalt playfulness, but they are determinedly unplayful. They are attracted to Brown's theories of the adult body as fundamentally erotogenic, but in describing their participation in various erotic rites, Cohen lapses into a parody of Brown that ultimately suggests Cohen's skepticism. Cohen presents a series of hysterical passages in which characters make love by stuffing their index fingers in one another's ears, to the amazement and dismay of a conventionally jealous husband: "You did it to each other? With your bare fingers? You touched ears and fingers?"/ "You begin to learn."/ "Shut up. What did her ears feel like?" /"Tight."/

"Tight!"/ And so on. Notions of orgasm are to be expanded to include a wide range of sensation: "All flesh can come! Don't you see what we have lost? Why have we abdicated so much pleasure to that which lives in our underwear? Orgasms in the shoulder! Knees going off like fire crackers!"

In fact, the range of human sensation may be extended by a conscious and habitual application of such principles to one's experience, but what this cannot do is counteract other tendencies in experience which tend to desexualize human beings and to detach them from the roots of human behavior. The industrialization of Cohen's native Canada involves a destruction of the primitive cultures that Cohen associates with the American Indians. "They are pouring roads over the trails," his character cries, and later, "I've poisoned the air, I've lost my erection." For Cohen, one cannot separate existence into discrete categories of things which do not interact. What Cohen wants, but knows he cannot have, is a reassertion of the possibilities of love among men, but he feels that such possibilities must remain remote so long as we commit ourselves to them only tangentially. What Cohen ideally envisions is a humanity prostrate before all varieties of experience, yet still somehow able to discriminate, to make choices based on a perception of what is most authentic.

Sexuality will involve a thrust toward an impossible, because complete, engagement with the love object, which may be a real person or an imaginary projection of various ideal qualities. What matters for Cohen is the individual's willingness to accept immolation as a necessary concomitant of genuine engagement. All distinctions between subject and object must cease to be operative, as one becomes what he envisions through the act of willing and naming the terms of his immolation.

Sexual activity is an enabling agent in this process, for as it gratifies, it also makes one receptive to the possibility of harmony among things. For Cohen, however, one does not achieve this purely on an imaginative level, through a passive receptivity potentiated by the release of sexual energies. Unlike Mailer's, Cohen's is an activist ethic, in which sexuality must ideally bring one back to the world, and back to the body, but a body which is loved to the degree that it incorporates qualities of all bodies, and is a pathway to the love of all men. Cohen's activist ethic has a communal basis, and sexual activity, as part of this ethic, must implicate masses of men in a process which renews them as individuals and unites them as a collectivity.

In *Beautiful Losers,* Cohen's protagonist is thrown against a girl in the midst of a swarming political rally. Without a word passing between them, they grope for and find each other's sexual organs, as the frenzy of the crowd begins to mount. As Cohen puts it, "We began our rhythmical movements which corresponded to the very breathing of the mob, which was our family and the incubator of our desire." For Cohen, sex is gratifying insofar as it directly involves men in the task of rebuilding their society. It is a beautiful thought, and if it ignores what we have come to take for granted in human behavior, perhaps it is time that we began to envision possibility in the image of our desire.

In any case, what our best writers and artists have demonstrated is that the engagement of the creative imagination with the materials of sexual experience can be a fruitful process, both for art and for our appreciation of the range of human resources. Though it has been impossible here to do more than suggest certain broad tendencies, it is clear at least that, for our most gifted people, human sexuality cannot be considered apart from other essential elements of the human personality. Where the vision of sexual encounter has been reducible to the grating of organs, at least we have been made aware of our impoverishment as men. We can say with gratitude that we have not been taken lightly.

Sex Education and the Roles of School and Church

By MARY S. CALDERONE

ABSTRACT: When sex education is properly recognized for what it is, a birth to death continuum, the increase of awareness of and involvement in it as a process, on the part of society's institutions, school and church, is striking in recent years. This involvement is looked upon as complementary and supplementary to the role of the family, and is being recognized as requiring didactic and pedagogic preparation. Thus, the number of schools, public, private, and parochial, engaged in developing sex education programs is increasing daily, as are teacher-training programs in institutions of higher learning. Movement away from emphasis on details of reproduction and into the area of the dynamics of male-female roles and relationships has been spearheaded by the major religious communions, which can be expected to continue and expand their leadership roles at both national and community levels. Other professional disciplines, especially in medicine, are also studying their roles in education for sexuality.

Mary S. Calderone, M.D., M.P.H., New York City, is Executive Director, Sex Information and Education Council of the United States (SIECUS). From 1953 to 1964 she was Medical Director of the Planned Parenthood Federation of America. She is a member of the American Medical Association's Committee on Human Reproduction, and of the Commission on Family Life, National Council of Churches of Christ in the United States of America. She was editor of Abortion in the United States (1958) and of Manual of Contraceptive Practice (1964) and author of Release from Sexual Tensions (1960) and of a number of articles in professional and lay publications.

IN the past three years, there has occurred a veritable torrent of interest in, and concern for, the subject of sex education. All responsible agencies dealing with the welfare of human beings, particularly those on the way to maturity, have involved themselves, and, strikingly, nearly always in terms of a rational and sober approach at a working level, rather than in terms of polemics or moralizations.

OVERVIEW: WHAT IS HAPPENING?

That this has been most striking in the case of the churches, as perhaps the last ones from which such an approach might be expected, is because of the unawareness of many people of the giant strides being taken by religion in its efforts to comprehend the phenomenon of changing man in his changing society. This kind of approach was signalized in a revealing transcript of a thoughtful, almost brooding, inter-reactive discussion between nine of the nation's leading liberal clergymen and theologians and Mr. Hugh Hefner, the whole of which was published in the July 1967 issue of *Playboy*. A Catholic priest, a rabbi, and representatives of several Protestant denominations, as well as theologians and deans or professors at theological schools took part. During the long colloquy, many puzzling or controversial aspects of human sexual behavior were discussed, but standouts were the sharp questions that were posed, such as the following: "What is the ultimate purpose of human sexuality?" "What is the meaning of this experience?" "How much inner meaning must the relationship have for us in order to make the outward expression of sex appropriate?" "Can the church expect young people to abstain completely from sexual activity for the ten or fifteen years of their lives when the sex drive is strongest, and then suddenly enter into a sexually mature and well-adjusted marriage?" "What do we have to say to a man or a woman in a situation where sex with the marriage partner is impossible?"[1]

Not only in the pages of *Playboy*, but in retreats, at annual conventions of various denominations, and in symposia, W. H. Genné writes that "members of the various communities of faith are engaging in a vigorous dialogue among themselves and with the secularists in our culture regarding the meaning of human sexuality and its fulfillment." Mr. Genné discusses the recent Joint Statements on Marriage and Family Life in the United States adopted on July 8, 1966 by the National Catholic Welfare Conference, the National Council of Churches, and the Synagogue Council of America, and remarks that "one implication of this statement is that school teachers and administrators can count on more support and cooperation of all these faith groups in any responsible effort to provide a base of study in sex education for the total community."[2]

That such responsible efforts are indeed being made by educators can be attested to very easily, for the number of school systems engaged in developing sex education programs is increasing daily. Although some would like to find a ready-made article that they could simply move comfortably into with a minimum of effort, like the hermit crab which adopts an empty snail shell for his home, others demonstrate the vigor and individualistic independence that has always been considered to be characteristic of the American character, as working committees in most schools and communities do their own homework. That such a process may

[1] The Playboy Panel, "Religion and the New Morality," *Playboy* (July 1967), pp. 55 ff.

[2] William H. Genné, "The Churches and Sexuality," *SIECUS Newsletter 2*, No. 3 (Fall 1966).

result in duplication of effort, and certainly in unevenness of results, is obvious, but the disadvantages are well overbalanced by the gains that accrue from self-involvement and intensive study by as many individuals as possible.

Although no standards for evaluation of school sex education programs have been developed, it is not difficult to observe that a number of communities have outlined, and are well on the way to achieving, totally integrated kindergarten through twelfth-grade sex education programs. There is also evidence that some of the broadest and most creative approaches are in those systems that have started fresh quite recently, rather than in those that have had a program going for a number of years.

All kinds of schools are involved—public schools in small towns and big urban areas, private day and boarding schools, and parochial schools as well. The National Association for Independent Schools gave the private schools a giant boost forward by circulating many source materials, and with an afternoon's symposium at its annual meeting, when representatives of four different schools described their programs, each one different from the other.[3]

Teacher educational institutions are recognizing the important stake they have in this field, and a number of training workshops have been conducted, covering various lengths of time, many of them for in-service credit, with prospects of many more to come in 1968. As an example of the breadth and depth of approach, it is worth noting some of the topics covered in the summer of 1967 in a Family Life

[3] Mary S. Calderone, "Planning a Program of Sex Education," Annual Conference, National Association of Independent Schools (NAIS), Boston, April 1967.

Institute conducted by the Department of Child Development and Family Relations, University of Connecticut at Storrs, over a six-week period. Only 76 graduate students of the many qualified applicants could be accepted. Enrolled were teachers, social workers, clergy, nurses, health educators, social agency personnel, physicians, and school administrators and counselors. Each day's major presentation by an outside consultant was followed by open discussion, and the afternoons were devoted to regularly scheduled discussion groups (1 hour 3 times per week), and to permanently assigned sensitivity groups ($2\frac{1}{2}$ hours 3 times per week) in which the dynamics of group interaction, and individual reactions to such interaction, were not only experienced but discussed and analyzed.

A more condensed six-day Seminar on Sex Education, conducted by the University of Massachusetts in October 1967, covered topics very similar in range to those of the longer symposium in Connecticut:

Transition in Sex Values; Implications for Education.
The Sexual Revolution and the American Family.
Sexual Learning and Sexuality in the Child.
Sexual Learning and Sexuality in the Adolescent.
Co-ordination of Sex Education with Development Stages.
Integration of Sexuality in the Personality.
Premarital Sex Standards in Today's Society.
Sex Education in the Context of Family Life Education.
Role of the School in Sex Education.
Resources and Materials for Sex Education.
The Goals of *Healthy Sexuality* and *Responsible Morality*.

It is notable that in connection with developing understanding of this as a major area of concern in education, several institutions are already planning the development of courses leading to

M.A. and Ph.D. degrees in family life and sex education.

Other professional schools have also become involved: in the summer of 1967 faculty representatives from twenty-eight medical schools of the United States and Canada attended a training seminar in marriage, the family, and human sexuality, at the Behavioral Sciences Center of the Bowman Gray School of Medicine; and the Ecumenical Continuing Education Center at Yale University announced that among its planned conferences on topics of relevance to the contemporary renewal of the church, such as worship, the arts, urbanization and others, were conferences on Theology and Sexuality, and Masculinity and Femininity. The former conference in May 1967, "after hearing Dr. William Masters' report on his researches on human sexual responses, recommended that funds be raised to have a theologically trained person work with Dr. Masters and develop a dialogue with the churches." [4]

A number of state medical societies and academies of general practice, as well as the Student American Medical Association, have taken advantage of the generous administrative and financial support of Lederle Laboratories to mount hugely successful one-day symposia on Sexual Problems in Medical Practice. In four states (Alaska, Colorado, Hawaii, and Oregon) these meetings commanded the largest attendance of any medical meeting in their history. This was true of most summer sex-education workshops, whether for teachers, clergymen, or physicians—almost every one was greatly oversubscribed.

GOALS AND EVALUATION

General understanding of the goals of a sex education program have moved very rapidly from the relatively limited aims of reducing unwed pregnancies or venereal disease rates, to the much more comprehensive goal of providing the kind of knowledge and opportunity for learning and discussion that will develop the ability of young people to make rational and responsible decisions in their personal lives. Cyrus R. Pangborn, Chairman of the Department of Religion at Douglass College of Rutgers, New Jersey, remarks that what the "new morality" calls for is "an end to the isolation of sex as a set of external acts and an integration of enriched notions of sexuality into our view of what comprises whole, complete personhood." [5]

It is certainly clear from such books as Myron Brenton's *The American Male* and Charles Ferguson's *The Male Attitude* that among the broad goals of sex education should be exploration of the whole realm of evolving and unanswered questions on the nature of marriage and of the changing roles and relationships of men and women today.

Inevitably, the question arises of how to evaluate the results of a sex education program: How and in what terms are its successes and failures to be identified and measured? Obviously, here one must differentiate between examination and testing for factual knowledge and the far more subtle question of evaluating changes in beliefs and attitudes. On this point, Seymour L. Halleck observes:

An important need is to help our youth understand those conditions which favor and those conditions which interfere with a permanent relationship. If students were more capable of gauging the depth of commitment in their relationships, they would be in a better position to make the initial decisions as to their premarital sexual behavior. [6]

[4] *Marriage and Family Life Newsletter*, National Council of Churches, *VII*, No. 2, New York (April-June 1967).

[5] Cyrus R. Pangborn, "Sex and the Single Standard," *Christian Century* (May 1967).

[6] Seymour L. Halleck, "Sex and Mental

One wonders whether evaluation of the results of sex education programs can ever be made, in view of the fact that the actual subject of judgment and evaluation will not be these, but society itself. In this connection, it should be remarked that to take the adolescent out of the context of the whole society, as we have been doing, and to focus our primary indictments on this age group, betrays the lack of a sense of balance and proportion as well as of involvement on the part of us adults. What is really at stake today is the changing roles and relationships of men and women, with the attending tensions and stresses, and adolescents are bearing the brunt of the resulting confusions and distortions. Furthermore, if it is the roles and relationships that are changing, then, in point of fact, man himself is *not* changing as fast as are his institutions and his world, and one is left to speculate about the obsolescence of man in relation to the technology that he himself has developed.

This speculation bears directly and specifically on the question of sex education, for in considering the long psychodynamic process by which the virtually sexually undifferentiated infant is turned into a mature man or woman, the question must arise whether it, the process, can be speeded up or automated without damage to itself and consequently to the human organism. There is strong evidence that it cannot be, or at least that our knowledge of the nature of the process is too imperfect to permit us to do so with impunity. Therefore the psychosexual maturation process of the human being continues to be carried on hit-or-miss, with pre-wheel-era standards and methods, while the organism itself is living under space-age tempo and impact. Studies that might

lead to an understanding of change and its impact on man, as in the Harvard University Program on Technology and Society, have barely begun; yet, as its executive director Emmanual Mesthene has observed, "Change is the new reality."

If man as he is, is obsolescent, then what kind do we want to produce in his place and how do we design the production line? In essence, that is the real question facing those who are concerned with sex education—what it is, how to do it, who does it. This is why the wide variety of the groups and professions engaged in dialogue about, and movement in, sex education is so encouraging, and this is also why the increasing dialogue on sexuality and sexual roles that is being encouraged among young people themselves and between young people and older ones, is of critical essentiality, for the young people are the very ones who will be living the change. Mesthene says it well:

The challenge to education is clear and staggering. Teachers who have been brought up to cherish the stable must take the children of parents who have been brought up to cherish the stable, and try to teach those children that the stable, the unchanging, is unreal, constraining, a false goal, and that they will survive in an age of change only to the degree that they become familiar with change, feel comfortable with it, understand it, master it, and control it.[7]

Here is where the leadership role of the churches is making itself most felt, for church leaders of all persuasions are proving themselves .to be more ready for the play of the mind over the vast implications of changes in the man-woman relationship than the other institutions such as education and medi-

Health on the Campus," *Journal of the American Medical Association,* 200, No. 8 (May 22, 1967).

[7] Emmanuel G. Mesthene, "On Understanding Change: The Harvard University Program on Technology and Society," *Technology and Culture, VI,* No. 2 (Spring 1965), pp. 222–235.

cine. The person who reads only the popular press cannot think or react from the same broad point of view as such a student in the history of social thought as Father Joseph Walsh, Catholic Chaplain of Brandeis University, who, in discussing the problem of making the Roman Catholic Church relevant to the needs of our society, remarked:

In reading . . . studies, you come away with an awareness of a profound cultural process taking place. . . . You see a culture in the process of rejecting a long-held, if not always well-observed moral position, searching for new standards, while often veering in the direction of self-indulgence; *a culture struggling, especially in its younger generation, to give birth to a new way of being human and sexual.* [Italics added.][8]

In the process of trying to learn how to help our younger generations in this struggle, many of us still make the mistake of offering to provide them with answers, which simply does not work. What, without any question at all, works and works well, at least as a starter, is to extend to our young people free and open access to such knowledge as we have about human sexuality and sexual behavior, including direct access to the very best and most valid studies available. When we do this, their response is everything we could wish for, as exemplified in the following result, in the words of the students themselves, of two and a half days spent by me on the campus of a boys' prep school.

(From the report):

"Throughout the discussions, to the relief of all, [she] took neither the coldly-clinical nor the sickly-sweet 'birds and bees' approach. From the beginning she made it clear she was not here to sanction a code of free love or in general to give answers."

"It was reassuring to all that she was willing at times to mention her convictions."

"She agreed with the students that contraceptives should not be handed out to teenagers unless through doctors who first discussed the situation fully with their patients."[9]

(From the Editorial):

"Students and Masters alike greeted Dr. Mary Calderone full of inhibition, skepticism, and perhaps even embarrassment. Four days later, when all the lectures and crowded, informal discussions . . . were over, boys were still talking openly and inquisitively about sexual behavior, the "new morality" and society's unjust reactions. The previous sneers and chuckles had disappeared. A milestone in understanding and communications had been reached."

"She communicated naturally on the level of the boys, spoke their language, appreciated and reciprocated their feelings, and *trusted their judgment. The respect was mutual.*" [Italics added.]

"Such a free and encouraging atmosphere could only result in a long-awaited outpouring of questions and pent-up feelings. But will such genuine communication on so vital a subject continue? Will the School seek to assuage this hunger for discussion only through a course in cold biology? . . . Masters and boys must not allow the present fervor to pass without capitalizing on *its ability to improve their relationship.*" [Italics added.][10]

One might postulate from the above that such a reaction, one that obviously has the possibility of much forward movement for everyone concerned, might be expected from a picked group of boys of highest educational status. But only two months later exactly the same kind of spirited and intelligent reaction was experienced with a group of Upward

[8] Father Joseph L. Walsh, "Sex on Campus," *Commonweal, LXXXV,* No. 20, February 24, 1967.

[9] *The Pelican,* St. Paul's School, Concord, N.H., May 3, 1967.
[10] *Ibid.*

Bound students, assembled after only twenty-four hours together on a Midwest campus. After the end, not of two and a half days, but of one hour of presentation and one hour of discussion, these high school young people, about equally divided as to color and sexes, were fervently discussing *with each other* the meaning of love and how to define maturity, and it was later reported that this discussion continued in the dormitory for over two hours. In retrospect, both experiences merge not only in terms of respect, dignity, real knowledge exchanged, and shouts of shared laughter at the *double-entendre* bloopers that are inevitable to such sessions and that are usually made by me, but also by the hard tingle that comes from the satisfying play of many intelligences on a subject of great mutual interest.

The prospect of well-planned backup reading for future discussions for the first group could turn their experience into true and continuing education. With the second group, all that could be said was that a door had been opened a crack and that was all, yet the potentialities for education were poignantly there. Presumably the Upward Bound young people were ones who had been having one or another difficulty, whether intellectual or behavioral, with regard to their schooling. There is a good deal of evidence that anxiety and tensions of various kinds can be the root causes of such difficulties, and, as highlighted by Michael Duane in an article on his own experience in a British school in a depressed area, school performance and behavior have often been noted to improve markedly when anxiety due to unanswered questions about sex is reduced.[11]

11 Michael Duane, "Sex Education—A Small Experiment," *Family Planning, II,* No. 2 (July 1962), London. (Available as a SIECUS reprint.)

SUMMARY

The roles of the school and the church as to sex education may be separate, but surely they are equal, for these are the two institutions that have been specifically charged by society with the development of quality human beings, by means of such consciously engineered processes as society's own best minds can blueprint. In these days of violence and dropouts, it is hard to say whether the failures we see are the minds' in what they have blueprinted, or the institutions' in their incapacity to carry out the blueprints, or the epoch's—or all three.

But the failures should not obscure the successes—those many young people who, in spite of little help from us, and much hindrance in the shape of obsessed, distorted, and exploitive sexual messages from the communications media, yet manage to achieve stable sexual maturity. The wonder is that these are as many as they are.

A listing of schools and churches which have stated that they are carrying on sex education programs would be long indeed but quite uninformative as to the nature or caliber of the programs. Just as pointless at this time would be the publication by SIECUS,[12] or any organization, of a "model" curriculum, for this might tend to stifle the very creative thrust that we now see happening in so many schools and communities, as responsible leaders engage in reading

12 The SIECUS purpose: *To establish man's sexuality as a health entity*—to identify the special characteristics that distinguish it from, yet relate it to, human reproduction; to dignify it by openness of approach, study, and scientific research designed to lead toward its understanding and its freedom from exploitation; to give leadership to professionals and to society, to the end that human beings may be aided toward responsible use of the sexual faculty and toward assimilation of sex into their individual life patterns as a creative and re-creative force.

and discussions, and arrive at patterns that in their judgment best fit the needs of their particular communities. Additionally, such efforts mean a far more dynamic involvement for each individual who participates actively in the process—and there is no substitute for this kind of involvement, if rapid movement forward is to happen.

Therefore, SIECUS has refused to prepare or to recommend any specific sex education curricula, although it has been involved in a consultative capacity in the development of not a few. Its first Study Guide, however, did set down in concise form what the multidisciplinary SIECUS Board considered to be the nine primary objectives for sex education and also six broad areas of emphasis that should be included in a comprehensive sex education program. The nine objectives are:[13]

1. To provide for the individual an adequate knowledge of his own physical, mental and emotional maturation processes as related to sex.
2. To eliminate fears and anxieties relative to individual sexual development and adjustments.
3. To develop objective and understanding attitudes toward sex in all of its various manifestations—in the individual and in others.

[13] Lester A. Kirkendall, *Sex Education,* SIECUS Study Guide No. 1 (New York: SIECUS, 1965).

4. To give the individual insight concerning his relationships to members of both sexes and to help him understand his obligations and responsibilities to others.
5. To provide an appreciation of the positive satisfaction that wholesome human relations can bring in both individual and family living.
6. To build an understanding of the need for the moral values that are needed to provide rational bases for making decisions.
7. To provide enough knowledge about the misuses and aberrations of sex to enable the individual to protect himself against exploitation and against injury to his physical and mental health.
8. To provide an incentive to work for a society in which such evils as prostitution and illegitimacy, archaic sex laws, irrational fears of sex, and sexual exploitation are nonexistent.
9. To provide the understanding and conditioning that will enable each individual to utilize his sexuality effectively and creatively in his several roles, e.g., as spouse, parent, community member, and citizen.

If the school and the church play their roles in driving hard and intelligently toward these objectives, they will find their best partners to be the very ones for whom they have primarily undertaken these efforts: our eager and capable American young people.

Sexual Patterns in Three Ethnic Subcultures of an American Underclass

By BERNARD ROSENBERG and JOSEPH BENSMAN

ABSTRACT: Three American ethnic subcultures, all consisting of transmigrated groups living in poverty, were studied and the sexual patterns of the youth described. The groups consisted of white Appalachians living in Chicago, Negroes in Washington, D.C., and Puerto Ricans in New York. Sharply differentiated patterns of sexual behavior, involving conquest, sex education, sex misinformation, attitudes toward females, responsibility, and affect were discovered, and these patterns are reflected in the language of the subcultures, particularly in their argot. The underclass sexual mores differ from those of the American middle class, but not more than they differ from each other among the three ethnic groups. Sexual practices are related to general life styles, and reflect ghettoization, subcultural isolation, and short-range hedonism in groups only recently transplanted from their rural areas of origin.

Bernard Rosenberg, Ph.D., New York City, is Professor of Sociology at the City College of New York and guest professor at the New School for Social Research. He is coauthor of Mass, Class, and Bureaucracy (1964), The Vanguard Artist (1965), coeditor of Mass Culture: The Popular Arts in America (1957), editor of Analyses of American Society (1966), and author of numerous articles that have appeared in Dissent, Commentary, and many sociological journals.

Joseph Bensman, Ph.D., New York City, is Associate Professor of Sociology at the City College of New York and has taught at the New School for Social Research. He is coauthor of Small Town in a Mass Society (1958) and author of Dollars and Sense (1967). Dr. Bensman has frequently contributed to sociological journals.

NO American who wishes to discuss love and sex can avoid the long Western tradition from within which we, knowingly or unknowingly, come by all our perspectives. Jerusalem, Athens, Rome, and their several sequelae constitute, or symbolize, that tradition. From it, that is to say, from the Hellenic and Judaeo-Christian past, Western man derives not only certain prescriptions and prohibitions, but a whole framework of ideas, concepts, and theories that are his heavy cultural burden. Diffusion and dilution notwithstanding, the sexual analyst and those he discusses share that burden. To be sure, neither need recognize or acknowledge the connection that binds them together in an inescapable matrix.

We have come to our present sexual pass through devious and tangled paths, still strewn with innumerable laws, parables, images, aftereffects, and reflections. In this brief statement, we can do no more than touch upon a few highlights which may illuminate part of our rich and varied background.

For example, the poems of Sappho and those of Ovid, like a score of other such sources—including philosophical schools, and religious cults—have in common that they celebrate erotic joy. All of them say to us that love (as in the story of Ruth) and sex (as in the mythopoeic figure of Priapus) should involve deep feeling or great pleasure. This notion is currently fashionable among many otherwise disenchanted, proudly "rational," and highly sophisticated people. At the same time, they are affected by those provisions of the Decalogue, as interpreted by Talmudic and Scholastic commentators, that set severe limits upon love and sexuality while emphasizing the responsibilities inherent in sacramental and indissoluble relationships whose purpose is solely reproductive.

With *eros* and *agape,* Plato spiritual-ized sex. St. Augustine, and, later on, many of the Schoolmen who introduced Aristotelian modifications, took over these Platonic ideas. In various guises, they became essential to both the Catholic and Protestant world view. The Christian churches also fashioned sexual codes of their own which, even when they were systematically violated, produced discrete and historically specialized sexual behavior. In Europe and America, sexual renunciation, with deep intellectual and religious roots, always seems to have had an obverse side, or to have proceeded in dialectical sequence to eroticism. Thus, to condemn the pleasures of the flesh may itself entail, or simply lead to, precisely those pleasures. The medieval denial of sex was in no way incompatible with chivalry and romantic love as practiced at the courts of Aquitaine and Provence. Here, if anywhere, as Denis de Rougemont has shown, are the beginnings of a romantic conception made universally familiar in our time by way of Hollywood films. Dante and Beatrice, Tristan and Iseult, or Romeo and Juliet are prototypic cases in which sexual desire feeds upon the loved one's permanent inaccessibility.

Seventeenth-century Puritanism and nineteenth-century Victorianism, each in its complex and contradictory manner, left us with a dualistic dogma whose force is not yet fully spent. Mind and body (therefore, love and sex) were pitted against each other. As the underside of Victorian life is subjected to increasing exposure, one beholds not only the sexually etherealized woman of virtue, but her fallen sister, whether given to prostitution or not, who is cynically and mercilessly exploited. As hitherto unpublishable memoirs reach the contemporary reader, he comes to know the moralistic upper-class gentleman who collects pornography, indulges in exotic, probably inverted and polymorphous, perverse sexual tastes while practicing hypocrisy, if not perfecting it to a high art.

Victorianism and the revolt against it are our immediate antecedents. And that revolt is largely ideological. The exaltation of eroticism tends to be academic. Proponents of "sexual freedom" contrast it favorably with artificial and hypocritical Victorian conventions. Beginning with feminism as a political movement, proceeding in the 1920's under banners like companionate or trial marriage, through a strident call for emancipation and liberation, to the present "sexual revolution," learned men have set forth their ideas. Hedonists and rationalists, champions of homosexuality, of a return to infantile gratification with "love's body" and no mere fixation on genital pleasure: here is a peculiar gamut from Bertrand Russell to Albert Ellis, Herbert Marcuse, and Norman O. Brown. None of them, the logician, the psychotherapist, the Hegelian, or the Classical scholar, is primarily interested in the restoration of "natural" sexuality. All of them are passionately interested in proving or disproving theories.

Even Sigmund Freud, who did more than anyone else to free Western thought from the straightjacket of Victorianism, was himself a puritan—in perhaps the best Biblical sense of the term. Furthermore, Freud, in his sexual speculations and investigations, drew heavily upon Greek philosophy, specifically the ideas of *agape, eros,* and *caritas.* Freud's "scientific" attitude toward sex is actually permeated with several of the oldest concepts of antiquity—with which they are perfectly continuous. Insofar as Freudian psychology fuels the sexual revolution, it is directed not at the demolition of Western norms, but only at one narrow version of a complicated social heritage.

Like speech, dress, manners, and a score of other visible stigmata, conduct in the sexual sphere has always been class-bound. To speak of the mores dominant in any period is necessarily to be elliptical. For example, the Victorian double standard was, in its own time, mainly an upper-middle-class phenomenon, rarely affecting higher and lower social strata. Similarly, the revolt against it seems to have liberated segments of the middle class at least from the idea of sexual repression. For some time now, as Theodore Dreiser noted over and over in his early novels, the relatively stable blue-collar working class has best exemplified puritanical prudery and sexual hypocrisy.

All the while, romantic writers, artists, and social scientists have been searching for "genuine" or "natural" sexuality, embodied in an eroticized and newly ennobled savage, uncontaminated by that odious sophistication which reduces the physical expression of love to *le contact de deux épidermes.* Thus occurs the idealization of peasants, "earthmen," primitives, those sexually spontaneous and unalienated humans who —when viewed from a safe distance— look so free and easy in all their ways. Are there such groups of people within the underclass of our own society? Does their alleged culture of poverty so far remove them from Western civilization that research in their midst will reveal what love and sex are really like when they are emancipated from history and intellectuality?

THE THREE ETHNIC SUBCULTURES

These are some of the questions implicit in the material that follows.[1] Three miserably, and more or less equally, impoverished areas in New

[1] This essay stems from a much larger study conceived and directed by Bernard Lander under multiple sponsorship, including the President's Committee on Juvenile Delinquency and Youth Crime, Notre Dame University, and the Lavanburg Corner House Foundation.

York, Chicago, and Washington, D.C., were selected for prolonged study. Lander and his associates held poverty constant and introduced ethnicity as the variable. They concentrated on all the inhabitants of one social block (with dwellings that face each other) in each of the three cities. In New York, most of the subjects were Puerto Ricans, in Chicago, Appalachian whites, and in Washington, Negroes. Intensive non-directed "tandem interviews" (with two interviewers and one respondent) yielded the qualitative data about adolescent youth that we cite and sift in our analysis.

All three of these ethnic groups are composed largely of recent migrants, who had come to the urban centers from other parts of the United States (including Puerto Rico), and who had brought with them many of their ways of life, perhaps even accentuated by contrast with their new environment and their new neighbors.

A common culture presupposes that those who belong to it speak the same language. There is such a language for all Americans as there is an overarching culture that unifies urban dwellers and farmers, the young and the old, the privileged and the underprivileged. Subcultural segmentation produces "special languages" within the larger linguistic community, and they are intelligible only to initiates, that is, members of ethnic, occupational, regional, and religious groups. That the broadly conceptualized culture (or subculture) of poverty is somewhat illusory can be demonstrated by the variegated speech patterns characteristic of poor Appalachian whites, Negroes, and Puerto Ricans. Indeed, for each of our populations, it would be possible to assemble a glossary of terms widely used by insiders but meaningless to most outsiders. How luxuriant local variation takes place (in meaning, accent, and

value) is the proper subject matter of a highly technical discipline called ethnolinguistics. It is not our intention to turn that discipline loose on data gathered for other purposes. Nevertheless, this much must be said: each group living in its own slum moves towards a certain linguistic homogeneity, bringing ancestral speech ways, borrowing symbols from the larger society, and synthesizing them into distinctive configurations. Peculiarities of speech are a rough index of differential association and cultural isolation. Unique idioms emerge from intense in-group living, and disappear at the opposite pole of full acculturation. In between, we find a complex mixture reflecting uneven exposure to the wider institutional order, which is itself in constant flux. A few illustrations from the heterosexual sphere may be in order.

Chicago

In our sample, the adolescent males among the New York Puerto Ricans and Washington Negroes are unresponsive to questions about dating. The word does not appear in their lexicon, and, as it turns out, this fact points to a substantive difference in behavior between these boys and those in Chicago. Every respondent among the Chicago Appalachian whites knows what a date is. One at first defines it as "goin' out with a fox," then adds, "You just go out driving, make some love, catch a crib—and that's all." Here, indeed, are the cadences, the inflections, and the semantics of a special language in which "fox" means girl and "crib" stands for house or apartment, which, in turn, signifies a trysting place that one "catches" along with the "fox." Such expressions may have their origin in the hill country of Kentucky and Alabama, whence they were transplanted to the Midwest and, merged with much else, produced a dynamic amalgam that cannot be duplicated elsewhere.

There are fuzzy edges around every word that is variously defined not only at different levels of the social hierarchy, but within any one level. For those who generalize in the grand manner, dating is understood to be "an American" phenomenon; the more sophisticated family sociologists (who prepare textbooks for college students) see it as a peculiar ritual, a courtship pattern, practiced by middle-class youth in the United States. In our samplings of the underclass, only the poor white teen-agers date, and they do so in ways similar to and dissimilar from those of their middle-class counterparts. The telephone, for instance, plays no great part in their activities, as it does among more privileged adolescents, but the automobile is central. Neither matters much with Puerto Ricans and Negroes.

The Chicago boys, who will sometimes commit crimes to get a car, and need it to commit other crimes, and whose vocabulary is rich with the knowledge they have of car parts, may be said to live in a car complex. This circumstance provides them with a degree of physical mobility far greater than that of any other economically deprived group we have studied. In a crisis, occasioned, say, by the impregnation of a girl friend (scarcely a rare occurrence), they can always take to the road, ranging widely over Illinois and adjacent states. The automobile liberates them, up to a point, not only from their constricted neighborhood, but from the metropolis itself. And, given the car, they are able to date girls in a more or less conventional manner. The "portable bedroom" can be used for preliminary sex play most conveniently at drive-in movies, where two or three couples commonly occupy one car. Asked what he usually does on a date, a fifteen-year-old Chicago boy replies,

in part:

If your friend's got a girl he's taking to the drive-in, you take her with him. And you take your girl to the show, go out to eat, dance, stuff like that.

On the average, what does a date cost?

Well, if you go to a show, you won't have to spend but about, at the most, five, maybe six dollars. . . . If you go to the drive-in, you spend a dollar and a half for each one to get in. That's three dollars. Give the kid who's driving the car a buck, split the gas bill, you know, help to pay for some of the gas—and you eat. Oh, it costs you about six dollars.

Bowling and roller-skating are other diversions deemed to be suitable on dates in our Chicago sample. Neither is a popular boy-girl pastime in the other cities—where boys like sports that they play with other boys. Pick-ups are made on the street from a car, in neighborhood movie houses, and in teen-age bars which are frequented with great regularity only by the Appalachians.

All of this sounds a great deal like the textbook account, even to a general preference for double-dating. Yet, the reasons behind that preference give us a clue to something different, and specific to the Chicago group, namely, that a heavy streak of violence is woven into the texture of their heterosexual behavior. Hence: "I like to go out with other couples because it's better when you travel together. When you're alone, there's always other guys trying to start trouble." You date, but you appear alone with a girl at your own peril, as this little vignette makes clear:

I saw her walking down the hall with another boy, and I got pretty jealous. I started saying, "If you like that guy so much, go ahead and go out with him," and he walked up and started smartin' off to me. So I hit him, and then I beat him up. She turned around and slapped me. She called me a brute or something. . . . So that didn't hit me just right, and I said, "Forget it."

If a date culminates in sexual inter-course, it is also useful to have someone else along:

> I was going with a girl. She was sixteen. She squealed on me, and they tried to get me on statutory rape. And, oh, she gave 'em a big long story, trying to get me into a lot of trouble. But there was another kid along with me on that date. And she claimed that he held her down and that I held her down. But this boy's stories matched and hers didn't. Otherwise, I would have been sunk.

With dating, there go the lineaments of a rating-dating complex, which does not precisely parallel Willard Waller's fam-ous description of a widespread campus phenomenon, but does imply a measure of respect for the girls one dates, by contrast with the disrespect accorded girls and older women who are nothing but sexual objects. The following ex-ample is somewhat extreme but highly indicative:

> I consider a girl you go out with and a girl you have intercourse with two differ-ent kinds of girls. There's a girl I date. I like to hold hands with her and make out with her, kiss her, but that's as far as I want to go with any girl I take out. If I like the girl, I don't want to mess her up. But then, there is the other girls I just don't care about because they give it to the other guys—which means they don't care too much for theirselves.

The type of boy who makes this pro-visionally puritanical division between good girls (with lovers who hold back from final consummation) and bad girls who "give it to the other guys," is yet capable of treating "good girls" with even greater harshness. This double standard means that there are separate norms; less is expected of the promis-cuous girl, much more of the girl you date who may, after all, become your wife. If so, unquestioning submission to male authority is expected:

> What if you married a girl who talked back to you? What would you do?
> Shut her up.
> How?
> Well, I'd fix her where she wasn't able to talk too much.

The specter of violence is omnipresent. It may issue from association with either type of girl, and although there are always two types, criteria for establish-ing them vary. (Asked whether he still considers girls decent if they go to bed with him, a Chicago boy answers, "It's a matter of how hard I have to work. If I have to work real hard I think a lot of them. If they give it to me right off I think they're pigs.") Infidelity in a girl friend will ordinarily provoke a physical assault of some sort. What to do if the woman you marry is unfaith-ful? "Beat the shit out of her" is the semiautomatic response.

Acts of aggression connected with sex are, no doubt, intensified by heavy con-sumption of alcohol. Sex, liquor, and violence form a *Gestalt* in Chicago not nearly so discernible in New York or Washington. In another context, whis-key and beer act as a catalyst for serious fighting, possibly with recourse to knives and firearms. In the sexual context, alcohol is also believed to be useful as a means of emboldening the boy and rendering the girl more compliant to his advances:

> Do the girls get pretty wild when they've had a few drinks?
> Yes.
> Do most of the guys try to get the girls loaded?
> Yes.
> How often are you successful?
> We're not very successful at getting them loaded. I mean that takes a little money.

Beer is cheaper than whiskey and favored for that reason; a low alcohol content notwithstanding, it is believed to serve the purpose. Girls plied with beer are considered "better," that is, more available, than those who remain unlubricated. They can more easily be "cut"—which is typical and revealing Chicago argot for the sex act.

New York City

In the New York sample, there is no "cutting." The first few interviews with Puerto Rican youth revealed little about sex, a topic concerning which we had not anticipated that there would be unusual reticence. The breakdown in communication turned out to be no more than terminological. Once in possession of key words and phrases, the interviewers encountered no serious resistance to the free discussion of plain and fancy sex. There are taboo topics, notably religion as it shades off into magic, but sex is not one of them. The linguistic breakthrough occurred in this matter when a resident observer advised us to ask about "scheming." We did so, causing faces to light up that had remained blank as long as we struggled vainly to find the right conventional or unconventional sexual expression. "Scheming" was that expression. Equivalent, in a way, to "cutting" which suggests sex-and-sadism, "scheming" has mildly conspiratorial overtones. It stands for kissing, necking, petting, and full sexual consummation, everything from prepubertal exploration to real coitus, which is secret, exploitative, and pleasurable, but seldom brutal. With appropriate language, much information can be elicited, and comic misunderstandings are left behind. (To the question, "Did you ever have a girl sexually?" the young Puerto Rican respondent answers by asking, "Did I ever have a girl *sectionally?*" And some minutes are consumed, to no avail, in disentangling the adverbs. We want to know from another boy whether he goes to bed with girls, whether he sleeps with them, and he takes us literally: "No. I sleep by myself, in my own bed.")

Scheming is initiated at parties, and parties are called sets. They function as substitutes for going out, picking up, and dating. Young people at or around twenty may have apartments of their own which, like any of many vacant apartments on the block, can be used for sets, as they can be and are used for private or collective sexual adventures. At sets, boys and girls meet, play records, dance, drink beer or whiskey more or less moderately, smoke cigarettes and take pot more or less immoderately, and, under dim colored lights, engage in uninhibited foreplay. With twenty or more in attendance, sets seem to be fairly large affairs, and while some are organized during the week by hedonistic truants, there are sure to be others around the clock on week-ends. Since the youngsters use stimulants and depressants that are costly, and Saturday is the traditional day for pilfering small objects whose sale produces money with which to buy supplies, the best sets are most likely to occur on Saturday nights. You drink a little, you smoke a lot, you are high, a girl offers to dance with you, and by and by, when the dim lights go out altogether, you fondle her. Presently, you step outside with your girl and scheme in the hallway, at her place if no one is at home, on a rooftop—this one, or another at the nearby housing project. And:

If you got a really good friend, and the girl is willing if she's really bad off or somethin', you know what she will do? *She'll pull the train.*
Pull the train?
Yes, that's what we call it: pulling the train. You take one chance. Then another guy takes a chance. You know.
Usually, how many guys are there?
Two.

Not like ten guys with one girl?

Oh, depends like on what kind of a girl. . . . I been in a situation with about six guys.

"Pulling the train" is by no means an everyday occurrence. Sets are. They may be regarded as a spontaneous expression of youth culture, an informal device contrived by teen-agers for their own pleasure, a technique for circumventing official and established organizations, an escape from uplift sponsored by benevolent adults. Sets provide an arena—or constitute a preparation—for scheming, which, in most cases, means private and secret sexual activity. Boys do boast, with a probable admixture of phantasy and exaggeration, about sexual conquests, but they are loath to name names and thus cause "trouble" for themselves or their girl friends. The set in which they begin to participate at about age fifteen is understood to be somewhat illicit. It may become a pot party or a sex party (our respondents are ambivalent and divided among themselves about which they like best) —and either one, if publicized, can lead to unpleasant sanctions.

Washington, D. C.

Boy-girl relations in the Washington poor Negro community are neither as car- and show-centered as in the Chicago white group nor as party-centered as in the New York Puerto Rican group. In Washington, the school, despite all its deficiencies, is much more pivotal than we would have supposed. Young people attend school dances now and then, meet classmates formally and informally, and, while ungoverned by any particular protocol, they begin to "go out" with one another. Soon there is sex play, and, in many cases, real sexual involvement. Things tend to begin in school, and there, too, the "facts of life" are transmitted most frequently and most effectively. Only in our Washing-

ton Negro sample do high school children use technical (now and then garbled) scientific terms for the sex act and the sex organs. They describe human reproduction as it has been explained to them by their biology teachers:

We had it in school. I know how the sperms come down, when a boy is having sex relations with a girl; they meet the egg, go up through the vagina, stay in the womb and grow month after month. And then after a period of time, the woman have a baby.

We're supposed to do that next half, after we finish with music (find out where babies come from and things like that).

Well, I know the process of starting—I mean, you have to have two unions, I mean a fusion of, uh, male and female, between the two organs. I mean the vulva and the, um, penis. The vulva and the penis. And, um, it takes a union of sperm and meeting with the egg. And after that, I know the situation of—what do you call it?—the embry—yeah, embry—and that's the first stage of the child. . . . And the food which the child receives comes from the navel of the mother. It's connected to the child, I believe mouth-to-navel, something like that. And after a nine month period, the child's supposed to be born.

A boy whose parents told him "all about it" at age twelve, says:

They explained it to me, that it was the entrance of the penis into the woman's vulva. I mean, they used other terms, but that's the terms I would use because, let's say, I'm more up on it now, on this education.

Again:

Well, uh, let's see, when the sperm, I think goes into the vagina, something like that, then, it meets the other sperm I think, and it starts doing something.

However imperfectly they may have absorbed their biology lessons, these teen-agers show a degree of sophistication unavailable to their counterparts among the New York Puerto Ricans and in Chicago, where sexual knowledge is more likely to be associated with the street—and its earthy language—than with the classroom. (With the Puerto Ricans, a self-taught, semi-demi-social worker has helpfully taken it upon himself to provide some sex instruction in yet another linguistic style—largely Spanish, partly English argot.) For children to seek or parents to offer information, even when it is urgently needed, seems to be a rare occurrence. (We suspect that parent-youth embarrassment on this score is a class phenomenon. There is reason to believe that the middle-class parent now speaks freely to his children about the facts of life while evading questions about the facts of death.) The young mother of two illegitimate children in Washington tells us that she developed early: "At the age of twelve I was as developed as any girl of fourteen or fifteen. Being young, I never paid too much attention to it, but older people in the community noticed." As she recounts it, men got fresh; some began to follow her home, and she took to making "smart" remarks. Then, after awhile, "I had one man run me home from school." She ran and found sanctuary on a neighbor's porch, and "the man started to come after me till he looked up and spotted a lady and another man on the porch. After that my mother came over, and we told her about it, and the three of them walked around, but they didn't see him." This incident was but the first of several, including one "proposition" from a preacher, about which the mother was informed. She still divulged nothing to her daughter, and the daughter observes, "I just could not bring myself to look up at my mother and ask her what was happening."

The whole story, "the nitty gritty," came from experience with "fellows,"

who, however, were judged to be stupid, as well as girls on the street and an older sister. From her own account, but never officially, she was a sexual delinquent by age thirteen.

On the other hand, in Washington, a Negro boy may experience sexual initiation under his father's auspices. If there is an older woman who wishes to "come some," that is, who wishes to have a sex partner, the father sometimes encourages his son to co-operate. We have one such case on record:

She (the older woman) came down to see my sister, and she started liking me. She started paying my way to the movies and all that. So my father told me to go on and do it. So I did. . . . He say, "I know you going to do it when I ain't around." So he gave me a protector, and I go on and do it. . . . He say we were going to do it behind his back anyhow, and that he just wanted to help me along. I ain't never used the protection, though.

Attitude comparisons

Although he tends to confuse protection against venereal disease with protection against pregnancy, the Negro teen-ager is generally more knowledgeable about this, too, than his Puerto Rican or poor white age mate. He more often recognizes and applies terms like contraceptive, diaphragm, coil, prophylactic, or rubber—for one reason, because he more often knows what they mean. Not that he or his girl friend is much inclined to use any of these objects, for their interposition threatens the individual with loss of his "cool"— an important but amorphous quality which must be maintained at all times. Although among all three ethnic samples, only a minority favor contraception, the Negro youth understand best, and Puerto Rican youth least, just what it is that they habitually decline to use. And, while amorality or *anomie* tends to prevail in sexual matters, it assumes a degree of egocentricity among the poor white boys unequalled elsewhere. In this exchange, we have an extreme but not atypical expression of the Chicago attitude:

Do you ever use contraceptives?
Nope.
How about women? Do they ever use anything?
Nope.
Do you ever think about it?
Nope.
Are you afraid of what might happen?
Nope. *They can't touch me. I'm under age.*

Seeing it exclusively from his own standpoint, and then only insofar as his conduct may lead to legal jeopardy, he is not afraid of making girls pregnant. Later on, when he does come of age, in order to avoid possible charges of statutory rape, such a boy will prefer sexual relations with older women. Even then, this respondent insists, he "ain't gonna use anything." Told by the interviewer about diaphragms and how they work, he vehemently protests against their use. They would interfere with his pleasure: "Might get in my way." To be sure, without contraception, it is possible to spawn an illegitimate child, something he at first claims to have done at least once—before second thoughts cause him to cast doubt on the "mother's" veracity. This is his complete verbatim statement on the matter:

She told me we were gonna have a kid. I said "Tough." She said, "Ain't it though?" I said, "What you gonna do about it?" She said, "I ain't gonna do nothin' about it. How about you?" I said nothin'. She said, "That's good." I said goodbye and she said goodbye. And that's the last I saw of her. I mean I *saw* her in school. She's still goin' to school. I don't believe that we had a kid, though. She just said we did.

Risk or no risk, boys are generally hostile to the idea of prophylaxis. One objection is phrased purely in terms of the pleasure principle, most colorfully by a Chicago boy who explains why he never uses anything like a rubber, "I tried it once. It's like riding a horse with a saddle instead of bareback." Is he afraid of "knocking a girl up?" Answer: "Sure. *I worry about it afterwards.* I guess I'm lucky so far. That's all." The cost factor appears again in Chicago where the poor-white boys are markedly more reluctant than the Negroes and Puerto Ricans in Washington and New York, respectively, to spend money on contraceptive frills. At the climactic moment, their impecuniosity can be frustrating. As a rule, in the white population, girls are no more eager than boys to insure against pregnancy, but once in awhile they are:

Oh, I've used them a couple of times. Like one time, a broad got all worried, and she told us to lay off. . . . We had her pants off and everything. She ask me if I didn't have some rubbers. Uh-uh. "Get off." I had to wait a little longer. I didn't have any money either.

In the Chicago underclass, there is, then, a minimum of anxiety about the consequences of sexual intercourse, a strong disinclination to take any responsibility for what happens. Most boys are poorly informed and unconcerned about measures taken or not taken by their sex partners. "I wouldn't know if they did or not [use anything to prevent pregnancy]. I don't care if they do or not." Does he know what girls might do to protect themselves? "Well, there's with the hot water, like that. Then, there's, they press on their stomachs someplace . . . on some cords, usually when you get done, the girl has to go to the bathroom. She goes in, she presses here and there, and it all comes out. They claim that's one of the best ways." Ignorance of the facts should not be discounted, but knowledge may or may not be correlative with action. Even if a girl asks for restraint, so that she will not have to cope with unwed motherhood, the boy is likely to refuse:

Do many girls ask you to stop before you come?
Most don't. Some do.
They don't want to get pregnant?
That's right.
Do you usually oblige them?
Well, not usually, no.

Biologists like Ashley-Montagu have established the existence of adolescent sterility, a period after the onset of puberty during which reproduction presumably cannot take place. Widespread premarital sexual experimentation, not always related to courtship, among "primitive peoples" to whom puritanism is unknown, has been noted for over a century. Adolescent sterility helps anthropologists to account for the smoothness with which such relations occur. In ever larger sectors of our own society, birth control has "sterilized" teen-agers, thereby insuring them against the many complications of illegitimacy. Neither of these mechanisms seems to be significantly operative in any of our cities. Adolescent *fertility* is high, and respondents (males only slightly more so than females) express a very nearly uniform distaste for every kind of contraceptive device. Significant differences are, in the first instance, more attitudinal than behavioral. How much responsibility does a boy who has got his girl with child feel? Some in the Puerto Ricans and Negroes of New York and Washington; virtually none in the whites of Chicago. That unimpeded sexual contact can and does lead to babies is something a transplanted Appalachian white boy is likely to know

only too well. For the most part, he "couldn't care less"; the interviewer asks such a boy: "What's stopping you from knocking up girls?" Answer: "Nothin'. I've got four kids, maybe five. Two here in Chicago, two in Wisconsin, and when I left Wisconsin, I heard there was one more." Does he support any of them? "Shit no." After getting a girl pregnant, "I just take off."

Less able to "take off," as careless but more likely to be "trapped," hemmed in on every side, the New York Puerto Rican boy generally finds insemination of his girl friends a worrisome matter. It is seldom a question of direct responsibility to the "victim"—which would presuppose a kind of socialization or internalization of standards evident neither among "good boys" nor among "bad boys." What if the girl has a baby? "Maybe the parents might make him marry her." Coercion under these circumstances into unwanted matrimony is a nightmare in the New York group to the like of which no one in Chicago ever alludes. We pursue the issue one step farther: "Suppose they didn't make you. Would you marry her anyhow?" The response is a derisive, "Nah!" But then we want to know whether he would support the baby, and to this the answer is a subculturally typical *yes*. Even if, in order to do so, he would have to quit school (and this respondent values school)? Yes, even so, although, "that would be pretty bad."

The qualitative difference we wish to point up is more than a matter of nuance. Lloyd Warner and his associates were able to rank people, whom they interviewed in Yankee City, by class-typed responses to interview questions. We, in turn, can situate boys and girls (and could do so "blind," that is, without any accompanying data) in one of three impoverished subcultures, by their responses to a variety of straightforward, nondirective, and projective questions. Thus, a Puerto Rican boy who presents a tougher "front" than the one just quoted above is still unmistakably a Puerto Rican, and not an Appalachian or Negro boy:

Do you try to avoid getting a girl pregnant or don't you care?
I try to avoid it.
Suppose you did, and she found out where you lived?
I'd have to marry the broad.
Would you like that?
No, that's a hell of a mess.

The less insouciant type, a boy, for instance, whose presentation of self is somewhat gentler, simply says of the hypothetical girl he has impregnated: "You've got to marry her," leaving implicit why you have got to.

Since precautions to avert childbirth are unpopular, and pregnancy takes place willy-nilly, abortions should be common. If so, boys in Chicago tend to feel that it is no business of theirs. How different is the attitude that emerges in New York where, to select one of many examples, an advanced adolescent remarks apropos a girl friend who might get pregnant, "If I liked the girl enough I would marry her, or something." Suppose he didn't like her all that much, would he still feel obligated? "Yeah." In what way, we wonder. Would he arrange for an abortion? "No. That would mess her up too much. . . . Cause some ladies, they just do it to get money out of it; they don't really do it to help a person at all." Nonmedical abortionists, charging about eighty dollars a job, are said to abound on the street. Nevertheless, the white boys recoil from availing themselves of these services, obviously not for financial reasons, which are important in Chicago, since the stated alternative, assuming marital or nonmarital responsibility for support, would be so much costlier than disposition of an undesired fetus.

The differential warmth, involvement, and concern for "the other" in sexual affairs, while significant, should not be exaggerated. It is nonetheless present whatever tack we take. The myth of *machismo*, incorporating an alleged need for constant dramatic assertions of masculinity, notwithstanding, our Puerto Rican teen-age boys do not preen themselves on their virility. Most of them accept the code which prohibits tattling "to other guys about girls they have schemed with." Some do engage in invidious talk about "street girls" whose well-known promiscuity makes it impossible to take pride in having "scored" with them. Similarly, the reaction to betrayal is a mild one. Violent assault on a girl may occur if she is suspected of having squealed to the police about stealing or fighting—not so about sexual defections. When they occur, New York boys say, "I walk away," "I tell her not to do that again," "I call it quits." The gorge does not rise very high, one's manhood is not called into question, and violence flares up but rarely. Likewise, the readiness to spare a girl friend undue embarrassment—or to share it with her by prematurely shouldering the parental responsibility—is quite exceptional. Commenting on the large number of unmarried girls with babies that boys refuse to support, a respondent explains, "Maybe one guy has her, then another, and then another. She doesn't know who the father is." Then what? "The last guy gets the blame." And getting the blame, more often than not, seems to mean accepting the blame, which, in turn (age permitting), means marriage. In this realm, as elsewhere, *fatalismo* apparently counts for more than *machismo*.

Sexual experience, which begins early and mounts in frequency, if not intensity, should not be equated with sexual sophistication. Indeed, the manifest naïvete is sometimes monumental. So:

How do you avoid getting girls pregnant? (Long pause) I don't really know.
Nobody ever told you about that?
Nobody ever told me.
Well, how do you keep the girl from having a baby?
I guess you kill the baby.
Do you know about killing babies?
I don't know, but . . .
Is that what they do around the block?
If they gonna kill the babies, they gonna kill theirself.
So you never heard about protection? Like a rubber?
What did you say? Girdle? Maybe that's the only way. I know a girl lives in my neighborhood. She had a baby, but you couldn't tell, and after awhile they found out she had a girdle on. But she still had a baby. I don't really know how you could stop it. The only way, I suppose, is wearing a girdle.

Another boy reports making a girl pregnant, but there was no baby, "because she took it out." How he does not know or will not say. Yet another, asked what he would do if he got his girl friend pregnant, replies, "There's nothing I could do," and, for lack of options, lets it go at that.

Early marriage ensues, in a spirit best described as resignation. This "solution" becomes all the more irrational whenever boys protest, as they do with great vehemence, that it is the one thing that they wish, above all, to avoid. They speak of no marriage or late marriage, drawing the lesson of delay and circumvention from their own experience in unsatisfactory family relations. And, pointing to others all around them, they declaim against too many people marrying too soon, having too many children. It is on this basis that they diagnose most of their own trouble and most of the ills that others encounter in a slum environment. It all starts, they say, when a young man fathers a child he does not want—whose conception he will do nothing to prevent. Here, indeed, for one part of the underclass is the way of all flesh: fully aware of the danger, our young man tumbles headlong into it, doing exactly what he had sworn not to do, classically entering a scene he had resolved to sidestep, with some, no doubt, unconscious, propulsion into a trap he professes to abhor.

A finer distinction must be made among Appalachians in Chicago. There, group-affiliated males show a consistent unwillingness to marry, holding out for very long, while, among the unaffiliated, there is a noticeably higher incidence of early marriage. When it takes place, males tend to be several years older than females, even if both are still in their teens. In the majority of cases, delay is secured through reinforcement of a powerful male peer group that seemingly functions much like the one analyzed by William Foote Whyte in *Street Corner Society*. It is the opinion of two long-time resident observers in Chicago that "most of the males find it impossible to maintain regular and satisfying experiences with a girl and quickly withdraw their attention and return to the male peer group." They also indicate that despite a well-nigh-universal claim to early sexual experience, many of the male youths admit to prolonged periods of disengagement both from overt heterosexual activity and coed sociability. Much of the sexual play that does take place involves a group of boys who exploit one or two females, many of them "young runaways" or disillusioned young wives, viewed as "easy scores" for all. After a week or so of intensified sexuality with one such female, she usually disappears. Then the males resume their involuntary celibacy. Later, they embark once again on the same cycle. All of this is absolutely affectless.

Appalachian girls in Chicago stress early marriage as a female adjustment,

They hope for husbands who "won't be unfaithful," "won't drink," "will be nice," and "will work hard." Demographic findings and intimate observation make it clear that, personal preference apart, a girl often marries the first young male adult with whom she has a steady relationship. Our resident observers also tell us that their "noncodified observations yield another interesting pattern of marital relationship in the next older group," which they feel may have a bearing on "the essentially brittle relations of the teen-agers." During our study, a number of marriages have been observed to dissolve into a peculiar pattern of realignment, such that: Male A, aged thirty-five, establishes a liaison with Female X, his own age or older; wife of A establishes a liaison with unmarried Male B, aged twenty-five or thirty or with a formerly married male, aged twenty-five to thirty who, in turn, has separated from his younger wife. Consequently, for the second marriage, or for sexual adventures after a first marriage, the male is ordinarily younger than the female. We find, in short, that, parallel to the traditional form (older husband, younger wife), there is a deviant form that leaves separated, divorced, and unfaithful women with younger husbands and lovers. There is a certain distinctiveness in this duality.

CULTURAL VALUES COMPARED

We suspected at the outset of our inquiry that the rhetoric and the activity of impoverished American subcultures would be far removed from traditional Western ideas of love and sex. They are. Middle-class standards, in all their present disarray, carry those ideas (or reactions against them) in a confusing mélange that can only bewilder young people who are their residuary legatees. Not so in the underclass, where, with all its diversity, these ideas appear—if at all—only in mutilated form.

With a mixture of envy and indignation, middle-class people often impute pure sensual pleasure to their social inferiors, who are thought to pursue this objective heedlessly, if not monomaniacally. There is no warrant for this judgment. Puerto Rican youth in New York seem, somewhat more than the other groups, to stress sensual pleasure, but even they are manifestly more interested in *collective* fun, in "the set" itself, than in pure hedonism. All the same, insofar as "scheming" is an act of rebellion against authority, it does not much differ from taking pot or ingesting alcohol. In any class, youthful manifestations of defiance are a tacit acknowledgement of that coercive culture which some choose to resist. On the face of it, a Puerto Rican boy willing to "accept the responsibility" of marriage to, or help for, the girl he has impregnated, responds in accordance with one element of the Western Catholic tradition. For him, heterosexual dalliance imposes an obligation, but only if "the worst should happen," and then only when he is actuated by a sense of fatality rather than by love or duty. Chance has dealt him a heavy blow, rendered him powerless to fight back, left him a plaything of mysterious forces, destroyed his capacity to act as a free agent.

That culturally induced responsibility for one's sex acts cannot be taken for granted is clear enough in the other two groups, whose members refuse to do what the New York Puerto Rican boy feels that he must do. In this milieu, a residue of the declining tradition may still be observed. Not so in the Washington and Chicago samples of Negroes and Appalachian whites.

Given time, any group encapsulated in a constricted ghetto can be severed, not just from the mainstream of a larger culture but from its ancestral subculture as well. The unique circumstances of isolation and contact, impoverishment and opportunity, continuity and rupture with the past, will produce new codes, new standards, new articulations, and new behavior patterns. The Appalachian whites and the Washington Negroes are in most ways slightly less "Westernized" (that is, made into middle-class people) than Puerto Rican youth in New York. All, however, have rural, but by no means identical, origins. And all have moved into hideous urban ghettos where, to varying degrees, they are shut off from the major values of Western society. For people from the Southern hill country or the Southern plantation, lack of contact with outsiders is an old story. Urbanization, even in ghettos, reduces their isolation. The Appalachian white may have been culturally on his own since the pre-Revolutionary settlement of this country. For lower-class Negroes, isolation may have begun with the capture of their ancestors in Africa, and continued through Southern slavery to Northern segregation. The Negro subclass has had practically no exposure to Western sexual ideals, and the Appalachian white's exposure occurred so long ago that its effects are virtually inoperative.

For these submerged peoples, our dominant sexual ideologies have little relevance. Neither emotional and material responsibilities, nor their opposite, pure joy in unrestrained sexuality, is much in evidence. Sexual fulfillment is experienced merely as a physical release —the "friction of two membranes"— in which the female is the necessary but unequal partner. Otherwise, sexual conquest provides a trophy calculated to enhance one's prestige in peer-group competition. Masculinity is affirmed as part of a game whose competitors must incessantly prove themselves before an audience of others engaged in the same pastime. Since it is a competitive game, the boy who plays cannot expect to earn points for scoring over an easy mark, a "pig." Victory consists in overcoming the largest possible number of inaccessible girls. The conversion of females into trophies reduces them to nonpersons. Their personal, sexual, or simply human, needs do not matter. They exist to be tricked, deceived, manipulated—and abandoned. Skill in all these techniques is a sign of stylistic virtuosity. For a boy to abuse his sexual partner in many ingenious ways makes him a big winner. To all this, the lush rhetoric and varied responses elicited from our interviews are ample testimony. Customary allusions to Western concepts of love and sex are "foreign" to people who cannot express them verbally or in terms of their actual conduct. They are historically and personally alienated from the amorous and sexual context that Western idealism, with all its twists and turns, has to offer. That condition, for which no single urban ghetto is a carbon copy, can only deepen as subcultural segregation runs its course.

Investigation of ethnic underclass sexual mores in our own society, while it points to important differences, certainly does not provide us with examples of "natural," spontaneous, unrepressed, and nonneurotic sensual pleasure. Sexual practices are indissolubly linked to nonsexual aspects of life-style. For this reason, it would in any case be impossible to transfer the really illusory freedom of slum sex codes to an academic and bureaucratic world. If in that world, "intellectualized," "artificial," and "abstract" standards prevail, they cannot be banished by sexual personalism. No more than primitive or peasant society do subcultures of poverty offer us solutions to our sexual dilemma.

Sex Behavior and the American Class Structure: A Mosaic

By Theodore N. Ferdinand

ABSTRACT: Close parallels in ancient Rome and present-day America suggest that the sexual revolutions in both societies were significantly influenced by the existential conditions that they confronted at the height of their powers.   At the same time, each was constrained in its sociocultural responses by the nature of its social-class structure.   In America we must examine the ethos of each of six broad strata to comprehend in detail the nature of the American sexual revolution.   When we do, we see that many of the changes in our sexual mores and behavior can be traced to recent changes in the social-class structure. The spread of higher education among the middle class has meant that a substantial portion of American adolescents are regularly exposed to a social setting in which their sexual behavior is governed essentially by the adolescents themselves. Such a situation could not help but be more permissive than that which prevailed before the modern period.   Moreover, since a substantial portion of the population is now embraced by the middle classes, a growing portion of the population is exposed to this permissive sexual environment.   The sexual revolution in America, therefore, is largely a blend of existential and structural pressures impinging upon only a segment of the total population.

Theodore N. Ferdinand, Ph.D., Boston, Massachusetts, is Associate Professor, Department of Sociology-Anthropology, Northeastern University, where he was Assistant Professor from 1961 to 1965.   During 1966–1967, Dr. Ferdinand was Research Analyst, Community Progress, Inc., New Haven, Connecticut, and he is the author of Typologies of Delinquency (1966), of numerous articles in professional journals, and of a functional analysis of the American society (in press).

THERE is a haunting similarity between the situation of modern America and that of ancient Rome at the height of its imperial powers. While the young men of both societies were busy defending the civilized world against barbarian hordes, the population at home was turning more completely to the diversions of the banquet and the bed. The harsh ascetic standards of the founding period were crumbling in favor of an opportunistic code in which the future and its obligations were gladly sacrificed to the pleasures of the moment. And among the sources of pleasure, none was pursued with greater intensity than those of a sexual nature. Both societies had their symbols of eroticism and their ardent spokesmen for the "new morality," as well as their outraged critics who denounced the decay of traditional values and practices.[1] In short, the points of agreement between Rome in the first century A.D. and America in the twentieth century are striking and numerous.[2]

[1] In America, of course, movie starlets strive reflexively to become sex symbols; Hugh Hefner, the publisher of *Playboy*, has become the high priest of the "new morality"; and there are countless commentators who see the sexual revolution as undermining the foundations of society. See, for example, Pitirim A. Sorokin, *The American Sex Revolution* (Boston: Porter Sargent, 1956).

In Rome Clodia, wife of Caecilius Celer a provincial governor in the first century, inspired an epic poem by Gaius Catullus in which her erotic charms were minutely described, and Julia, the only child of Augustus Caesar, became so notorious for her fast and furious sex life that she was finally exiled by her father to the isle of Pandateria. In addition to Catullus, the poet Ovid helped shape the Roman sexual revolution with his lengthy poem, *The Art of Love,* in which the proper approach to sensual love was intimately described. Among those who denounced the changing sexual mores of first-century Rome were Seneca and Tacitus.

[2] In addition to the similarities noted above, we might mention also that as both nations moved to the center of the world stage, both turned inexorably from a kind of collective

We cannot, in this short essay, give close attention to the similar historical paths which both societies traced, but there can be little doubt that their similarities derive to some extent from the fact that both developed in their formative years in much the same way. During their formative periods, both peoples were dedicated to an ascetic ideal of stringent self-discipline. And in this early period, severe adversity gave this ethic definite meaning. But as both societies advanced to the front rank, the pressure of adversity diminished and the ethic of self-discipline began to lose its relevance. Thus, in America today, many of those who were born after the Second World War, that is, nearly half the population, have never known a national disaster like the Great Depression or the strong likelihood that a world war would drastically interfere with their lives. Hence, many Americans today live in the present, confident that the future will take care of itself. For them, an ethic of indulgence is more meaningful than one of self-discipline.

Existential explanations of historical events—and this is an existential explanation—are only partly successful, however, because they tend to ignore the structural restrictions that inevitably limit the alternatives available to an individual or a society in confronting its situation. And in this particular case, although the structural restrictions of ancient Rome may never be fully known, the structural features of American society that constrain its existential responses are well understood. To a large extent, they derive from the social-class structure and the encourage-

leadership in which authority was distributed among a number of centers to a much more centralized governmental structure; both nations became increasingly skeptical of traditional religious teachings; and, finally, both nations devoted considerable attention to the development of their legal institutions.

ment it gives to those at different status levels to deal with the universal problem of sexual behavior in different ways. Thus, it would be a mistake to suggest that the sexual mores of the *American society* have grown more permissive in the twentieth century. Rather, certain social classes have always endorsed loose sexual standards; others continue to endorse a puritanical sex code; and only a portion of society has actually relaxed its views regarding sexual behavior. Thus, in drawing an estimate of the sexual mores of America, it is important to recognize that there are several social classes, each with its own situation and its own values and practices.

THE AMERICAN CLASS STRUCTURE

There has been considerable argument among sociologists regarding the nature of the American class structure. There is disagreement, for example, regarding the definition of the class structure. Shall we consider, first, the "hard" facts of income, education, and occupation in defining a social class, or should we be concerned primarily with such qualitative patterns as its life style? And, further, shall we regard the class structure as a series of discrete steps in which the several levels are clearly distinguishable from one another, or should we consider it as a continuum with each class grading imperceptibly into its neighbors? These issues have troubled social scientists for years, but they are not as intractable as many have assumed. For example, there is considerable similarity between the class structure that we find by focusing upon the hard variables of income, education, and occupation and the class structure that we get by using life style as the basic criterion of class. Also, whether you regard the class structure as a series of discrete steps or as a single continuum depends to a large extent upon your

purposes. If you are interested in defining the structure itself, abstracted from the unsettling effects of class mobility, you will probably develop a discrete version of the class structure. But if you are interested in defining a class structure that actually approximates the American situation today, with all its upward mobility, you will probably develop a model that emphasizes the continuity of the classes. In this essay, I shall define the class structure as a series of discrete social classes, each with its own distinctive life style and its own solution to the problem of sexual behavior.

The upper-upper class

The upper-upper class has only recently emerged in the American class structure. Before the Civil War, there were so few families in the North with old wealth that they were negligible in comparison with those with new wealth, and in the South during the War and Reconstruction, the plantation aristocracy was decimated. Thus, the upper-upper class did not make its appearance until those families that had accumulated wealth during the ante bellum period weathered the postwar period and mellowed in the process. The boundaries of the upper-upper class were further sharpened by the sudden emergence after the Civil War of a new generation of business leaders with aggressive and sometimes indictable views on certain public issues.[3] Although these leaders and their families often commanded greater fortunes than those families already in the upper-upper class, the differences in life styles between these two groups were too great to ignore. Consequently, soon after the

[3] See E. Digby Baltzell, *The Protestant Establishment* (New York: Random House, 1964), pp. 73–76; and Cleveland Amory, *The Proper Bostonians* (New York: E. P. Dutton, 1947), pp. 39–55, for a discussion of the evolution of the American upper-upper class.

Civil War, the upper-upper class made its appearance as a distinct and self-conscious class in this country.

What is the life style of the upper-upper class? There is no single social pattern that all members of this class can be said to endorse, since the upper-upper class is as influenced by regional differences as most other groups. The New England upper-upper class differs from the Middle Atlantic upper-upper class which, in turn, is readily distinguishable from the Southern or the Midwestern pattern. But, taken as a whole, it is possible to identify a core pattern that describes the basic values and attitudes of most upper-upper-class members in this country.[4] First, the typical upper-upper-class person regards quality, rather than ability or dedication, as the quintessence of virtue.[5] Quality in this context refers to a capacity to excel by virtue of one's inherent excellence rather than by an accelerated effort or an extra desire to excel, and it is readily discernible in the natural ease with which the typical upper-upper-class person discharges the most difficult of tasks.[6]

A second facet of the life style of this class is an unshakable confidence that the way of life of the upper-upper class is superior to anything found in the other classes. There are, of course, no objective criteria by which such questions might be weighed, but, nevertheless, the typical upper-upper-class person regards the compulsive industriousness of the lower-upper and upper-middle classes, the moralistic conservatism of the lower-middle classes, and the unbridled impulsiveness of the lower classes with disdain and contempt. The upper-upper-class person, therefore, is not governed by the same moral restraints as the other classes in most of his relationships, including those of a sexual nature.

These particular emphases in the life style of the upper-upper class contain several implications for the manner in which the members of this class conduct themselves sexually. First, the view that the upper-upper-class person is naturally superior tends to discourage relationships, sexual or otherwise, with members of other classes, and even when such liaisons do occur, they often carry invidious overtones. Second, the need to display quality in word and deed forces the typical upper-upper-class person to strain for a type of individualism that indicates unmistakably his innate excellence. This individualism, of course, colors his relationships with the opposite sex and imparts an intensity and self-consciousness that is not common in the other classes. In effect, this means that he enters most serious liaisons with the aim of developing an awesome, historic love affair.

But this striving for the heights in his relationships means that inevitably he must awaken a similar response in his feminine partner. Her personality, of course, is an essential ingredient in the relationship, and to insure her fullest response he must honor her wishes and preferences. This consideration for the feelings of the partner, however, means that sexual relationships will only occur when both are in substantial agreement.

---

[4] For some insight into the life style of the upper-upper class, see E. Digby Baltzell, *Philadelphia Gentlemen* (New York: Free Press, 1958), pp. 52–64; Nathaniel Burt, *The Perennial Philadelphians* (Boston: Little, Brown, 1963), pp. 37–76 and pp. 584–588; Amory, *op. cit.*; and A. B. Hollingshead, *Elmtown's Youth* (New York: Science Editions, 1961), pp. 84–90.

[5] The ethos of this class is not unlike that attributed by Nietzsche to the nobleman. See Friedrich Nietzsche, *The Genealogy of Morals,* trans. Francis Golffing (Garden City, N.Y.: Doubleday Anchor Books, 1956).

[6] John Lindsay, mayor of New York City, nicely illustrates the simple grace that many upper-upper class individuals bring to the most difficult and corrosive of tasks. John Kennedy while he was President also displayed some of these same qualities.

For example, premarital intercourse would be unlikely if the young lady had serious reservations, or bizarre sexual experiments would not occur if it meant terrible anguish for one of the partners. But where both ardently agree to such relationships, the absence of deep commitments to conventional standards of morality means that there is little to prevent their consummation. Thus, in his sexual relationships, the typical upper-upper-class person attempts to display an elegance and quality that is appropriate for someone of his position. He eschews tawdry or unworthy affairs, and although, at times, he may be regarded as immoral by the community, it is unlikely that he would ever be exploitative or inconsiderate in his sexual relationships.

There are some variations in this pattern depending upon the way in which marriage and the educational system arrange the lives of members of this class. For example, since the younger members of this class are not ordinarily educated in coeducational secondary schools, they have little opportunity to engage and relate with members of the opposite sex. Hence, they are forced to resort to masturbation to an unusually high degree.[7] At the same time, since upper-upper-class ladies are more likely to remain spinsters than ladies in other classes, they, too, are forced to seek outlets other than intercourse for their sexual drives. In their case, they turn to homosexuality and masturbation to an extraordinary degree.[8] Curiously enough, married females in this class also turn to homosexuality relatively

frequently.[9] This fact may reflect their exposure to unmarried friends and relatives who have such inclinations, as well as a greater emancipation from conventional mores and a willingness to experiment sexually in unorthodox ways.

In sum, then, the typical upper-upper-class person enters sexual relationships with an implicit expectation that they will offer an opportunity for expressing another dimension of his excellence. At the same time, he is mindful of his responsibilities in the relationship and careful not to violate the sensibilities and preferences of his partner. Finally, although he is not preoccupied with the physical aspect of sexuality, he regards it with a lively interest, and he is willing to undertake a wide degree of experimentation to heighten his appreciation of it.

The lower-upper and upper-middle classes

These classes differ from the upper-upper class in that they regard ability, perseverance, and aggressiveness as highly admirable qualities.[10] The typical lower-upper-class person has achieved his position via intensive competition, and he has sometimes been forced to adopt immoderate and unbecoming tactics as he has advanced. There is, therefore, a certain raw quality to his behavior that repels the typical upper-upper-class person. In addition, the typical member of the lower-upper class generally endorses and actively participates in the conventional moral and social patterns of the community. Members of the lower-upper class are often lay leaders of their churches, active in United Fund cam-

[7] See Alfred C. Kinsey et al., Sexual Behavior in the Human Female (Philadelphia: W. B. Saunders, 1953), Table 25, p. 180. Also see Alfred C. Kinsey et al., Sexual Behavior in the Human Male (Philadelphia: W. B. Saunders, 1948), Table 82, p. 340.

[8] Kinsey, Sexual Behavior in the Human Female, Table 25, p. 180, and Table 127, p. 490.

[9] Op. cit., Table 143, p. 500.

[10] For a discussion of the life style of the lower-upper and upper-middle classes, see John R. Seeley, R. A. Sim, and E. W. Looseley, Crestwood Heights (New York: Basic Books, 1956), p. 120; and Hollingshead, op. cit., pp. 90–95.

paigns, and much sought after as speakers for high school and college commencements.

The upper-middle class follows much the same pattern, although they have generally not been quite so effective in their occupations, and their impact upon the community has been much less. The typical lower-upper-class member is well known in the community, and not infrequently he is known nationally as well, but the upper-middle-class person is generally known only to a narrow circle of colleagues, friends, and neighbors. Whereas the lower-upper-class person is typically at or near the top of his profession or occupational category, the upper-middle-class person is only at the middle levels.

The view that these classes hold toward sexual behavior is powerfully shaped by the fact that nearly everyone has been exposed to a large university in which Greek-letter societies closely govern relationships between the sexes. Within these fraternities and sororities, sex, in one way or another, enters nearly every decision and policy, and in such an atmosphere, it is hard to imagine how a preoccupation with sex could be avoided. Hence, the typical lower-upper-class or upper-middle-class young man learns during his years in college that sexual experience is the ultimate of human values, and he pursues it with all the ingenuity and intensity that his father displays in pursuing professional recognition and advancement. In the process, he comes to differentiate the physical aspects of sexual behavior from the loved person, while continuing to endorse, at some level, the traditional belief that sex is immoral and repulsive, especially when it is extra- or premarital. Thus, it is in these classes that the sharpest ambivalence toward sexual behavior is displayed. There are very powerful forces propelling the members of these classes toward inten-

sive sexual involvement, but, at the same time, many of them also sincerely endorse the traditional moral sanctions against doing so.[11]

In general, those who have examined this problem empirically find that there is a large amount of premarital sexual relations among the younger members of this class in college.[12] Their interest in the physical aspect of sex, however, falls off rather rapidly in middle age, so that little attention is given it among those who have been married for some time.[13] Extramarital affairs do not count heavily in the behavior patterns of these classes, but when they do occur, they often exhibit the same compulsive quality that is found among fraternity men.[14] Homosexuality is not common in this class—perhaps because of the value attached to an assertive masculine manner, but masturbation is almost universal among both sexes.[15]

The lower-middle class

The lower-middle class includes those who perform the routine white-collar

[11] This ambivalence apparently gives rise to two quite distinct patterns among the members of this class. Those who endorse liberal political views tend to follow a sexually permissive path while those who endorse conservative views tend to follow a puritanical path. See Ira L. Reiss, "Social Class and Premarital Sexual Permissiveness: A Re-Examination," *American Sociological Review,* Vol. 30 (October 1965), pp. 747–757.

[12] Winston Ehrmann, *Premarital Dating Behavior* (New York: Henry Holt, 1959), chap. v; Kinsey, *Sexual Behavior in the Human Female,* Table 80, p. 337; and Sidney Goldstein and Kurt B. Meyer, "Illegitimacy, Residence, and Status," *Social Problems,* Vol. 12 (Spring 1965), pp. 428–436.

[13] John F. Cuber and Peggy B. Harroff, *The Significant Americans* (New York: Appleton-Century-Crofts, 1966), chap. vi.

[14] *Op. cit.,* chap. viii.

[15] Kinsey, *Sexual Behavior in the Human Male,* Table 90, p. 360, and Table 82, p. 340; and Kinsey, *Sexual Behavior in the Human Female,* Table 25, p. 180.

tasks of society.[16] They are the sales-men, the office workers, and the school teachers who are largely interchangeable and, therefore, anonymous to the com-munity as a whole. Their lives are rarely brightened by recognition for noteworthy accomplishment, nor do they ordinarily seek such excitement or fame. They prefer predictability and stability to uncertainty, security to op-portunity. They support the conven-tional community groups and values with perhaps the greatest enthusiasm but the least insight of any of the classes. For all their devotion, how-ever, they rarely rise to leadership po-sitions in these groups. Their position in the community rests more upon the support which they give to the basic institutions than on anything of a unique or creative nature that they bring to the community. Hence, their ethos is based upon social insecurity and is defined rigidly in terms of the orthodox morality of the community.

With regard to sex behavior, this class is probably the most puritanical of all. For them, sex is an ugly aspect of the human situation, and they do their best to ignore it. They try to suppress it in their teen-agers, and they take a detached, utilitarian attitude toward it in marriage. Extramarital affairs occur infrequently, and the mem-bers of this class masturbate relatively little.[17] If they enter college, they are not often caught up in the hypercharged sexual atmosphere of the Greek-letter so-cieties, and they are generally on the periphery of the clubs and cliques that govern teen-age relationships in high school. Thus, they have most of the

moral reservations of the orthodox com-munity regarding sexual behavior, but fewer erotic stimulants than the higher classes. They approach sex, therefore, gingerly, and they attempt to keep it at arm's length.

The upper-lower class

The working class is distinctive in several respects.[18] The typical working-class person is convinced that basic truths are best revealed through intui-tion and emotion and that lengthy, intricate analyses are likely to be ir-relevant or dishonest. He trusts his feelings, and he suspects the motives of those who cannot establish a rapport with him at this level. Moreover, the typical working-class person is quite aware of the level at which society places his class, and he is especially sensitive to contemptuous or invidious comments regarding his personality or situation. He will not accept evalua-tions that reflect on his worthiness, and he is easily goaded into physical vio-lence in response to such evaluations. Finally, he looks with deep resentment upon the mores and social patterns of the upper classes, for he regards the members of these classes as exploitative, self-satisfied, and undeserving. The Sermon on the Mount captures his sentiment quite nicely in that the typical working-class person regards it as a great injustice that the most de-serving in society, that is, the working class, fare so poorly, whereas those who are most unworthy, that is, the in-sincere, self-serving, and largely inconse-

[16] For a description of the life style of the lower-middle class, see C. Wright Mills, *White Collar* (New York: Oxford University Press, 1951), pp. 224–228; pp. 254–258; and Hollingshead, *op. cit.*, pp. 95–102.

[17] Kinsey, *Sexual Behavior in the Human Female*, Tables 100 and 101, pp. 399–400, and Table 25, p. 180.

[18] See Hollingshead, *op. cit.*, pp. 102–103; S. M. Miller and Frank Riessman, "The Working Class Subculture: A New View," *Social Problems* (Summer 1961), pp. 86–97; Walter B. Miller, "Lower Class Culture as a Generating Milieu of Gang Delinquency," *Journal of Social Issues*, Vol. 14 (April 1958), pp. 5–19; and Herbert J. Gans, *The Urban Villagers* (New York: Free Press, 1962), pp. 28–32.

quential members of the higher classes, receive rich rewards from society. In the hereafter, says Christ, these wrongs will be righted.

These views have a rather characteristic impact on sexual relations in the working class. In the first place, relationships between the sexes often develop a mildly combative tone in which sympathy and tenderness play little part.[19] Both males and females are vigilant lest their honor or ability be questioned, and since sexuality is the medium through which both qualities are regularly tested, it is almost inevitable that relationships between the sexes should develop a combative pattern in which defensive attitudes are common on both sides.[20] Thus, although there is a great amount of premarital intercourse—a large majority of the adolescents of both sexes have had intercourse before the age of eighteen— and although extramarital intercourse is a common occurrence, at least among the males, very little appreciation or understanding grows among the sexes.[21] Moreover, since the working-class person typically regards coitus as the sole aim of sexual relationships, he views most forms of foreplay as perverted.[22] Hence, sex relationships, even among marriage partners, tend to fall into a matter-of-fact routine in which little effort is made to heighten or prolong

enjoyment. The fact that this class utilizes prostitutes more frequently than any other, both before and after marriage, merely confirms the impersonal tone that pervades relationships between the sexes.[23]

All in all, then, the members of the working class regard sexual behavior as a dangerous arena in which one's worth as a person comes under careful and often critical scrutiny. This scrutiny, in turn, provokes a defensive reaction on both sides which tends to anticipate and neutralize critical judgments when they come. But this defensiveness also stands as a barrier isolating the individual from meaningful human relations. Curiously enough, homosexuality seems to be a common experience among the males of this class.[24] The reasons behind this pattern are, no doubt, quite complex, but one factor may be the rather mechanical, impersonal pattern that heterosexual relations have fallen into in the working class.

The lower-lower class

The cultural pattern of the lower-lower class is largely determined by the fact that they are physically present but not part of society.[25] Economically, politically, and socially, they are ignored or shunned, and accordingly they have little stake in the moral and economic concerns of the rest of society. They share the emotional impulsivity of the upper-lower class, but they have none of the stabilizing effects of a reasonably steady and satisfactory income.

[19] Jackie Gleason has captured this tone quite nicely in his television show "The Honeymooners." See also Nathan Hurvitz, "Marital Strain in the Blue Collar Family," in Arthur B. Shostak and William Gomberg (eds.), *Blue Collar World* (Englewood Cliffs, N.J.: Prentice-Hall, 1964), pp. 92–109.

[20] Lee Rainwater, "Some Aspects of Lower Class Sexual Behavior," *The Journal of Social Issues*, XXII (April 1966), pp. 96–108.

[21] Kinsey, *Sexual Behavior in the Human Male*, Table 85, p. 348; and Kinsey, *Sexual Behavior in the Human Female*, Table 80, p. 337, and Table 115, p. 440.

[22] Kinsey, *Sexual Behavior in the Human Female*, Tables 100 and 101, pp. 399–400.

[23] Kinsey, *Sexual Behavior in the Human Male*, Table 87, p. 352.

[24] *Op. cit.*, Table 90, p. 360.

[25] See Michael Harrington, *The Other America* (New York: The Macmillan Company, 1963), pp. 133–137; Michael Schwartz and George Henderson, "The Culture of Unemployment," in Shostak and Gomberg (eds.), *loc. cit.*, pp. 459—468; and Herman Lantz, "Resignation, Industrialization, and the Problem of Social Change," *Ibid.*, pp. 258–270.

Hence, their life style is guided essentially by an opportunistic, hedonistic ethos in which pleasure and comfort are viewed as the basic aims of life. They see little point in preparing for the future or for developing their own human qualities. They are cynical about society and its values, and they refuse to conform without a compelling reason. In sum, the members of this class take their pleasure when and in whatever form they can, and they pay little heed to the usual proprieties in doing so. They are not vicious in an aggressive sense, just thoroughly opportunistic.

The best evidence on their sexual behavior indicates that the members of this class follow the same pattern as the upper-lower class except that there is somewhat greater willingness to indulge in practices that the higher class regards as abnormal. Homosexuality and incest, for example, are relatively common in this class.[26] The stable family with husband and wife present is a rarity, and with such a fluid family structure, the distinction between marital, premarital, and extramarital intercourse becomes largely meaningless. The callousness of the upper-lower class also pervades sexual relationships here, but in this case it dominates most other relationships as well. For members of this class, then, sexuality is just another facet of their total way of life, and they approach it in the same way they approach anything else—with a dispirited eye for making the best of a bad situation. They do not wall off sexuality, romanticize about it, or embellish it. It is just there, and they use it as they will.

SOME CONCLUSIONS

In sum, it appears that a large part of the revolution in sexual behavior in

[26] Oscar Lewis, *La Vida* (New York: Random House, 1966).

America can be attributed to two fundamental changes in the American social structure. First, a very large segment of the middle and upper classes are now exposed to a social milieu, that is, the large state university, in which sexual relationships have become a pre-eminent aim of virtually all its members. With the spread of higher education among these classes, the ascetic ethos of their ancestors has given way to a frankly hedonistic one in which sexual relations have become the keystone. The upper-upper class has endorsed a humanist, expressionistic ethos since its emergence in America in the post-Civil War period, and life in the lower classes seems to have continued relatively unchanged since the Industrial Revolution. Thus, the spread of higher education among the middle and upper classes has been a crucial factor in the American sexual revolution.

A second factor is the extraordinary growth in the relative size of the middle classes in the American social structure. There is general agreement that the broad shift from blue-collar to white-collar jobs in the occupational structure and the general rise in real income has produced a much broader middle class in America, with the result that a much larger proportion of the population has progressively come under the influence of its life style. Hence, as the middle classes have changed their evaluation of sexuality, they have also embraced a broader share of the American people, producing what appears to be a sexual revolution.

There can be little question, of course, that the absence of a crisis atmosphere in America throughout the last generation has also contributed to the general relaxation in asceticism, and certainly the diffusion of the automobile in the last half-century has aggravated considerably the problem of sexual relations. But there can be little doubt that the major momentum for the sexual revolution in America has come from the changes that have occurred in the middle classes over the last fifty years.

Whether corresponding changes occurred in Rome during the first century of the Empire cannot be finally determined. But we do know that Rome underwent a sexual revolution not unlike our own and that it seemed to engulf the upper and middle classes, much as our own has done. Certainly, both societies were influenced by the disappearance of serious external threats during their periods of pre-eminence, but we have also seen that the general disenchantment with traditional ideals in America is a reflection of broad structural shifts, and the inference is probably safe that corresponding shifts were also at the roots of the sexual revolution in Rome as well.

The "Sexless Older Years"—A Socially Harmful Stereotype

By Isadore Rubin

ABSTRACT: The stereotype of the "sexless older years," which has placed its stamp upon our entire culture and which, in many cases, acts as a "self-fulfilling prophecy," has done considerable damage to our aging population. Although no studies of sexual behavior and attitudes of the aging have been done on a sufficiently representative sample to provide us with norms, a growing body of research makes clear that there is no automatic cutoff to sexuality at any age and that sex interests, needs, and abilities continue to play an important role in the later years. This is true not only for the married, but also for the single and widowed. Unless our entire culture recognizes the normality of sex expression in the older years, it will be impossible for older persons to express their sexuality freely and without guilt.

Isadore Rubin, Ph.D., New York City, has been Editor of Sexology magazine since 1956. Since its inception, he has also been an officer and member of the Board of Directors of the Sex Information and Education Council of the United States (SIECUS), as well as chairman of its publications committee. He is a Fellow of the Society for the Scientific Study of Sex, an Affiliate of the American Association of Marriage Counselors, and an Executive Board member of the Tri-State Council on Family Relations. He is author of Sexual Life After Sixty (1965); coeditor of 150 Sex Questions and Answers (1960) and of Sex in the Adolescent Years: New Directions in Guiding and Teaching Youth (1968); and author of a number of articles in various publications.

IT has been suggested that our culture has programmed marriage only until the child-raising period has been completed.[1] If this is true of marital roles in general, it is especially true of sexual roles in the later years. Society has not given genuine recognition to the validity of sexual activity after the child-bearing years, creating a dangerous stereotype about the "sexless older years" and defining as deviant behavior sex interest and activity which may continue vigorously into these older years. Thus, for example, the opprobrious term "lecher" is never coupled with any age group but the old; the young are "lusty" or "virile."

A SELF-FULFILLING PROPHECY

This stereotype has until recently placed its unchallenged stamp upon our culture. In the late 1950's, undergraduates at Brandeis University were asked to take a test to assess their attitudes toward old people.[2] Those taking the test were requested to complete this sentence: "Sex for most old people. . . ." Their answers were quite revealing. Almost all of these young men and women, ranging in age from seventeen to twenty-three, considered sex for most old people to be "negligible," "unimportant," or "past." Since sex behavior is not only a function of one's individual attitudes and interactions with a partner, but also a reflection of cultural expectations, the widespread belief about the older person being sexless becomes for many a "self-fulfilling prophecy." Our society stands indicted, says psychiatrist Karl M. Bowman, of grave neglect of the emotional needs of aging persons:

Men and women often refrain from continuing their sexual relations or from seeking remarriage after loss of a spouse, because even they themselves have come to regard sex as a little ridiculous, so much have our social attitudes equated sex with youth. They feel uncertain about their capacities and very self-conscious about their power to please. They shrink from having their pride hurt. They feel lonely, isolated, deprived, unwanted, insecure. Thoughts of euthanasia and suicide bother them. To prevent these feelings, they need to have as active a sex life as possible and to enjoy it without fear.[3]

Most of our attitudes toward sex today still constitute—despite the great changes that have taken place in the openness with which sex is treated publicly—what a famous British jurist has called "a legacy of the ascetic ideal, persisting in the modern world after the ideal itself has deceased."[4] Obviously, the ascetic attitude—essentially a philosophy of sex-denial—would have far-reaching effects upon our attitude toward the sexual activity of those persons in our society who have passed the reproductive years. Even so scientific a writer as Robert S. de Ropp, in his usually excellent Man against Aging, betrays the unfortunate effects of our ascetic tradition when he says:

For sexual activity, enjoyable as it may seem in itself, still has as its natural aim the propagation of the species, and this activity belongs to the second not the third act of life's drama.[5]

In addition to our tradition of asceticism, there are many other factors which undoubtedly operate to keep alive a strong resistance to the acceptance of

[1] E. Cumming and W. E. Henry, Growing Old (New York: Basic Books, 1961), p. 155.
[2] P. Golde and N. Kogan, "A Sentence Completion Procedure for Assessing Attitudes Toward Old People," Journal of Gerontology, Vol 14 (July 1959), pp. 355–363.

[3] K. M. Bowman, "The Sex Life of the Aging Individual," in M. F. DeMartino (ed.), Sexual Behavior and Personality Characteristics (New York: Citadel, 1963), pp. 372–375.
[4] G. Williams, The Sanctity of Life and the Criminal Law (New York: Alfred A. Knopf, 1957), p. 51.
[5] R. S. de Ropp, Man against Aging (New York: Grove Press, 1962), p. 252.

sexuality in older people. These include our general tradition of equating sex, love, and romance solely with youth; the psychological difficulty which children have of accepting the fact of parental intercourse; the tendency to think of aging as a disease rather than a normal process; the focusing of studies upon hospitalized or institutionalized older people rather than upon a more typical sample of persons less beset by health, emotional, or economic problems; and the unfortunate fact that—by and large—physicians have shared the ignorance and prejudices equally with the rest of society.[6]

It is significant, however, that centuries of derogation and taboo have not been successful in masking completely the basic reality that sex interest and activity do not disappear in the older years. Elaine Cumming and William E. Henry point out that our jokes at the expense of older people have revealed considerable ambivalence in the view that all old people are asexual.[7] The contradictory attitude which people possess about sexuality in the later years is also well illustrated by the history of the famous poem "John Anderson, My Jo," written by Robert Burns almost two centuries ago. In the version known today, the poem is a sentimental tribute to an old couple's calm and resigned old age. The original folk version—too bawdy to find its way into textbooks—was an old wife's grievance about her husband's waning sex interest and ability which makes very clear that she has no intention of tottering down life's hill in a passionless and sexless old age.[8] It is also

interesting to note that sexuality in older women was an important part of one of Aristophanes' comedies. In his play Ecclesiazusae ("Women in Parliament"), Aristophanes described how the women seized power and established a social utopia.[9] One of their first acts was to place sexual relations on a new basis in order to assure all of them ample satisfaction at all times. They decreed that, if any young man was attracted to a girl, he could not possess her until he had satisfied an old woman first. The old women were authorized to seize any youth who refused and to insist upon their sexual rights also.

THE HARMFUL INFLUENCE OF THE MYTH

A British expert in the study of aging has suggested that the myth of sexlessness in the older years does have some social utility for some older women in our society who may no longer have access to a sexual partner.[10] However, the widespread denial of sexuality in older persons has a harmful influence which goes far beyond its effect upon an individual's sexual life.[11] It makes difficult, and sometimes impossible, correct diagnoses of medical and psychological problems, complicates and distorts interpersonal relations in marriage, disrupts relationships between children and parents thinking of remarriage, perverts the administration of justice to older persons accused of sex offenses, and weakens the whole self-image of the older man or woman.

A corollary of the failure to accept sexuality as a normal aspect of aging has been the tendency to exaggerate the prevalence of psychological deviation in

[6] H. I. Lief, "Sex Education of Medical Students and Doctors," Pacific Medicine and Surgery, Vol. 73 (February 1965), pp. 52–58.
[7] Cumming and Henry, op. cit., footnote, p. 21.
[8] R. Burns, The Merry Muses of Caledonia, ed. J. Barke and S. G. Smith (New York: Putnam, 1964), pp. 147–148.

[9] H. Einbinder, The Myth of the Brittanica (New York: Grove Press, 1964), p. 94.
[10] A. Comfort, Review of Sexual Life after Sixty, by Isadore Rubin, British Medical Journal, II, March 25, 1967, p. 750.
[11] Isadore Rubin, Sexual Life after Sixty (New York: Basic Books, 1965), chap. i.

the sexual behavior of older men and to see in most old men potential molesters of young children. Seen through the lenses of prejudice, innocent displays of affection have often loomed ominously as overtures to lascivious fondling or molestation. It is common, too, to think of the exhibitionist as being, typically, a deviation of old age.

Actually, the facts indicate the falsity of both of these stereotypes. As research by Johann W. Mohr and his associates at the Forensic Clinic of the Toronto Psychiatric Hospital showed, "contrary to common assumption the old age group is the relatively smallest one" involved in child-molesting.[12] The major age groups from whose ranks child-molesters come are adolescence, the middle to late thirties, and the late fifties. The peak of acting out of exhibitionism occurs in the mid-twenties; and, in its true form, exhibitionism is rarely seen after the age of forty.

In relatively simple and static societies, everyone knows pretty much where he stands at each stage of life, particularly the older members of the group. "But in complex and fluid social systems," notes Leo W. Simmons, "with rapid change and recurrent confusion over status and role, no one's position is so well fixed—least of all that of the aging."[13] For many aging persons, there is a crisis of identity in the very sensing of themselves as old, particularly in a culture which places so great a premium upon youth. David P. Ausubel notes that, just as in adolescence, the transition to aging is a period where the individual is in the marginal position of having lost an established and accustomed status without having acquired a new one and hence is a period productive of considerable stress.[14] Under such conditions of role confusion, aging persons tend to adopt the stereotype which society has molded for them, in sex behavior as in other forms of behavior. But they do so only at a very high psychic cost.

For many older people, continued sexual relations are important not so much for the pleasurable release from sexual tension as for the highly important source of psychological reinforcement which they may provide. Lawrence K. Frank has said:

Sex relations can provide a much needed and highly effective resource in the later years of life when so often men face the loss of their customary prestige and self-confidence and begin to feel old, sometimes long before they have begun to age significantly. The premature cessation of sexual functioning may accelerate physiological and psychological aging since disuse of any function usually leads to concomitant changes in other capacities. After menopause, women may find that continuation of sexual relations provides a much needed psychological reinforcement, a feeling of being needed and of being capable of receiving love and affection and renewing the intimacy they earlier found desirable and reassuring.[15]

THE GROWING BODY OF RESEARCH DATA

Gathering data about the sexual behavior and attitudes of the aging has not been an easy task. To the generalized taboos about sex research have been added the special resistance and taboos that center around sexuality in older persons. For example, when the New England Age Center decided to

[12] J. W. Mohr, R. E. Turner, and M. B. Jerry, *Pedophilia and Exhibitionism* (Toronto: University of Toronto Press, 1964).

[13] L. W. Simmons, "Social Participation of the Aged in Different Cultures," in M. B. Sussman (ed.), *Sourcebook in Marriage and the Family* (2nd ed.; Boston: Houghton Mifflin, 1963).

[14] D. P. Ausubel, *Theory and Problems of Adolescent Development* (New York: Grune and Stratton, 1954), pp. 53 ff.

[15] L. K. Frank, *The Conduct of Sex* (New York: Morrow, 1961), pp. 177–178.

administer an inventory to its members, they included only nine questions about sex among the 103 items.[16] The nine questions were made deliberately vague, were confined largely to past sexual activities, and were given only to married members. Leaders of the Center felt that if they had asked more direct questions or put them to their unmarried members, these people would not have returned to the Center. In California, a study of the attitudes of a sample of persons over sixty years old in San Francisco during the early 1960's included just one general open-ended question about sexual attitudes, apparently because of the resistance which many of the researchers had about questioning subjects in the area of sex.[17] Psychiatrists reporting on this research before the Gerontological Society noted that the people involved in research in gerontology are being hamstrung by their own attitudes toward sex with regard to the elderly in much the same way in which the rest of society is hamstrung with regard to their attitudes toward the elderly in such matters as jobs, roles, and those things which go into determining where a person fits into the social structure.

Fortunately, although no sample has yet been studied that was sufficiently broad or typical to present us with a body of norms, a sufficient amount of data now exists which leaves no doubt of the reality of sex interests and needs in the latter years. While it is true that there are many men and women who look forward to the ending of sexual relations, particularly those to whom sex has always been a distasteful chore

or those who "unconsciously welcome the excuse of advancing years to abandon a function that has frightened them since childhood,"[18] sexual activity, interest, and desire are not the exception for couples in their later years. Though the capacity for sexual response does slow down gradually, along with all the other physical capacities, it is usually not until actual senility that there is a marked loss of sexual capacity.

With the research conducted by William H. Masters and Virginia E. Johnson, who observed the anatomy and physiology of sexual response in the laboratory, confirmation has now been obtained that sexual capacity can continue into advanced old age.[19] Among the subjects whose orgasmic cycles were studied by these two investigators were 61 menopausal and postmenopausal women (ranging from 40 to 78) and 39 older men (ranging from 51 to 89). Among the women, Masters and Johnson found that the intensity of physiologic reaction and the rapidity of response to sexual stimulation were both reduced with advancing years. But they emphasized that they found "significant sexual capacity and effective sexual performance" in these older women, concluding:

The aging human female is fully capable of sexual performance at orgasmic response levels, particularly if she is exposed to regularity of effective sexual stimulation. . . . There seem to be no physiologic reasons why the frequency of sexual expression found satisfactory for the younger woman should not be carried over into the postmenopausal years. . . . In short, there is no time limit drawn by the advancing years to female sexuality.

[16] E. B. Armstrong, "The Possibility of Sexual Happiness in Old Age," in H. G. Beigel (ed.), *Advances in Sex Research* (New York: Hoeber-Harper, 1963), pp. 131–137.

[17] E. H. Feigenbaum, M. J. Lowenthal and M. L. Trier, "Sexual Attitudes in the Elderly," Unpublished paper given before the Gerontological Society, New York, November 1966.

[18] W. R. Stokes, *Married Love in Today's World* (New York: Citadel, 1962), p. 100.

[19] W. H. Masters and V. E. Johnson, *Human Sexual Response* (Boston: Little, Brown, 1966), sec. on "Geriatric Sexual Response," pp. 223–270.

When it came to males, Masters and Johnson found that there was no question but that sexual responsiveness weakens as the male ages, particularly after the age of sixty. They added, however:

There is every reason to believe that maintained regularity of sexual expression coupled with adequate physical well-being and healthy mental orientation to the aging process will combine to provide a sexually stimulative climate within a marriage. This climate will, in turn, improve sexual tension and provide a capacity for sexual performance that frequently may extend to and beyond the 80-year age level.

These general findings have been supported by various types of studies which have been made over the course of the years. These studies include the investigation by Raymond Pearl in 1925 into the frequency of marital intercourse of men who had undergone prostatic surgery, all over the age of 55;[20] Robert L. Dickinson and Lura E. Beam's studies of marriages and of single women, including a number of older single women and widows;[21] the Kinsey studies of the male and the female;[22] older men studied at outpatient clinics by urologists at the University of California School of Medicine at San Francisco;[23] extended study by Duke University psychiatrists of Negroes and whites living in the Piedmont area of North Carolina;[24] Joseph T. Freeman's study of older men in Philadelphia;[25] a study of patients attached to a geriatric clinic in New York;[26] a survey of veterans applying for pensions;[27] a questionnaire survey by Sexology magazine of men over 65 who were listed in Who's Who in America;[28] and a study of sex attitudes in the elderly at the Langley Porter Neuropsychiatric Institute in San Francisco.[29]

NO AUTOMATIC CUTOFF DATE

All of these studies indicate the continuation of sex needs, interests, and abilities into the later years despite the gradual weakening that may take place. The Kinsey group, quite contrary to general conceptions of the aging process in sex, found that the rate at which males slow up sexually in the last decades of life does not exceed the rate at which they have been slowing up and dropping out of sexual activity in the

[20] R. Pearl, *The Biology of Population Growth* (New York: Alfred A. Knopf, 1925), pp. 178–207.
[21] R. L. Dickinson and L. E. Beam, *A Thousand Marriages* (Baltimore: Williams & Wilkins, 1931), pp. 278–279, 446; and R. L. Dickinson and L. E. Beam, *The Single Woman* (Baltimore: Williams & Wilkins, 1934), p. 445.
[22] A. C. Kinsey, W. B. Pomeroy, and C. E. Martin, *Sexual Behavior in the Human Male* (Philadelphia: W. B. Saunders, 1948); and A. C. Kinsey, W. B. Pomeroy, C. E. Martin, and P. H. Gebhard, *Sexual Behavior in the Human Female* (Philadelphia: W. B. Saunders, 1953).
[23] A. L. Finkle *et al.*, "Sexual Function in Aging Males: Frequency of Coitus Among Clinic Patients," *Journal of the American*

Medical Association, Vol. 170, July 18, 1959, pp. 1391–1393.
[24] G. Newman and C. R. Nichols, "Sexual Activities and Attitudes in Older Persons," *Journal of the American Medical Association*, Vol. 173, May 7, 1960, pp. 33–35.
[25] J. T. Freeman, Sexual Capacities in the Aging Male," *Geriatrics*, Vol. 16 (January 1961), pp. 37–43.
[26] L. Friedfeld, "Geriatrics, Medicine, and Rehabilitation," *Journal of the American Medical Association*, Vol. 175, February 18, 1961, pp. 595–598; and L. Friedfeld *et al.*, "A Geriatric Clinic in a General Hospital," *Journal of the American Geriatrics Society*, Vol. 7 (October 1959), pp. 769–781.
[27] L. M. Bowers, R. R. Cross, Jr., and F. A. Lloyd, "Sexual Function and Urologic Disease in the Elderly Male," *Journal of the American Geriatrics Society*, Vol. 11 (July 1963), pp. 647–652.
[28] I. Rubin, "Sex over Sixty-five," in H. G. Beigel (ed.), *Advances in Sex Research* (New York: Hoeber-Harper, 1963).
[29] Feigenbaum *et al., op. cit.*

previous age groups.[30] For most males, they found no point at which old age suddenly enters the picture. As far as females were concerned, the Kinsey investigators—like Masters and Johnson later—found little evidence of any aging in their capacities for sexual response.[31] "Over the years," they reported, "most females become less inhibited and develop an interest in sexual relations which they then maintain until they are in their fifties or even sixties." In contrast to the average wife, the responses of the husband dropped with age. Thus, many of the younger females reported that they did not desire intercourse as often as their husbands. In the later years of marriage, however, many of the wives expressed the desire for coitus more often than their husbands were then desiring it.

The Duke University survey—reported by Gustave Newman and Claude R. Nichols—found that only those persons who were seventy-five or older showed a significantly lower level of sexual activity.[32] This study found that Negro subjects were sexually more active than white subjects; men were more active than women; and persons lower in the social and economic scale were more active than those in the upper-income group. A possible explanation of the greater activity reported by males lies in the fact that men and women of the same age were reporting on different age groups. The wives, on the average, would be reporting on sex activity with a husband who was perhaps four years older.

Despite the fact that masturbation has been usually considered an activity that ends with maturity, for many older persons, this practice apparently con-

tinues to serve as a satisfactory form of release from sexual tensions when a partner is, for one reason or another, not available.[33]

Several of the studies suggest a correlation between early sex activity and a continuation into the late years. The Kinsey group found that, at age fifty, all of the males who had been sexually active in early adolescence were still sexually active, with a frequency about 20 per cent higher than the frequency of the later-maturing males.[34] They report:

Nearly forty years maximum activity have not yet worn them out physically, physiologically, or psychologically. On the other hand, some of the males (not many) who were late adolescent and who have had five years less of sexual activity, are beginning to drop completely out of the picture; and the rates of this group are definitely lower in these older age periods.

They conclude:

The ready assumption which is made in some of the medical literature that impotence is the product of sexual excess, is not justified by such data as are now available.

Freeman [35] found that the sex urge of persons in advanced years correlated strongly with their comparative sex urge when young, and a similar finding was reported by the Duke University survey.[36]

Masters and Johnson report the same finding, with additional emphasis upon regularity of sexual expression as the essential factor in maintaining sexual capacity and effective performance for both males and females:[37]

[30] Kinsey et al., Sexual Behavior in the Human Male, pp. 235–237.
[31] Kinsey et al., Sexual Behavior in the Human Female, pp. 353–354.
[32] Newman and Nichols, op. cit.

[33] Rubin, "Sex over Sixty-five"; and Dickinson and Beam, A Thousand Marriages.
[34] Kinsey et al., Sexual Behavior in the Human Male, pp. 319–325.
[35] Freeman, op. cit.
[36] Newman and Nichols, op. cit.
[37] Masters and Johnson, op. cit.

When the male is stimulated to high sexual output during his formative years and a similar tenor of activity is established for the 31–40-year range, his middle-aged and involutional years usually are marked by constantly recurring physiologic evidence of maintained sexuality. Certainly it is true for the male geriatric sample that those men currently interested in relatively high levels of sexual expression report similar activity levels from their formative years. It does not appear to matter what manner of sexual expression has been employed, as long as high levels of activity were maintained.

FACTORS RESPONSIBLE FOR DECLINING SEX ACTIVITY

On the basis of present data, it is not possible to sort out the emotional element from the purely physiologic factors in the decline in sexual activity of the older male. Some animal experiments have shown that changes in the external environment can result in changes in sexual drive. When aging rats had the opportunity for sex activity with a number of partners, for example, the number of copulations increased considerably.[38] However, as soon as male rats reached a certain age, they failed to respond to females.[39]

Many men also find that, with a new partner, a new stimulus is given to their virility.[40] However, often these men return to their old level within comparatively short periods of time.[41] Present data lead us to conclude, with the Kinsey investigators:

[38] J. Botwinick, "Drives, Expectancies, and Emotions," in J. E. Birren (ed.), Handbook of Aging and the Individual (Chicago: University of Chicago Press, 1959), pp. 739–768.

[39] L. F. Jakubczak, Report to the American Psychological Association, August 31, 1962.

[40] J. Bernard, Remarriage (New York: Dryden, 1956), p. 188.

[41] Kinsey et al., Sexual Behavior in the Human Male, pp. 227–229; and A. W. Spence, "Sexual Adjustment at the Climacteric," Practitioner, Vol. 172 (April 1954), pp. 427–430.

The decline in sexual activity of the older male is partly, and perhaps primarily, the result of a general decline in physiologic capacity. It is undoubtedly affected also by psychologic fatigue, a loss of interest in repetition of the same sort of experience, an exhaustion of the possibilities for exploring new techniques, new types of contacts, new situations.[42]

Masters and Johnson, on the basis of their clinical work with older males, describe six general groups of factors which they believe to be responsible for much of the loss of sexual responsiveness in the later years: (1) monotony of a repetitious sexual relationship (usually translated into boredom with the partner); (2) preoccupation with career or economic pursuits; (3) mental or physical fatigue; (4) overindulgence in food or drink; (5) physical and mental infirmities of either the individual or his spouse; and (6) fear of performance associated with or resulting from any of the former categories.

The most constant factor in the loss of an aging male's interest is the problem of monotony, described by the Kinsey group as "psychologic fatigue." According to Masters and Johnson, many factors may produce this: failure of the sexual relationship to develop beyond a certain stage; overfamiliarity; lack of sexual interest on the female's part; aging and loss of personal attractiveness of the female.

A major deterrent for many men is preoccupation with the outside world and their careers. Overindulgence in food and drink, particularly the latter, takes a high toll. According to Masters and Johnson, secondary impotence developing in the late forties or early fifties has a higher incidence of direct association with excessive alcohol consumption than with any other single factor.

[42] Kinsey et al., Sexual Behavior in the Human Male, pp. 226–235.

As each partner ages, the onset of physical or mental infirmities is an ever-increasing factor in reducing sexual capacities. The harmful effect of this is sometimes multiplied by the negative or discouraging attitude of the physician. Once a failure in performance has occurred because of any of the factors, the fear of failure becomes an additional factor in bringing about withdrawal from sexual activity. "Once impotent under any circumstances," remark Masters and Johnson, "many males withdraw voluntarily from any coital activity rather than face the ego-shattering experience of repeated episodes of sexual inadequacy."

The very scanty data concerning the sexual attitudes of older persons suggest a more positive attitude toward sex among men than among women, with women being more "culture-bound" and still showing strong evidences of the effects of the Victorian age in which they acquired their attitudes toward sex.[43] A study of dreams of residents of a home for the aged and infirm, on the other hand, indicates a contrasting difference in emotional tone of the sexual content of the dreams of men and women: "Whereas in men sexual dreams revealed anxiety, failure, and lack of mastery, in women they usually depicted passive, pleasurable gratification of dependent needs."[44]

THE UNMARRIED HAVE SEX NEEDS TOO

It is not only the married who have sexual needs. Aging widows, widowers, and single persons, who make up an increasingly large segment of our population, face even greater problems in respect to sex than do the married. In the survey by Newman and Nichols,

only seven of the 101 single, divorced, or widowed subjects reported any sexual activity with partners.[45] Apparently, the strength of the sexual drive of most elderly persons is usually not great enough to cause them to seek a sexual partner outside of marriage in the face of social disapproval and the difficulties of such an endeavor. Interestingly, however, thousands of older couples were reportedly living "in sin—or what they think is sin" because marriage would mean loss of social security payments.[46]

Dickinson and Beam reported that in their study of widows ranging from sixty to eighty years of age there was evidence of masturbation.[47] They reported that when these women underwent pelvic examinations they showed such marked sexual reactions that they found that "it is desirable to relieve the patient's embarrassment by hurting her, lest she have orgasm." Since many older women are quite troubled by their practice of masturbation, marriage counselors have stressed the importance of helping older persons to accept this practice as a valid outlet when they feel the need for it.[48]

THE GREAT NEED FOR INFORMATION

Persons who have worked with "senior citizens" and "golden age" clubs have reported the great need for knowledge, the confusion, and the eager hunger for information about sex shown by persons in these clubs.[49] The many perplexing problems that they raise indicate the extent to which such in-

[43] Feigenbaum et al., op. cit.

[44] M. Barad, K. Z. Altshuler, and A. I. Goldfarb, "A Survey of Dreams in Aged Persons," Archives of General Psychiatry, Vol. 4 (April 1961), pp. 419–424.

[45] Newman and Nichols, op. cit.

[46] New York Times, January 12, 1965.

[47] Dickinson and Beam, A Thousand Marriages.

[48] L. Dearborn, "Autoerotism," in A. Ellis and A. Abarbanel (eds.), The Encyclopedia of Sexual Behavior (New York: Hawthorn, 1961), pp. 204–215; and L. Hutton, The Single Woman (London: Barrie & Rockcliff, 1960), p. 58.

[49] Feigenbaum et al., op. cit.

formation is needed to help people solve broader questions of remarriage and interpersonal relationships during their later years. The growing incidence of disease states in these years—each of which may require a difficult readjustment in sexual and other relationships— makes it essential that older people be provided with this information openly and consistently.[50]

It should be clear, however, that unless our entire culture recognizes the normality of sex expression in the older years, it will be impossible for older persons to express their sexuality freely and without guilt. Physicians are particularly crucial in this respect; unless they are convinced of the psychological

importance of sexual functioning in the later years, they can do irreparable harm to their patients' sexuality.[51] Fortunately, at long last, medical schools and medical publications have begun to take steps to correct the glaring lacks in the education of medical students, which have in the past resulted in the creation of a body of medical practitioners who, by and large, shared the general prejudices of our society concerning sexuality in older persons.

[50] Rubin, *Sexual Life after Sixty*, chaps. xi–xiii.

[51] J. S. Golden, "Management of Sexual Problems by the Physician," *Obstetrics and Gynecology*, Vol. 23 (March 1964), pp. 471–474; and A. L. Finkle and D. V. Prian, "Sexual Potency in Elderly Men before and after Prostatectomy," *Journal of the American Medical Association*, Vol. 196, April 11, 1966, pp. 139–143.

Sexual Manifestations of Emotionally
Disturbed Behavior

By Albert Ellis

ABSTRACT: It is difficult to define sexual disturbance today because concepts about emotional disturbance in general and sexual disorder in particular have recently undergone significant changes. Sexual disorders may be seen in terms of (a) specific aberrant acts or (b) the psychological and philosophic causes that underlie such acts. It would appear to be more meaningful to define them largely in relation to the self-defeating ways in which and reasons for which an individual behaves sexually rather than in terms of the concrete behaviors he performs. When so viewed, the basic causes of sexual disorders seem to be quite the same as those of most general emotional difficulties. Societal reaction to disturbed individuals with sexual problems has improved in recent years but is still much too condemnatory and punitive. At the same time, some social thinkers, in a misguided effort to prevent the persecution of sexually troubled and deviant individuals unrealistically refuse to face the facts of their intrinsic neurosis or psychosis and trace all their upsets to social persecution. Sexually disturbed persons are not easy to treat successfully for a variety of reasons, especially by conventional psychoanalytic methods. But if a hard-headed therapist actively-directively intervenes in their lives and induces them to challenge and work against their irrational value systems, he may achieve effective results in a relatively brief period of time.

Albert Ellis, Ph.D., New York City, is Executive Director of the Institute for Rational Living and for the last two decades has been in the private practice of psychotherapy and marriage and family counseling. He has been Chief Psychologist for the New Jersey Diagnostic Center, Chief Psychologist of the New Jersey Department of Institutions and Agencies, and has taught psychology at Rutgers University and New York University. He is the author of more than 250 articles and of 26 books and monographs, including Sex Without Guilt (1958), The Art and Science of Love (1960), Reason and Emotion in Psychotherapy (1962), and Homosexuality: Its Causes and Cure (1965).

IN the good old days, it was conveniently clear what a sexually disturbed person was. Obviously, he was someone who went against the prevailing code of sexual morality and practice, and who engaged in such "unnatural" or "perverted" activities as masturbation, oral-genital relations, or homosexuality, or who even practiced normal heterosexual relations to "excess." According to this rigorous standard, it is a little difficult to see who was *not* sexually aberrated; and, if we are to believe the secret diaries and other honest revelations of, say, the 1800's, it would appear that most healthy young males and not a few young females of the day actually did consider themselves more than slightly abnormal.

CHANGING CONCEPTS OF DISTURBANCE AND MENTAL HEALTH

Today, conditions have changed radically in this regard. The concept of emotional disturbance is far from what it used to be only a couple of decades ago; and many authorities are questioning whether unconventional behavior is really indicative of neurosis or psychosis. Psychologists such as Timothy Leary and Richard Alpert and social thinkers such as Paul Goodman (who also happens to be a former psychotherapist) and Lawrence Lipton are stoutly contending that it is the traditionalists and the conformists who are really sick and that the truly healthy person is self-directed rather than other-directed, is much happier when he rebels against American middle-class mores, and should even go to the extreme of "turning on, tuning in, and dropping out" of his silly social order if he is fully to actualize himself as a healthy human being.

In a more professional way, but with almost equal vehemence, Thomas Szasz[1] has recently been attacking the entire concept of "mental illness." He contends that people who act peculiarly in their social milieu, and who are carted off to mental hospitals because they are presumably "sick," have in many or most cases only selected idiosyncratic ways of expressing their individualities; and that these "disturbed" people are being persecuted unjustly by society in order to censor them and to exert undue and unfair control over their behavior. Szasz is, to some extent, echoing the stand of Otto Rank,[2] who, a generation ago, pointed out that the person whom we call "neurotic" may really be a highly creative, self-actualizing person who in many respects is more "normal" than the nonneurotic; and he has many followers, such as Siebert,[3] who vehemently go along with him, and then even a few steps further.

On the other hand, there are vigorous dissenting voices, too. David Ausubel, who is both a psychiatrist and a highly reputable research psychologist, stoutly protests that "personality disorder *is* disease."[4] And the present author, in a recent article, "Should Some People Be Labeled Mentally Ill?",[5] indicates that if we will eliminate the negative, condemning connotations that we usually include under the term "mental illness," we may very well be left with a valid concept of emotional disturbance that goes well beyond the somewhat Pollyannaish limits that Szasz, Rank,

[1] Thomas S. Szasz, *The Myth of Mental Illness* (New York: Hoeber, 1961).

[2] Otto Rank, *Beyond Psychology* (New York: Dover Publications, 1958).

[3] L. A. Siebert, *Are You My Friend?* (Portland: By the Author, 1967).

[4] David P. Ausubel, "Personality Disorder *Is* Disease," *American Psychologist*, Vol. 16 (February 1961), pp. 69–74.

[5] Albert Ellis, "Should Some People Be Labeled Mentally Ill," *Journal of Consulting Psychology*, Vol. 31 (October 1967), pp. 435–446.

Siebert, and other apologists would like to set for this condition.

WHAT CONSTITUTES SEXUAL DISTURBANCE?

Modern writers have had great difficulty in coming to any unanimity of opinion as to what constitutes sexual disturbance, and will probably continue to have such difficulty as long as they use two different and somewhat conflicting criteria: (a) a standard of what emotional disturbance in general is and (b) a standard of sexual aberration in itself. The former standard is usually approached in terms of what the psychodynamic or philosophic core of an individual's neurosis is; and it is fairly clearly understood that a large variety of symptoms—such as phobias, depressions, psychosomatic disorders, and characterological deficiencies—may all stem from a few basic causes (for example, from perfectionistic demands of the individual and his consequent need to impress others with his greatness). The standard of sexual aberration, however, frequently pertains to the kinds of specific sex behaviors in which the individual indulges and how far from some supposed statistical norm these behaviors happen to be. Sexual disturbance, therefore, is viewed *peripherally* and *symptomatically*, while general emotional disturbance is viewed *centrally* and *causally*; and the two just do not seem to be very closely related.

I have often suggested, instead, that sexual neuroses be logically catalogued as subheadings under the same basic headings as general emotional disorders —for the obvious reason that unless they can be so conveniently catalogued, there is no evidence that they really *are* aberrations.[6] If—to take deliberately

an extreme case—a man fairly regularly engages in intercourse with corpses, but enjoys several other kinds of sex outlets as well, is not guilty about his necrophiliac or other sex acts, is not driven to necrophilia by his fear of other kinds of relationships, is not obsessively-compulsively attached to penile-corpse relations, and is not defeating himself in any way by engaging in such "bizarre" practices, we would honestly have to wonder (if we were truly objective about observing him and labeling his behavior) if he were actually disturbed—or if, instead, he were not merely highly idiosyncratic.

Sexual aberrations, in other words, do not seem merely to consist of the *modes* of activities to which people resort but to the *ways* in which and the *reasons* for which they perform these acts. And this, of course, is just as true of nonsexual behaviors. The two main forms of general disturbance are: (a) inhibited, rigid, pain-inflicting actions, which are typically associated with anxiety, guilt, feelings of inadequacy, and fears of failure and (b) underinhibited, overly impulsive, undisciplined actions, which are typically associated with childish grandiosity, hostility, and low frustration tolerance. In the sexual area, the same two basic forms of disturbance exist. Anxious, guilt-ridden, self-deprecating individuals tend to limit themselves to an overrestricted, often exclusive mode of sexuality (such as masturbation or homosexuality); and childish, demanding, hostile individuals often refuse to accept societal proscriptions and impulsively or compulsively

---

[6] Albert Ellis, *Reason and Emotion in Psychotherapy* (New York: Lyle Stuart, 1962); Albert Ellis, *The Art and Science of Love* (New York: Lyle Stuart and Dell Books,

1965); Albert Ellis, *Sex Without Guilt* (New York: Lyle Stuart and Grove Press, 1966); Albert Ellis, *The Search for Sexual Enjoyment* (New York: Macfadden-Bartell, 1966); Albert Ellis, *If This Be Sexual Heresy . . .* (New York: Lyle Stuart and Tower Publications, 1966); Albert Ellis, *Homosexuality: Its Causes and Cure* (New York: Lyle Stuart, 1965).

engage in self-defeating sex acts (such as incest or exhibitionism).

Can sexual disturbances be accurately classified? Probably not too accurately, in terms of the acts themselves. However, we can attempt a rough categorization along these lines: (a) inability to perform sexually: for example, impotence and frigidity; (b) inability to perform sexually except under unusual conditions: for example, fetishism, sadomasochism, and exclusive masturbation; (c) obsessive-compulsive interest in activities which do not lead to orgasmic fulfillment: for example, teasing, exhibitionism, peeping, and tranvestitism; (d) obsessive-compulsive occupation with conventional heterosexual acts: for example, nymphomania and satyriasis; (e) preoccupation and/or overt involvement with peculiar or socially banned sex objects: for example, pedophilia, homosexuality, incest, and necrophilia; (f) extreme antisexuality: for example, complete abstinence and sexual self-mutilation; (g) delusion that one is or should be a member of the other sex: for example, homosexuality that includes sex-role inversion or transsexualism; (h) adequate sex functioning with appropriate partners, but with feelings of severe guilt, shame, or inadequacy: for example, feelings of guilt after successful marital congress; (i) love aberrations: for example, inability to love, fear of emotional involvement, dire needs for a love relationship, and erotomania.

The difficulty with this kind of classification of sex acts that are presumably indicative of emotional disturbance is that most of the activities just listed may in some or many instances be statistically normal or emotionally healthy. Thus, innumerable individuals are impotent or frigid in their early sex experiences; exclusive masturbation is exceptionally common in our sexually restricted society, especially among young people; some degree of peeping is a healthy component of the adolescent male; occasional homosexual episodes are not in the least unusual or unhealthy in the lives of average individuals; and almost every normal father at some times thinks about and is sorely tempted to have sex contact with his attractive teen-age or adult daughter. So, again, it is misleading rigidly to label any sex act as "abnormal," "deviated," or "disturbed." It is more meaningful, instead, to inquire about the manner, conditions, and extent of the individual's performing such an act and to designate him as exhibiting emotionally-sexually disturbed behavior only if he is needlessly self-defeating, distinctly sabotaging his own sex-love potential, or unduly harming others.

THE CAUSES OF SEXUAL DISTURBANCE

Most modern psychologists have attributed emotional disturbances in the area of sexuality to early childhood conditioning. Thus, the Freudians and their psychoanalytic followers have insisted that the individual becomes sexually aberrated because his normal tendency to develop from pregenital, latency, and homosexual stages to a fully adult genital stage of sexuality is interrupted or fixated by his traumatic experiences in regard to toilet training, sibling rivalry, an Oedipus complex, or various other interfamilial experiences.[7] The behaviorists and their heirs have held that early learning influences, within and outside of the family setting, condition many individuals to later sexual-emotional disturbances.[8] Disagreement exists, however, because the Freudians have held that human neurosis and psychosis stem from sexual traumas of

[7] Sigmund Freud, *Collected Papers* (New York: Collier Books, 1963).

[8] H. J. Eysenck (ed.), *Experiments in Behaviour Therapy* (New York: The Macmillan Company, 1964).

early childhood, while neopsychoanalysts, such as Jung, Adler, and Horney, have contended that sexual disturbances stem from general neuroses.[9]

There is much reason to believe, today, that neither the psychoanalytic nor the conditioning theories of the etiology of sexual neurosis fully explain the observed facts. First of all, they largely ignore the pronounced physiological factors that often are significant in the causation of sexual disorders. Inadequate or deviated individuals may have unusually low or high sex hormone levels, may be physically handicapped, may be suffering from arteriosclerosis of the brain, or may have peculiar physiological sensitivities which importantly contribute to their behaving in an aberrated manner.

More importantly, emotional disturbance itself, as research findings increasingly indicate, may partly or mainly stem from the individual's biological predisposition to be disturbed. Although few, if any, sexually disturbed persons may be born with a clear-cut tendency to be homosexual, exhibitionistic, or necrophiliac, most of those who are seriously aberrated may well be born with a predisposition to be *generally* neurotic or psychotic; and they may therefore be much more prone to sexual traumas than are other members of the populace, and may frequently become deviated.[10] As Anthony Storr notes:

Clinical experience suggests that the majority of patients who seek help from a psychiatrist because of sexual deviations were, as children, particularly impressionable. Most of these people belong to the introverted or dysthymic type. They tend to be withdrawn and unsociable, to substitute thought for action, and, especially in the sexual sphere, to live in a world of phantasy which may be quite unrelated to any real possibility of sexual fulfillment. It has been shown experimentally that, in introverted people, conditioned reflexes are more easily established.[11]

A second reason why the usual psychoanalytic and conditioning theories offer far from definitive explanations of the causes of sexual disturbance is that they largely fail to consider the immense self-training tendencies of human beings. Man is not merely the kind of animal who is indoctrinated, early in life, with certain attitudes and action-tendencies; he is, much more than this, the kind of being who actively *interprets* the events of his life, who makes generalized and vastly *important* (and often quite false and illogical) *conclusions* about these happenings, and who thereafter specifically *re*indoctrinates himself with his early-fabricated ideas, attitudes, and philosophies about himself and the world. It is therefore not what happens to an individual, at point A, which causes his emotional upsets and aberrations, at point C; rather, it is what he thinks, imagines, and *tells himself*, at point B, about the occurrences at point A that truly affects him and largely determines his subsequent neurotic or unneurotic behavior.[12]

[9] C. G. Jung, *Two Essays on Analytical Psychology* (New York: Pantheon Books, 1953); H. L. Ansbacher and Rowena R. Ansbacher, *The Individual Psychology of Alfred Adler* (New York: Basic Books, 1956); Karen Horney, *The Neurotic Personality of Our Time* (New York: W. W. Norton, 1937); Karen Horney, *New Ways in Psychoanalysis* (New York: W. W. Norton, 1939).

[10] Stella Chess, Thomas Alexander, and Herbert G. Birch, *Your Child Is a Person* (New York: Viking, 1965); Albert Ellis, *Reason and Emotion in Psychotherapy* (New York: Lyle Stuart, 1962).

[11] Anthony Storr, *Sexual Deviation* (Baltimore: Penguin Books, 1965), p. 22.

[12] Moses Hadas (ed.), *Essential Works of Stoicism* (New York: Bantam Books, 1962); Albert Ellis, *How to Live With a Neurotic* (New York: Crown Publishers, 1957); Albert Ellis, *Reason and Emotion in Psychotherapy* (New York: Lyle Stuart, 1962); Albert Ellis, *How to Prevent Your Child from Becoming a Neurotic Adult* (New York: Crown Pub-

Man's so-called "emotional" responses, as Magda Arnold and a good many other psychological thinkers have pointed out in recent years, are largely dependent on his cognitive appraisals of himself and others; and these, in turn, are only partly dependent on his early childhood conditioning.[13]

Because of his innately predisposed *and* early acquired tendency to think irrationally about himself and the world around him, and because of his concomitant tendency to sustain his false assumptions uncritically (rather than to question and challenge them in the light of empirical evidence), it can fairly accurately be said that most (though hardly all) of man's ostensibly sexual disorders are actually the result of love or acceptance problems. The three basic ways in which he needlessly upsets himself are these: (1) He refuses to accept himself as a fallible, imperfect creature, but instead demands that he practically always be adequate and competent and that he win the almost universal approval of others. (2) He refuses to accept other human beings as error-prone individuals and blastingly condemns them when they do not behave in the way that he thinks they *should* or *ought* to behave. (3) He refuses to accept the usual difficulties and limitations which the world imposes on him and angrily and rebelliously condemns it for being *too* hard and frustrating. These three ways of ir-

rationally condemning and damning himself, others, and the world result, in turn, in the individual's feeling (a) self-deprecating, anxious, guilty, ashamed, and inadequate; (b) inordinately angry, hostile, vindictive, and sadistic; and (c) childishly grandiose, demanding, overrebellious, unco-operative, self-pitying, lazy, and avoidant. Any one or any combination of these irrational, self-defeating, neurotic reactions may easily lead the crooked-thinking individual into sexual disturbance.

Take, as a case in point, the typical fixed, exclusive male homosexual, who rarely or never enjoys sex relations with females. There is, as noted above, nothing necessarily disturbed about his sex *acts*—since almost half of our males at one time or another (especially when they are isolated from females) engage in occasional homosexual practices. But the fact that he rigidly, obsessively-compulsively, and persistently practices homosexuality in a social milieu which (albeit unfortunately and unfairly) frequently penalizes him for doing so almost invariably means that he is not merely doing so because he healthfully *prefers* or *desires* such relations but because he unhealthfully thinks he *needs* or *demands* them. More concretely, he frequently has all three of the love or acceptance problems listed above: (1) He cannot accept himself with his own imperfections, believes that he should immediately and always succeed with females sexually, and that it is too painful and shameful if he does not; so he withdraws from the entire field of heterosexual risk-taking. Also: he thinks that he must be an ideal, supermasculine male; feels that he can never attain this perfectionistic goal; so he worships other "masculine" males, desperately tries to win their approval, and thereby deludes himself that he can magically acquire supermanhood. (2) He bitterly resents

lishers, 1966); Albert Ellis and Robert A. Harper, *A Guide to Rational Living* (Englewood Cliffs, N.J.: Prentice-Hall, 1961; and Hollywood, Calif.: Wilshire Books, 1967); Albert Ellis and Robert A. Harper, *Creative Marriage* (New York: Lyle Stuart, 1961; and New York: Tower Publications [under the title, *The Marriage Bed*], 1966).

[13] Magda Arnold, *Emotion and Personality* (New York: Columbia University Press, 1960); V. J. McGill, *Emotions and Reason* (Springfield, Ill.: Charles C Thomas, 1954); E. Lakin Phillips, *Psychotherapy* (Englewood Cliffs, N.J.: Prentice-Hall, 1956).

females for the kinds of demands that they frequently make on males in this society; and he also hates heterosexual males who easily succeed in the regular sex rat-race and who do not fully accept and approve him. (3) He thinks that the world is much too rough on him, that he should not have to compete for sexual favors and for other goals in life, and he frequently avoids life responsibilities, adapts to a lower vocational level than he is capable of achieving, and sees himself as too lazy to accomplish much, particularly in the sexual area.

The basic causes of this individual's fixed, compulsive homosexuality, therefore, are not truly sexual. Rather, he does not *relate* adequately to himself, to others, or to the world around him. Similarly, other sexual neurotics are usually motivated by (a) short-range hedonism, or the refusal to give up present pleasure for future gains; (b) addiction to an easier, avoidant behavioral pathway; (c) terrible fear of failure, in case they risk taking one of the regular sex routes and are not successful; (d) guilt caused by their belief that certain sexual acts are wrong or sinful; (e) hostility stemming from their views that others have not treated or will not treat them well enough; (f) compulsive or overimpulsive behavior originating in the notion that they *must* follow some urge or that they *need* what they *want*. For reasons such as these, most sexually disturbed individuals adopt an overly channelized mode of sexuality and then rigidly stick to it; or else they refuse to become sufficiently socialized in their community and thereby do themselves more harm than good. These aberrant individuals, because they are so immature and self-defeating, are hardly distinguishable from nonsexual neurotics, who are equally anxiety-ridden, phobiac, hostile, and obsessive-compulsive, but who just

happen to have somewhat different symptoms of their irrational basic value systems.

SOCIETAL REACTION TO SEXUAL DISTURBANCE

Until very recently, society has reacted with extreme prejudice and persecution to all kinds of deviants, sexual and nonsexual. Such individuals have been derided and defamed, kept from holding certain kinds of employment, unfairly jailed, or put into mental institutions, and otherwise discriminated against. During the last few decades, this attitude has changed considerably as far as nonsexually disturbed individuals are concerned; they are now often looked upon with relative kindness, held little accountable for their antisocial behavior, and encouraged to go for treatment, rather than being condemned and punished. Much progress has also been made, in this regard, concerning the acceptance of sexually disturbed individuals; but society still has a long way to go here.

As the Kinsey research group showed two decades ago, and as it has recently reaffirmed, as many as 95 per cent of American males could still technically be jailed for committing sex acts, at one time or another during their lives, which are against state and federal statutes.[14] And, of course, every year, thousands of our citizens are prosecuted for sexual behavior which is, at the very worst, neurotic and which, if it were being acted out in an equally disturbed nonsexual way, would never come to police attention. Several organizations, such as the Mattachine Society and the

[14] Alfred C. Kinsey, Wardell B. Pomeroy, and Clyde E. Martin, *Sexual Behavior in the Human Male* (Philadelphia: W. B. Saunders, 1948); Paul H. Gebhard, John H. Gagnon, Wardell B. Pomeroy, and Christina V. Christenson, *Sex Offenders: An Analysis of Types* (New York: Harper and Row, 1965).

Society for Individual Rights, keep crusading against this kind of sexual discrimination; but the progress that they are making is agonizingly slow.

On the other side of the fence, in a sort of misguided attempt to counterbalance the unfair persecution of sexual nonconformists, there is a modern movement which insists that most sexual deviants are really not disturbed and that they only become neurotic *because* of society's persecutions.[15] Individuals who take this point of view are largely do-gooders who believe that if deviated individuals are neurotic and if they themselves are somewhat responsible for becoming and keeping themselves neurotic, there may be some justification for condemning them; therefore, it is better to assume that they have normal, though statistically different, preferences for their homosexual, pedophiliac, or exhibitionistic behavior, and that society will just not sanely accept their normality.

This is silly. If an individual is seriously disturbed emotionally and his choices for a certain kind of sexual behavior are therefore compulsive rather than preferential, he is, if anything, less responsible for his acts than he would be if he were performing them out of sheer preference. So, if anything, he should be less condemned and punished for them. If, moreover, a person is highly responsible for his acts and he willfully keeps repeating behavior that is socially aberrant and that can easily get him into trouble, he *still* need not be

condemned or punished—since he has a right, as a fallible human, to be wrong, and is not a villain or a demon for being so. Although society may justifiably criticize his acts, and, if necessary, place him in protective custody if he continues to perpetrate antisocial performances, it is still mistaken if it condemns him as a person, and if it theologically holds that he *should* not do what he does (instead of sanely holding that *it would be better* if he did not do so).

The defenders of sexual deviants would, therefore, be far wiser and more humanely consistent if they held that even if a deviant *is* emotionally aberrated, there is no good reason for damning him. For these defenders to contend, in contradistinction to considerable clinical and experimental evidence, that sex deviates are rarely neurotic or psychotic constitutes lack of realism, and, at times, a kind of intellectual dishonesty, on their part.

THE TREATMENT OF SEXUAL DISTURBANCE

Once an individual becomes sexually disturbed, he is often quite difficult to treat successfully. Sexual inadequacy is not easily overcome, even by intensive treatment; acute love problems, such as erotomania, are sometimes impossible to cure; and the usual kinds of deviation, such as fixed homosexuality and transvestism, are frequently not reached by any known form of psychotherapy or drugs.

There are probably several reasons why this is so: (1) Many sexually disturbed individuals are ashamed to admit that they are disturbed or to come for treatment even when they do admit this to themselves. (2) A good many of them erroneously believe that they were specifically born the way they are and that nothing can be done to change themselves. (3) A considerable number

[15] Harry Benjamin, *The Transsexual Phenomenon* (New York: Julian Press, 1966); O. Benson, *In Defense of Homosexuality* (New York: Julian Press, 1965); John H. Gagnon and William Simon (eds.), *Sexual Deviance* (New York: Harper and Row, 1967); Evelyn Hooker, "The Adjustment of the Male Overt Homosexual," *Journal of Projective Techniques*, Vol. 21 (January 1967), pp. 18–31; Wardell B. Pomeroy, "What Is Normal?", *Playboy* (May 1965).

of sexually aberrated persons obtain considerable pleasure, or neurotic gain, from their behavior patterns. (4) Sex deviants are frequently seriously disturbed in general, and treating their sexual symptoms is not really too helpful, while treating their underlying disturbance is most difficult and discouraging. (5) A great many sexual neurotics and psychotics are formidable avoiders or "goofers," and will refuse to work at psychotherapy just as they will at so many other aspects of their lives. (6) During the last half-century, the treatment of sexually disturbed individuals has largely been psychoanalytic; and there is considerable evidence that passive, prolonged, indirect methods of analytic therapy are generally ineffective and are certainly not likely to work with difficult patients such as sex deviants, while more active-directive, persuasive-philosophic methods of therapy, which have been rarely used in recent years, are likely to be more effective.

In spite of the difficulties of treating sexually neurotic individuals, some success in doing so has been reported by a good many psychotherapists; and this has even been true in the case of severely disturbed and therapy-resistant homosexuals.[16] Usually, treatment has tended to be psychoanalytic, and therefore it has been prolonged and expensive. But psychotherapists such as E. Lakin Phillips and Daniel N. Wiener [17] and Albert

Ellis [18] have reported relatively short-term active-directive methods of therapy that have proved to be quite effective with individuals suffering from sexual inadequacy and deviancy; and several behavior therapists have reported unusual success with from a few to a score of sessions of deconditioning procedures.[19] Fairly inexpensive methods of treating sexually disturbed individuals with group therapy have also been outlined by several therapists.[20]

In order for therapy with this type of patient to be effective, several requisites are usually in order: (1) The therapist should be a nonmoralistic individual who is himself free of sexual puritanism and is noncondemning of individuals who have severe problems in this area. (2) He should be realistic in his expectations and not demand that his patients make 100 per cent changes in their sex proclivities. His main goal should not necessarily be to eradicate all the aberrant or neurotic tendencies of the disturbed individuals, but to help them to increase their range of enjoyable activities, so that they are no longer compulsively, exclusively, and fearfully held to an arbitrarily limited number of outlets. Thus, if he helps a confirmed peeper to overcome his

[16] Clifford Allen, The Sexual Perversions and Abnormalities (London: Oxford University Press, 1949); Irving Bieber et al., Homosexuality (New York: Basic Books, 1962); Edmund Bergler, Homosexuality (New York: Hill and Wang, 1956); J. A. Hadfield, "The Cure of Homosexuality," British Medical Journal, Vol. 1, June 7, 1958, pp. 1323–1326; Benjamin Karpman, The Sexual Offender and His Offenses (New York: Julian Press, 1954); L. S. London and F. S. Caprio, Sexual Deviation (Washington, D.C.: Linacre Press, 1950).

[17] E. Lakin Phillips and Daniel W. Wiener, Short-Term Psychotherapy and Structured

Behavior Change (New York: McGraw-Hill, 1966).

[18] Albert Ellis, Reason and Emotion in Psychotherapy (New York: Lyle Stuart, 1962); Albert Ellis, Homosexuality: Its Causes and Cure (New York: Lyle Stuart, 1965); Albert Ellis and Edward Sagarin, Nymphomania: A Study of the Oversexed Woman (New York: Gilbert Press, Grammercy Books, and MacFadden-Bartell, 1965).

[19] K. Srnec and K. Freund, "Treatment of Male Homosexuality through Conditioning," International Journal of Sexology, Vol. 7 (May 1953), pp. 92–93; H. J. Eysenck (ed.), Experiments in Behaviour Therapy (New York: The Macmillan Company, 1964).

[20] Daniel Cappon, Toward an Understanding of Homosexuality (Englewood Cliffs, N.J.: Prentice-Hall, 1965).

compulsive voyeurism, to enjoy heterosexual participations that he has not formerly had the courage to try, he need not also expect that the patient will be completely without voyeuristic tendencies for the rest of his life, but will be content with the fact that he is able to keep these under noncompulsive control. (3) The therapist should often be quite interventionist, see that the patient is persuaded to go at times beyond the point where he would spontaneously wish to go, and encourage him to make basic personality changes rather than be content only with symptomatic improvement.

The therapist who treats sexually disordered individuals has several important questions on which he has to take a fairly definite stand. First, he has to decide whether the person who comes to him for help is truly disturbed emotionally or whether he merely has certain idiosyncracies which do not happen to be very popular in his society. Second, the therapist has to judge whether the individual with a distinct sex problem has a relatively minor disability or whether he has a symptom of a deep-seated general disturbance. Third, the therapist has to estimate whether it is feasible, in a given case, to tackle the sexual symptom or to try to cure the basic neurosis or psychosis which lies at the base of it. If he makes all these decisions correctly and strives relentlessly for the best feasible therapeutic result he may (or may not) help the patient considerably; in any event, he will have the satisfaction of working in a highly challenging and as yet relatively uncharted area.

Sexual Deviance in Contemporary America*

By John H. Gagnon and William Simon

ABSTRACT: Sexual deviance was traditionally seen within the framework of a society's definition of morality and sin; today it is being viewed from the vantage point of the society's definition of mental health and emotional disturbance. A typology of categories of sex deviance is suggested, using three variables: incidence or frequency, the level of invoked sanctions, and the existence of a specialized social structure that may arise out of the deviant behavior or may be necessary to support it. It is suggested that the deviant subcultures do not attain their new adherents by recruitment, but rather by enlistment. Several shifts in the patterns of deviant behavior are noted.

John Gagnon and William Simon are Senior Research Sociologists and Trustees of the Institute for Sex Research of Indiana University. Mr. Gagnon and Mr. Simon edited Sexual Deviance (1967), and they have recently published articles on homosexuality in The Journal of Health and Social Behavior, Social Problems, and The Dublin Review; on pornography, in Trans-Action; and on sex education, in Saturday Review. Other recently published articles covered problems of the American small town, urban development, and poverty programs. They are currently completing research projects dealing with postchildhood socialization, homosexuality, and the effects of sex education.

* Support for the research for this paper was from United States Public Health Service Grants MH-07742 and HD-02257.

THERE is no form of sexual activity that is not deviant at some time, in some social location, in some specified relationships, or with some partners. Truly, one can say that sexual deviance covers a multitude of sins. As a consequence of this variety, sexual deviance as a category includes behaviors that call forth societal responses that range from tacit encouragement to almost incalculable ferocity. It is important, therefore, that the term "sexual deviance" be approached somewhat less globally. Moreover, in discussing several possible subcategories of sexual deviance, it is important that a careful distinction be made between deviant sexual behavior as it occurs and the image that the society has of the behavior. The image, including the motives imputed to the deviant actor and the societal definition of deviance which is the implicit guide to the social response, exists in a complex and only indirect relation to the behavior.

SOCIAL CHANGE AND THE DEFINITION OF SEXUAL DEVIANCE

Before considering subcategories of sexual deviance, it is important to sketch in summary fashion some of the evident changes in the American contemporary scene that most significantly relate to the definition of and response to sexual deviance. The first of these is a manifest shift from a rhetoric imbued with moral or theological judgments to one expressive of essentially psychiatric judgments. As part of this trend, the society moves from defining the deviant actor as morally defective toward a view of the deviant actor as psychologically defective. The appropriate imagery of societal response correspondingly shifts from punishment to treatment, though the commonly available forms and contexts of "treatment" often turn out to be as punishing as,

if not more punishing than, those conceived for serving the ends of punishment.[1] At the same time, however, this shift does allow for increased rationality in responding to deviance, making it possible, for example, to define some forms of sexual deviance as unpleasant or unhealthy without necessarily defining them as wicked, immoral, or depraved and, ergo, criminal and dangerous to society.

A second trend has been the marked increase in mass media representations and discussions of sexuality in almost all of its forms. The *New York Times,* which in 1948 refused to carry advertising for the initial volume by Professor Kinsey and his associates, now carries ads for publications that were generally considered to be pornographic. The *Times'* drama critic may now devote a full column to a discussion of the effect of the homosexual playwright on the Broadway theater. In its magazine section, models in lingerie ads retain possession of their navels. Generally, the representation of heterosexual activity in the mass media has become, depending on one's orientation, either more honest or more blatant, but, in any case, far more explicit. Moreover, with general liberalization of public representation and discussion of sexuality, there have been comparable increases in the representation and discussion of what are generally defined as deviant practices. Mass magazines and even network television openly consider the problem of homosexuality and the problems of the homosexual—sometimes with considerable sympathy. Problems of pre-, post-, and extra-marital sexual relations are widely discussed in the public media. In general, then, there is a growing public language for describing essentially private behavior.

[1] Thomas Szasz, *The Myth of Mental Illness* (New York: Harper & Row, 1961).

Parenthetically, one might add, what may be missing is a corresponding growth of private language.

A third trend involves the ways in in which sexual behavior is styled. Clearly, there is a growing tendency to be more "elaborate" or "sophisticated" in managing sexual activity. A number of years ago, Nelson Foote pointed to the potential use of sex in marriage as a form of play.[2] With an increasing separation of the sexual function from the procreative function, sexual activity becomes more explicitly a basis for establishing relation-stabilizing patterns of reciprocity and, of increasing significance, a basis for reciprocal validation of competence.[3] In other words, sex can become an activity which requires progressively greater elaboration, not unlike woodworking or outdoor gourmet cooking. Moreover, in at least some segments of the middle class, a rigidly stylized division of roles in sexual activity may begin to break down, and this, in turn, might provide for a more aggressive commitment of females to sexual activity and a greater need for sexually committed females on the part of males. Part of this shift may be seen in the widespread interest in Masters' research on female orgasm.[4] Even the relatively conservative Catholic position with reference to sex now extends to cover many forms of sexual technique. For example, a fairly recent Cana Conference manual suggests that in marital sexual activity it is legitimate for "all parts of the body to touch all parts of the other's body" so long as the sex—now expressing the Church's stand on the birth control issue—culminates in penetration of the vagina.[5]

One obvious consequence of this elaboration of sexual activity (one might now more literally refer to it as sex play) is that it narrows the gap between what sexual performers who define themselves as conventional are actually doing and what they assume many persons with sexually deviant commitments are doing. As sexual activity is elaborated, it moves beyond an exclusively or nearly exclusively genital focus and, consequently, increasing numbers of essentially conforming sexual actors find themselves doing things that many others still consider "unnatural acts"; indeed, doing things that most state jurisdictions define as "crimes against nature" or "sodomy." Mouth-genital contact or oral sex is an excellent case in point. In many cases, this trend must surely act to lessen the sharpness of distinction between conforming sexual behavior and some forms of deviant sexual behavior, though, given absence of systematic data, it is difficult to assess the impact upon societal attitudes and practices.

These three trends are manifestly not independent of one another. Indeed, they not only bear directly upon each other, but also tend to reflect other trends in the society that are of possibly greater significance. Thus, one could point to the growth of urban or metropolitan centers and the penetration of nonmetropolitan areas by urban culture through increasing reliance upon mass media systems. The rising educational level of the population and the increased secularization and commitment to modernity that generally is expected to accompany increases in education is another trend that is related to our discussion. A third would be the

[2] Nelson Foote, "Sex as Play," *Social Problems*, Vol. 1, No. 4 (April 1954), pp. 159–163.

[3] Talcott Parsons, "The Kinship System of the Contemporary United States," in *Essays in Sociological Theory* (rev. ed.; Glencoe, Ill.: Free Press, 1954), pp. 177–196.

[4] William Masters and Virginia Johnson, *Human Sexual Response* (Boston: Little, Brown, 1966).

[5] Walter Imbiorski (ed.), *The New Cana Manual* (Chicago: Delaney, 1957), pp. 84, 116.

TABLE—Sexual Deviance: Three Variables

Incidence		High to Moderate		Low	
Level of Invoked Sanctions		Weak	Strong	Weak	Strong
Existence of specialized social structure	No	Masturbation Premarital coitus Postmarital coitus Extramarital coitus Noncoital genital contacts		Exhibitionism Peeping Fetishism	Incest Offenses against children Rape
	Yes	Female homosexuality Female prostitution	Male homosexuality	Social nudism	"Hard-core" pornography*

* Not treated in this paper.

increased affluence of many segments of the society's population, which should serve not only to lower relative costs of extended sexual activity (marriage and divorce, pregnancy and abortion becoming economically less significant) but also to increase leisure and the possibility of experiencing what Durkheim referred to as the anomie of prosperity.[6] Both of these latter trends place a new emphasis upon the exploratory and innovative in interpersonal behavior in general. It is in the context of these trends, then, that our examination of several subcategories of sexual deviance should proceed.

Categories of Sexual Deviance

There are several ways of approaching the subcategorization of sexual deviance. Since many forms of deviance or deviant practice appear to the conventional observer as exotic or bizarre, most typically, categorization fixes upon the sexual activity itself. Thus, attempts

[6] Emile Durkheim, *Suicide* (Glencoe, Ill.: Free Press, 1951 [originally 1897]), pp. 246–258.

at categorization tend to focus upon attributes of the object or objects of sexual desire or specific sexual practices. This, in turn, leads to a kind of specificity that makes social analysis (as opposed to analysis for criminological or psychological purposes) extremely difficult. Instead, we propose to group and consider particular forms of sexual deviance using three variables: the degree of social structure attending or necessary to the practice, the estimated incidence of the behavior, and the severity of societal response (sanction). (See Table.) On the basis of this approach, four fairly gross subcategories may be described. The first contains those behaviors which have relatively high incidence, weak societal responses, and relatively little facilitating social structure. This subcategory might almost be labeled "normal deviance," and would include masturbation, pre-, post-, and extra-marital intercourse, and noncoital genital forms of heterosexual activity in and out of marriage. The second would be characterized by moderate incidence, strong to weak societal responses, and a substantial amount of facilitating social structure. This subcategory would include female prostitution and homosexuality, as instances of behavior which are relatively weakly sanctioned, and male homosexuality, which is strongly sanctioned. The third subcategory, characterized by low incidence and the requirement of a specialized social structure, contains social nudism, for which sanctions are relatively low. Another set of behaviors in this subcategory, with stronger sanction, is hard-core pornography, the content of which will not be dealt with in this paper. The fourth subcategory contains those behaviors which have relatively low incidence, strong to weak societal responses, and relatively little necessary social structure. This category would include incest, child-molesting, and rape, all of which meet with strong societal sanctions, and exhibitionism, voyeurism, and fetishism, for which the societal responses are weak.

Even this approach produces considerable heterogeneity within each subcategory and does not always eliminate ambiguity in assignment. Typical of problems of assignment is group involvement in husband-wife extramarital activity. The major defense to be made for this approach is that it facilitates a summary discussion that is more immediately referential to the changing character of the larger society and allows for linking the behaviors themselves to social structures outside of the sexual domain.

Normal deviance

The largest subcategory of sexual deviance, both in terms of the number of persons involved and in terms of the frequencies of the behavior, consists of those behaviors that must be considered normal in character. This conception may be defended on at least two levels. The first is purely statistical, in that

there are relatively vast numbers of actors engaged in the behavior. While a statistical definition is not an adequate defense of the morality of a behavior, when large numbers of a population are involved in norm-violating behavior, it suggests that the violations of the norms involved are directly linked to the maintenance of other systems of behavior that are approved and that there exist mechanisms, both social and psychological, for the neutralization of the guilt which is consequent on the violation of such norms. This is a major basis for considering these behaviors normal deviance. The second ground on which to make this case is lack of evidence of other major psychopathology resulting from engaging in these activities, even though there may be some evidence of guilt and anxiety on the part of actors engaging in them. As will be suggested, there may be sufficient amounts of guilt and anxiety evoked by some of these behaviors to result in forms of secondary deviance; however, in most cases such manifestations are handled without recourse to specialized psychiatric or mental health aid.

Masturbation. The most widespread form of sexual deviance in this society is masturbation, especially as it occurs among males. There is substantial social-class variation in the incidence of masturbation even during adolescence, but it occurs in at least three-quarters of males who go to elementary school and upwards of 90 per cent of those males who enter college.[7] Among these latter, masturbation continues into marriage not only as a form of gratification in the absence of coitus, but also as an autonomous source of sexual pleasure. Masturbation occurs at fairly high rates during adolescence and then declines in

[7] Alfred C. Kinsey *et al., Sexual Behavior in the Human Male* (Philadelphia: W. B. Saunders, 1948), pp. 497–509.

frequency with the onset of regular heterosexual contacts either before or during marriage.

The shift in attitude toward sexual behavior noted at the beginning of this paper is most noticeable in regard to masturbation. While masturbation was severely condemned on religious and moral grounds as well as on certain spurious physical- and mental-health grounds (masturbation would lead to physical weakness or insanity because of the loss of valuable bodily fluids or to mental deterioration because of the intensity of the orgasmic experience), in most instances it is now considered a necessary form of adolescent sexual expression which, in the psychologically healthy, will cease with adulthood.[8] Rarely, however, is masturbation suggested or approved of as a good thing for either adolescents or adults. It continues as a clandestine alternative to heterosexual contact among middle-class males and is, in general, not controlled except by the invocation of indirect norms or sanctions.

There is some evidence that a commitment to masturbatory rather than social sexual outlets may be linked to social mobility and the reinforcement of a complex sexual fantasy life. Indeed, it is possible that the masturbatory fantasy may serve both middle-class and upwardly mobile working-class male youth as contexts within which they learn to invest symbols with affect and to derive gratification from the imaginative manipulation of symbols.[9]

For females, the picture is profoundly different. Until recently, masturbatory rates were far lower for females than for males. Kinsey reports that only two-thirds of females ever masturbated and that the frequencies tended to be substantially lower at all levels of the life-cycle.[10] Moreover, unlike the male experience, the initiation of this behavior among women tends to occur late in adolescence or the early adult years. Also, in distinction to the male experience, approximately half of the women who masturbated began doing so only after having experienced orgasm in some form of sociosexual activity.[11]

If contemporary sexual behavior is expressive of change on this level, it is clearly change among females that would be significant. Current research at the Institute for Sex Research suggests that change in female masturbatory behavior—both in terms of starting earlier and in terms of doing it more often—may, in fact, be occurring. While the sociocultural forces that restrict the young female in the expression of many emotions and behaviors that are accepted as legitimate for young males still operate powerfully, the general societal shift toward greater freedom for females may represent a countervailing pressure resulting in earlier self-exploration of a sexual nature. If this shift toward earlier experience with sexuality is, in fact, occurring, then we might entertain thoughts of profound social change waiting in the wings. The masturbatory experience may turn out to be a stronger determinant of ultimate sexual commitment than is the experience of initial coitus.

Premarital coitus. The second largest area of normal sexual deviance is that of premarital coitus. The patterns for males and females are quite different and must therefore be discussed separately. There is evidence that male patterns of sociosexual commitment and masturbatory behavior are in-

---

[8] Steven Marcus, *The Other Victorians* (New York: Basic Books, 1966), pp. 1–33.

[9] Kinsey *et al., op. cit.,* pp. 417–436.

[10] Alfred C. Kinsey *et al., Sexual Behavior in the Human Female* (Philadelphia: W. B. Saunders, 1953), pp. 132–190.

[11] Cornelia V. Christenson and John H. Gagnon, "Sexual Behavior in a Group of Older Women," *The Journal of Gerontology,* Vol. 20, No. 3 (July 1965), pp. 351–356.

versely related; that is, lower-class males begin heterosexual relationships in mid-adolescence or earlier, with a consequent decrease in masturbation, while middle-class males begin heterosexual contact in the late teens and early twenties, commonly in the context of family-forming behavior, with masturbation remaining a significant portion of sexual experience.[12] In contrast to these male patterns, there are few variations among females in the incidence or frequencies of premarital coitus by social class. About 50 per cent of the females who ever marry have coitus before marriage, and this rate has been stable for some forty years. Of those females who do have premarital coitus, about half confine their experience to the man they ultimately marry, and a large proportion of the remainder have coitus with less than five males. The proportion of females who have coitus with six or more males before marriage is lower than 10 per cent of all females.[13] It is this small proportion of females who are the sexual targets for the males who have coitus before marriage and from which the recruits to prostitution generally originate.[14]

The evidence is that there are still fairly strong norms against premarital coitus and that these norms continue to be much stronger for females than for males. There is also evidence that males continue to make distinctions between girls with whom one has intercourse under conditions of no affection and girls with whom one has intercourse only before marriage when in love. Ehrmann suggests that males who are in love with a female are less likely to

desire coitus with her than males who are not in love with a female.[15] The current situation appears to be one in which the female allows increasing levels of sexual intimacy in exchange for increasing levels of emotional commitment on the part of the male.[16] While the coitus does not become legitimate in the eyes of the larger society, it is legitimate for the participants because they are in love and because they are going to get married. This particular process of mate-selection seems to be the outcome of the decline of the arrangement of marriages on the basis of propinquity in terms of neighborhood, family, or religion, and the declining strength of parental control over mate-selection. This is a fundamental readjustment in the processes of mate-selection resulting from increasing autonomy of females that began in the 1920's.

At present, there are uneven signs of a shift in rates of premarital intercourse in our society—a shift toward increasing incidence of premarital intercourse on the part of females. However, an increase in incidence of premarital intercourse—even one of substantial proportions—need not imply a proportionately significant shift in the meaning of the sexual experience or the ways in which it relates to general social life. As long as the greater proportion of premarital intercourse occurs within the context of family-forming behavior, little need change on either the personal or social level. When a significant amount of sexual activity is detached from family-formation, we might be able to talk in terms of major change. This would be evidenced by greater sexual access under conditions of lower levels of affective

---

[12] Kinsey et al., Sexual Behavior in the Human Male, pp. 547–557.

[13] Kinsey et al., Sexual Behavior in the Human Female, pp. 285–345.

[14] John H. Gagnon, "Prostitution," International Encyclopedia of the Social Sciences (New York: The Macmillan Company, 1967).

[15] Winston W. Ehrmann, Premarital Dating Behavior (New York: Henry Holt, 1959).

[16] Robert R. Bell, Premarital Sex in a Changing Society (New York: Prentice-Hall, 1967), pp. 80–85.

investment, which, in turn, should produce larger numbers of sexual partners. Higher rates of masturbation by females might be an effective predictor of such a change, as it would mark the advent of a larger number of females entering adult life with a stronger and symbolically more complicated commitment to sexuality.

Postmarital coitus. The third major category of sexual deviance which can be called normal is that of coitus which occurs among the widowed, divorced, and separated. There is a good deal of evidence that coitus is far more likely to occur among males and females who have been married than among those never married, and that among females, coitus is more likely to occur among those divorced than among those widowed.[17] Given the high rates of remarriage among these groups, especially those of younger age, much of this behavior may be seen as facilitative of forming new families rather than as a fundamently uninhibited and lusty desire for sex. There is a good deal of sexual deinhibition in these populations; however, the primary forces involved, especially among females, would seem to be those of remarriage. The normative constraints against such coitus appear to be rather unspecific and rarely enforced, though the behavior itself can be construed as either illegal or immoral. The more powerful norms against such behavior among the never-married are quite obvious. The number of females who are generally available for coitus will increase if there is any increase in the divorce rate; however, this rate has been relatively stable for two or three decades.

The detached male and female, such as the divorced or widowed, have frequently been viewed by the society as being more sexual than persons conventionally attached; they are defined, as it were, as being both sexually experienced and socially less constrained. Even though rates of activity are higher, the motives imputed to this population are more a projection of what might be called collective fantasy needs. Suggestive of this is the fact that many of the representations of the divorced and widowed (the gay divorcee, the merry widow) in popular culture have been marked by strong ambivalences; more often than not, they were viewed as temptations that opened the door to social and personal disaster.[18] However, more recently, there have been some shifts in perspective, and the individual moving outside of conventional family arrangements is increasingly viewed more sympathetically and as being legitimately active sexually. This is, of course, consistent with the greater affluence of the American middle class where social detachment becomes more easily manageable both economically and socially. For the first time, there is visible evidence of available rhetoric for support of such a social position. This does not mean that actual rates of postmarital sexual activity will automatically begin to rise substantially; however, at the same time, there have been many other points in social history where "life has copied art."

Noncoital genital contacts. Another major area of normal deviance involves those sexual techniques which are not coital and which fall under the sodomy and crimes-against-nature statutes in many jurisdictions, even when practiced between husband and wife. In the case of mouth-genital contact, whether fellatio or cunnilingus, the most likely situation for its practice is between

---

[17] Paul H. Gebhard, "Postmarital Coitus among the Widowed and Divorced," in Paul Bohannon (ed.), *Divorce and After* (in press).

[18] William J. Goode, *After Divorce* (Glencoe, Ill.: Free Press, 1956).

husband and wife.[19] These techniques commonly begin in premarital contacts in the form of mutual genital petting among dating couples, and mouth-genital contact is relatively rare. It is in marriage that an increase of mouth-genital contact occurs. These techniques are commonly arrived at in non-verbal ways, and there is little talk about them, even between married couples, though they may be part of routine sexual contacts. There seems to be a considerably greater incidence of these techniques in higher social classes, while lower-class men view them as appropriate only during contact with prostitutes.

While most of these contacts are worked out between individuals operating in private, there is considerable social support for the behavior in the marriage-manual and sexual-technique literature. It is at this point that a major tension between conventional norms as expressed in the law and the private quality of sexual adjustments becomes most apparent. There is direct opposition between the literature on sexual adjustment in marriage and the law in these matters. What appears to be true is that couples involved in such behavior are often not aware of the legal sanctions that exist, and, if they are aware of them, the context of marriage or love is sufficient to reduce the guilt that might arise from such behavior. Indeed, for many males, the fact that the behavior has been sanctioned in the atmosphere of the informal peer group may serve to make it more arousing and erotic. The connection between degradation and eroticism often seems to be quite clear. In any case, the context of love and affection makes the behavior legitimate, in part because it is seen as a service given to the

partner rather than something that is arousing in itself.

Extramarital coitus. The final major area of normal deviance is that of extramarital coitus. The Kinsey data suggest that about half the males and about a quarter of the females who ever marry have coitus during marriage with someone other than their spouse.[20] This does not account in any way for sexual contacts short of coitus that arise from cocktail parties and other social gatherings where there is a certain permissiveness about the extent of physical contact between the sexes. In the main, there are substantial sanctions about extramarital coitus which are not legally enforced but which may have extensive impact on the marital situation. The timing of extramarital coitus seems to vary with social class. The lower classes seem to begin such behavior relatively early in marriage and continue into the thirties, with a consequent decline after the mid-thirties. The middle-class pattern in those marriages that survive the first few years is that extramarital coitus begins after five to eight years, often after the birth of children.[21] In most cases, such coitus is relatively sporadic, occurring in periods away from home, while the individual is detached from the environment. To the degree that the coitus is regular or frequent, there is danger of emotional involvement and disruption of the family.

While extramarital coitus most commonly occurs without the knowledge of the spouse and in detachment from the marriage, there are a small number of

---

[19] Kinsey *et al., Sexual Behavior in the Human Female,* pp. 257–258, 361–362.

[20] Kinsey *et al., Sexual Behavior in the Human Male,* pp. 584–589; Kinsey *et al., Sexual Behavior in the Human Female,* pp. 416–422.

[21] William Simon and John H. Gagnon, "Heterosexuality and Homosociality: A Dilemma of the Lower-Class Family," 1966 (Mimeographed.)

persons who, for various reasons, engage in extramarital coitus either with the knowledge of the spouse or with the participation of the spouse. This appears to be a secondary form of deviance attendant upon the problems of managing the guilt of the usual individual pattern of extramarital coitus— to manage the guilt, the spouse is required to engage in the deviance. Such activity commonly occurs only within the limited situation of mutually selected partners and with the consent of the spouse. What is interesting about these patterns is that they convert the family into a deviant unit and must, of necessity, increase the communication of the husband and wife about sexual matters.

In all but the last of the categories noted above, it can be seen that the deviant behavior itself serves to facilitate the management of conventional forms of sexuality. Thus, masturbation serves as an alternative to unacceptable heterosexual relationships, and premarital coitus facilitates family-formation, as does coitus during intermarital periods. All of these behaviors are normatively sanctioned, but the sanctions are rarely enforced and then only upon the unwary. The case of extramarital coitus is more complex and of potentially greater danger to the marital unit if it becomes known to the spouse. In some sense, it may contribute to family equilibrium by funneling off the male's desire for variety in sexual contacts and reinforcing his conception of masculinity.

None of the above behaviors (except for wife-swapping) require the interaction of more than a pair of persons, nor do the behaviors themselves require that the participants have particular and peculiar psychological adjustments. The behaviors arise from routine social-psychological adjustments requiring no special facilitating social structure for either the initiation into the behavior or the maintenance of the behavior. The values and attitudes of the participants will not differ a great deal on any major dimension from those who do not participate, and indeed the potential for any of the behaviors will, by and large, rest on values and attitudes that are independent of the behavior itself (for example, religious devoutness, social class, and education).

Socially structured forms of deviance

Four forms of sexual deviance, and, potentially, a fifth, have developed subcultural patterns that either facilitate entry into deviant roles or maintain persons within the roles after entry. The first four are male homosexuality, female homosexuality, female prostitution, and social nudism. The potential fifth is the currently small-scale, but possibly increasing, phenomenon of collective extramarital coitus. Of the four, only male homosexuality exists under threat of strong sanctions and police pursuit. Female prostitution generally results in moderate sanctions on the females involved, weak sanctions on the persons who are linked to the work situation of the prostitute (cab drivers, bellboys, and the like), and no sanctions for the male customers. Female homosexuality rarely results in the invocation of legal sanctions (in one jurisdiction the courts have interpreted the sodomy statute to exclude female homosexuality), and even though there are normative sanctions against the behavior, they are only invoked on an interpersonal level. Female homosexuality, unlike male homosexuality, does not arouse anxiety and anger among nondeviants, and its presentation in "pulp" fiction is often primarily an aphrodisiac for essentially heterosexual populations. Social nudism is often ideologically aggressively nonsexual, but the public definition is commonly sexual in nature. The nudist groups have had their greatest difficulty at the point of greatest public visibility, the sale of nudist publications.

Male homosexuality. The incidence of male homosexuality is commonly overestimated, partially because of a naïve interpretation of the Kinsey statistics by those heterosexuals who see the world in terms of a homosexual revolution and those homosexuals who wish that there were more homosexuals. A reanalysis of the Kinsey figures suggests that about one third of the males interviewed have had a single homosexual experience, but that one half of this number had the experience between age 12 and 14, and no further experience later, while about 35 per cent had the homosexual experience between age 12 and 18. This leaves only 15 per cent of those males who ever had a homosexual experience (or between 4 and 5 per cent of the total male population) with extensive adult commitment to homosexuality.[22]

The patterns by which males become homosexuals seem to vary a great deal. Disordered familial structure is one of the sources, but certainly not the exclusive mechanism. In contrast to other deviant careers such as drug addiction or crime, there does not seem to be a specialized subgroup of peers or a value system through which persons are recruited to homosexual careers. In the words of R. Laud Humphreys, the problem seems to be one of enlistment rather than recruitment.[23] However, there does exist in most large cities a specialized kind of community whose most prominent institution is the bar. It serves as a sexual market place as well as gathering place where the homosexual may socialize with other men who have similar sexual interests.[24]

One of the consequences of the deviant commitment is that the sexual element tends to become of major importance in the organization of the homosexual's life style, and he may tend to organize his friendships, leisure time, and occupational adjustments around the homosexual community and around homosexual friends.[25] The existence of the homosexual commitment serves to detach the homosexual from heterosexual contacts and relationships, and the intensity of the heterosexual sanctions against his behavior makes him seek out almost exclusive relationships with other homosexuals.

The future does not augur an increase in the number of exclusively homosexual men, given the fact that the process of becoming homosexual lies, in most part, outside of the existing collectivity of homosexuals. Unlike addiction, which has the potential for spreading from one person to another within the confines of a peer group, adult homosexuality does not have this character. Thus, one may conclude that an increasing tolerance of homosexuality through the reform of sex laws will not increase the incidence of homosexuality, though it may allow those males who have not, due to fear of the law, engaged in homosexual contact, to enter into such relationships. At the same time, there may be a countertendency. The lowering of sanctions

[22] John H. Gagnon and William Simon, "The Sociological Perspective on Homosexuality," *The Dublin Review* (In press, 1968).

[23] Letter from R. Laud Humphreys, 1967.

[24] Evelyn Hooker, "The Homosexual Community," in John H. Gagnon and William Simon (eds.), *Sexual Deviance* (New York: Harper & Row, 1967), pp. 167–184; Maurice Leznoff and William A. Westley, "The Homosexual Community," *Ibid.*, pp. 184–196; Nancy Achilles, "The Development of the Homosexual Bar as an Institution," *Ibid.*, pp. 228–244.

[25] William Simon and John H. Gagnon, "Homosexuality: The Formulation of a Sociological Perspective," *Journal of Health and Social Behavior*, Vol. 8, No. 3 (September 1967), pp. 177–185.

and the decrease in stigma may reduce the barrier between the homosexual and heterosexual worlds, and this may allow some persons in the homosexual world to develop an interest in heterosexual adjustments. One of the consequences of the intensity of sanctions is that it decreases the capacity of persons to move from one social role to another and impedes communication between the two social groups.

Female prostitution. Aside from pornography, prostitution is probably the form of collective sexual deviance that is most intermixed with and linked to the conventional social order. There is an intimate relationship between the practice of prostitution, the agencies of criminal justice, a variegated and complex number of supportive personnel, and the conventional citizens who are the clients of the prostitute.[26] Much like male homosexuality, there is no systematic process of recruitment of females into the role of prostitute. The majority of the females are from lower-class and upper-lower-class homes and have had careers of relative sexual promiscuity during adolescence. Once again, we are dealing with the phenomenon of enlistment rather than recruitment.

Prostitution, of all the forms of sexual deviance, has probably changed the most over the years due to shifts in other patterns in the society. With the increase in the proportion of conventional females who have premarital coitus, there has been a decrease in prostitution as a form of premarital outlet for males, and with the substantial decrease at all class levels in the number of never-married and unattached males in the society, there has been a systematic decline in the amount of sexual experience that males have with prostitutes. This shift, at least until 1948, had not affected whether a male would ever have gone to a prostitute

[26] John H. Gagnon, "Prostitution," *loc. cit.*

(with substantially higher rates for lower-class men than for those of the middle or higher social classes), but the frequency of going to the prostitute has declined substantially.[27] At the same time, the very structure of prostitution has shifted. The old-style brothel has nearly disappeared from the American scene except for holdovers in towns which service large populations of migrant males and for sections of the southeastern and southwestern parts of the United States. Most prostitution today takes place in the bar or on the street and involves men who are currently detached from normal familial contexts. The other major shift in the practice of prostitution has been the movement to the call girl, who services higher-class populations in large urban centers for relatively high prices. Again, the activity is commonly restricted to convention and vacation locations, with a smaller proportion of clients who remain regulars.

The prostitute provides a source of sexual satisfaction that the client may enjoy because of the lack of responsibility, and, in some cases, sufficient sexual degradation is involved so that the sexual act is viewed as more erotic. Because the prostitute plays an explicitly sexual role, she becomes the focus for fantasy of the conventional population so that she is viewed as being far more sexual than she is. The contact with the prostitute is thus divested of its normal social trappings and is allowed, unlike sexual contacts with conventional others (the wife, the mistress, the girl friend), to be more nearly purely sexual. In this situation the client may ask for services that he would not feel free to ask of a partner who has a more complex social relationship to him.

As a consequence of this societal definition and the nearly exclusively sexual

[27] Kinsey *et al., Sexual Behavior in the Human Male,* pp. 597–604.

occupational role, the prostitute lives nearly entirely in a world of other persons who are linked in some way to the life of prostitution.[28] Friendship, leisure time, and occupational success and adversity are shared with persons who are intimately linked with clandestine and criminal concerns. This embedding in a deviant situation results in the great difficulty which females have in getting out of "the life" since there are few conventional others with whom a major source of life experience may be shared.

Female homosexuality. Female homosexuality is the least public of the forms of collective sexual deviance. It attracts less attention and is probably less frequent than either male homosexuality or prostitution. Like them, however, it is also a career made up of enlistees rather than recruits. One of the crucial elements in the minimum sanctions against female homosexuality is the fact that for unmarried women, the society has a number of available nondeviant roles that are defined as nonsexual. Unlike unmarried males, females may live together, they may kiss and touch each other affectionately, and they may seek each other's company without attracting any undue notice. Further, because of the lower levels of general sexual commitment in females, it is possible for them to live with lower levels of sexual desire and sexual contact than appear to be required by males. One of the major consequences is that the female homosexual is probably better integrated than the male homosexual into other conventional relationships such as the family of origin, work, religion, and conventional leisure-time pursuits. Thus, a larger proportion of female homosexuals live outside the overt homosexual community and outside of the bar culture.[29]

Like male homosexuality, female homosexuality will probably remain relatively stable over time, in terms of incidence and the numbers of adult committed deviants. Given the low order of sanctions and the relatively low visibility of most Lesbians, changes in the law will have minimal consequence for the participants, even though there may be good reason for a re-evaluation of the statutes as they relate to behavior among consenting adults.

Social nudism. Social nudism is rarely mentioned as a form of sexual deviance; yet it has historically been involved in conflict with the law in terms of the protection of areas where collective nudism may take place and in legal cases involving the propriety of either the public sale or the mail distribution of nudist publications. The rights of places of collective nudism are now protected under the right of private property, and there are now national organizations of nudists as well as organizations of camp proprietors. In addition, the nudist magazines have won most of their legal cases and now send through the mails materials showing the nude genitalia of males and the pubic hair of females.

In an important sense, there is a direct conflict between the image that the public has of the nudist movement and the image that most of the nudist movement has of itself.[30] The view of the unsophisticated public is that the nudist movement is prosexual and that the

[28] James H. Bryan, "Apprenticeships in Prostitution," *Social Problems,* Vol. 3, No. 2 (Winter 1965), pp. 278–297; N. R. Jackman, R. O'Toole, and G. Geis, "The Self-Image of the Prostitute," *The Sociological Quarterly,* Vol. 4, No. 2 (April 1963), pp. 150–161.

[29] William Simon and John H. Gagnon, "The Lesbians: A Preliminary Overview," in Gagnon and Simon (eds.), *Sexual Deviance,* pp. 247–282.

[30] Fred Ilfeld, Jr., and Roger Laver, *Social Nudism in America* (New Haven, Conn.: College and University Press, 1964).

nudist camp is a hotbed of sexual activity. A more sophisticated public conceives of the nudist movement as essentially antisexual, since it is recognized that the sexual patterns of nudists are similar to those of the larger society, but there is still the expectation that collective nudity should produce higher rates of deviant sexual activity among members of the movement. The contention of the movement is that nudity and sunbathing in a collective situation are independent of sexual activity and that the body is beautiful without any consideration of sexual matters. What is important here is the ideological character of the claims of the nudist movement that nudism is a way of moving away from the society's obsessive concern with sexuality to a more moral set of relationships between the sexes. Within the nudist movement, there are conflicts between those groups who see nudism as an avant garde of sexual freedom and those who conceive of it in the older terms of reordering the relationship between nudity and sexuality. It should be clear that persons come to nudism for a variety of reasons: some come out of what are originally sexual motives; others, out of concerns for health; and still others, out of an interest in sex education for their children. From this welter of original concerns, the experience in the nudist camp shapes an ideology which is relatively common to all: that social nudism is a health activity. For most of those who join the nudist movement, this is the most extensive commitment to sexual deviance. However, for a small minority, there is a greater interest in sexual activity itself, and in many cases this results in an involvement in extramarital coitus on either an individual or a collective basis. This accounts for the history of nudist activity that one finds among persons who are involved in libertarian sexual groups. The nudist move-

ment is a way station for more extensive sexual involvement for this small minority. When this further commitment is made the persons often drop out of the nudist movement itself. It is suggested by some observers of the nudist scene that some camps are more likely than others to offer an opportunity for this escalation of deviance, while in the majority of cases the conventional nudist injunctions about the separation of nudity and sexuality are strongly enforced.

In the bulk of the cases, the nudist movement probably serves as a coping mechanism for those persons who have interests in sexual deviance, and for whom the ideology of the movement allows segregation of the nudist commitment from their sexual concerns. For many males in the nudist movement, there is likely to have been in the beginning of the nudist career a basic voyeuristic concern; however, the ideology and the socialization processes of the camp turn this interest into a socially approved interest in the conventional values of the nudist community.

Individual deviance

Of all the forms of sexual deviance, individual deviance has the lowest incidence, is the most severely sanctioned by the law and by public reaction, and is the most difficult to explain, especially in essentially sociological terms. There are a few forms of individual sexual deviance that attract a certain amount of public horror but, by and large, result neither in intense public pressure on the police nor in police action to apprehend the offenders. These are exhibitionism, window-peeping, and fetishistic behavior involving theft. (Certain baroque forms of fetishism and sadomasochism that are conducted in private between adults—often involving payment—are of such rarity that they require no discussion.) Except when the exhibitionism involves children or when the window-peeper has a pattern of entering dwellings, the offender is categorized as a form of public nuisance and is treated as such by the police. In certain jurisdictions, laws that were passed to deal with the sexually dangerous person (criminal sexual psychopath laws) are sometimes used to coerce such offenders into psychiatric treatment.[31] For the bulk of these offenders, the offense is not repetitive, and in some cases seems to be a stress reaction to the inaccessibility of legitimate coitus. However, there is a substantial minority of offenders who act out of a compulsive need to peep or exhibit, who account for the majority of the offenses known to the police, and who have extensive histories of recidivism.

There are three forms of sexual deviance that are most intensely condemned by both the public and the police. These are those offenses that involve incest (the most common form being father-daughter or stepfather-stepdaughter and, less commonly, brother-sister— other forms being extremely rare, though, as in all human situations, it is possible to find a single case of all combinations); offenses involving the sexual approach of or sexual contact with children of either sex; and, finally, offenses that involve the use of force in obtaining sexual gratification. The norms relating to the first two categories are explicit and clear, and though there is some evidence that children might in some cases be willing accomplices to the offense, or might indeed be seductive, the onus is always on the offender and pursuit by the police is commonly quite vigorous. The relationship of force and sexual relationships is more ambiguous since there is evidence that charges of rape may grow out of

what is at the beginning a conventional sexual situation or from having to disclose a consenting sexual contact to persons such as parents. In cases where there is not a great deal of physical damage, where the partners are known to each other, where the female and the male have a minority-group status, or where the female has a "bad" reputation, the police have a tendency not to interpret the offense as being rape.

While most of the individual deviance offenses discussed above are performed by unattached persons operating alone and without the social support of others, in a minority of rape cases there is a plurality of offenders and usually a single victim. These offenses commonly arise from an all-male situation in which most of the males present participate in a gang rape of a single female, commonly in a situation that could have been defined as potentially sexual (for example, a lovers' lane, with a pick-up, and the like).[32] Except for these cases of gang rape, the conditions and behavior of the individual sexual deviant appear to be idiosyncratic and primarily a function of a failure of sexual socialization. There is evidence for a wide variety of specific antecedent conditions and specific precipitating events for these kinds of offenses.[33]

Shifts in the patterns of these kinds of offenses would appear unlikely, and their increase will probably be dependent on increases in population rather than on basic shifts in norms with reference to sex.

Summary

The three dimensions selected to categorize sexual deviance better—the incidence of the behavior, the existence of

[31] Edwin H. Sutherland, "The Sexual Psychopath Laws," *Journal of Criminal Law and Criminology*, Vol. 40, No. 5 (January-February 1950), pp. 543–554.

[32] W. H. Blanchard, "The Group Process in Gang Rape," *Journal of Social Psychology*, Vol. 49 (1959), pp. 259–266.

[33] Paul H. Gebhard *et al., Sex Offenders* (New York: Harper & Row, 1965).

a specialized social structure in which to carry it out, and the intensity of sanctions invoked—seem to have heuristic value in assessing the linkage of the deviant activity to larger forms of social behavior. A series of trends seem to be identifiable, especially with reference to the shifts in values that were mentioned in the beginning of the paper: a shift from a concern for the sinfulness of the behavior to its healthiness, the shift from an absence of discussion of sex to chronic overdiscussion, and, finally, a shift in the styling and contexts of sexual performance.

One major trend is the increasing recognition and discussion of premarital coitus, masturbation, and coitus between marriages—if not as good things, at least not as evil. The discussions of extramarital coitus are beginning to take on some of the main concerns. At the same time, there is increasing consideration of legal reform with reference to sexual contacts between consenting adults, which would relieve most homosexuals, both male and female, from certain difficulties with the law, though there is some evidence that there would still be substantial police activity against male homosexuality, and continuing dangers of public exposure. In any case, there is a tendency to begin to conceive of these problems as lying in the purview of moral authorities and mental health persons rather than the criminal law. Finally, with reference to individual sexual deviance, there is an increasing interest in the notion that sex offenders are psychiatric casualties and should be treated as such rather than as criminals. In a few states, there are attempts to implement this in practice, though in no jurisdiction is there an adequate program that is designed and organized to treat these populations.

Two fundamental dilemmas remain, even in the face of what are quite clearly liberalizing trends in the society.

The first of these is the difficulty of translating changes at the public level (for example, sexual law reform increasing the domain of private consent in the sexual area, law reform with reference to abortion, and the increasing availability of contraception) into changes at the level of norms and mores. While the public discussion of sexuality becomes freer, there does not seem to be a great deal of evidence for a flow of this liberalizing sentiment into the private capacities of the individual to talk about sex. Thus, the general sociological evidence that changes at the mass media level, in order to be effective at the private level, require mediation by interpersonal relationships, suggests that there will be substantial difficulty in moving toward a greater ease in dealing with sexual matters at the personal level.[34] Thus, homosexual law reform may not result in increasing levels of personal tolerance for homosexuals, and, indeed, may not ease the problems of the homosexual in dealing with the guilt and anxiety that result from his own deviance. This same dilemma may also make attempts at sex education for the young problematic, given the conflicts that older persons in the society have with reference to sex. Regardless of the inadequacy of the informational content of the peer group as a source of sex education, it at least reinforces sexual expression and sexual activity in a way achieved by few adults.

The second basic dilemma is the imagery with which we confront sexuality. All too often, the sexual impulse is conceived as a beast held in check only by the application of immense societal sanctions, and much that is both destructive and creative in the human

[34] Elihu Katz and Paul Lazarsfeld, *Personal Influence* (Glencoe, Ill.: Free Press, 1955); James Coleman, Elihu Katz, and Herbert Menzel, *Medical Innovation: A Diffusion Study* (Indianapolis: Bobbs-Merrill, 1966).

experience is believed to arise from this tension between biological impulse and social contract. Thus, the act of freeing the sexual impulse is thought of by some persons as increasing human freedom and by others as creating the conditions for social collapse. In this sense, we have overloaded the meaning and the power of sexual acts, and what is likely to be discovered is that the significance of sexuality is exactly in proportion to its perceived significance; that is, without the imagery of power and danger, the sexual impulse is no more potent than any other biological component. In the process of freeing sex, we may also deprive it of its capacity to have major social consequences; for what we may be preparing for is our own disappointment with it.

Prostitution in the United States

By T. C. ESSELSTYN

ABSTRACT: Currently, the demand for suppressing prostitution is far less insistent than it used to be. Some cities have experienced an apparent revival in prostitution, but this appearance is due chiefly to the visibility of the young, aggressive, attractive streetwalker. The prostitute now moves freely through all layers and areas of the community. While there is no census of prostitutes in the United States, it is believed that their numbers have not changed recently. About the same proportion of men patronize prostitutes as three decades ago, but their contacts are less frequent. The slack is taken up by nonprostitutes, in keeping with the greater sexual accessibility of women of all classes. Women become prostitutes for a complex of reasons, most of them quite rational. Men seek out prostitutes from a variety of long-recognized motives. The male prostitute is a youth who has sex relations with men. Much less is known about him, but he has been sufficiently studied to permit a rough profile. Currently, he is a potent source of venereal infection. Future public policy toward the female prostitute might include her under Social Security. Policy toward the male prostitute should start with educational measures and heightened concern for youth generally.

T. C. Esselstyn, Ph.D., San Jose, California, is a Professor of Sociology at San Jose State College. The following article is part of a long-term interest which he has developed in the female offender. As a consultant to the President's Crime Commission, he prepared a special paper on the violent offender. He has published articles on the social organization of correctional systems and is currently engaged with Alvin Rudoff, Ph.D., in a four-year study of the work-furlough program for jail inmates administered by the Sheriff of Santa Clara County, California. He was former Staff Director of the United States Board of Parole.

THE following discussion will review the fields of both female and male prostitution—women and men who are prostitutes, who their clients are, the basis for prostitution in each case, and related matters. Most of the discussion will center on female prostitution. As the male prostitute has not been reported upon extensively, much less is known about him.

This account refers to the situation in continental United States. However, brief comment must be made about prostitution elsewhere. Conditions in other parts of the world affect the United States. Americans traveling abroad take their sex practices with them and, to some unmeasured degree, probably modify domestic sex behavior upon their return.

The chief concern here is with prostitution on the contemporary American scene—roughly, since World War II. Space limitations mean that even this must be selective and must emphasize those aspects of the topic that command the greatest interest and that appear to be the most crucial.

WOMEN AS PROSTITUTES

Definition of prostitute

Webster defines a prostitute as "a woman given to indiscriminate lewdness for hire." Overlooking the quaint verbiage, three elements are present here: sex relations with anyone on a contract basis. A fourth element is frequently added—emotional indifference, with the prostitute thought of as frigid to all but her pimp and seldom experiencing orgasm.[1] Often, however, the element of emotional indifference is omitted or is debated.[2] What constitutes hire has also been debated, and so, too, has the meaning of such words as *indiscriminate, promiscuous,* and the like. While recognizing that any definition presents difficulties, the word *prostitute* will be used below, as in the Kinsey *Male* Report, to mean a woman who accepts sexual relations with almost anyone who pays her in money.[3] This seems to be the sense of much popular usage and of most serious studies of prostitution as a form of behavior.

Public attitudes toward prostitution

While the above definition is, in itself, neutral, prostitution is loaded with negative connotations in America. In the nineteenth and twentieth centuries, through World War II, prostitution was generally regarded by legislators, social reformers, and vast masses of citizens as an evil to be suppressed. Vice crusades were launched periodically to stamp out the brothels, the red-light districts, and the traffic in women. The prostitute was seen as a focus of venereal infection, a corrupter of young men, and a threat to the family. Closely linked to prostitution in popular imagery were the sale of liquor, gambling, drugs, and the operation of dance halls and disorderly premises. These were the

[1] Marshall B. Clinard, *Sociology of Deviant Behavior* (New York: Holt, Rinehart and Winston, 1963), p. 249. Maryse Choisy, *Psychoanalysis of the Prostitute* (New York: Philosophical Library, 1961), p. 41. Benjamin Karpman, *The Sexual Offender and His Offenses* (New York: Julian Press, 1954), pp. 641–645, summarizing Glover.

[2] Harry Benjamin and R. E. L. Masters (eds.), *Prostitution and Morality* (New York: Julian Press, 1964). See their Chapter 1 for an extensive review of attempts at definition. Alfred C. Kinsey, Wardell B. Pomeroy, Clyde E. Martin, *Sexual Behavior in the Human Male* (Philadelphia, W. B. Saunders, 1948), p. 595. (Hereinafter this work will be cited as the Kinsey *Male* Report.) J. DeSans Coderche, "Psychodynamic Structure of Prostitution," *Revista de Psiquiatría y Psicología médica de Europe y América latina* (Barcelona) (*Rev. Psiquiat. Psicol. méd.*) Vol. 6, No. 7 (1964), pp. 5–37 *passim*, summarized in *Excerpta Criminologica* (1965), p. 469.

[3] Kinsey *Male* Report, *op. cit.,* p. 595.

greater social threats. The prostitute herself was the lesser and, while sometimes this ranking was reversed, at no time has the prostitute or her profession been widely popular or publicly approved in America.[4]

Condemnation of prostitution has become less strident in recent years, although in some cities, such as San Francisco and New York, public outcries have become very marked—chiefly against public solicitation rather than against prostitution *per se*. However that may be, prostitution continues to be discouraged, not encouraged; regarded as regrettable and undesirable, not as a community asset. While, perhaps, no one today "saves fallen women," still the prostitute is seen as one who should be "rehabilitated" or otherwise deflected into some other career or mode of behavior. In brief, attitudes toward the prostitute and her calling stretch out on a continuum from enthusiastic approval by a few at one extreme to indignation and dangerous hostility by a few at the other, with a rather high and broad plateau of vague, generalized mass discomfort and disapproval somewhere in the middle.

However strong or mild, how is this negative view explained? One approach is that societies everywhere link sex behavior to some form of stable social relationship—enduring affection or setting up a family being the most common, although peripheral pleasure is not ruled out. Accordingly, sex conduct is to be aimed at group survival. When sex is not so linked and not thus focused, the group interprets this as a threat to its continuity. Not being able to accept such a threat, it condemns it. The group senses the seeds of social collapse in promiscuous, commercialized, and uncontrolled sexual congress and

disapproves of it for this principal reason. When the prostitute has some additional way of making her living, when she exercises a degree of choice over her clients, or when she uses her income from prostitution for some socially approved purpose, she suffers lesser degrees of social censure. But none of these accord her a secure status in the larger society. At best, she is tolerated, not accepted.[5]

Crudely put, what this seems to say is that folk wisdom commands that no one should make love for money. Whoever does is a menace because the rewards of love-making are perceived as nonmonetary. If one gets money for it, one is rewarded twice or one accords the perceived rewards second billing. In either case, one is a cheat. And society fears the cheat: his (her) behavior cannot be predicted. This is the basic reason for hostility to prostitution. All other arguments—vice, crime, disease, white slavery—are important, but actually they are disguises.

This highly cogent approach is open to several criticisms. It accords to a complex mode of behavior a simple unitary explanation. It assigns priority to enduring social relationships apparently as we judge them today—which position is either ethnocentric, tempocentric, or both. It imputes a conscious rationality to sex and its limitations which it does not really have—everywhere, sex is suffused with the unconscious and nonrational. Yet, such criticisms as these do not destroy the "social threat" explanation for widespread hostility to prostitution. They say merely that societies look chillingly upon prostitution for many reasons, and prominent among these are the fear of the prostitute as a

[4] Roy Lubove, "The Progressive and the Prostitute," *Historian*, Vol. 24, No. 3 (May 1962), pp. 308–330.

[5] Kingsley Davis, "Sexual Behavior," in Robert K. Merton and Robert A. Nisbet (eds.), *Contemporary Social Problems* (New York: Harcourt, Brace and World, 1966), pp. 348–355.

kind of ill-defined social parasite and an incapacity to accept her as an authentic social servant.

Volume and trends

Public attitudes toward prostitution fluctuate, and this has an effect on volume, rates, and trends. Yet the data are seldom reliable and what one is left with is a series of informed impressions based on nonstatistical evidence.

In colonial and postcolonial New England, the incidence of sex contact outside matrimony was high, if one may judge from the number of public confessions and the variety of penalties imposed. Yet, the incidence of prostitution was low. "Adultery and fornification were so prominent as to render the prostitute not only unwelcome but almost superfluous." [6] Elsewhere in early America, prostitutes do not appear to have been numerous because of the presence of many indentured servants and others from easily exploited classes.[7]

The nineteenth century saw the expansion of great cities in America, the rise of commerce and industry, an influx of immigrant streams, and the now-familiar process of profound social change. Prostitution became a fixture on the moving frontier, where the genuine pioneer woman was really a prostitute. Some cities, such as Galveston, Chicago, and New Orleans, acquired an international fame for the number and variety of their prostitutes. This was perhaps the heyday of the bordello, the brothel, and red-light district, and it lasted until the close of World War I. It was also the heyday of graft and corruption. It was the great age of the vice crusade and of the rising strength of the prohibition movement. Thus, in

the official folk-belief system of America, prostitution became imbued with the coloration of all other great social evils. There were no collective efforts to extract it from this context and to approach it with some other philosophy.

The era following World War I brought a decline in older sex rigidities. However, the drive against prostitution continued. The objective was seldom prostitution per se—it was more likely to be organized crime and the corruption of local police forces, with the prostitute being regarded as their helpless and hapless tool. Public sentiment was perhaps more protective toward her than punitive. Suppression efforts were revived in World War II, when large numbers of prostitutes were seen as posing several kinds of hazards to servicemen as well as to the civilian labor force which had moved into new war-industry areas.

By the close of World War II, prostitution had become gradually less visible. Brothels were less numerous, red-light districts had disappeared from many cities, police raids became all but unheard of. As prostitution receded from view, there was a widespread tendency to believe that it had declined. About twenty years ago, the number of full-time prostitutes in the United States was estimated to be about 600,000, with an equal number of women who served as prostitutes on a part-time basis.[8] There is no way to verify this or to determine whether the actual number has changed since that date. Arrests for "prostitution and commercialized vice" totaled 18,995 women in 1960. This figure had increased in 1965 to 26,331. The percentage of nonwhites was higher than the percentage of

---

[6] Fernando Henriques, Prostitution in Europe and the Americas (New York: Citadel Press, 1965), pp. 242–243.

[7] Ibid., p. 245.

[8] Walter C. Reckless, The Crime Problem (New York: Appleton-Century-Crofts, 1955), p. 268, quoting another source. In his 1967 edition, Reckless does not attempt a later estimate.

whites.[9] The recent outburst of street-walking in some cities and the public pressure upon police for arrest and control measures have, no doubt, puffed local estimates in 1966–1967.

This represents an increase in the rate of arrests of women for this offense from 10.6 to 13.3 per 100,000. Whether it also represents an actual increase in prostitution and commercialized vice is open to question.

It is the opinion of several observers that, notwithstanding recent police interest, the number of prostitutes and the number of their clients have not changed appreciably in the past two or three decades. On the contrary, what seems to have occurred is a decline in the frequency with which men patronize prostitutes. Evidence also suggests an increase in the frequency of sex relations by men with women who are not prostitutes.[10]

There are several explanations. The suppression drives of the past have had the effect of forcing prostitution underground and of encouraging a clandestine, rather than a segregated but open, type of operation. The change in sex mores and the availability of effective means of contraception have increased the sexual accessibility of women of all classes, thus increasing the opportunity for heterosexual outlet for both men and women, even though the number of prostitutes remains unaffected. A raising of the level of social tolerance for deviants of all types has facilitated the

mobility of the prostitute and has occasioned a redefinition of sex as a feature of life. Additionally, there is the enormous growth of cities and the spread of anonymity in urban areas. All of these considerations make it likely that the number of prostitutes is about the same as it has been, but that men have greater opportunity for heterosexual experience outside of prostitution.[11]

Significant, too, are certain new elements which have crept into prostitution. One is the rise of the call-girl and the call-girl system accompanied by a gradual decline in the prominence of the older-type madam. With this has come a decline in the extrasexual functions of the prostitute. It seems also to have ushered in a period when prostitution in America is increasingly an individual undertaking rather than a vocation practiced in close association with others. Teen-age prostitutes seem to have emerged as a survival in some cities of the V-Girl problem in World War II. The ubiquity of the motel is believed to facilitate prostitution as well as other forms of extramarital sex experience. The number of part-time prostitutes may have increased, as well as the number of full-time prostitutes who develop conventional job skills. College women who are prostitutes while pursuing degree programs are not numerous, but, on the other hand, they are far from unknown.[12] While still active in prostitution, organized crime seems less concerned with this as a side line today than in former years. As suggested above, the demand is less readily manipulated, and the supply of nonprostitutes is increasing. Further, organized crime has more lucrative and less perilous enterprises available to it.[13] While it is

[9] U.S., Department of Justice, Federal Bureau of Investigation, *Crime in the United States: Uniform Crime Reports* (Washington, D.C.: U.S. Government Printing Office, 1930——[annually]), 1960–1965 (derived from tables showing total arrests by sex).

[10] Alfred C. Kinsey, Wardell B. Pomeroy, Clyde E. Martin, and Paul H. Gebhard, *Sexual Behavior in the Human Female* (New York: Pocket Books, 1965), p. 300. (Hereinafter this work will be cited as the Kinsey *Female* Report.)

[11] *Ibid;* also Henriques, *op. cit.*, pp. 346–366.
[12] *Ibid.*
[13] Davis, *loc. cit.*, p. 365. See also U.S., President, Commission on Law Enforcement and Administration of Justice, *Task*

not clearly an accompaniment of the type of prostitution discussed in this section, mention should be made of the rise of venereal disease in the United States and in other countries as a consequence of what might be called heightened sexuality, world-wide.[14]

Types of prostitutes

There is no single typology of female prostitutes. Writers have developed different classification schemes depending upon their own background and the criteria they employ. Some have delineated types on the basis of the area in which they solicit or practice. In 1934, the Gluecks classified delinquent girls according to their degree of promiscuity. One scheme turns on the degree to which the prostitute relies on the services of her pimp.[15] The call-girl, as one type of prostitute with many subtypes, is described in the well-known work by Harold Greenwald.[16] At least one writer holds that there is no way in which distinctions can be made between prostitutes satisfactorily.[17] The Kinsey *Male* Report classifies prostitutes, both male and female, into four types but does not classify female prostitutes except as to those who have relations with males and those who have relations with females.[18] The Kinsey *Female*

Report does not present data on prostitutes as a special category.[19]

Benjamin and Masters describe fifteen different varieties of prostitutes; but the criteria employed to separate these types are not explicit, and some seem to overlap: [20]

Call-Girl	"Beat"
Streetwalker	Elderly
Bar girl	"Gimmick"
Brothel	Fricatrice, fellatrice
Camp follower	Fetishist, sadomasochist
Interracial	Adolescent
"Fleabag"	Child
Dance Hall	

In summary, there appears to be no agreement on the types of prostitutes operating in the United States. It may even be doubted that a classification system could be developed or would be useful. It would probably be outdated shortly after it was devised either by the collapse of some categories and the appearance of new ones or by the movement of occupants from one category to another, as time worked its changes upon the individual.

The attraction of prostitution to women

Why do women become prostitutes? What are the reasons? What are the causes of prostitution? These are unsatisfactory ways to put the question. If, however, one asks how does prostitution "call" to women, one can talk about both reason and cause and much else.

If one accepts the view that all societies regulate sex behavior in some way and to some degree, then it can be seen that these very regulations create the opportunity for their own breach. The more complex the society, the more likely the breach. It is mathematically impossible to devise ways to regulate sex so as to provide for the demands of all

Force Report: Organized Crime (Washington, D.C.: U.S. Government Printing Office, 1967), p. 4.

[14] As summarized in *Excerpta Criminologica* (1960–1965), sec. 6.13, for all years.

[15] For a summary of the above typologies, see Paul F. Cook, "The Prostitute," in T. C. Esselstyn (ed.), *The Female Offender* (San Jose, Calif.: Spartan Book Store, 1966), pp. 46–49.

[16] Harold Greenwald, *The Call Girl* (New York: Ballantine Books, 1958).

[17] Karpman, *op. cit.*, pp. 641–645. It is not wholly clear whether he means that there are no discrete types of prostitutes, or whether he means that there is no distinct type of woman who is more likely to become a prostitute than some other type of woman.

[18] Kinsey *Male* Report, *op. cit.*, p. 596.

[19] Kinsey *Female* Report, *op. cit.*, p. 79.

[20] Benjamin and Masters, *loc. cit.*, pp. 121–170.

members in all circumstances without extinguishing the society itself. With breach of the sex code actually assured by its own drafting, that breach will take many forms. One of these forms is prostitution, and hence prostitutes appear in consequence of the very measures designed to outlaw them. Suppose there were no codes. There has never been such a society, and none is in view. Hence prostitution is inherent and inevitable in organized social life.[21]

On a more obvious plane, women are attracted to prostitution in contemporary America because the income is high and because it affords an opportunity to earn more, buy more, and live better than would be possible by any other plausible alternative. If this seems like economic determinism, it can be said that no writer in America today holds that women become prostitutes to keep from starving. Added to this economic reason is the hope of meeting interesting men. This is not unrealistic. Many of the most prominent men throughout history have been clients of prostitutes. On the reverse, many prostitutes complain that the corps of eligible mates in their community of origin did not include many appealing choices. There are other obvious reasons. Included here are, for example, an unhappy love affair, the enticement of a persuasive pimp, early life as a girl surrounded by prostitutes as approved role models, an occupation where she is vulnerable to seduction and sexual attack, and the lack of stable family ties.[22]

Clinicians have traditionally sought other kinds of explanations. Thus, then, the prostitute's motivation has been found in an impulse toward self-debasement and self-destruction because of early failures to charm her father, or to gain revenge on a father who refused to

bestow love upon her as a child. Mother hatred, unconscious homosexuality, sado-masochistic impulses as a compound of parental neglect and indifference, the long-delayed reactions in the adult woman to serious frustrations as a child at the hands of her parents, no practice in expanding the infantile concepts of the self—these are some of the underlying reasons which clinicians advance to explain why women become prostitutes and which account for the readiness of many young girls in the "larval group" to answer the "call." [23]

Clinicians also commonly call attention to the great number of prostitutes who are frigid and who hate their clients as a psychosexual residue of deprivations such as those just suggested.[24] Other clinicians find no basis for this, regard such conclusions as unsupportable and absurd, believe that frigidity is lower than among nonprostitutes, and find that the majority are quite free of neurotic involvements and experience orgasm frequently.[25]

A rhythm of knowledge is evident here. In an earlier day, when prostitution was officially abhorred, investigators found that prostitutes abhorred their clients. Today, when prostitution is not too markedly condemned, investigators find that prostitutes do not condemn their clients so uniformly.

It is difficult to generalize on why or how women and girls are introduced to "the life . . . the business . . . working." Completely absent from current surveys of prostitution in America are references to seduction, the procurer, the white-slaver, spoiled goods, or the melodrama about the girl who suffered a fate worse than death. It is doubtful whether they ever were accurate, for the number of willing volunteers seems al-

[21] Davis, loc. cit., pp. 359, 370 ff.
[22] Benjamin and Masters, loc. cit., pp. 91–93; De Sans Coderche, loc. cit., p. 470.

[23] Karpman, op. cit., pp. 641–645.
[24] Choisy, op. cit., p. 41.
[25] Benjamin and Masters, loc. cit., p. 209; De Sans Coderche, op. cit., p. 469.

ways to have been enough to meet the demand and maybe more. Two of the women interviewed for this report said that they became professionals after having had several enjoyable sex episodes and after learning from girl friends how to ask for money. This confirms the recent observation that the new girl acquires the techniques of a prostitute by undergoing a period of training in the company of a girl who is already competent, or occasionally under the supervision of a pimp. The point emphasized is that it is a case of "each one teach one." The knowledge and skills necessary for success in prostitution are learned and are transmitted in a social group.[26] No one accomplishes this by herself. The *readiness* to learn is a psychosocial resultant.

It mistakes the case to say that the prostitute loathes her work and is attracted to it because it affords her an opportunity to seek retribution and revenge for the way she was mishandled as a child. The evidence that she does is no longer convincing, either with respect to prostitutes as a class or with respect to prostitutes compared to non-prostitutes. Most women say that they are prostitutes because it is lucrative; the work is not unpleasant; they are quite independent, and have a good chance to meet a client whom they can marry. Their avowed reasons deserve a more respectful hearing than they have received in these changing times.

Omitted from the above is any discussion of the role of the pimp. It is questionable whether women are drawn to prostitution by pimps in any substantial number, although this may happen in individual cases. The pimp seems to appear later. Generally, he functions as an agent or manager after the girl has taken the first several steps toward her

calling on her own initiative. There are many lurid accounts of the duplicity of the pimp, how he exploits the prostitute, encourages her dependency needs, is brutal to her, and prevents her from giving up the life even if she wants to. These characterizations seem one-sided and overdrawn. Undoubtedly, there is a wide variety of pimps, and it is questionable whether they all fit the rather unflattering characterizations now made of them.[27] Even the word *pimp* is loaded. The European term, *souteneur*, has connotations far less hostile than this, and it actually defines his role more accurately—although most of the recent Continental legislation on *soutenage* seems quite harsh.

The attraction of prostitution to men

Psychiatrists who have observed the clients of prostitutes report much symbolism and an attempt to fulfill several unconscious needs. A basic motive of the client is seen as mother hatred. In patronizing the prostitute, he strikes back at his mother by possessing a woman who is officially defined as bad and whom he now further soils and defiles. Good women are to be revered, worshipped. One may look at them and love them, but one may not feel passion for them. Passion is shameful and may be vented only with shameful women. Thus, many a client is sexually neutral or impotent with his wife and erotic or potent with a woman he can safely degrade—usually a prostitute. Latent sadism is thus present in the client, and in the prostitute there is a strong current of guilt and masochism. The relations between the two are reciprocal. "So self-debased and debaser meet in sadomasochistic coitus. Two neurotics

[26] James H. Bryan "Apprenticeship in Prostitution," *Social Problems*, Vol. 12, No. 3 (Winter 1965), pp. 287–297.

[27] Benjamin and Masters, *loc. cit.*, pp. 215–239. See also *The Autobiography of Malcolm X* (New York: Grove Press, 1965), pp. 108–125.

can thus unite for the sake not of creating but of destroying." [28]

A catalogue of the less symbolic and more conscious motives which attract men to prostitutes would probably begin with men who are temporarily separated from their women—soldiers on leave, sailors ashore after long sea duty, salesmen, and other classic examples. Included here might be conventioneers and youths responding to peer pressures, although their motives may not be the same as the first group. Some clients feel that the danger of venereal disease is less with a prostitute than with a pick-up. Others want sex relations, but have neither the time, the opportunity, the freedom, nor the inclination for a protracted courtship. The responsibility for pregnancy and its entanglements are eliminated if one visits a prostitute. She herself, in her person alone, without regard for her techniques, is a welcome change from the monotony of monogamy, and there is often the likelihood that she will provide types of desired sex experiences not provided by one's wife or lover. Clergymen struggling with their vows find relief from sex tension with her and a way to reestablish their poise. Men between marriages, men who feel sexually gauche with, or who are sexually blackmailed by, their wives, men who are physically repulsive to women of their own group—all these have sexual needs which underlie the appeal which prostitutes have for them.

Yet, as mentioned earlier, the frequency with which men seek out prostitutes, while varying by population segment, is actually declining as a result of increased sexual accessibility of women from all walks of life. As to volume, Kinsey and his associates estimated that 69 per cent of the white male population visits prostitutes once or twice.

Not more than 15 to 20 per cent go more than a few times per year over a five-year span. About one-third of the white population never go at all.[29]

An important insight into the motives of the prostitute's clients has been provided recently by Charles Winick. He interviewed 732 men who had patronized prostitutes, and he probed for their estimates of both the prostitutes and themselves. The sample included whites and Negroes of various ages and a wide range of occupations.[30]

Something of the complex and inconsistent pattern which characterizes the motives of clients can be seen in the way these respondents described the prostitute. Nineteen themes ran through these descriptions. Arranged in order of declining frequency, the five themes most frequently mentioned are shown below in a form slightly revised from the original:

TABLE 1—HOW CLIENTS SEE PROSTITUTE

RECURRING THEME	PER CENT OF RESPONDENTS EXPRESSING IT
1. A sex partner different from the usual one	73
2. A colorful woman, interesting career and life-style	71
3. Like mother or wife: cold, remote, takes but does not give	65
4. Pimp—never seen, but sure he is there. Gets her money	56
5. Mass media portray prostitute as attractive	54

When asked to describe themselves as they saw themselves after their last visit to a prostitute, the five themes mentioned most often out of a total of sixteen were the following, compressed and revised from the original:

[28] Choisy, op. cit., p. 63; Karpman, op. cit., p. 641 ff.

[29] Kinsey Male Report, op. cit., pp. 597–606.
[30] Charles Winick, "Prostitutes' Clients' Perceptions of Prostitutes and of Themselves," International Journal of Social Psychiatry, Vol. 8, No. 4 (1962), pp. 289–297.

TABLE 2—HOW PROSTITUTES' CLIENTS
RECALLED THEMSELVES

RECURRING THEME	PER CENT OF RESPONDENTS EXPRESSING IT
1. Felt different than with non-prostitutes, but not clear how	78
2. Empathy, felt closely identified with her, understood her needs	74
3. Felt closely identified with pimp. Never saw him, but wanted to *be* him	71
4. Know she has other clients "Fellow-Travelers," mutually involved	70
5. Might fall in love with her. She would then charge others but not me	66

If space allowed the inclusion of all themes on both lists, the conflict and inconsistency between them would be even more marked. The conclusion is that the prostitute taps complex and self-contradictory motives in her clients, and ministers to a complicated network of conscious and unconscious needs, urges, and fantasies. Few clients could describe what the prostitute looked like, which suggests that her symbolic value transcends her reality. The perceptions and motives summarized here do not vary significantly by age or social class, nor do they vary as between Negro and white clients. However, this is tentative, and Winick calls for further investigation to establish it firmly.[31]

MALES AS PROSTITUTES

The male prostitute is one who engages in sex relations with other males. Occasionally, males are paid a fee by

women for sexual purposes; but this is rare, and there are obvious physical limitations which diminish its utility as a way for the male to make his living. As used below, the male prostitute is thought of as one who gets a fee for providing sex outlets for other males, not females.

Profile

A recent account by Harold Call makes it possible to draw a profile of the white male prostitute and to derive an understanding of some of his activities, at least as these have been described for one part of the United States.[32] There does not appear to be any way at present to tell whether this portrait is recognizable in other parts of the country, but, on the other hand, there is little reason thus far to suspect that it varies substantially from a standard pattern.[33]

The white male prostitute is between 15 and 25 years old. He may be between 25 and 30, but this is unusual. He is not obviously effeminate. Like others similarly engaged, he may strive for an emphatic masculine image in clothing, posture, and musculature. Many in his ranks have a high school education; some have gone to junior college. He is quite likely to have been homosexually seduced as a child. He is not now employed and has a limited job history. He has registered for the draft but will avoid induction somehow, probably by saying he is a homosexual even though he denies he is in all other cir-

---

[31] *Ibid.*, pp. 296–297. On the subject of inability to recall what the prostitute looked like, see the discussion of dulled sensory perceptions among men when approaching orgasm, Kinsey *Female* Report, *op. cit.*, p. 614.

[32] Howard Call, "Male Prostitution on the West Coast," in Benjamin and Masters, *loc. cit.*, pp. 311–324. See also pp. 290–299.

[33] However, compare with D. E. J. MacNamara, "Male Prostitution in American Cities," *American Journal of Orthopsychiatry*, Vol. 35, No. 2 (1965), p. 204, summarized in *Excerpta Criminologica* (1965), p. 471. The profiles by Call and MacNamara seem to agree more than they differ.

cumstances. He has average intelligence or above.

He solicits male customers by a language of gestures, generally in "meat blocks"—areas of a city known to be frequented by males interested in homosexual services. He solicits also in bars, theaters, and hotel lobbies. Occasionally he works in an all-male bordello, or "peg house," but this is less common than soliciting on the move. He may also work as an added attraction in a female bordello and is present also as an attendant in public baths, athletic clubs, and massage parlors.

The more successful, upwardly mobile, and opportunistic of his ranks become "kept boys," living a life comparable to that of the well-established mistress. Here he is disguised as a secretary, boat or auto driver-mechanic, and business assistant to well-to-do men desiring homosexual outlets exclusively or as a diversion.

The prostitute allows his client to fellate him, sometimes to the point of his (the youth's) orgasm but more often not. He may also fellate the client or may offer himself for anal penetration. At the present time, it is not clear which form of sexual approach is most frequently employed, but it is clear that some youths are very rigid in the form they will permit. Any departure may lead to a violent attack upon the client.

The youth's fee averages between $2.00 and $5.00 per contact, but this often varies with the age and appearance of the client—the older the client, the higher the fee. Sometimes there is no fee—an evening meal, lodging for the night, a shave the next morning, and breakfast being the substitute. Far higher fees are not uncommon.

There is conflict of view as to whether he will "cross over" fully or whether he will discontinue prostitution and lead a preponderantly heterosexual life as an adult. Meanwhile there is great likelihood that he will contract a venereal disease and spread it principally, although not exclusively, among male clients. Some of the recently reported rise in venereal disease rates is attributable to this source.

Extent of male prostitution

It is very difficult to judge how numerous male prostitutes are. Gebhard and his associates found that 15 per cent of their sample of 136 convicted adult homosexual offenders against minors had been prostitutes. Twenty-nine per cent had paid for homosexual contacts at some point in their histories, but had never been paid. Sixteen of their sample of 199 convicted adult homosexual offenders against other adults had been prostitutes, and 25 per cent had paid, but had never been paid, for homosexual advances. This indicates the proportion of male prostitutes within categories of convicted sex offenders, but unfortunately provides no clue as to the proportion outside those categories.[34]

There is persuasive argument that male prostitution is widespread among juvenile and youthful gangs, the gang member making himself available to adult male fellators. The gang member enters the relationship for money. As long as he applies a commercial interpretation to his relations with the adult, he is not defined by his peers, and he does not define himself, as homosexual —irrespective of the definitions of conventional society and irrespective of the sexual satisfaction he himself may derive. This type of prostitution is part of the versatility of the gang. It is but one of their many activities. It tends to terminate as the gang member ages, and is passed on down to newer boys

[34] Paul H. Gebhard, John H. Gagnon, Wardell B. Pomeroy, and Cornelia V. Christenson, *Sex Offenders* (New York: Bantam Books, 1967), pp. 316, 347.

as part of the traditions and lifeways of their social world.[35]

PROSPECTS

In bringing this discussion to a close, certain suggestions seem to be warranted as a guide to further debate in the formulation of public policy.

The female prostitute

The use of contraceptive pills among women in prostitution needs to be vigorously encouraged. Veneral-disease control and treatment measures require review so as to include the new and the part-time prostitute. Some consideration needs to be given to steps which will encourage full-time prostitutes to file income tax returns and make indicated Social Security payments as persons who are self-employed. Many prostitutes achieve an enduring security through marriage. Others do not, and it is important that they be provided for through appropriate modifications in the existing machinery of public security.

While they probably know more about the meaning of the bizarre sex appetites of some of their clients than they have been given credit for, still a case could be made for a review of some of this with prostitutes in a group setting. It would have to be arranged discreetly and handled sympathetically. The advantages are that a series of such sessions would forewarn the prostitute of possible abuse and danger to herself. Another advantage is that it would aid law enforcement.

Laws stipulating that apartments and homes may not be used for purposes of prostitution require updating. Such laws seem to be used now to enable neighbors to file complaints which may really be unwarranted if the prostitute's

conduct is circumspect. Elsewhere, they are used to facilitate harassment by the police. Both usages are ultimately self-defeating.

The male prostitute

Obviously, one starting point here is a step-up in venereal-disease control and propaganda to saturate youths with a thorough comprehension of venereal infection and their own role in it. Youths of all classes also need a consistent and continuing exposure to education on the physical, arrest, and career hazards of public solicitation. Many youths are supremely confident of their invulnerability in such situations and supremely ignorant of how close they are to violent catastrophe.

The larger issue, however, is: How can youth be converted into something other than a useless surplus commodity? A large number of youths are prostitutes because they are aimless, because there is nothing else to do, no other way to make money, and no real guidance on how to address the job world or how to become an adult. A clue to the control of youthful prostitution would, therefore, seem to lie with the questions: "Why do we have youths anyway? What do we want them for? What purpose do they serve?" Until these questions are faced and until their comprehension is internalized universally, with all their painful and unsettling implications, youth will continue to perplex the social order with its libidinous nihilism.

General

Two prostitutes who were interviewed for this report complained about young men.

I don't like young unmarried men. They are arrogant. They are assaultive and abusive. They don't know what they want.

[35] Albert J. Reiss, Jr., "The Social Integration of Queers and Peers," *Social Problems,* Vol. 9, No. 2 (Fall 1961), pp. 102–120.

Younger men are trouble. They are nervous and awkward. I can usually make them calm down but you never know what they are going to do to you.

Speaking in the same vein, Sara Harris reports that Japanese *geishas* complain that young American servicemen are incompetent and inept at love-making. The Americans are not tender, and the *geishas* trace this to fears and inadequacies in American women.[36]

While these are insufficient sources,

[36] Sara Harris, *House of 10,000 Pleasures* (New York: E. P. Dutton, 1962), pp. 132–134.

there can be little doubt that continued experiments are needed with the American sex ethic. We stand in need of a much broader type of sex education in home, school, shop, and lunch counter than we have now. Steps need to be taken to modify the idolatry with which most American men surround their wives. Both American men and American women seem to stand in urgent need of less tyrannical and less demanding definitions of sexual success. Prostitutes will be with us forever. Meanwhile, they have these great lessons to teach us.

Abortion

By EDWIN M. SCHUR

ABSTRACT: As part of the increasingly open discussion of sexual matters in our society, new public attention has been focused on the abortion "problem." In America, induced abortion (which medically can be a simple procedure) has been subject to legal proscription and administrative control. The current narrow legal exception for "therapeutic abortion" does not accord with accepted standards of good medical practice, and is now being challenged by medical practitioners and organizations. Instead of curbing abortion, the criminal-law ban simply diverts the demand for such services to illicit sources. The results are a thriving illegal business; subjection of abortion-seekers to the dangers of criminal abortion; a process of "criminalization"; and—for women in the lower socio-economic strata—discriminatory treatment, according to their financial and informational resources. An important trend toward liberalization of abortion laws is related to broader currents of social change in our society—involving norms governing private sexual behavior, fertility control, and the social roles of women. The keynote of such change is the extension to women of areas of free choice hitherto not accorded them. How far this trend will be carried with respect to freedom of abortion remains to be seen.

Edwin M. Schur, Ph.D., LL.B., Medford, Massachusetts, is Professor and Chairman of the Department of Sociology at Tufts University. A participant in the Planned Parenthood Federation of America's national conference on abortion (1955), he is currently a member of the Scientific Advisory Committee of the Association for the Study of Abortion. He is the author of Narcotic Addiction in Britain and America (1962), Crimes Without Victims (1965), and Law and Society: A Sociological View (1968), and is editor of The Family and the Sexual Revolution (1964). He is an Associate Editor of the American Sociological Review, and previously was an Associate Editor of Social Problems. During 1963–1964 he was a Russell Sage Foundation Resident at the Center for the Study of Law and Society, University of California, Berkeley.

THE practice of induced abortion (intentional destruction or expulsion from the womb of the fetus, before it attains viability) and the norms defining and limiting its acceptability are matters of great concern to the student of human social life. The prevalence and distribution of abortion, and the nature and extent of informal and formal means of social control governing the practice, seem to reflect (and may serve as partial indicators of) certain central values of a society. Abortion is important sociologically because of its planned or unplanned effects on population trends, because of its relation to social definitions of approved patterns of sexual behavior and of appropriate roles for women, and because of the moral dilemmas it may pose.

Although increased openness about sexual matters has recently produced widened public discussion of the abortion "problem" in the United States, intentional abortion is a new phenomenon neither in this society nor in any other, nor is it unique to any particular kind of society. An authoritative survey of cross-cultural data revealed that "there is every indication that abortion is an absolutely universal phenomenon, and that it is impossible even to construct an imaginary social system in which no woman would ever feel at least impelled to abort." [1] Reasons for which women in diverse cultures have sought to rid themselves of unwanted pregnancies are myriad, as are the methods they have adopted to effect this purpose. Furthermore—and notwithstanding the need of every social system to ensure adequate population—there has been wide variation in the conditions under which abortion has been considered acceptable in particular social orders. To the sociologist, these societal reactions to abor-

[1] George Devereux, A Study of Abortion in Primitive Societies (New York: Julian Press, 1954), p. 161.

tion are probably of even greater interest than is the practice itself—since, in an important sense, it is the society's dominant reaction to such behavior which shapes the conditions under which it occurs and which really determines whether (or to what extent) abortion is to be considered a "problem."

THE PRESENT STATUS OF ABORTION IN THE UNITED STATES

In modern American society, as in most Western societies today, the question of abortion lies at an intriguing but perplexing crossroads where social, psychological, legal, medical, and religious considerations and forces interact or at least intersect. Given this interplay, and the fact that in our particular society the tendency clearly has been to view abortion as a "social problem" and not simply as a predictable occurrence, the values and practices of individuals occupying positions of power in several institutional realms significantly color the abortion situation. In this connection, the roles played by the medical profession, the legal profession, and by religious organizations and functionaries are of particular interest. While individual physicians may well vary in their views as to when induced abortion is indicated, the operation itself is generally recognized to be a standard medical procedure. From this standpoint alone, it need no more constitute a social "problem" than does appendectomy, X-ray treatment, or administration of pain-relieving drugs. The usual hospital abortion (a procedure known technically as dilatation and curettage) is a relatively simple surgical intervention which, when performed in the early weeks of pregnancy, is quite harmless. As a leading obstetrician-gynecologist noted some years ago, "There is little scientific evidence that in the United States today . . . any marked deterioration in the physical condition of women, aborted for therapeutic reasons in a hospital setting, will take place." "If the operation is properly performed," this expert added, "it will have no effect on either the health of the woman or her reproductive future." [2] Many features of our present abortion situation must be seen as deriving not from any medical considerations, but rather from the social meanings that we attach to intentional interruptions of pregnancy and to institutionalized practices associated with those meanings.

Therapeutic abortion

In the United States, abortions performed by qualified medical practitioners in reputable hospitals (and not challenged by law-enforcement officials) are termed "therapeutic." From this statement, it should be evident that, with respect to surgical interruption of pregnancy, the determination of appropriate medical practice has become partly an administrative and legal matter. As will be seen below, there have been signs, during the past few years, of significant public and professional pressure in favor of broadening the legal indications for therapeutic abortion. To date, however, induced abortion remains illegal in most states except when necessary to preserve the life of the mother.

In terms of modern medical practice, this exception to the ban on interrupting pregnancies is not very meaningful. Because of major advances in the management of conditions which at one time constituted serious dangers in pregnancy, it is now relatively rare that an abortion must be performed because of a strictly medical condition.[3] On the other hand, recently recognized conditions which physicians widely regard as

indicating abortion do not satisfy the typical legal criteria for permissible therapeutic abortion. This is true, for example, of German measles early in pregnancy—which has been known since 1941 to give rise to a substantial risk that the child will be born with a congenital abnormality. Likewise, eugenic risks arising from certain drugs taken by the mother have not been covered by American abortion laws—as was pointed up a few years ago by the much-publicized Arizona case of Mrs. Sherri Finkbine.[4] Nor does the legal exception for therapeutic abortions typically allow the operation where pregnancy has resulted from rape or incest, or where pressing socioeconomic conditions may suggest the advisability of interrupting the pregnancy. And while physicians have shown an increased willingness to approve abortion on psychiatric grounds, under the "life of the mother" provisions, only convincing evidence that the mother will otherwise commit suicide legally justifies medical intervention.

In recent years, there has been a tendency for American hospitals to establish special administrative machinery for the processing of therapeutic-abortion applications. Today, perhaps half or even more than half of the major hospitals in the United States have special abortion boards (usually consisting of senior staff members from several medical departments) which pass upon all requests for therapeutic abortion. There is little doubt that these mechanisms have been developed at least partly as a result of medical concern about the legal status of practitioner decisions and hospital practices. They serve the additional function of relieving any one physician from bearing the psychological burden of sole responsi-

[2] Alan F. Guttmacher, "The Shrinking Nonpsychiatric Indications for Therapeutic Abortion," in Harold Rosen (ed.), *Therapeutic Abortion* (New York: Julian Press, 1954), p. 12.

[3] *Ibid.*

[4] For details of the Finkbine case, see Edwin M. Schur, *Crimes Without Victims* (Englewood Cliffs, N.J.: Prentice-Hall, 1965), pp. 11–12.

bility for denial of an abortion request. All available data indicate that institution of abortion boards has contributed to a decline in the performance of hospital abortions. For example, a Therapeutic Abortion Board was established at Sloane Hospital for Women in New York City in September of 1955. During a five-year period following this date, the rate of abortions performed (as expressed in the ratio between therapeutic abortions and deliveries) declined to almost precisely one-third of what it had been during the five years preceding the advent of the board.[5]

The changing medical indications for abortion and the widespread use of abortion boards have combined to produce declining rates of therapeutic abortion. Thus, a recent study found a "consistent downward trend" in the incidence of therapeutic abortion in New York City during a twenty-year period (1943–1962), a decline in the nature of 65 per cent. The total number of approved abortions performed in all boroughs of that city during the three-year period 1960–1962 was 875.[6] The estimated annual national total for hospital abortions is now around eight thousand. One commentator on the national situation (who places particular emphasis on the restrictions produced by the abortion board procedures) refers to "a drastic reduction resulting from one of the greatest cases of jitters ever to afflict the medical profession."[7]

The possible validity of this assessment is highlighted by the same author's discussion of experience in two particular hospitals in which a decision was reached not to adopt a special committee procedure, but rather to rely solely on the obstetrical staff's judgment as to what constitutes good medical practice. These hospitals simply instituted liberal abortion policies, and refused to be intimidated by the possibility of legal interference. As a result these hospitals have shown a rising rate in over-all abortions performed, and have also been especially willing to "stretch" the legal provisions to cover a variety of situations believed by the staff to justify interruption of pregnancies.[8] Indeed, it should be noted that—despite the law's impact in limiting the total number of approved abortions—of the eight thousand or so therapeutic abortions performed annually in the United States, perhaps only a small fraction are actually in accord with the letter of the law. According to a report based on information from twenty-nine hospitals in California, "many routinely performed therapeutic abortions fall outside any possible statement of the legal justification, while more are at best of dubious legality."[9] German measles early in pregnancy, and a variety of psychological disturbances (the assessment of which may often include indirect consideration of socioeconomic and other situational factors), are probably at present the primary bases for this informal medical loosening of the legal restrictions. Most studies now show that mental disorders have become a major (perhaps the major) indication for therapeutic abortion in recent years.

Illegal abortion

Although there is no way of being certain of exactly how many abortions

[5] Robert E. Hall, "Therapeutic Abortion, Sterilization, and Contraception," *American Journal of Obstetrics and Gynecology*, 91, February 15, 1965, p. 518.

[6] Edwin M. Gold *et al.*, "Therapeutic Abortions in New York City: A 20-Year Review," *American Journal of Public Health*, 55 (July 1965), pp. 965–966.

[7] Lawrence Lader, *Abortion* (Indianapolis: Bobbs-Merrill, 1966), p. 24.

[8] *Ibid.*, pp. 150–151.

[9] Herbert L. Packer and Ralph J. Gampbell, "Therapeutic Abortion: A Problem in Law and Medicine," *Stanford Law Review*, 11 (May 1959), p. 419.

are performed each year in the United States, an authoritative estimate (made by a statistical committee of abortion experts) in 1955 stated that the annual number of induced abortions could be anywhere between 200,000 and 1,200,-000.[10] These figures, and that of 8,000 for therapeutic abortions, indicate the dimensions of the traffic in illegal abortion. Indeed, the demand for these relatively scarce services is so great that the illicit practitioner finds himself in a highly favorable economic market situation, perhaps akin to that of an unchallenged monopolist.[11] High profits, in turn, enable him to perform the operation with a greater degree of safety to the woman, and also to absorb the costs of protecting his underground practice—including the purchase of police protection, when that becomes necessary.

While provision of these illicit services has at times reached high levels of organization (in the form of abortion "mills" and "rings"),[12] many abortions are, in fact, performed by individual practitioners operating on the fringes of (or even mainly engaged in) legitimate medical practice. No definite statistics exist concerning the proportion of criminal abortions performed by trained physicians, but recent studies suggest that the completely untrained and un-

scrupulous "butcher" abortionists may even be in the minority. A study by the Kinsey Institute (in which the sample admittedly overrepresented women who would be in a position to obtain better than average abortion services) found that about 85 per cent of induced abortions had been performed by physicians.[13]

Perhaps the most noteworthy general point about illegal abortion is the patent unenforceability of the laws against it. The abortion situation represents but one of a number of instances of what I have elsewhere termed "crimes without victims"—in which an attempt is made to proscribe through criminal law the willing and private exchange between adults of socially disapproved but widely demanded goods or services.[14] Prohibition was the classic case; current attempts to regulate prostitution, homosexuality, drug addiction, and gambling would also fall into this category. Of course, the victimless nature of these forms of behavior might well be debated, but the designation does not focus on whether or not any individual is in fact victimized. Rather, it is meant to highlight the fact that the "offenses" in question represent transactions between (more or less) willing buyers and sellers. From the standpoint of law-enforcement consequences this consensual element is crucial. Citizens do not come forward to complain to the police of these transactions in which they have been involved. As a result, enforcement activity is hamstrung for lack of evidence.

In the case of abortion, even women who have found the experience extremely distasteful and frightening are most reluctant to co-operate in enforcement efforts. Usually, criminal abor-

[10] Mary S. Calderone (ed.), *Abortion in the United States* (New York: Hoeber, 1958), p. 180.

[11] See Herbert L. Packer, "The Crime Tariff," *The American Scholar*, 33 (1964), pp. 551–557; also Thomas C. Schelling, "Economic Analysis and Organized Crime," in U.S., President, Commission on Law Enforcement and Administration of Justice, *Task Force Report: Organized Crime* (Washington, D.C.: U.S. Government Printing Office, 1967), pp. 114–126.

[12] Jerome Bates, "The Abortion Mill: An Institutional Analysis," *Journal of Criminal Law, Criminology, and Police Science*, 45 (July–August 1954), pp. 157–169; also Jerome Bates and E. S. Zawadzki, *Criminal Abortion* (Springfield, Ill.: Charles C Thomas, 1964).

[13] Paul H. Gebhard *et al.*, *Pregnancy, Birth, and Abortion* (New York: Hoeber, 1958), p. 197.

[14] Schur, *op. cit.*

tion comes to the attention of enforcers only through the death or hospitalization of an aborted woman. Extensive long-term investigation may build a case for prosecution of an illegal practitioner, but juries and judges often are unwilling to convict and pass harsh sentences on abortionists (especially those who are trained physicians). It is not surprising, then, that enforcement is largely limited to sporadic "drives" and "exposés," or that the annual numbers of prosecutions and convictions are negligible. It is not surprising either if abortion law provides an invitation to police corruption. Policemen who recognize the public demand for abortion services and the ambivalence about strong enforcement of the laws, and who are also aware of the discretion that they enjoy in determining when an "offender" against the abortion laws will be officially recognized as such, may well succumb to the temptation to participate in the profits.

SOCIAL DYSFUNCTIONS OF PRESENT POLICY

Dangers of illegal abortion

While the use of antibiotics and an improvement in the care that abortionists provide their patients have, over the years, caused the degree of risk to decline, there is still a considerable amount of mortality and morbidity associated with crudely performed abortions. Recent estimates have placed the number of abortion deaths at a minimum of 1,000 annually and a maximum of 10,000. A survey in New York City has indicated an increase (during the period 1951–1962) in the proportion of total maternal deaths due to abortion—with almost half of all maternal deaths being attributed to this cause in the most recent years studied.[15]

[15] Gold et al., loc. cit., p. 965.

It is impossible to calculate the incidence of medical complications short of death; even among hospitalized cases, some instances of abortion undoubtedly go unrecognized, and a great many complications never lead to hospitalization.

One of the most dangerous consequences of restricting legal abortion is that many women themselves attempt to induce interruption of pregnancy. Understandably, data on self-induced abortion attempts are hard to come by, but most observers report widespread use of a variety of techniques. Few of these methods (whether they be manual or chemical) are likely to terminate a pregnancy effectively unless undertaken in such manner that they also seriously endanger the woman's life. Very likely the greatest dangers exist for poorly educated women of the lower socio-economic strata, who may be among the most desperate and the most inadequately informed about the likely consequences of "home remedies" and techniques touted by the informal social "grapevine." However, some studies reveal that even well-educated and better-situated women also try to interrupt their own pregnancies. Given a social situation in which they often are impelled to maintain the utmost secrecy concerning their pregnancies, or their desires to terminate such pregnancies, it may well be that most abortion-seekers in our society attempt self-induction before seeking out an abortionist—and, possibly, in some instances, even prior to exploring the chances of obtaining therapeutic abortions.

Socioeconomic differentials

With respect to both therapeutic and illegal abortion, under our current policies the treatment that women receive bears a direct relation to socioeconomic status. Once a decision to terminate a pregnancy has been reached, women in the various strata have unequal resources at their disposal. A considerable amount of education and general "know-how" will usually be necessary to recognize the possibility of obtaining a therapeutic intervention, to take the initial steps needed to set the therapeutic abortion-seeking process in motion, and to present one's case in such a manner as to maximize the likelihood of approval. Theoretically, decisions regarding performance of therapeutic abortions should be made on the basis of medical judgment (in which, if anything, low socioeconomic status might be a factor weighing in favor of approval of an abortion request). It is true that, as just noted, there probably is a self-selection determining the social-class distribution of women requesting legal abortion—and even of women bringing their situations to legitimate medical attention. Nonetheless, such factors seem inadequate to account for the striking socioeconomic differentials in the actual performance of hospital abortions. One researcher recently reported that "the over-all frequency of therapeutic abortions at 60 outstanding American hospitals is 3.6 times higher on their private services than on their ward services."[16] Similarly, the New York survey cited earlier found:

Therapeutic abortion occurs most frequently among the white population by a considerable margin. The white ratio is more than five times that among the nonwhites and 26 times that among the Puerto Ricans. (Well over 90 per cent of all therapeutic abortions in New York City are performed on white women.)[17]

The causes of such differentials have not been precisely established, but it is safe to assume that they reflect more general socioeconomic differentials in access to and receipt of medical care. An-

other significant differential in granting of therapeutic abortions involves the treatment accorded married and unmarried applicants. All other things being equal, a married woman usually stands a better chance of obtaining legal abortion than an unmarried one; the unmarried woman of low socioeconomic status is in a particularly unfavored category in this regard.

For those women who have no access to legal abortion facilities, or who fail in efforts to obtain the needed approval, socioeconomic status is a major determinant of the quality of criminal abortions obtained. Partly, this is a matter of sheer economics. It is widely recognized that, whereas the woman of relative means may obtain the services of a skilled medically trained practitioner, the lower-class woman may be consigned to the care of an untrained unscrupulous operative. (Such abortionists have been known to exploit patients in every possible way, even sexually; and cases often are reported of "operations" on women who mistakenly believed they were pregnant when actually they were not.) Naturally, as quality goes down, risk goes up. Although complete national statistics on the socioeconomic distribution of deaths from abortion are unavailable, it is suggestive that, in New York City, one of every two maternal deaths among nonwhites and Puerto Ricans is attributed to abortion, whereas among whites the figure is one out of four.[18]

Locating adequate illegal abortion services requires not only financial resources, but also access to a special kind of scarce information. Such access, in turn, varies according to involvement in certain subcultures and in specific acquaintance networks. Even for a relatively sophisticated middle- or upper-middle-class woman, following the path from initial source of information

[16] Hall, *op. cit.*, p. 519.
[17] Gold *et al.*, *loc. cit.*, p. 966.

[18] *Ibid.*, p. 965.

to final success in obtaining the type of service desired may be a lengthy and intricate process.[19] Although there has not been systematic research on social-class differences in this process, it seems likely that the lower-class woman in our society—as well as not being in a financial position to get a competent abortion—suffers from inadequate intimate contact with knowledgeable informants who can lead her to skilled practitioners.

Criminalization and guilt

In the United States, current law pushes most abortion-seekers into criminal situations and, in some jurisdictions, even renders the woman herself technically a law-violator (for which violations, however, prosecutions are very rare and convictions virtually non-existent). It is difficult to assess the social-psychological impact which this has on the women involved. The fact that women violate this particular law in such numbers could be held to imply a repudiation of the legal proscription and a refusal to be in any way intimidated by it. Such data as we do have suggest that few aborted women seriously regret the decision to abort, and many (of those fortunate enough to locate skilled operators) even express considerable respect for and gratitude toward the abortionist. Yet under prevailing conditions in this country, at the very least, the immediate social situation of obtaining the abortion is, for a great many women, an extremely unpleasant one. The condition of extreme vulnerability, the awareness of danger, and the need for secrecy color the experience in a way which cannot but affect the woman's self-conceptions. Some trained illegal practitioners do, of

course, perform their services in a professional and considerate manner. And certain well-organized abortion facilities seek to cloak the potentially harsh realities of the situation with a "front" and "rhetoric" of respectability and professionalization which may be superficially comforting.[20] Nonetheless, some elements of sordidness usually cloud the situation. Even where serious psychiatric disturbance does not arise following abortion (and the Kinsey study—again, it should be stressed, of a select sample—found little adverse psychological reaction), the possibility of subtle and long-term psychological consequences of "criminalizing" these women should not be discounted. While psychiatrists sometimes attribute post-abortal guilt to thwarting of woman's "basic nature" in the abortion process,[21] there is much evidence (for example, from studies showing little adverse psychological reaction in countries with less restrictive social policies on abortion)[22] that abortion guilt is, in large measure, culturally determined.

ABORTION AND SOCIAL CHANGE

The trend toward liberalization

For many years, individual critics—including distinguished physicians and jurists—have called attention to the hypocrisy of American abortion laws and to the social damage that such laws produce. Recently, the criticism has intensified, and it now includes official spokesmen for prominent legal and medical organizations. A 1955 conference on abortion, sponsored by the

---

[19] Nancy Howell Lee, "Acquaintance Networks in the Social Structure of Abortion," unpublished Ph.D. dissertation, Harvard University, 1967.

[20] Donald W. Ball, "An Abortion Clinic Ethnography," *Social Problems,* 14 (Winter 1967), pp. 293–301.

[21] See Helene Deutsch, *The Psychology of Women* (New York: Grune and Stratton, 1945), Vol. 2; also discussion in Calderone, *loc. cit.,* pp. 116–128.

[22] See various studies cited in Gebhard *et al., op. cit.,* Appendix.

Planned Parenthood Federation of America, was instrumental in focusing attention both on the dimensions of abortion as a public issue and on the legitimate and strong concern of several professions and scientific disciplines in this area.[23] Also extremely important has been the recommendation of the American Law Institute (ALI) (in its Model Penal Code) that abortion by a licensed physician should be deemed legal if there is "substantial risk that continuance of the pregnancy would gravely imperil the physical or mental health of the mother or that the child would be born with grave physical or mental defect," and also in cases of pregnancy resulting from rape, incest, or "other felonious assault" (including illicit intercourse with a girl below the age of sixteen).[24] During the past ten years, many medical organizations have issued statements in opposition to the present laws, and in June of 1967, the American Medical Association itself (through its House of Delegates) stated its support for legal revision along the lines of the American Law Institute's proposal. At the same time, systematic surveys of professional and public opinion have indicated strong sentiment for abortion reform. In one of the most important medical surveys, of obstetrician-gynecologists in New York State, 85.3 per cent of the 1,350 respondents were found to favor (in 1965) modification of New York's abortion law in accordance with the ALI model.[25] Results in this poll helped to provide the impetus for the formation of the Association for the Study of

Abortion, a national organization promoting education and research on abortion and serving as a clearinghouse for information on the topic. Action organizations, openly devoted to effecting reform of the criminal law on abortion, also have arisen in several cities.

In the most significant survey of public opinion on the topic (conducted by the National Opinion Research Center in December of 1965), a representative sample of 1,484 adult Americans were questioned as to the conditions under which they would approve legal abortions. The percentage approving, for each of the six sets of circumstances presented in the survey, were as follows: If the woman's own health is seriously endangered by the pregnancy, 71 per cent; if she became pregnant as a result of rape, 56 per cent; if there is a strong chance of serious defect in the baby, 55 per cent; if the family has a very low income and cannot afford any more children, 21 per cent; if she is not married and does not want to marry the man, 18 per cent; if she is married and does not want any more children, 15 per cent.[26] It is particularly interesting that close to half of the Catholic men and women questioned in this study were in favor of allowing legal abortion in the first three instances (despite the fact that none of the circumstances would justify it according to official Catholic doctrine). Clearly, there is strong public support for the ALI recommendation, and, undoubtedly, recognition of this support (and of the accompanying professional pressure for reform) partly accounts for the fact that, in the past year or so, several states have liberalized their abortion statutes. Reform

[23] Calderone, *loc. cit.*, is a complete report of the proceedings of this conference.

[24] American Law Institute, *Model Penal Code,* Proposed Official Draft (Philadelphia: American Law Institute, 1962), pp. 189–190.

[25] Robert E. Hall, "New York Abortion Law Survey," *American Journal of Obstetrics and Gynecology,* 93, December 15, 1965, pp. 1182–1183.

[26] See Alice S. Rossi, "Abortion Laws and Their Victims," *Trans-Action* (September–October 1966); and Rossi, "Public Views on Abortion," Committee on Human Development, University of Chicago, 1966. (Mimeographed.)

proposals also were initiated, but defeated, in a number of other jurisdictions—including New York.

Social sources of change

The development of an increasingly liberal outlook on abortion in our society reflects broader and quite complex patterns of social change. Aspects of the practice of induced abortion cause it to be implicated in and responsive to emerging patterns with respect to the norms governing private sexual behavior, the intentional control of fertility, and the social roles of women in modern society. In all of these areas, the hallmark of the changes that are taking place is the increased emphasis placed on individual free choice—in particular, a socially approved extension to women of areas of freedom hitherto not accorded them.[27] Indeed, freedom of abortion—and hence control over maternity—has, at times, been considered to be the touchstone of a complete emancipation of woman,[28] and it is often remarked that men have enacted the abortion laws while women have suffered from this action. (It is interesting, however, that in the national survey cited earlier, men were somewhat more liberal in their attitudes toward abortion than women.)

To some extent, changes relating to abortion may reflect a general reaction against attempting to use the criminal law to "enforce private morality," for we are seeing today a questioning of policy in many of the "crimes without victims" areas. However, each of these behavioral proscriptions gives rise to

special kinds of situations, and, to some extent, each "offense" is probably evaluated in terms of its peculiar characteristics. Thus, one small-scale attitude survey found that the respondents' views on abortion seemed a good deal more "liberal" than their views on homosexuality and on drug addiction.[29] At the same time, attitudes regarding any one of these types of behavior may, of course, themselves be differentiated in terms of responses to varying sets of circumstances in which the behavior occurs. Thus, as we saw above, in the national survey on abortion, a majority of respondents supported legal abortion for the conditions covered in the ALI proposal—but did not approve of it on the grounds of poverty, unmarried pregnancy, or simple decision that the child was not wanted.

Reference was made before to the convergence of medical, legal, and religious factors on the issue of abortion. Perhaps in all three of these realms we are beginning to see (not simply with respect to the matter of abortion) the reflection of broad trends toward secularization and rationalization in modern American society. Traditional answers are questioned; rational assessment of the real consequences of alternative policies is attempted. Functionaries in these three spheres of society, moreover, increasingly display a strong sense of social consciousness and social responsibility. Perhaps particularly noteworthy is the ferment within American religious bodies concerning the role of the church with regard to major social problems. The creation by twenty-one ministers and rabbis of a Clergy Consultation Service on Abortion, following defeat of an abortion reform bill in New York, is one indication of heightened

---

[27] See William J. Goode, *World Revolution and Family Patterns* (New York: Free Press, 1963); also Edwin M. Schur (ed.), *The Family and the Sexual Revolution* (Bloomington: Indiana University Press, 1964).

[28] Simone de Beauvoir, *The Second Sex*, tr. H. Parshley (New York: Alfred A. Knopf, 1957).

[29] Elizabeth A. Rooney and Don C. Gibbons, "Social Reactions to 'Crimes Without Victims,'" *Social Problems*, 13 (Spring 1966), pp. 400–410.

religious involvement in such public issues.

Moral considerations

A major obstacle to reform of abortion laws has, of course, been the position of the Roman Catholic Church.
Under Catholic doctrine, intentional
abortion (including one performed on
allegedly therapeutic grounds, even
where the life of the mother may be at
stake) is considered a form of "direct
murder of the innocent" and hence intrinsically immoral.

Whether inflicted upon the mother or upon
the child, it is against the precept of God
and the law of nature: "Thou shalt not
kill." The life of each is equally sacred,
and no one has the power, not even the
public authority, to destroy it.[30]

The sole concession to medical necessity
is the rule of "double effect," under
which a fetus may be aborted where
necessary as a secondary consequence
of another, morally acceptable, surgical
procedure; to date, this rule has been
narrowly interpreted.[31]   At present,
there are no indications of significant
modification of the Church's ban, notwithstanding the evidence (in virtually
all systematic studies) that very large
numbers of Catholic women in this country (as well as in other, predominantly
Catholic, countries) do obtain abortions.
Perhaps the major possibility for change
lies in the increased willingness (on the
part of at least some Church spokesmen)
to lessen Church pressure for the impo-
sition of Catholic doctrine on non-Catho-
lics through public policy measures.

[30] Pius XI, *Casti Connubi* ("On Christian
Marriage"), December 31, 1930.

[31] For excellent general discussion of the
development and present status of Roman
Catholic doctrine on abortion, see Glanville
Williams, *The Sanctity of Life and the Criminal Law* (New York: Alfred A. Knopf, 1957);
John T. Noonan, Jr., *Contraception* (Cambridge, Mass.: Harvard University Press,
1965).

Since other religious organizations in
the United States have been much less
restrictive in their statements on therapeutic abortion,[32] agreement by the
Catholic Church that legal enactments
should emerge out of America's religious
pluralism could have an important impact on the abortion situation.

It is sometimes overlooked that
spokesmen for Catholicism have no mo-
nopoly on viewing abortion as a problem
in morality. With respect to actual
"necessary to save the mother's life"
situations, many observers—including
both laymen and theologians—insist it
is immoral to sacrifice the mother's life
in order to save the fetus. But going
well beyond that, critics of present abortion policy assert that the immoral consequences of denying desired abortions
exceed any that may follow from termi-
nating such pregnancies. As one biolo-
gist has stated:

If a woman *wants* an abortion—and this is
the only case we are considering—then we
can predict that the cost of *not* aborting
will be very high indeed. With various
degrees of probability, it will take the
forms of marital strife, divorce, child
abandonment, psychological breakdown of
the mother, impoverishment of the children, child battering, delinquency and
crime. . . . The drawbacks of a wanted
abortion are, by comparison, trifling.[33]

Furthermore, as noted above, denial of
a legal abortion most often simply constitutes what we might call "indirect
referral" to a criminal abortionist.
Neither Church spokesmen, nor medical practitioners who have co-operated
in the legal restrictions on abortion,
have produced a satisfactory rationale
for coping with the moral implications
of such referral—or of the direct referral which often accompanies the physician's refusal himself to help the woman.

[32] Lader, *op. cit.*, chap. xi.
[33] Garrett Hardin, "A Scientist's Case for
Abortion," *Redbook* (May 1967).

Prospects

It seems likely that, as part of more general patterns of social change, abortion statutes in a large number of jurisdictions may soon be modified in accordance with the ALI formulations. Some observers suggest that this change will affect only a limited proportion of women currently seeking abortion—unwanted pregnancies among single women, and among married women who feel they cannot afford or handle (or who simply do not want) another child, would not be covered. And, it is argued, to deny woman mastery over her own body (and to make her beg for abortion, as she would have to do under abortion-board systems and other legal arrangements) is an affront to human dignity.[34] Nothing short of legal abortion on demand can satisfy the latter objection. With respect to the former, however, it is not at all clear that such extension of therapeutic abortion through legal revision could not

[34] Garrett Hardin, "Abortion and Human Dignity," Public Lecture, University of California, Berkeley, April 29, 1964; also Rossi, loc. cit.

substantially improve the over-all abortion situation. To the extent that abortion comes increasingly to be viewed as a medical question, to be managed by the medical profession—and given the inclusion of mother's "health" (physical and mental) as well as "life" among the excepting criteria in most reform statutes—it is quite possible that broad interpretation could gradually extend legal abortion to cover most (admittedly not all) abortion-seekers.

The future status of abortion relates also to trends in the dissemination and effective use of contraceptive information and techniques. Notwithstanding the serious obstacles to developing anywhere near completely effective use of contraception in all sectors of our society, improved contraceptive practice could appreciably reduce the demand for abortions. It could not, however, eliminate all the situations in which abortion would be desired. But as the secrecy and misinformation which have clouded the question of abortion recede, and as a medically oriented approach to abortion gains ascendancy, rational policies for coping with the continuing demand may be forthcoming.

Sex Offenses and Sex Offenders

By Donal E. J. MacNamara

Abstract: Sex and sex-related conduct is rigidly circumscribed by law in the United States, and rigorous penalties are provided for deviations from the limited forms of sexual expression (or choice of sexual partners) permitted. These laws reflect a puritanical sociosexual culture, strangled in taboos, but do not accurately depict either the incidence or modes of sexual conduct. They do, however, create a body of sexual offenders (perhaps exaggerated as to numbers and certainly exaggerated as to degree of social danger) who are differentially subjected to hysterical, almost sadistically punitive sanctions by public, police, courts, and corrections authorities. Little research and experimentation is supported in this field, and less treatment is provided in the nation's penal institutions. While sex acts committed by force or threat, and sexual advances to very young children, must be restrained by penal sanctions (at least in the absence of effective therapeutic techniques), many of the sex statutes punishing consensual or autoerotic conduct, or nuisance manifestations of minor sexual pathology, might well be repealed. This would permit the development of a legal code more consistent with the changing sociosexual mores and folkways of our culture.

Donal E. J. MacNamara, M.P.A., New York City, is President of the American League to Abolish Capital Punishment and a past president of the American Society of Criminology. He is Assistant Professor in charge of the corrections sequence, John Jay College of Criminal Justice, City University of New York.

THE criminal law, despite Lord Devlin's contrary dictum, should distinguish between those acts prohibition of which is necessary for the protection of society (and of its specially vulnerable charges, for example, children, the mentally ill, and confined persons) and those acts, sexual or otherwise, which are matters of private moral choice, individual taste, or of differential cultural conditioning. The sexual provisions of American penal codes, derived in large part from English common law and highly responsive to Judaeo-Christian Biblical taboos, are extremely puritanical in attempting to repress with overly severe penalties both normal sex relations not theologically sanctioned (for example, contraception, seduction, fornication, and adultery); unconventional sex play even between married couples (cunnilingus, fellatio, and anal intercourse); consenting homosexual acts committed in private between adults; and, in some jurisdictions, even such secret autoerotic practices as masturbation or the possession of pornographic materials. Not only are many acts prohibited and severely punished that are not socially dangerous, but legislatures, police, judges, correctional authorities, the press, the public, and many behavioral scientists (including some criminologists) have approached sex "crimes" and sex "criminals" emotionally, moralistically, and subjectively, rather than pragmatically, scientifically, and objectively.

Although there are some indications of enlightened change (for example, challenges to birth control and abortion laws, elimination of criminal penalties for consenting homosexual acts committed by adults in private in England, in Illinois, and in the Model Penal Code, more open discussion both in the classroom and in the communications media, court decisions holding alcohol-ism and drug addiction to be noncriminal *per se*, and less rigorous police persecution of prostitutes, homosexuals, and other sex deviants in many cities), sex—other than face-to-face copulation in private between a legally married heterosexual couple—is often illegal in the United States.

Eventually, our overly limiting, too rigorously punishing antisex laws will change in response to changing sex attitudes and sex mores. Sin may always be sin, but it will no longer be categorized as crime when we have convinced ourselves that the consequences of many prohibited and punishable sex crimes are private rather than public, individual rather than societal. While the United States, the Soviet Union, and Germany still apply Biblical sodomy laws, Denmark, Holland, Sweden, and Switzerland do not distinguish in their penal laws between homosexual and heterosexual acts, and such Catholic countries as France, Italy, and many Central and South American nations make little attempt to enforce by criminal law all that the canon law denounces as sinful. The American Civil Liberties Union has only recently adopted a policy statement to the effect that while "the state has a legitimate interest in controlling by criminal sanctions public solicitation for sexual acts and sexual practices where a minor is concerned . . . the right of privacy should extend to all private sexual conduct . . . [which] should not be a matter for invoking the penal statutes."

State sodomy, adultery, fornication, transvestitism, and other sex statutes may well be abolished by legislation, declared in violation of constitutional rights by the courts, or deleted in penal-code revisions, just as miscegenation, birth control, and abortion laws have been discarded in the past decade, even though, as Webster Schott has so aptly prophesied,

a society as schizophrenic about sex as ours, pandering to the drive in all media of communications yet restricting by law its practice to forms of expression suited to Mayflower pilgrims, will struggle and sweat as it consigns to the realm of sin what it cannot enforce as law. . . . [Sex] laws . . . will change because a moral revolution is invading the institutions of American life, the church, the family, schools, political organizations, and dramatically altering what we think of as right and wrong.[1]

That society has the right, and indeed the duty, to protect itself against sexual violence, and to prevent sexual aggression or seduction directed at its young, is incontestable. That society may rightly discourage or prevent sexually motivated nuisance conduct is equally defensible. That highly restrictive laws and rigorous penal sanctions contribute to the realization of these objectives is not demonstrable. A new approach (preventive and therapeutic) is therefore indicated.

The complete catalogue of prohibited and punishable sex or sex-related acts cannot be treated in the limited compass of this paper. Aborton, homosexuality, and prostitution are discussed specifically elsewhere in this volume. "White slavery," compulsory prostitution, maintaining a brothel, living off the proceeds of prostitution, "pimping," procuring, manufacturing, distributing, or possessing obscene or pornographic materials, and similar violations of what are loosely referred to as our "sex laws" are not *sex crimes*, but rather the provision of commodities or services, albeit sex-related and illegal, as a normal business activity. No doubt, a Freudian might well find significance in the occupational choice, but the illegal acts can hardly be considered sex acts. The esoteric deviations (necrophilia, zoo-

philia, coprophilia, nonassaultive fetishism, partialism) are statistically and criminologically insignificant. Cunnilingus is now widely accepted among sexologists as normal precopulative sex play, while transvestitism is rapidly becoming the victim of changing hair and clothing styles which are erasing external distinctions between male and female. Masturbation, fornication, and adultery are in twentieth-century America considered "crimes" only by legislative, judicial, and canonical anachronisms; and seduction, statutory rape (as distinguishable from forcible rape and carnal abuse of children of very young age), consensual adolescent sex experimentation, miscegenation, plural marriage (polygamy), and geographical and jurisdictional violations (for example, of the Mann Act) are not, for the purposes of this discussion, considered "sex crimes"; nor, of course, are such frequency delineators as nymphomania and satyriasis. Frotteurism (touching) and voyeurism (peeping) and the acts of the sexually disturbed telephone-caller or letter-writer, while constituting public nuisances and necessitating police action to apprehend the perpetrators in order to make them available for treatment, will be considered only briefly, as will exhibitionism.

Hence, the major emphasis of this presentation is directed toward an understanding of the dangerous sex offender: the assaultive rapist; the child-molester; the perpetrator of such sex-related dangerous and destructive crimes as pathological fire-setting; the sex deviant as the victim of assaults, blackmail, and thefts; and those who commit forcible sodomy, the latter largely confined to incidents in penal and mental institutions, although occasional attacks on boys are reflected in police records.[2]

[1] *New York Times*, November 12, 1967.

[2] Crime statistics are approached with a healthy skepticism by most criminologists. Sex crime statistics must be dealt with even

RAPE

Rape is the only sex crime included among the "crime index offenses" in the Federal Bureau of Investigation's Uniform Crime Reports (although a number of homicides and felonious assaults undoubtedly entail a sexual element). Briefly, there were some 22,467 rapes "known to the police" in 1965 (with an approximate 10 per cent increase in 1966 and a further 8 per cent increase during the first six months of 1967). California had the highest state rate (21.2 per 100,000) and the western states the highest regional rate (17.2 per 100,000); the lowest state rate was reported from Hawaii (0.8) and the lowest regional rate from New England. Of 10,734 males arrested for rape in 1965, only 3,386 were formally charged with that crime. Of these, 30.7 per cent were convicted of rape; 13.4 per cent were convicted of a lesser offense; 32.5 per cent were acquitted; and 23.4 per cent were referred to juvenile court. Of those arrested, 4,485 were white; 4,665, Negro; and 85, Indians. Repeaters numbered 983, of whom 85 per cent had had one previous rape arrest, 13 per cent had been arrested twice, and 2 per cent had three or more previous rape arrests. Of those arrested for rape in 1965, 14 per cent were boys under 18 years of age.

Gebhard and his associates found their rapists to include the *sadistic-*

more cautiously. Adultery, fornication, and sodomy are consensual acts, and, there being no victim, are seldom made known to the police; incest is intrafamilial and mostly unrecorded; and the victims of rape and other forcible sex crimes all too often, for reasons ranging from embarrassment to fear, make no reports of their traumatic experiences. On the other hand, experienced police officers feel that a very high percentage of "peeping tom" reports and a lesser but significant percentage of other reported sex criminality reflect the fantasies and fears (and sometimes the malice) of sexually neurotic individuals.

aggressive assaulters, for whom sexual gratification must be preceded, accompanied, or followed by physical violence. These men are women-haters, usually act alone, frequently use weapons, are indifferent to the physical attractiveness of their victims, and are often unable to complete the coital act. A second variety is the *amoral delinquent* whose concept of the female is that of an object for his sexual pleasure. He is hedonistic, deficient in social controls, and neither sadistic nor hostile to his victim, although he will use force to overcome resistance. There is, too, the *drunken aggressor* (the relationship of alcohol to the loss of inhibitions controlling socially unacceptable sex behavior of every variety is well-known, but there is little evidence that narcotics, other than cocaine and perhaps methedrine, have a similar effect). The conduct pattern of these alcohol-influenced rapists may range from clumsy attempts to gain acceptance from females whom they mistakenly believe to be amenable, to those men in whom alcohol has the effect of releasing potentially pathological violence.

Rape is sometimes committed as an explosive act by men for whom such sexual aggression is sudden and seemingly inexplicable, although thorough study often discloses evidence of psychosis. There are also those rapists who apply the double standard, differentiating the good female from the bad and rationalizing the use of force or threats to compel the latter to make good on her implied promise (when she accepted his drinks, got in his car, visited his apartment, or permitted liberties with her body). These men are likely to be normal, of low socioeconomic status, and likely to engage in group sexual activity, sharing one or more females with their fellows. Very frequently, rape by this type of offender is in response to what he construes to be provocative or "teasing" behavior by the female. The rapist may also be mentally defective, psychotic, or a mixture of the types described here.

Gebhard *et al.*, in summarizing their findings on heterosexual aggressors against adult victims, state:

The majority of aggressors against adults may be succinctly described as criminally inclined men who take what they want, whether money, material or women, and their sex offenses are by-products of their general criminality. Aside from their early involvement in crime, there are no outstandingly ominous signs in their pre-sex-offense histories; indeed their heterosexual adjustment is quantitatively well above average. There are occasional hints of underlying violence and sadism, but these are manifest in only a minority of individuals. In the sex offense itself, however, one can frequently see a basic pathology revealed by unnecessary violence, bizarre behavior, and self-delusion. A minority of aggressors against adults are not the amoral and anti-social individuals often involved in criminal activities, but are seemingly rather ordinary citizens leading conventional or even restrained lives. Actually many are suffering from personality defects and stresses which ultimately erupt in a sex offense. A few aggressors against adults appear to be statistically normal individuals who simply misjudged the situation.[3]

NUISANCE OFFENDERS AND PSYCHOTICS

The voyeur, frotteur, and exhibitionist create nuisances and psychological insecurities among both adults and children, and their activities must be restrained by the police. There is no evidence that the immature, largely passive and ineffective, sometimes mentally defective offenders in these cate-

[3] Paul H. Gebhard, John J. Gagnon, Wardell B. Pomeroy, and Cornelia V. Christenson, *Sex Offenders: An Analysis of Types* (New York: Harper & Row, 1965), pp. 205–206.

gories escalate to more violent and more serious sex misconduct. Like the obscene phone-caller and letter-writer, they achieve minimal sexual gratification by peeping, touching, or showing, and have no compelling need for more complete sexual expression. These men (females are seldom involved in this type of activity) benefit little from penal confinement (nor does society). Out-patient psychiatric care, group psychotherapy in a voluntary setting, and commitment to specialized psychiatric facilities for recalcitrant cases would seem indicated.

The criminal fetishist whose compulsion involves either personal assault (as removal of hair or clothing directly from the victim) or associated criminality (frequently burglary, often entailing assault, arson, malicious damage, and sometimes, as in the case of Heirens, homicide) is a more dangerous offender. Often there is a strong sadomasochistic element. Generally there are castration fears, excessive masturbation, a dominant fantasy life, and desire for incestuous gratification, sometimes of a homosexual nature. The fetishist is frequently aggressive, assaultive, obsessively guilt-ridden, concentrating on a substitute sex object as but one manifestation of a highly pathological mental state.

ACTS WITH AND AGAINST CHILDREN

Society reacts angrily against those who look to young children for sexual gratification, whether the sexual approach be seductive (that is, designed to elicit voluntary participation) or forcible, or indeed merely responsive to the sexual initiative of the child. Legal definitions as to the age groups especially protected differ from jurisdiction to jurisdiction, as do the very rigorous penalties. The prohibited acts are not spelled out in the laws, but the inclusive language covers all bases from giving a minor an alcoholic beverage, showing him or her obscene pictures, fondling or touching, particularly, but not exclusively, the buttocks or the genitalia, to consensual or forcible sodomy or intercourse. The acts are described under such terms as "carnal abuse of a minor," "impairing the morals of a minor," "sexual assault on a minor," "contributing to the delinquency of a minor," as well as "incest" and "statutory rape."

The offenders in this category cover a wide range, from senile old men, through drunken aggressors, to psychotic pedophiles, mental defectives, and adventitious offenders. The Lolitalike "teeny-boppers" and adolescent (even preadolescent) prostitutes attract males so socially inept as to be uncertain of their capacity to approach or satisfy adult females; the prepubescent, nonsexually aggressive or adventuresome girl may awaken biological urges by her uninhibited affection for a male relative, acquaintance, or neighbor who, if his social inhibitions are weak because of loneliness, depression, alcohol, or other emotional state, may respond sexually.

The aggressive pedophile who uses or threatens force to secure the child's compliance with his sexual approaches is considered to be the most heinous of all sex offenders. These men are less likely to be senile or sociosexually underdeveloped. Many of them are alcoholics or at least heavy drinkers, usually of low socioeconomic status, from broken homes, and manifesting mental pathology or mental defect. Their adult sexual activity, not overly frequent, is largely confined to prostitutes. They are, as a group, asocial, with a high recidivistic potential.

In the prison community, the sex assailant of children ranks lowest in the pecking order and is himself likely to be subjected to sexual assaults by other prisoners as retribution.

THE ROLE OF THE VICTIM

Prostitutes, both male and female, frequently are involved in associated crimes against their clients (thefts, assault, blackmail), and are as frequently the victims of a class of criminals who prey on society's rejects, capitalizing on the reluctance of such victims to seek the aid of the police. Assaults and thefts are also committed against prostitutes and homosexuals by psychotic individuals exercising moral judgment on them, often as a defense mechanism against latent desires of their own or as a rationalization of their sadistic and larcenous acts. Occasionally, such conduct is wholly pathological (hostility to females) or it is a reactive vengeance for some real or fancied wrong (for example, contracting a venereal disease, impotency, genital anomalies, or even racial discrimination).

Of great danger to society is the offender who seeks sexual gratification in the warmth, noise, flames, and excitement of set fires. The pathological fire-setter may also be seeking opportunity to "prove" his masculinity by discovering and assisting in the fighting of a conflagration which he has himself ignited. These "hero complex" fires are frequently set in institutions (schools, hospitals, homes for the aged, juvenile-detention facilities, jails, and prisons), almost as often by the staff as by inmates. Occasional instances of such fires involve outsiders, not infrequently volunteer firemen. The role of deficient masculine self-image in the occupational choice of fire, police, and military careers is insufficiently appreciated. Psychological screening of candidates for such services would protect the public from much sex-motivated violence, improve the services' public image, and increase public co-operation.

The role of the victim in attracting, even enticing, the sexual attack has been inadequately studied. Were we to apply the civil law doctrines of contributory or proportionate negligence in many rape cases, either the victim would incur punishment equal to that of the perpetrator or the latter would have imposed upon him a much reduced sentence. In many cases of carnal abuse of minors, incest, or statutory rape, and of other sex crimes, the initiative in the act was taken by the "victim," frequently for financial reward. Certainly, the young male prostitute who solicits actively for customers or the husky young serviceman who makes himself obviously available for solicitation by frequenting "gay" bars is not a blameless victim implicitly in need of the law's solicitous protection. On the other hand, the patron who is robbed or assaulted by a prostitute is not entirely blameless for the manner in which the ephemeral relationship terminated, although he certainly is in need of the protection of the law.

A recent case involving sadomasochistic sex rites in New Jersey resulted in the conviction and imprisonment of the lady flagellant, but no prosecution of her all-too-willing "victims"—victims who differ little in their guilt-ridden, self-destructive need for punishment from those males and females who select their sex partners consciously or unconsciously for their potential for abusive, assaultive, and larcenous behavior after the sex act has been completed.

Despite the enactment of "sex psychopath" laws (providing, in New York, for example, an indeterminate sentence of from one day to life) based on the assumption that sex offenders need something more than just a term of confinement if society is to be protected, there is little evidence that sex offenders receive any especially effective therapy in our penal institutions. Aversion therapy, glandular injections, various psychiatric approaches, surgery (sterilization and castration), narcotherapy, and hypnotherapy have been employed in some programs, but the abnormality of sex interaction within our monosexual institutions, the prevailing punitive orientation (maximized when the prisoner is a sex offender), the shortage of qualified therapeutic staff, and the lack of public sympathy and support for experimental programs combine to make the prognosis pessimistic.

The New Jersey Diagnostic Center at Menlo Park, the California Correctional Research Institution at Vacaville, and George Sturup's sex-offender facility at Herstedvester, Denmark, might well serve as models for minimal approaches by other correctional systems. A national sex-offender facility, a center for therapeutic research and experimentation, receiving both voluntary and penal commitments, operated by the National Institute for Mental Health and/or the United States Public Health Service in conjunction with a university strong in both medical and behavioral science faculty, should be a matter of high priority.

SEX IN PRISON

Sexual expression within the penal community, whether juvenile-detention facility, jail, or prison, by its very nature constitutes an offense against the penal laws; but even when serious cases (for example, forcible sodomy) are discovered, they are usually handled administratively within the institutional disciplinary system and only infrequently prosecuted in the criminal courts or recorded in the nation's crime statistics.

While many attempts have been made (architectural, disciplinary, segregational, dietary, and physical programming) to reduce sex drive and the opportunity for its expression within prison walls, and while some recent experiments with the conjugal visit, family furlough, and, in other countries, visits to prostitutes have attracted the attention of those concerned with the sexual pathologies developed by many during their terms of confinement, experience convinces us that this problem is best avoided by institutionalizing only those whose records indicate no potential for rehabilitation by extra-institutional processes and confining

them for the shortest terms consistent with the protection of the public.[4]

[4] The voluminous literature on sex offenders and sex offenses ranges, with two notable exceptions, from the inadequate, through the nonsensical, to the dangerous. The serious student is directed for his basic introduction to this important area of behavioral science to: Benjamin Karpman, *The Sexual Offender and His Offenses: Etiology, Pathology, Psychodynamics, and Treatment* (New York: Julian Press, 1954); and to Paul H. Gebhard, John J. Gagnon, Wardell B. Pomeroy, and Cornelia V. Christenson, *Sex Offenders: An Analysis of Types* (New York: Harper & Row, 1965).

Book Department

EUROPEAN GOVERNMENT AND HISTORY

FERENC A. VÁLI. *The Quest for a United Germany.* Pp. xii, 318. Baltimore: Johns Hopkins Press, 1967. $8.50.

Throughout most of history there have been many or at least several Germanies. Today we find the same phenomenon. There are today at least three Germanies which differ by their prevailing traditions and their ways of life: the Federal Republic of Germany, the German Democratic Republic, and the Austrian Republic. All three were briefly united in Hitler's short-lived Great German Reich. The first two were united in the Bismarck-created, Prussian-dominated German Reich from 1871 to 1945, a very late, but hardly the necessary or most fortunate outcome of one thousand years of Germany history. That they are no longer united is the unexpected result of the German invasion of Russia in 1941. Their unity did not assure the peace of Europe, neither in 1941 nor in 1939, instead, it increased international tensions from 1890 on. This situation had been foreseen by the leading German political scientists of the late eighteenth century.

This plurality of Germanies, "natural" before the middle of the nineteenth cen-

tury, appears "unnatural" to many Germans in the middle of the twentieth century. But this division, a "stalemate over Germany," is only a part, and not the cause, of a world-wide stalemate, a balance of terror, or a balance of powers, whatever the student of international politics wishes to call it. How long it will last, no one knows. No one foresaw the end of the Bismarck-Hohenzollern Reich in 1918 or the Hitler Reich in 1945. The present division of Germany can not account for German animosity toward the Soviet Union or the Communist camp. The animosity of the very much united Germany from 1933 to 1939 was also directed against the Soviet Union or the Communist camp. The animosity was directed even before then not only at communism but also at Poland, which was not until 1939 a Communist country, but rather the very opposite of it, yet it bore the brunt of German animosity during the years of the Weimar Republic.

Thus things seem rather complex, if one goes back a few decades in history. Equally complex is the right of self-determination, which can be put to many uses. It was used by Hitler in his demand for the Sudetenland and for Danzig, but not for the German South Tirol; it was refused among others to the Austrian Germans in the Treaty of Versailles, as it was refused to the Arabs of Palestine in 1919. There are many problems connected with a solution of the at-present insoluble problem of several Germanies. But nobody can foresee the changes that the future may bring. The present situation would have seemed fantastic in 1938, as would the prosperity and power of both Germanies in 1946.

Professor Váli has written a very thoughtful and carefully documented book —though documented more from western German than from Polish or Russian sources—on this important problem. This problem was created by the destruction of Poland in 1939, for Poland filled the important role of a buffer state between the two giant neighbors, Germany and Russia. These neighbors were seriously weakened in 1918, but had recovered their strength by 1940. Both Poland and Czechoslovakia felt then, rightly or wrongly, that they were abandoned by their Western friends and allies. It is against this background that the present situation ought to be seen. Professor Váli's stimulating book will acquaint the reader with many aspects of this situation, though he views them frankly from a West German point of view. Perhaps, this presentation of a clear-cut point of view in a scholarly fashion enhances the value of the book, which also has a good index and an excellent bibliography.

HANS KOHN

Professor of History
University of Texas

KURT P. TAUBER. *Beyond Eagle and Swastika*, Vols. I and II: *German Nationalism since 1945*. Pp. xxiv, 1,598. Middletown, Conn.: Wesleyan University Press, 1967. $35.00.

Beyond Eagle and Swastika is a monumental work. Kurt P. Tauber, an associate professor of political science at Williams College, has examined hundreds of groups, separate youth movements, many newspapers, and scores of books with a nationalist tinge. His patience was inexhaustible. He spent almost all of 1958 studying the Deutsche Reichs-Partei

(DRP). Despite the assurance of positive support from the leaders of the Party, not one of the 1,400 questionnaires involved in the study was ever returned to him. But the other material he found enabled him to fill two giant volumes. The second volume of 602 pages is devoted entirely to notes and references, appendixes, a bibliography, and indexes.

The author's main concern is not the German democratic forces after 1945, but rather the antidemocratic counterforces: their nature, development, strength, and potential. He seeks to answer this specific question: "How dead is antidemocratic nationalism?" He is not interested in the question: "How alive is democracy?"

The problem is much deeper than the simplified story of the sinister rebirth of neonaziism. There exist in contemporary Germany many forms of antiparliamentary nationalism not related to neonaziism. Dr. Tauber suspects that a basic sociopolitical conservatism continues to hold the imagination of many Germans and sets out to prove it.

There are further aims. The author is interested in the historical sources of German conservatism. He analyzes those factors that have contributed to its survival, as well as those that have prevented its decisive return to power. In addition, he examines in detail the rise of postwar nationalist leaders, their political parties, and their influence.

The book is organized in six major sections. In part I the author treats the background from the antiliberal Wilhelmian legacy to the Nuremberg trials. In Part II he is concerned with the first stirrings of a revived nationalism under Allied occupation. Radical nationalists were preparing to challenge the more moderate conservative nationalists for leadership and political power. Part III is devoted to extraparliamentary politics from 1949 to 1953, with emphasis on nationalist neutralism, rearmament, and resurgent nationalism.

In part IV he examines in detail postwar German youth at the crossroads, as well as ideas and literature of the new nationalism. In part V the author discusses parliamentary politics, with attention to the Socialist Reich party, politics on the extreme right, and the quest for a united nationalist opposition. And in part VI, the final major section, he treats the problem of renazification or reunification.

Dr. Tauber warns against being tricked by the authoritarian image of National Socialism into accepting current German nationalism as monolithic. The real force at work is a temporary alliance of the most diverse antidemocratic, antiliberal, and antiparliamentary forces. "Heterogeneity, not monolithity," conflict and tension, not order and harmony, characterized the Nazi movement. After Hitler's death, conglomerate naziism was shattered, in Tauber's opinion, and was never to be restored. Some observers of the German scene will not readily accept this conclusion. The future is already charted: "In a Germany where the liberating catharsis never took place among broad layers and the skeptics and fellow-travelers of democracy have climbed back into the seats of affluence, prestige, and power, where a climate of smug self-satisfaction and bumptious *arriviste* pride has impeded wide commitment to humane values, there the defenders of an open pluralist society and of a progressive, egalitarian polity must anticipate sharp challenges" (p. 995).

This book, the fruit of ten years' study, is a model of painstaking scholarship. No scholar of German nationalism can afford to ignore it. The organization is excellent: little of importance has escaped the eye of the author. The style is attractive—the narrative flows smoothly, with crisp, well-structured paragraphs and sentences, and without unnecessary padding. The conclusions merit attention, even if they are not accepted in toto. These two volumes are indispensable for the scholar and general reader interested in understanding the course of German politics since 1945.

LOUIS L. SNYDER
Professor of History
City College of the
City University of New York

JOSEPH NYOMARKAY. *Charisma and Factionalism in the Nazi Party.* Pp. 161. Minneapolis: University of Minnesota Press, 1967. $5.00.

One of the satisfactions of the specialist comes from the opportunity to read technical monographs which only a specialist is in a position to evaluate. Probably few general readers will want to spend time on the relatively obscure subject of Nazi factional disputes in the 1920's and 1930's. These conflicts were soon forgotten by the Nazis themselves, and they played no major role in subsequent Nazi history. The commanding presence of Adolph Hitler prevented undue consequence to all such wrangles. Nevertheless for the specialist, Nyomarkay's study is exceptionally useful. It brings together a wide variety of data on early Nazi history, focuses systematically on several significant turning points in the Nazi party's grasp for power, and then proposes an analytical framework of concepts to develop a theory of factional antagonisms in totalitarian movements.

In this monograph, the term "factionalism" does not refer to those ordinary kinds of intragroup disagreements that remain personal and transitory. Rather it defines all those internal power struggles that center on issues affecting some basic party policy, that endure over a period of time, and that have some organizational independence. Nyomarkay discusses a number of factional crises: the early disputes in the Nazi party over Hitler's absolute leadership, the *völkisch* idea, middle-class socialism, and the merits of putschism; the controversies caused by the northern factions from 1925 to 1930; and the more serious insubordinations of the stormtrooper factions from 1926 until the purge of 1934. In each case there were important differences in the types of programmatic issues, contending personalities, and eventual outcomes. Moreover, the changing class composition and orientation of the Nazi party—at one time or another influenced by the working classes, demobilized soldiers, armed bohemians, activist intellectuals, *völkisch* nationalists, radical socialists, conservative revolutionaries, and big business capitalists —made each factional conflict nearly unique. Yet the main common denominator, as seen by Nyomarkay, was the charismatic authority exercised by Hitler over his quarreling political lieutenants. Thus each faction presumed to be Hitler's

France, Germany, and the New Europe, 1945-1967

REVISED AND EXPANDED EDITION

F. ROY WILLIS

First published in 1965, covering the period 1945–1963. "As suits the subject, the writing of Willis is lively and interesting. His history of the events leading up to Franco-German cooperation and his detailing of the problems faced are thorough and scholarly. In fact, if one is looking for a work that has the mark of excellence on its every page he need look no farther. . . . This is a superb book."—*World Affairs*. "A profound presentation of the beginning of European integration. . . . [A] definitive study."—*The Annals*. $12.50

Politics and the Labor Movement in Latin America

VICTOR ALBA

This book is a comprehensive history of the Latin American labor movement with emphasis on the political factors, both national and international, that have so largely shaped and been shaped by the movement's course. For this edition, the author has added a chapter on the probable future of the Latin American labor movement. The original Spanish text, published in 1964, has been corrected, reorganized, updated, and edited for this English edition. $12.50

The Uniting of Europe

POLITICAL, SOCIAL, AND ECONOMIC FORCES, 1950-1957

ERNST B. HAAS

A reissue, with a new Preface. "It is a pleasure to say without equivocation that this work by Professor Haas is not only by far the richest book on the unification movement in Western Europe and on the European Coal and Steel Community as a political mechanism and process, but also a significant theoretical contribution to the study of community formation across national boundaries. The book represents a most impressive combination of meticulous empirical and imaginative theoretical effort."—*The Annals*. $12.50

Order from your bookstore, please

STANFORD UNIVERSITY PRESS

representative of the true idea of National Socialism and sought to win him over to its side. Once it came into conflict with Hitler, the faction lost its support and collapsed. Hitler himself fostered many of these factional rivalries for tactical reasons. As ultimate arbiter and benevolent judge, he elevated himself above most party splits and maintained his undisputed authority in threatening situations. This study adds a great deal to the deeper understanding of both Nazi Germany and the nature of factional conflicts in totalitarian movements.

RICHARD M. HUNT
Lecturer on Social Studies
Harvard University

GIANFRANCO POGGI. *Catholic Action in Italy: The Sociology of a Sponsored Organization.* Pp. xv, 280. Stanford: Stanford University Press, 1967. $8.00.

One of the significant responses of the Roman Catholic church to increasing secularization has been the sponsoring of laymen's organizations under the ultimate direction and control of the hierarchy. This book is a case study of Azione Cattolica Italiana (ACI)—Italian Catholic Action—the largest organization in Italy dedicated to bringing the Church's influence back into all spheres of Italian life. It is focused on the period from 1944 until 1958—in other words, the last two-thirds of the pontificate of Pius XII. The author, who is now a lecturer in sociology at the University of Edinburgh, suggests that ACI entered a "vastly different phase" with the advent of John XXIII, but he resolutely declines to speculate on the modifications that have occurred since then.

Professor Poggi hastens to point out that his study is not a historical one. This reviewer wishes that it were, for the brief historical excursuses in the book are far more interesting—and probably more important—than the sluggish sociological analysis that characterizes the rest of the book. In clarifying his purpose, the author states that he is not concerned with ACI's activities as a pressure group, though he drew the bulk of his data from a study of pressure politics while working in 1957–

1958 with Professor Joseph LaPalombara under a grant from the Social Science Research Council (SSRC). Nor is the author concerned with religious sociology, though the "parameters of the analysis" are provided by "one of the most important—and most controversial—hypotheses in the literature on religious sociology, the 'secularization hypothesis.'" The proper framework of his analysis, Poggi declares, is "organizational sociology." The study "emphatically adopts a sociological, not a sociographic, perspective." The author has developed at length a tentative new construct, the "sponsorship relation" existing between the Church and ACI, and he has drawn from a pioneering work by Philip Selznick some features of a model that emphasize an organization's external commitments and its competence for fulfilling them. Poggi's basic analytical concern is to discover to what extent and in what manner the Church-ACI relationship has affected the relationship between ACI and the wider society.

Much of this study served as a doctoral dissertation, and portions of it appeared earlier in Italy under the title, *Il clero di riserva: Studio sociologico sull'Azione Cattolica Italiana durante la presidenza Gedda* (Milan: Feltrinelli, 1963). The book is divided into four parts, in which the author seeks to appraise the Church's appeal to the layman and the sponsorship relation; the impact of the requirement of control on ACI's structure; the impact of the requirement of faithfulness on ACI's culture; and aspects of ACI's policy after the war. Those who have the persistence to slash through the colorless thicket of jargon will learn that the author, whose attitude towards ACI and the Church is generally hostile, concludes that ACI is "a relatively incompetent" though "not an absolutely incompetent" organization for carrying out its mission in the world. It is the sponsorship relation between the Church and ACI that critically limits the latter's chances of accomplishing the very tasks for which it was organized. The author suggests in conclusion that the unresolved difficulties in the relationship between ACI and its environment reflect the deeper question of how the Catholic church, and perhaps institutional religion itself, is to meet the challenge of rampant secularization.

CHARLES F. DELZELL
Professor of History
Vanderbilt University

GEORGES BIDAULT. *Resistance: The Political Autobiography of Georges Bidault.* Translated from the French by Marianne Sinclair. Pp. xx, 348. New York: Frederick A. Praeger, 1967. $16.95.

Georges Bidault, who shared the French foreign ministry with Robert Schuman for ten years, and whom British Foreign Secretary Bevin called "that dear little man," is the leader in exile of the "Resistance" to de Gaulle's Republic, having been as well the leader of the Resistance to the German occupation. Not "standing high" physically like his arch-enemy, Bidault has stood firm, but in a way that is better described as "standing pat." "Part of a day gone by," and barely born into the nineteenth century, he has never quite left it. Admittedly, many can sympathize with his opposition to the public, propagandistic diplomacy of today; Bidault accepted open covenants, but not "openly arrived at." We can sympathize also with his pungent description on pp. 265 and 266 of the ways in which the modern press can distort the news, "managed" either by the government or by disruptive groups.

It is harder, however, to sympathize with Bidault's stereotypes, partly the result of his skill at and inclination toward speaking in aphorisms. For example, "we live in an age of accomplices"; "all men ever remember are their grudges"; or his attack on "those blind fanatics" who wanted a free Algeria.

Bidault's strongest suit is his concern for moral consistency; now, at least, he is not a political relativist. An admitted colonialist, he blames de Gaulle most for deluding the French in the process of stripping them of their colonies. Ample quotations from de Gaulle and his henchman Debré appear to attest to this volteface. Bidault refuses to bow to de Gaulle's "wind of history."

This former history teacher demands that men "practice what they preach." Yet did he? Resistance, he says, is refusal to compromise, but as a government minister he had said, "Government is conciliation." In my own study of the Mouvement Republicain Populaire (MRP) I found him to be much less a champion of the European Defense Community than he now claims to have been. He bowed to the pressures of the French bureaucracy in Morocco. "Quand on agit, on trahit."

It is too early, says Bidault, for this to be a set of memoirs; the picture in France —"a nation where men keep silent"—will change; the last battle is yet to come. His exile gives him an advantage over active politicians who have too little time to sit and think—and brood, one might add. Bidault does give credit to foreign leaders and programs and has kind words for many former colleagues; his vitriol is mainly confined to the Fifth Republic.

RUSSELL B. CAPELLE
Professor of Government
Norwich University
Northfield
Vermont

DAVID B. RALSTON. *The Army of the Republic: The Place of the Military in the Political Evolution of France, 1871–1914.* Pp. xiii, 395. Cambridge, Mass.: M.I.T. Press, 1967. $12.50.

As more and more of us Americans find our careers in the armed forces or in their support, it is appropriate that military history gain in prominence; this book's good qualities should help military history get its proper notice. Although his style needs a dash of verve and drama, Ralston writes clearly. In the Bibliography he lists many parliamentary and biographical sources and such journal materials as *Spectateur militaire* and *Correspondent,* though the biographies of Generals Gallieni and Lyautey and an article in French Historical Studies (1962) on the demography of conscription were not mentioned. That economics, foreign affairs, and colonies are too peripheral is at once a disappointment and an indication of Ralston's steady focus on the army in the politics of the Third Republic. In this book, army often means the officer corps, and sometimes the army is almost an abstraction rather than a living group of men. Although his sympathies are largely with the army, he does write with restraint and balance.

What Ralston does competently is to narrate the remarkable recovery of the French Army after Sedan; the establishment of a working entente between an inwardly authoritarian army and the Republic, as if they were almost separate entities; the breaking of the entente after l'Affaire Dreyfus; and the restoration of that entente as signalized by the rapid enactment of three-year conscription in 1913. He reveals strength in his knowledge of the details of parliamentary organization and of the army's command structure. He affirms the largely civilian character of the Boulanger movement and the tenacious loyalty of the army in contrast to the near disloyalty of the Republic's civilian enemies; charitably, he passes by the embarrassing death of Boulanger. The central issue in the Dreyfus case, he holds, was the autonomy of the army, something for which he has sympathy. Once again, the army remained loyal to the Republic even though some officers were promonarchist.

Ralston lays the ghost of a monarchist officer corps as a threat to the Republic. But republican politicians evidently believed in the threat; so unfortunately, such officers as Gallieni were fearful that attending mass regularly might lead to a demotion or a belittling transfer. This book should be the first volume of a trilogy. The second volume should trace the relations of the army and the Republic during World War I until the disaster of 1940; the last should narrate the rise of conditional obedience, the wars in Indo-China and Algeria, and the de Gaulle revolution and regime. This is history that our society needs.

GARLAND DOWNUM
Professor of History
Northern Arizona University

DAVID MACKENZIE. *The Serbs and Russian Pan-Slavism, 1875–1878*. Pp. xx, 365. Ithaca, N.Y.: Cornell University Press, 1967. $10.00.

In contrast to previous treatments of the Eastern Crisis of the 1880's, David MacKenzie examines closely Russia's relations with a single Balkan people and relies primarily upon unpublished materials. Historians, assisted by newly discovered or recently published materials, must continually reassess past events, and the complex Eastern Crisis is no exception. Aside from S. A. Nikitin's study (*Slavianskie komitety v Rosii v. 1858–1876 godakh,* Moscow, 1960), at least a generation has passed since six other studies (listed here by MacKenzie, p. ix) covering this period were completed. Here MacKenzie offers us a new interpretation of the Eastern Crisis as it affected Russia and the South Slavs, derived from his examination of the Ristić papers at the Archive of the Historical Institute, Belgrade, the vast collections of the Austrian State Archives in Vienna, and the Public Record Office in London, including also recent Soviet dissertations and other documents found in *Osvobozhendie Bolgarii ot tretskogo iga,* in the State Historical Museum in Moscow, the manuscript divisions of libraries in Moscow and Leningrad, the Archive of the Serbian Academy of Sciences and the State Archives of Serbia in Belgrade, and Russian and Serbian newspapers of the period.

MacKenzie's findings are most interesting. The Serbian people, many of whom were divided between the Ottoman and the Austro-Hungarian Empires, dreamed of achieving unity and independence. In the 1870's, when revolts against Turkish rule broke out in Bosnia and Herzegovina, Serbian nationalists looked to Russia—their traditional protector in foreign affairs—to deliver them from oppression. While MacKenzie stresses the bonds between Russians and Serbian nationalists, he cites two aspects of Russian policy that actually contributed to the political fragmentation of the Serbs: official Russia placed co-operation with the European powers above obligations to the South Slavs, and the Russian Pan-Slavs were more interested in fostering their personal careers and the national interests of Russia than in helping the Serbs achieve unity. Thus the vaunted ties of blood, culture, and religion proved less important than national and political differences.

Although the primary emphasis is on Serbia and its national aspirations, Bosnia, Herzegovina, Montenegro, and the Voivodina are also treated at some length. Since nationalist organizations and the press played significant roles in the events of the 1870's, the author devotes considerable attention to public opinion and the early use of mass media in forming national consciousness. He also examines the views and activities of such prominent Russian Pan-Slavs as Ivan Aksakov, M. G. Cherniaev, and N. P. Ignat'ev, and Foreign Minister Jovan Ristić of Serbia. The result of ten years of research, MacKenzie's study is a distinguished, if not a remarkable, contribution to American historical scholarship.

JOSEPH S. ROUCEK
Professor of Sociology
  and Political Science
Queensborough Community College
  of the City University
  of New York

BERNARD K. JOHNPOLL. *The Politics of Futility: The General Jewish Workers Bund of Poland, 1917–1943.* Pp. xix, 298. Ithaca, N.Y.: Cornell University Press, 1967. $8.75.

Professor Johnpoll in *The Politics of Futility* makes an important contribution to three areas of scholarly inquiry: the tangled history of Polish politics during the interwar years, the tragic history of East European Jewry, and the tortured history of European Socialism. The well-chosen title is equally applicable to all three areas, but the author has something more specific in mind: the history and fate of the Jewish Workers Bund itself, an organization in which these three currents dramatically merged.

The Bund was derived from the General Jewish Workers Bund of Poland and Russia, founded in Vilno in 1897, one year before the founding of the Russian Social-Democratic Workers party. It soon affiliated with the Russian Social Democrats (SD), but its relations with the party, both Bolshevik and Menshevik factions, were always troubled. The roots of conflict lay in the Bund's chosen role as representative of the Jewish workers of the Russian Empire, which conflicted with the more cosmopolitan approach of the Russian Marxists.

When an independent Poland was established in 1918, a similar conflict arose between the new Polish Bund and other branches of the Polish socialist movement. Specifically, the Bund's principle of national cultural autonomy for Jews and other minorities was unacceptable both to the quasi-nationalist Polish Socialist party (PPS) and to the antinationalist Communist party (KPP). Added to these important differences were the excessive moderation, from the Bund's point of view, of the PPS, and the evolving totalitarianism and subservience to Moscow of the KPP. Johnpoll deftly traces the zig-zag course of the Bund—which was itself divided into pro-Communist, radical democratic, and moderate factions—in its vain efforts over the years to reach an accommodation first with the Communists and then with the PPS. The failure to create a unified socialist camp, for which all parties shared responsibility, also meant the failure of democracy in Poland.

The Bund was engaged in a "politics of futility," according to the author, since standing alone, even if totally successful in winning the Jewish masses to its ranks, the Bund could never hope to win State power as representative of a minority group. Its ultimate choice was between joining forces with the PPS and thus abandoning the Jewish national character, which was the very basis for the Bund's existence, or remaining in weak isolation. As a form of "church militant," feeding on its own prophetic myths, the Bund was unable to choose the former course.

This work combines good scholarship with sympathy for the subject matter. It fails, however, to examine adequately the social and cultural situation of the Jewish workers, whom the Bund purported to represent, an investigation which would deepen our understanding of the approaches taken by the party's leadership. Surely the inability of the Bund to reach a permanent accommodation with the PPS was in part a reflection of strained relations between the Jewish and Polish-Catholic working classes.

REGINALD E. ZELNIK
Assistant Professor of History
University of California
Berkeley

RICHARD T. DEGEORGE. *Patterns of Soviet Thought: The Origins and Development of Dialectical and Historical Materialism.* Pp. xi, 293. Ann Arbor: University of Michigan Press, 1966. $6.95.

Professor DeGeorge divides his study almost equally between Marxism, Leninism, and post-Leninist Soviet philosophy. This evaluation is not intended to be negative, as the book is a ueseful compendium. It is, indeed, valuable to have a comprehensive and objective summary of the philosophic thought of Marx, Engels, Lenin, and Stalin, and of those who have regarded Marxism-Leninism as an official, state doctrine since the passing of the founder of bolshevism. This summary is remarkable for its comprehensiveness, balance, and clarity. Of course, it is not easy reading. If the author had tried to make it easy, he would have done a disservice to his readers. A conscientious effort has been made to outline the major tenets of the "classics" of Marxism-Leninism. The book is useful as a reference work, highly instructive for those not already familiar with Marxist and Leninist thinking.

Despite its considerable merits, the book can be criticized on various grounds. Its approach is primarily that of the technical philosopher. This reviewer is not competent to judge whether or not it is fully successful in conforming to the criteria of the technical philosopher. It impresses him as being competent and honest. More than most American studies of Marxism, it is written in a calm, careful tone. However, little effort is made to probe for the psychological and situational roots of the formal patterns which are summarized. This is not to say that the work is entirely and exclusively descriptive. It contains useful, contextual, and critical commentary. However, the critical element is subordinated to the descriptive. Perhaps because the author strives so earnestly to

be objective, the presentation is not very lively.

This reviewer would have welcomed more effort to relate the formal structure of thought, which is analyzed with considerable competence by DeGeorge, to political traditions and events. In particular, he would have welcomed a stronger interpretive position concerning such questions as the degree to which Leninism is in reality compatible with Marxism. Also, there is a striking vagueness in the book's position regarding the degree to which the thinking of Lenin, in particular, is genuinely systematic philosophy or, on the other hand, mere rationalization of action. It is really no solution to this problem to refer to the official Marxist doctrine of "The Unity of Theory and Practice." For the political scientist, the brief treatment given by Michael P. Gehlen in his recent study, *The Politics of Coexistence,* of the various functions of ideology in Soviet political behavior is probably more useful than the more extensive and systematic treatment furnished by DeGeorge. However, there is no doubt that DeGeorge has produced a worth-while study. Much valuable information is presented in brief compass. The book should be useful to teachers of philosophy, political science, and history, and not merely to specialists on communism. A careful reading of it helps one to understand why, despite its dullness and internal contradictions—not to mention its apparent irrelevance—Marxism-Leninism is still a formidable political force. This reviewer agrees with DeGeorge that Soviet thought still deserves to be taken seriously. In particular, he shares DeGeorge's view that the official doctrine of the Soviet Union performs an important political function as a political faith and as a legitimating and orienting scheme for political decisions and political relationships.

FREDERICK C. BARGHOORN
Professor of Political Science
Yale University

EDMUND BURKE. *The Correspondence of Edmund Burke,* Vol. VI: *July 1789–December 1791.* Edited by Alfred Cobban and Robert A. Smith. Pp. xxv, 494.

Chicago: University of Chicago Press, 1967. $13.50.

In January 1789 Edmund Burke was about to withdraw from public life; as it happened, he was on the threshold of the most significant phase of his career. In this latest volume of the definitive edition of all his known letters, it is the French Revolution and Burke's own *Reflections* which dominate the correspondence, overshadowing even personal concerns.

We have sometimes been led to believe that Burke only slowly developed an opposition to the Revolution; from the correspondence, it is evident that any support of the cause was in fact shortlived. Even in early August 1789, he is writing that "the old Parisian ferocity has broken out in a shocking manner"; in September he very much questioned whether the National Assembly "are possessed of any real deliberative capacity"; by October he was writing of "the portentous state of France —where the Elements which compose Human Society seem all to be dissolved." And in November a letter to the younger Dupont in Paris sets forth many of the arguments later elaborated in the *Reflections*.

Among other significant themes which may be followed in this volume is that of the growing breach between Burke and his fellow Whigs in England, especially Philip Francis and Charles James Fox. With Fox the final break did not come until June 1791, after a direct confrontation in the Commons at which time Fox "condemned that book [the *Reflections*] both in public and private, and every one of the doctrines it contained." Publication of the *Reflections* in November 1790 made the author both a European personality and a center of controversy. At home he was unduly sensitive to criticism, including that of the Prince of Wales "to Whose very existence the principles of that Book were necessary." In point of fact, the *Reflections* proved a powerful influence in the decline of sympathy for the Revolution in England and brought Burke into close association with French *émigrés*, a development which may now be closely followed for the first time in the correspondence with Richard, his son.

The unity given by the theme of the Revolution and the general knowledge, which the average reader has of both issues and letter writers, make this correspondence much more satisfactory to follow, letter by letter, than previous volumes. In a brief period of two and a half years—no volume hitherto concerned less than four years—we have 225 letters, of which 164 were written in whole or in part by Burke. Of these, seventy-nine now appear in print, in full, for the first time.

ALFRED F. HAVIGHURST
Professor of History
Amherst College

GEORGE HUNTSTON WILLIAMS. *The Radical Reformation.* Pp. xxxi, 924. Philadelphia: Westminster Press, 1966. $15.00.

G. H. Williams, now Winn Professor of Ecclesiastical History at Harvard University, has performed an important double service to scholars in all those historical disciplines that include, within their range of professional concern, the dynamics and meaning of social movements. In the first place, Professor Williams has brought within the scope of one volume, large but compassable, the results of a great mass of monographic scholarship on what may still be called the "left wing" of the Reformation. Here, in detail ample for most collegial uses, is a survey of "the tremendous movement at the core of Christendom" during the middle and later decades of the sixteenth century. There are thirty-one chapters that pay close attention to the particular conflicts of men and ideas. The author begins with movements, soon aborted, within Reformed Catholicism. We are then taken through the various missions and martyrdoms of Anabaptists, psychopannychists, spiritualists, anti-Trinitarians, and so forth. The volume is a veritable encyclopedia of names, places, dates, and events; as such, it can serve some of the purposes of a reference book.

But the encyclopedic character of this volume is not its outstanding characteristic. The second way in which Professor Williams has served scholarship in the historical disciplines is more important, I think, than the first. For he has collected this welter of forgotten names, places, dates, and sometimes scarifying events to plumb the consciousness, and peculiar strength, of what appears, on the historical surface, to be utterly defeated and futile movements. As Williams writes: "The whole of the Radical Reformation might be called abortive." This is certainly the surface-truth. What is left of these movements has a "limited appeal even to the direct descendents of the movement who today cherish above all their own spiritual lineage" (p. 862). But history, as it should be written, is not one-dimensional; surface-truth is not the only level of truth. Williams goes into what may be called the psychology of the movement, to the feelings shaped by and within the movement. Those feelings survived all kinds of defeat and contend still for a deeper sort of power to shape human decision. In this brief review, I can but note the relevant summative pages on this point for the interested reader. (See, especially, pp. 863–864). Nor are the tenets of the Radical Reformation quite dead. "It is a commonplace," writes Professor Williams, "that the . . . separation of church and state has long been accepted by American Christianity as a basic principle, a boon both for the churches and the state."

PHILIP RIEFF
University Professor of Sociology
University of Pennsylvania

ASIA AND AFRICA

FRANCIS G. HUTCHINS. *The Illusion of Permanence: British Imperialism in India.* Pp. xx, 217. Princeton, N.J.: Princeton University Press, 1967. $6.50.

When the Raj was young, the British seemed happy enough to contemplate its eventual dissolution in old age, just as Augustine once prayed to be made virtuous but not yet. The anomaly of government by a Company could be tolerated for a time, while drastic reforms were carried out: independence for an unreformed India was unthinkable. But the Mutiny taught the British that reforms could only come with infinite caution, if at all, and when the Queen had replaced the Company, it seemed disloyal to suggest that she could ever be unseated.

Such is the stereotype. Francis G. Hutchins does not try to disturb its outlines. But he has some elegant modifications to suggest and some rich details to add. He argues that the illusion of the permanence of the British rule was generated before the Mutiny, when reforming zeal had already flagged and when conditions of life had become more agreeable to Europeans. He also points to the changing image of India among the British. Early in the nineteenth century, reformers looked to India as a field for the improvements they despaired of seeing at home; later in the century, conservatives saw India as a realm fit for the authority and status that seemed threatened by democratizing experiments at home. "Once the target of reformers, India had now become the hope of reactionaries." At the same time, the Indian religions and customs that had been disliked and distrusted earlier in the century now came to be cosseted as cushions and props for British rule. All this made permanence seem more desirable and more practicable.

However, Hutchins' general outline cannot be effectively tested at any point without closer analysis. More specific questions must be asked and the attitudes to Empire, displayed by specific groups—for example, missionaries—over a coherent period, or the attitudes of various groups to specific issues involving Imperial purposes—for example, the Royal Titles Act—must be investigated. Another promising line of research would be through comparative studies of the attitudes displayed in different Imperial situations—for example, in South and Southeast Asia under different Imperial powers. Nevertheless, this is an enjoyable and stimulating book.

KENNETH BALLHATCHET
Professor of the History of South Asia
University of London

STANLEY A. WOLPERT. *Morley and India, 1906–1910.* Pp. x, 299. Berkeley and Los Angeles: University of California Press, 1967. $6.95.

Mr. Wolpert's book joins three previous ones to form a quartet on the Morley-Minto partnership in Indian affairs from 1906 to 1910, the others being Lady Minto's *India: Minto and Morley* (1934), M. N. Das's *India under Minto and Morley* (1964), and S. R. Wasti's *Lord Minto and the Nationalist Movement* (1964). It is in effect a reply to Lady Minto's picture of her husband as a wise statesman, harried and embarrassed by an irascible, irresolute, and vain Secretary of State. Mr. Wolpert's book is based on a close study of Morley's personal papers, not fully available before, and its purpose is a vindication of Morley in the light of them. The uninhibited use of both sets of papers enables him to show Minto as the delayer and reluctant reformer being alternately prodded, scolded, and wheedled by a farsighted and humane statesman. I think one can say that the case for Morley as the real inspirer of the reforms is proved as is the case for Minto's reluctance to move far and his subordination to the views of the bureaucracy. But in doing this, Mr. Wolpert has swung rather far against Minto. His picture of a man who preferred his stables to his council chamber is overdone and does not account for the Scotch shrewdness which delayed rather than opposed, obstructed rather than wrecked, and always gave way before a crisis, which might have enforced his resignation. An example of this tendency is on page 169 where he speaks of Minto with the typical insecurity of a mentally mediocre subordinate."

Morley's wisdom, patience, and management are by contrast also apt to be a little overdone. There was in him a strain of nervousness if not of timidity, a tendency to talk big and act small, which cannot be denied. Mr. Wolpert is also a little free with his whips on that very convenient modern whipping post, the old bureaucracy. There is some exaggeration, as on page 168 where he writes that "the blow Morley struck against British White supremacy was of shattering significance." But when these caveats have been made, the fact remains that Mr. Wolpert has produced a very able work, full of incisive thought and imaginative insight.

His quotations are effective, judicious, and illuminating. In addition, he adds to our understanding in a number of ways. He is the first writer to have grasped the relevance of the House of Lords to Morley's tactics. It was necessary to bring Minto along with him, if not to convert him, because of Minto's links with the Conservative majority, then in a militant mood which led to the rejection of the Budget of 1909 and the veto crisis of the following year. With Minto in support of the reforms, the Lords could do nothing. He brings out well Morley's initiative on the race issues and his deficiency, due to his Liberal principles, on economic matters. Altogether, the book is not only very readable but impressive in its scholarship and penetrating in its interpretation.

PERCIVAL SPEAR
Fellow of Selwyn College
University Lecturer in History
University of Cambridge
England

KHALID B. SAYEED. *The Political System of Pakistan.* Pp. viii, 321. Boston: Houghton Mifflin, 1967. $5.95.

Professor Sayeed's book ranks among "the classics" on Pakistan's political development. It compares very well with Keith Callard's *Pakistan: A Political Study,* Ian Stephen's *Pakistan,* William Metz' *Pakistan: Government and Politics,* and Leonard Binder's *Religion and Politics in Pakistan.* Indeed, it is even a distinguished advance on Professor Sayeed's own earlier work, *Pakistan: The Formative Phase.*

The primary orientation of the book is naturally political, but it also has a good deal of sociological and economic insight. Often the flavor is more journalistic than academic, yet all of the documentation and sound scholarship that one could desire is present. It gives a three-dimensional feel that is seldom found in a book of this kind. To add to everything else, it is beautifully written.

Some of the material is virtually unique. Chapter 2, "Muslim Separatism and Indian Nationalism," covers in detail the pre-independence alliance of the British civil service and the Muslim landowners. The

166a

Breakthrough in Burma
Memoirs of a Revolution, 1939–1946
by Ba Maw

Independence leader and first Prime Minister of Burma, Dr. Ba Maw provides in these memoirs the most complete account of his country's struggle against foreign domination in World War II to be written by any major Southeast Asian leader of the period. "In times like these when American involvement in the affairs of peoples all over the globe is growing, it is of great importance that we learn to understand what it is that we are doing and what the reaction is on the part of the peoples we are trying to help. . . . We have a lot to learn from this book." —From the Foreword by William S. Cornyn. **$8.75**

Britain and Russia in Persia, 1864–1914
by Firuz Kazemzadeh

During the half century preceding the First World War the interests of Russia and Britain clashed at many points from Turkey to China, but only in Persia did the imperialist giants meet face to face. The author describes that confrontation in an account exhaustively documented from the official records of the British Foreign Office, the India Office, and the Russian Ministries of Foreign Affairs and of War. **$15.00**

The Origins of Malay Nationalism
by William R. Roff

"A fascinating study of the roots of Malay national consciousness and sense of political identity in the half century before the Japanese captured Singapore . . . as a study of pre-war Malay political attitudes Dr. Roff's work is unique, based as it is on the author's remarkable knowledge of both Malay literary sources and Malay intellectual attitudes."—*Times Literary Supplement.* **$8.50**

Soviet Political Schools
by Ellen Propper Mickiewicz

"An important contribution to understanding the political socialization process as it is performed by the Soviet political system. [It] reflects understanding of several dimensions of relationships between the party structures and processes upon which it focuses and the overall structural and historical context within whch adult political socialization occurs in the USSR."—Frederick Barghoorn, Yale University. **$6.50**

 Yale University Press **New Haven and London**

**Communist
China**

COMMUNIST CHINA AND WORLD POLITICS

Harold C. Hinton
*Institute for Sino-Soviet Studies
The George Washington University*

Dr. Hinton's analytic interpretation of the objectives, methods, successes, and failures of Communist China's foreign policy and foreign relations is based on a decade of experience in studying and evaluating the primary and secondary materials on the subject. The book is divided into four major parts featuring: (1) a description of the historical, political, and ideological foundations of Communist China's foreign policy, (2) a consideration of her role in international politics beyond Asia, (3) a discussion of her role as an Asian power, and (4) an analysis of two interconnected events (the fall of Khrushchev and the first Chinese atomic test) and some reflections on how the United States might best cope with the challenge presented by Communist China.

527 pages, 1966, $7.50

**South
Asia**

SOUTH ASIA AND UNITED STATES POLICY

Norman D. Palmer
University of Pennsylvania

This thorough study of the internal dynamics and external policies of the major states of South Asia concentrates on India and Pakistan —their politics, mutual relations, problems of security and defense, relations with the Communist countries, and efforts at economic development. United States-South Asian relations are considered, taking into account the effects of American foreign aid, the dispute between India and Pakistan, and the Chinese attack on India. Dr. Palmer concludes his discussion with some significant recommendations for future United States-South Asian relations.

332 pages, 1966, Paper, $4.50

**Latin
America**

A SURVEY OF UNITED STATES–LATIN AMERICAN RELATIONS

J. Lloyd Mecham
University of Texas

This analytical survey text is the first in ten years to trace the evolution of the Latin-American foreign policy of the United States from its beginnings in the days of independence to the present time. The book is organized both historically and topically, with adequate coverage of both United States policies of general application and United States relations with individual countries.

487 pages, 1965, $7.75

Houghton Mifflin Company

Boston /Atlanta / Dallas / Geneva, Ill. / New York / Palo Alto reasons for the failure of the Congress party to attract Muslims is analyzed most effectively.

There is a vast amount of detail on the personalities and events of the last decade before 1947. There is also in Chapter 7, "Islam, Political Culture and National Unity," the best description this reviewer has seen of the orthodox and modernist trends in Islam as they have been played out in Pakistan.

This historical review has an interesting epilogue: the author's own survey of students, which shows the limitations of Islam as a unifying factor. The "East vs. West" program in Pakistan is treated objectively and comprehensively, including an especially useful chart pointing out some of the more important differences.

In general, this is a book about which scholars and general readers concerned with Pakistan can be enthusiastic. It should also be eminently useful in helping the people of Pakistan to comprehend better their own society and government.

JAMES W. SPAIN
Country Director
Pakistan-Afghanistan Affairs
Department of State
Washington, D.C.

LORNE J. KAVIC. *India's Quest for Security: Defence Policies, 1947–1965.* Pp. 263. Berkeley and Los Angeles: University of California Press, 1967. $7.95.

In view of the lack of satisfactory studies of India's defense policies, Mr. Kavic's contribution is particularly welcome. But the title suggests a far more comprehensive treatment than is actually given in this brief volume. It is essentially a description of the organization and equipment of the Indian Army, Navy, and Air Force during the period 1947–1962, and of India's "Himalayan policy," both diplomatic and military, during the same period. Only a few developments affecting defense since 1962 are mentioned. These include a chapter on the "new" Indian defense program, made public in early 1964, a brief reference to the Indo-Pakistan war of September 1965, and some critical comments in the concluding chapter on current pressures to embark on a nuclear

weapons program. Mr. Kavic feels that "the creation and maintenance of an imposing military establishment has become an obsession in India," and he is obviously unhappy over this situation.

Two chapters of particular interest deal with defense production, 1947–1962, and with civilian-military relations, especially during the years (1957–1962) when V. K Krishna Menon was Defense Minister. Nearly one-third of the latter chapter is devoted to "the Menon-Thimayya episode." In this episode, involving the controversial Defense Minister and the Chief of Army Staff, Lieutenant General Brij Mohan Kaul figures prominently, especially in discussions of the "promotions issue" and of the military debacle in the North East Frontier Agency (NEFA) in October-November 1962. Unfortunately, Mr. Kavic did not revise his comments on General Kaul in the light of Kaul's much-discussed book, *The Untold Story,* which has been available for several months.

This study reaffirms, although it throws no new light upon, the well-known complacency and inactivity with which Mr. Nehru and other top political leaders approached the problem of Himalayan defense, at least until 1959, and the general unpreparedness, military and nonmilitary, when the Chinese attack came in late 1962. There are tantalizing hints that India's "forward policy" in Ladakh and NEFA, and especially the cryptic order to the military in mid-October 1962, to expel the Chinese from Indian soil in NEFA, constituted a significant provocation for the Chinese attack.

Throughout the work problems of defense against Pakistan are curiously neglected. (In the Index the entry for NEFA is longer than that for Pakistan!) Apparently, Mr. Kavic does not consider this problem to be a serious one; in fact, he flatly states that "the only real military threat to India" is "that from China." This orientation helps to explain why he looks at India's defense policies almost exclusively from the point of view of Himalayan defense.

The eleven Appendices contain useful but outdated notes and tables. The seven maps are helpful, but badly executed.

Only one book listed in the Bibliography was published since 1963. The author of the famous "P" article in the January 1954 issue of *Foreign Affairs* is erroneously identified as Sir Narayana Raghavan Pillai.

NORMAN D. PALMER
Professor of Political Science
University of Pennsylvania

A. DOAK BARNETT, with a contribution by EZRA VOGEL. *Cadres, Bureaucracy, and Political Power in Communist China.* Pp. xxix, 563. New York: Columbia University Press, 1967. $12.00.

This volume, prepared by a professor of government at Columbia University and a senior scholar specializing on modern China, is essentially a government organization manual rather than a study of the Chinese political system in the post-1949 period. The author inventories and describes, frequently in vivid detail, agencies, political organizations, administrative functions, and operational behavior or practices of the Chinese Communist party and governmental structures from the national ministry level down to the rural villages. It does not deal directly with the highest levels of national government, administration, and policy-making—the National People's Congress, the top Party and government leaders and offices, the Communist party's Congress and Central Committee, the military forces and judicial agencies, country-wide political parties and groupings, and national domestic and foreign policy operations. China's progress and problems in achieving economic and technological development and in promoting social change are not discussed in over-all terms. The focus of this study is on the structure and operations of the political system, not on its policies and substantive activities. In places this approach gives the work a somewhat abstract quality. Except to the well-informed reader interested in technical details, this book probably will serve as an extremely useful and illuminating reference work rather than a volume to be read from cover to cover.

Half of the substantive part of this work —two hundred pages—is in Part II and concerns organization and operations of the Party and government in a county. This section, clearly the most substantial part of the book and the only detailed and authoritative account of county operations and administration that is yet available, was written jointly by Barnett and Ezra Vogel, Professor of Social Relations at Harvard University. Part I deals with an anonymous central ministry, and Part III with a commune and a brigade.

This work is presented as three case studies, each based primarily on data provided by one key informant, supplemented at points by documentary information and reports of secondary informants. In the case of the lower levels of administration, from the county down to the village, the need to protect the anonymity of the sources does not demand a withholding of concrete, case-study-type detail. In these sections, the introduction of references to substantive policy questions is possible without compromising informants because of the large number of units in each class.

In the case of Ministry M, however, the cost paid for protecting the anonymity of the informant comes high. To conceal the identity of the informant, the identity of the Ministry is completely suppressed. Hence, there is no discussion of the Ministry's eight substantive or operational bureaus (page 95). Thus we do not know why it existed, what functions it performed, and why it finally was abolished. The Ministry has no faces; it does not seem to enter the stream of political and policy activities and pressures. There are no dates or no issues. To understand the functional relations of the Ministry to the Central Committee of the Party and to the State Council, the reader needs some clues to its responsibilities and activities, whether related to high or low political and economic goals of the regime. A case study instructs by virtue of specificity and detail. Here we have an illustration of the frustrations and limitations imposed on the scholar who, in penetrating the Chinese scene, must deny to his readers necessary information as the price he pays to inform himself through private means.

This volume is a pioneering work on at least two counts. It is the first major study based primarily on data provided by

Kindly mention THE ANNALS *when writing to advertisers*

thorough interviewing, an art which has been increasingly cultivated by specialists on contemporary China, as published sources of information about developments in China have withered away. Secondly, this is the first monograph, both systematic and detailed, dealing with general party and government organization and operations of geographic administrative systems below the national level. Charts, tables, and a ninety-page glossary of terms, with Chinese characters, assure that this study will be pressed into immediate use as a reference and text by students of Chinese politics.

JOHN M. H. LINDBECK
Director
East Asian Institute
Columbia University

T. O. RANGER. *Revolt in Southern Rhodesia, 1896–97: A Study in African Resistance.* Pp. xii, 403. Evanston: Northwestern University Press, 1967. $12.50.

For many years students of African history have criticized the Eurocentric approach to African history. Instead, they have called for a reappraisal of traditional methods and value judgment, for studies that would pay more attention to local sources, give better prominence to the African side of the story, and thereby avoid the failings of imperialist historiography. In all too many cases, however, the "revisionists" have not proved conspicuously more successful than their Victorian predecessors. Works such as Endre Sík's *Histoire de l'Afrique Noire,* written from the Marxist-Leninist standpoint, or Robert I. Rotberg's *The Rise of Nationalism in Central Africa . . .* , a product of the liberal anticolonialist school, in many ways simply stand imperialist preconceptions on their head.

Terence O. Ranger's work is in a very different category. The author has thoroughly investigated the archival material available in Rhodesia and Great Britain. He is familiar with the anthropological literature concerning his subject. Despite a modest disclaimer that he must "remain excluded from many of the insights into Ndebele and Shona society which are needed for a truly balanced account," he has made good use of oral sources. He is familiar with colonial history of the more conventional kind. He tries to do justice to the White as well as to the Black actors in the grim drama he describes. Finally he attempts to place the rising into its wider setting. His book is, therefore, much more than a specialized monograph, but a major contribution to Rhodesian history.

Ranger's study will interest political scientists as much as historians. The author believes that modern nationalism in Rhodesia has obtained mass support by turning into a radical, almost millenarian movement, which looks to the past for inspiration but promises mastery of the future. According to the writer, "the mood of [present day] Southern Rhodesian nationalism is closer to the ambiguity towards the white world which characterized the risings and subsequent millenarianism than to the total acceptance of its values which characterized the new [African] associations of the 1920s and 1930s."

This reviewer disagrees with the author on a number of issues. The Matabele military monarchy, for instance, appears to have suffered from many more internal contradictions than the author would allow. Little is said concerning how some Africans adapted themselves to the new economic opportunities brought about by the white intrusion. (Between 1902 and 1913, for example, the number of native-owned cattle supposedly increased seven-fold. Ploughs and wagons gradually came into use; many African farmers began to sell maize and beef to the mines.) More might also have been made of the Chartered Company's postrebellion reforms in the fields of health and labor management; these may also have helped to reduce revolutionary tension. Despite these criticisms, however, Ranger's work represents a pioneering effort and will remain a classic of Rhodesian historiography.

L. H. GANN
Hoover Institution
Stanford University

JEAN MEYNAUD and ANISSE SALAH BEY. *Trade Unionism in Africa: A Study of*

Its Growth and Orientation. Pp. 242. New York: Barnes & Noble, 1967. $11.50.

This study, originally published in French in 1963, was one of the first global studies of trade unionism on the African continent. When the book was first published, it was a useful study, pulling together scattered sources on African unionism and presenting them systematically. Published in English four years later, its value and significance have dropped sharply. Part of the reason for this is that much of the book is now outdated. Equally, however, the translation is a poor one. The translator appears unacquainted with Africa and trade unionism. French spelling forms are used throughout—for example, M'Boya, N'Krumah, and the like —and French-language sources are usually cited, although many are readily available in English—for example, *Free Labour World.* Some English formulations are almost incomprehensible, and certain terms having specific meaning in French are translated literally thereby producing no sense—for example, *syndicat professionel* is translated as "professional union" but, in context, can only mean "industrial union."

The book is divided into three parts. The first part provides background information, dealing with the economic prerequisites for unionism in Africa. The various external influences and their effects on African developments are then examined. Part II focuses upon the politics of African unionism in the pre- and post-independence periods. The final portion deals with pan-African trade union developments and with the relationship between African unions and the International Labour Organization (ILO).

The basic thesis of the book rests upon a belief about the pre-eminence of politics in Africa: unions must deal with this fact of life by becoming politicized. This thesis, which has had broad support in the past has been challenged by a number of scholars in recent years—see, especially, the chapter by Berg and Butler in the volume edited by Coleman and Rosberg, *Political Parties and National Integration in Tropical Africa.* Indeed, a number of detailed studies in single countries have shown that successful unionism is marked by an avoidance of overt political action by the unions.

The strength of this book rests on its breadth of coverage. It is one of the few studies which is strong on francophonic and anglophonic Africa. Its documentation and coverage of the literature of the field are impressive although, paradoxically, basic reports from labor departments are hardly cited. It also provides good coverage of the Congo (ex-Belgian) and of the Maghreb.

The book is also marked by a number of shortcomings. The authors fail, for example, to achieve the high level of analysis they attempt from time to time. Thus, the typology of union-government relations (pp. 107–108) is handled neither clearly nor developed to its logical conclusions. With the heavy focus on political questions, the authors devote little or no time to a consideration of industrial relations practices of African trade unions. Finally, the book conveys a tone of having been commissioned by the International Labour Organization since the space devoted to the ILO's activities is far beyond the significance of that organization in Africa, in the opinion of this reviewer.

Although intended as an introduction to the study of trade unionism in Africa, this study will be too advanced for most readers without basic knowledge of the subject. Nor does the translation make for easy reading.

WILLIAM H. FRIEDLAND
Associate Professor of
  Industrial and Labor Relations
Cornell University

RICHARD P. STEVENS. *Lesotho, Botswana, & Swaziland: The Former High Commission Territories in Southern Africa.* Pp. 294. New York: Frederick A. Praeger, 1967. $7.50.

In 1968 Swaziland will gain its independence and thus bring to an end British colonial rule in Africa. Sobhuza II, certainly the longest reigning monarch active today, having been named king at the age of five months in 1899 and officially installed in 1921, will become ruler of the land. Bechuanaland and Basutoland became independent in 1966. With the independence of all three territories a *modus vivendi* with the Republic of South Africa, which would assure continued independence, had to be made. Internal consensus on constitutional arrangements and some understanding between the local governments and Britain on support for economic development was also required.

Professor Richard P. Stevens has primarily written a historic account of the development of the three territories, from the earliest contacts of African tribal societies with Europeans to independence. As a former Chairman of the Political Science Department at Pius XII University College in Basutoland, an institution which serves as the college for all three territories, the author knows well the governmental institutions and the political process operative there. The political forces —indigenous, British, and South African— their strategies, and their objectives are clearly analyzed. The dilemmas faced by African political parties and leaders are treated with sympathy.

The book presents a study of each territory treated seriatim. Dr. H. George Henry, a colleague of Professor Stevens at Lincoln University, provides a chapter for each country surveying their economic potential and economic problems.

Lesotho, Botswana, and Swaziland face problems typical of many newly independent African states. Conflict between modernizing and traditional leaders embitters political issues within each of the Territories. The need to demonstrate accomplishments in the field of economic development is an ever-present source of challenge to the ruling parties. But, over and above the problems faced by other African states, the question of South Africa is an immediate and crucial one for the three states dealt with in this volume. It was originally expected that the Territories would be incorporated into the Union of South Africa. Afrikaner racial policies precluded the fulfillment of this expectation. Through the 1940's and 1950's, the South African government insisted on incorporation, but by 1963 the Verwoerd government became reconciled to independence for the High Commission

Territories. At the onset of independence, each territory chose normal, correct, and even friendly relations with Pretoria. While their hearts were with their brethren of the Organization of African Unity (OAU) in feelings of distate for *apartheid*, their heads and their stomachs dictated noninvolvement in African efforts to end minority rule in the Republic of South Africa.

Professor Stevens' book deserves to be rated as a basic volume on the High Commission Territories. His study is rich in political data and is presented in a clear and straightforward manner. His insights are helpful. The dilemma of race conflict in southern Africa leads Professor Stevens to urge that Washington and other Western governments become more generous with assistance to Lesotho, Botswana, and Swaziland. Economic dependence on South Africa might thereby be reduced. This is a useful point to make; nevertheless, for reasons of geography and security, the three states must devise a policy toward South Africa. Having noted that tactics of prudence have been adopted in this respect, the author seems reluctant to challenge or to endorse such an approach. Having produced so valuable a contribution to our understanding of the countries involved, one might hope that Professor Stevens will provide intellectual leadership on this crucial issue as well.

J. LEO CEFKIN
Professor of Political Science
Colorado State University

LATIN AMERICA

ANDRÉS SUÁREZ. *Cuba: Castroism and Communism, 1959–1966.* Pp. xviii, 266. Cambridge, Mass.: M.I.T. Press, 1967. $7.50.

JOHN PLANK (Ed.). *Cuba and the United States: Long-Range Perspectives.* Washington, D.C.: Brookings Institution, 1967. $6.75.

These books are distinguished additions to the literature on "Castro" Cuba. To measure the Castro revolution in United States terms, the Brookings Institution book, edited by John Plank, will become an essential yardstick. The chapters by Wriston, Silvert, Baldwin, and Manning deserve special attention. Suárez's work is the first scholarly insider's report on Castro and his entourage since he came into power. As might be expected of a book under the auspices of the Interna-national Communism project at the Massachusetts Institute of Technology, whereby the author had access to every file in Washington, it is exceptionally well documented.

Henry Wriston tells more in the thirty-five pages of his "Historical Perspective" than many authors do in entire books. His piece on Cuba's "client status" is a masterpiece, as is his description of the denouement of Cuban democracy under Grau, Prio, and finally an insensitive Batista. His lessons on intervention—"it must be done skillfully enough and on a large enough scale to guarantee its success"—on the use and responsibility of power, and on the "fatal confusion" which results from linking recognition to the approval of governments, are classics in pragmatism. Wriston just stops short of saying that the weak American response to the Bay of Pigs led directly to a Soviet miscalculation and thus the missile crisis of 1962. I would say that it did. I can also state that one reason for United States support of the anti-Castro elements was precisely the fear that Soviets would place missiles in Cuba.

Bayless Manning offers an excellent summation in his "An Overall Perspective." He describes six critical problems that would have to be faced by the United States. "If the Castro regime were in some way to be unseated": (1) restoration of order, probably with United States and the Organization of American States (OAS) assistance; (2) claims settlement, possibly through a multilateral international procedure; (3) need for Cuban sugar to re-enter the United States market; (4) restoration of social and economic services; (5) decommunization of press, schools, and the like; and (6) need for capital without American predominance.

Ernest Halperin brilliantly states Suárez's main themes in the Foreword to the latter's book, concluding that "foreign policy con-siderations determined Castro's conversion to Communism and the transformation of Cuba into a Communist state." Suárez stops short of that position, carefully juxtaposing Castroism and communism, but seeing no convergence of the two. He asserts that "it is highly doubtful that the Cuban regime can legitimately be called Communist," apparently because the ideology and disciplined party apparatus heretofore associated with Marxist-Leninist regimes is missing—or invisible to him.

The Tad Szulc chapter in *Cuba and the United States,* "Exporting the Cuban Revolution," is sobering. While revealing no Castro successes, indeed a string of failures ranging all over the hemisphere, he shows, nevertheless, that the example of Castro has set in motion powerful currents of nationalism and extreme Leftist trends. Most chilling of all is Hanson W. Baldwin's chapter, "A Military Perspective," in which he points out that "what makes Castroism a potential strategic threat to the hemisphere is the backing of Soviet power." He concludes that "as long as Soviet Russia uses Cuba for its purposes, statesmen and military planners in the United States will have nightmares."

Both books were inexplicably delayed in going to press. Although two contributors told me that they submitted their chapters for *Cuba and the United States* in 1963, the timeliness of the book stands unimpaired.

R. RICHARD RUBOTTOM, JR.
Vice-President
Southern Methodist University

WENDELL BELL (Ed.). *The Democratic Revolution in the West Indies: Studies in Nationalism, Leadership, and the Belief in Progress.* Pp. xxiii, 232. Cambridge, Mass.: Schenkman, 1967. $8.95.

The main purpose of this collection of studies is to explore the attitudes which will influence the leaders in the former British West Indian colonies in dealing with what the authors call "the decisions of nationhood." Much of the book is devoted to an analysis of responses by 112 prominent citizens of the various islands to questions designed to elicit information about each individual's basic political and social philosophy.

In one chapter, for example, Mr. Moskos studies the attitude of these leaders toward political independence. He classifies them as "true nationalists," "acquiescing nationalists"—who may be "reluctant," "dutiful," or "opportunistic"—and "colonialists." He then investigates the relative strength of each group on each island and the apparent relationship between attitudes toward independence and age, education, wealth, color, and occupation. He finds that colonialists are apt to be older, more prosperous persons of white descent, while the true nationalists tend to be younger, darker, but often better educated. A substantial proportion of the leaders, ranging from 21 per cent in Jamaica to 43 per cent in Barbados and 47 per cent in Dominica, are colonialists, while less than 50 per cent are true nationalists, except in Guyana and Jamaica. Mr. Moskos also shows the relationship between West Indian nationalism and eighteenth-century revolutionary philosophy. By constructing an index of "enlightenment," based on attitudes toward political democracy, egalitarianism, and concern for the elimination of social barriers, he shows that 100 per cent of the most enlightened were true nationalists while 83 per cent of the unenlightened were colonialists.

In other chapters, Messrs. Bell and Moskos explore the attitudes of the same group of leaders toward democracy, "global alignments," and equality. They find that "the over-all level of egalitarianism among West Indian leaders was not overwhelmingly high," except among the true nationalists. Using material from other groups, Mr. Duke investigates egalitarianism among university and secondary school students in Jamaica, and Mr. Mau reports on the prevalence of belief in progress among leaders on that island.

The studies do not tell us a great deal about recent events or current problems. There is a good chapter by Mr. Oxaal on the background of the independence movement in Trinidad, and one would like to have a similar chapter on Jamaica. Except for Mr. Mack's study of "Race, Class, and Power in Barbados" and Mr. Phillips', of the attitude of labor in Antigua, both of which are interesting, there is little discussion of the problems of the smaller islands.

DANA G. MUNRO
Emeritus Professor of History
Princeton University

ROBERT T. DALAND. *Brazilian Planning: Development, Politics, and Administration.* Pp. viii, 231. Chapel Hill: University of North Carolina Press, 1967. $6.00.

"Is planning necessary, practicable, desirable or even possible under the conditions which exist in a developing society?" It is not the theoretical possibility of rationally determining the best means for achieving selected ends which is called into question by this book, but rather, the usefulness of gathering and maintaining a professional staff to write, implement, and supervise a comprehensive plan for economic development. Thus, Professor Daland's book is not about particular issues of economic policy-making but about the mechanics and style of plan-making. While methodological advantage is gained by thus restricting the scope of this study, severe problems in controlling the variables and identifying the relationships between them are engendered. This rather spare and circumscribed account of the evolution and impact of economic planning in Brazil since the revolution of 1930 is written with the intention of offering evidence on this question of planning's relevance to development.

The sources of the author's concern with the efficacy of planning in a developing society are political and social. Implementation of comprehensive national economic plans pursuing goals effecting the relative status of competing social groups and diminishing the influence of established branches of the bureaucracy in a society unable to achieve a consensus regarding goals, lacking a corps of trained and reliable civil servants, and incapable of placing a viable coalition at the head of state, will, in Daland's view, make economic planning a very heavy political burden to sustain. He hypothesizes that in such circumstances national economic plans will derive from the political needs of the regime in power, will be dependent for their implementation upon its political resources, and will be readily sacrificed to expediency as the regime daily negotiates its survival.

An account of national economic plan-formulation and implementation within the Brazilian federal government is offered in support of these hypotheses. The author also gives an analysis and recommendations made in successive plans: the narrowly focused infrastructure investment programming of the early postwar years, the heady optimism of Kubitschek's program of fifty years' progress in five, João Goulart's Three Year Plan (Plano Trienal) to harmonize development, stabilization, and reform, and the 1964 coup's effort to stabilize the economy and perfect market institutions to return Brazil to a more liberal (in the sense of Manchester liberalism) model of development under the aegis of a dominant Ministry of Planning. A lengthy chapter traces Goulart's Plano Trienal from its inception to its abandonment in the midst of the continuous political crisis of 1963 and 1964.

Daland's criteria of the successful conduct of planning are the degree of implementation the plan achieves, its impact upon development, and the continuity of the institutions it creates. Applying these criteria to his account of Brazilian planning, he concludes that "planning in Brazil is politically useful, but not for the purpose of achieveing development."

Despite the care with which the problem and research design have been formulated, its conclusions are not fully satisfactory. By systematically avoiding the substance of the economic policies which the various plans proposed, it fails to come to grips with the relationship of economic policy formation, politics, and planning in Brazil. Planning, in the very narrow sense considered by this book, was only a very small part of the economic policy-making engaged in by the federal government. The Kubitschek government did very little plan-making but promoted a broad economic policy of import substitution for

which there was a theoretical and technical rationale and which was implemented with a wide range of policy instruments. This policy was not only politically useful but also made a vital contribution to development. Whether under the tag "planning" or not it engaged in the purposive manipulation of economic policy instruments (planning?).

As a study of the efficacy of plan-making, this study is insufficiently detailed and has inadequately discounted the influence of the economic and political conditions under which particular governments labored to be able to distinguish the discrete effect of plan-making upon the progress of economic development. The Plano Trienal did fail. But did it really worsen the position of the Goulart government in what was an extremely precarious economic and political situation? Had Goulart conducted the same policies without a plan would his government's fate have been any different? Certainly no one connected with his plan was unaware of its political goals. The plan was an instrument of political mobilization to overcome instability. Its marginal contribution to the outcome can be determined only with far more sensitive tools than used and with a much more wide-ranging discussion of the entire political and economic situation.

PAUL I. MANDELL
Assistant Professor of Geography
Food Research Institute
Stanford University

ROBERT N. BURR. *Our Troubled Hemisphere: Perspectives on United States-Latin American Relations.* Pp. xi, 256. Washington, D.C.: Brookings Institution, 1967. $6.75.

JEROME SLATER. *The OAS and United States Policy.* Pp. viii, 315. Columbus: Ohio State University Press, 1967. $6.00.

With so many books appearing on Latin America, especially in its relations with the United States, there is bound to be considerable textual overlapping. Perhaps this is good since several viewpoints and interpretations are presented, and the organization of materials is dissimilar. But the story has already become monotonous with the same facts and the same references offered by different writers, laymen as well as scholars. Accounts are often fragmentary, disjointed, and badly organized. Many studies are too contemporary and current to have lasting value. Opinions rather than facts are assembled, and interpretations take the place of critical evaluations. Political scientists are most to blame for this state of affairs, but historians are not far behind. Much of the present-day history is still a mystery, and political science-fiction is still a problem. These two volumes are tinged with these characteristics, the second more than the first.

Professor Burr is a widely recognized historian, who has been engaged in teaching and research for many years, and his writings are highly regarded, so much so that in 1966 he received the Bolton Prize, established by the Pan American Foundation and awarded annually by the Conference on Latin-American History. His book is a question-and-answer presentation, concerning our current complex relations with the Latin-American countries; what our past policies have been; what our present relations are; what inherent contradictions exist; and what conditions create tensions. In a word: what is wrong, and what is the remedy? Dr. Burr believes that some of our policies have been made without planned direction or by indifferent misdirection. He asks: Why has this happened? Who is to blame? What can be done? And what changes can be attempted? He suggests more support for the Alliance for Progress; expanded power for the Organization of American States (OAS); and a campaign to increase knowledge, respect, and appreciation among business firms and even educational institutions for Latin-American culture, sensibilities, attitudes, and individual dignity. In brief, Dr. Burr proposes to provide the concerned layman with a basis for the critical reappraisal of United States "public policies—political, economic, and social—that seem of greatest consequence to the United States." This objective he has accomplished.

Dr. Slater is Assistant Professor of Political Science at the State University of New York at Buffalo. He asserts in his introduction that the events of the late 1950's "not only symbolized the failure of United States foreign policy toward Latin America, they also focused attention on the dismal state of scholarship on Latin American politics and inter-American relations." Consequently, the author proposes to make for these scholars "rigorous political analyses" of the OAS and to partially fill in the gaps in our Latin-American relations by "examining the role of the OAS" during the years 1947–1964. United States policy-makers are chiefly concerned with internal Latin-American political structures, international relations within the hemisphere, and relations of the hemisphere to the rest of the world. The United States "has attempted to influence the OAS to play one of three roles—that of a collective security system, of an anti-Communist alliance, or even on occasion of an anti-dictatorial alliance." Our Latin-American policy is divided into three phases: "the first from 1946–60, the second roughly coinciding with the Kennedy administration, and third beginning with the Johnson administration." In the author's opinion, the OAS has functioned with some success in supporting a collective security system, but in serving as an alliance it is relatively impotent.

This study is repetitious, but there are pertinent omissions. It is analytical, but not always objective. Many public documents are cited, but opinions of the author and others are often given factual status and are premature in consequence. Yet Dr. Slater has given a good indication of the direction that our Latin-American policy is now taking.

A. CURTIS WILGUS

Miami
Florida

ROBERT N. BURR. *By Reason or Force: Chile and the Balancing of Power in South America, 1830–1905.* Pp. 322. Berkeley and Los Angeles: University of California Press, 1967. $7.95.

This is a most useful diplomatic history.

The rise of Chile as a nation with an internal nationalism—that is, centralization—and a foreign policy based on national self-interest seems so clear and patent that it is hard to believe that this study is probably the first of its kind. The notion that there is a "Latin America," with a common language, a common background, and a Hispanic tradition is offset by the facts of boundary disputes, wars, and rivalries. Continental solidarity and intra-American co-operation have been ideals and principles, but Chile and the other countries are more firmly guided by security, national interest, and foreign policy.

Such a position has changed with history. It has been flexible in times of crisis and when the forces of one era have been replaced by other forces. Chile, however, began as a weak and internally chaotic country and emerged as a stable power. Material development and sea power aided this evolution, but the character of the people, their industry, and their readiness for expansion, war, and firm diplomacy combined to back up Chile's development.

Chilean nationalists were conscious of South American power, particularly among neighbors (Argentina), or were looking for a balancing factor (Brazil). At different times, the Chilean situation required adroit diplomacy and at other times war. With both reason and force Chile found the way to retain and advance her national interests. In the end, Chile achieved equilibrium with her neighbors, and by 1905 could turn her attention once again to internal growth and development.

Studies of nationalism are often too much concerned with nationalization, antiforeign aspects, street demonstrations, or romantic origins. Latin-American nations have permanent national self-interests which are basic to their existence and growth. Chilean interests are influenced by its geography, its history, its ambitions along the Pacific Coast, and the character of the people.

This study, although very largely dealing with terms of law, treaties, and diplomacy, points the way to insight into national forces in Latin America. There should be a series of national interest studies for Mexico, Brazil, Argentina, Colombia, and other leading Latin-American countries. These would show, as the study does, that there is meaning beneath revolutions, *caudillos,* violence, and the apparent disorder of the national period. The balance-of-power theme is one guideline, and the book follows that guide very well.

HARRY BERNSTEIN
Professor of History
Brooklyn College
City University of New York

EDWARD BAXTER BILLINGSLEY. *In Defense of Neutral Rights: The United States Navy and the Wars of Independence in Chile and Peru.* Pp. viii, 266. Chapel Hill: University of North Carolina Press, 1967. $6.00.

In a well-written, carefully researched, and objective account of some of the origins of United States relations with Chile and Peru, Edward Baxter Billingsley—a rear admiral, retired, and currently an assistant professor of history at the University of South Florida—notes that during the 1817–1823 period "both the administration and its naval arm placed the tangible interests of American commerce above somewhat nebulous ideological considerations" (p. 206). Ideological matters, however, when viewed by Latin Americans, were apt to seem more significant and less nebulous than when regarded by representatives of the United States. This difference in approach rendered friction inevitable.

Charged with defending their country's commercial interests and neutral rights, the commanders of United States ships in the far southern reaches of the Pacific often encountered more difficulty with the patriots than with Spanish royalists. This was particularly true when the patriots gained naval mastery over the royalists in 1818. Some of the main difficulties arose from the fact that the United States naval commanders were charged with enforcing the neutrality concepts, including the principle of effective blockade, and their young country found it convenient to regard this as international law. The patriots often found it convenient to their cause to advance different principles of international law.

In addition to the difficulties they encountered with the patriots, the North American officers were sometimes troubled by the edge which they thought the British might be gaining in commercial intercourse with the independence-seeking republics. More troublesome still were their clashes with such United States special agents as John B. Prevost. Assigned to Peru and Chile and an overt partisan of the patriot cause, Prevost felt that the first task was to foster sentiments of good will and that toward this end a more flexible and yielding attitude on protection of the neutral rights of commerce was in order.

Victims of cultural shock, as they came into initial contact with South Americans, many United States officers quickly formed adverse opinions about the Chileans and Peruvians. The character of the South Americans, it was often concluded, had been undermined by the Spanish colonial experience and by the ignorance and superstition allegedly associated with Catholicism. One officer complained also of the indecent and unladylike custom of the Chilean ladies of leaving their bosoms largely uncovered. It was generally accepted that it would be a long time before the patriots could gain virtue by learning to conform to United States standards.

Author Billingsley shows that the naval officers of whom he writes were, on the whole, men of quality and ability. If they generally fulfilled their assignments with efficiency and even distinction, they decidedly disappointed the patriots who had anticipated an unquestioningly friendly attitude from the United States and even positive acts of assistance. "When it became apparent that the North American naval forces in the Pacific would not extend aid at the expense of the interests of the United States, their [the patriots'] expectations turned to bitterness and resentment —vestiges of which linger to this day" (p. 209).

FREDERICK B. PIKE
Professor of History
University of Notre Dame

INTERNATIONAL RELATIONS

WILLIAM T. R. FOX and ANNETTE B. FOX. *NATO and the Range of American Choice*. Pp. xii, 352. New York: Columbia University Press, 1967. $7.95.

This book is the latest in the outstanding series sponsored by the Institute of War and Peace Studies of Columbia University. It can be distinguished from the plethora of recent volumes on the North Atlantic Treaty Organization (NATO) in both its orientation and its scholarly objectivity. *NATO and the Range of American Choice* is much more a study of the policy process than an evaluation of past policies, although the latter is implicit. While clearly identifying with their subject, the authors are nonetheless clinical in their analysis and dispassionate in their diagnosis. NATO partisans may well be overwhelmed with the dimension of reforms required to reinvigorate this regional organization, while NATO critics will be reminded of the continuing contribution of this institution to international relations, including the management of the German problem and the restraints that the member-states have placed on each other.

As the title suggests, the Foxes' book is primarily concerned with the impact NATO has had on the United States, and vice versa. It is the fifth in a series of comparable country studies—relations between NATO and Britain, Germany, Belgium, and Norway have been covered in previously published volumes. Separate chapters inquire into the changing American views, regarding the role of NATO and American participation in it. An attempt is made to assess the impact of NATO on the United States foreign policy, and subsequently to identify opportunities the United States missed in benefiting from membership in NATO. The discussion of the United States executive and Congressional decision-making process in respect to NATO is about the best in the book and has implications which reach far beyond United States participation in NATO. In rich detail, the authors illustrate Dean Acheson's observation that government itself is an alliance and its position is determined by what part of the elephant you tap. It would be expected that the impact of the United States on NATO's decision-making, discussed in the penultimate chapter, was sufficiently overwhelming to bring the authors to the recurring observation that the United States has not in any real sense relinquished its independent decision-making role for a collective regional process.

The Foxes have succumbed, less than other NATO scholars, to an implicit optimism concerning the organization's future role. Thus Robert Strausz-Hupé *et al* in *Building the Atlantic World* (1962) added a lengthy and rather unconvincing postscript to explain why they had not anticipated de Gaulle's rejection of Kennedy's Grand Design. For their part, the Foxes concluded their study with the observation that NATO is not the kind of organization which continually poses actual problems for United States officials, just as de Gaulle gave notice that all French forces would be withdrawn from NATO commands. But they may be right for different reasons; dynamic institutions, not moribund ones, are more likely to produce problems. In any event, history will record whether this incisive study by two outstanding scholars is to be valued as a prescriptive landmark for a revitalized NATO or as a comprehensive and definitive obituary of United States relations with the Atlantic organization.

MARTIN B. TRAVIS, JR.
Professor and Chairman
Department of Political Science
State University of New York
Stony Brook

J. D. B. MILLER. *Britain and the Old Dominions.* Pp. 286. Baltimore: Johns Hopkins Press, 1966. $6.50.

Professor Miller opens his book with a statement that has a nostalgic ring: "The Old Dominions are only a small part of the total British experience, but to them Britain is a massive and significant element in their whole range of existence."

Towards the end of his study, he suggests that "Britain's post-war problems of defense and foreign affairs have centered round its decline from the status of a great power to that of a major power ultimately dependent on the United States."

He concludes that "if Britain were attacked now, Australia, New Zealand and Canada would go to its aid; South Africa presumably would not. They would do so with some diminished sense of kinship, and with a fuller awareness of the strains of international politics than in 1914. They would be accompanied by the United States."

His urbane and competent study of the relations between Britain and what used to be the main body of the British Commonwealth is aptly summed up in the following statements: The Commonwealth, no longer British, is not the family affair it was before the First World War; but there is some family feeling left. The Old Dominions are not about to deny their ancestral heritage, but they are very conscious that for protection they must now rely on the United States. Professor Miller reflects these facts. He could not have used accurately the subtitle of a previous book in the series: "Requiem for Empire"; but what he describes could perhaps be titled "The Comonwealth in Decline."

There are sturdy imperialists in the Old Dominions who may dispute, and will certainly deplore, such a suggestion. The Commonwealth now has a secretariat. It has lost Eire and South Africa; but it has gained new members as colonies have become independent in Africa and Asia. It can still serve as a useful means of communication between its diverse communities. But those who dreamed of it becoming a powerful international instrument are now few. Fifty years ago its prophet could give to his book the title "Civitas Dei," and speak of the Commonwealth as the political expression of the City of God; but no one today would compare the Commonwealth with the City of God.

Professor Miller traces the uncertain and reluctant steps by which Australia, New Zealand, and Canada, while acknowledging their debt to the mother country, have developed independent attitudes and policies in realistic acceptance of a changed international situation. South Africa decided

NEW AND RECENT FROM . . .

POLITICS IN TRANSITIONAL SOCIETIES:
The Challenge of Change in Asia, Africa, and Latin America

Edited by HARVEY G. KEBSCHULL, *North Carolina State University at Raleigh.* Analytical and descriptive selections, accompanied by Professor Kebschull's extensive introductory notes, survey the political environment, processes, institutions, groups, ideologies, international relations, and major problems in what are referred to as the "developing areas."

April 1968   469 pages   illustrated   paperback $4.95 (tent.)

THE ART OF DIPLOMACY: The American Experience

THOMAS A. BAILEY, *Stanford University.* A compendium of the principles that have guided and misguided the conduct of diplomacy, each accompanied by brief illustrations from recent American experience, and recounted in a pungent and witty style.

January 1968   303 pages   paperback $2.50

THE SOVIET UNION: An Introduction

GEORGE ALEXANDER LENSEN, *The Florida State University.* A vivid description of contemporary Russia, providing introductory students with basic political, historical, geographic, and economic data on the growth and practice of Soviet communism.

September 1967   181 pages   31 photographs, 2 maps $1.95

WORLD TENSIONS: Conflict and Accommodation

ELTON ATWATER, KENT FORSTER, *and* JAN S. PRYBYLA, *all of The Pennsylvania State University.* An introductory, social science approach to world affairs, presenting the principal sources of—and various means of resolving—international tension and conflict. Instructor's manual available.

July 1967   396 pages   illustrated   paperback $3.95

CASES IN CONSTITUTIONAL LAW, 3rd Edition

Edited by ROBERT E. CUSHMAN, *National Historical Publications Commission; and* ROBERT F. CUSHMAN, *New York University.* Completely revised, reset, and reorganized. The most thoroughgoing and up-to-date casebook available today.

June 1968   1104 pages $10.00 (tent.)

CASES IN CIVIL LIBERTIES

Edited by ROBERT F. CUSHMAN. An inexpensive paperback version of the second part of Cushman and Cushman's *Cases in Constitutional Law, 3rd Edition.*

June 1968   500 pages   paperback $4.95 (tent.)

(Remember: Two annual Cushman supplements—*1964–1966* and *1966–1967*—already are in print.   Each $.95.)

Appleton-Century-Crofts

Kindly mention THE ANNALS *when writing to advertisers*

Kindly mention THE ANNALS *when writing to advertisers*

to drop out of the Commonwealth rather than to accept the censorious judgment of the new Asian and African members. The other Dominions could not defend its racial policies, nor could Britain. It was in South Africa that the Commonwealth idea was born. What survived the withdrawal of South Africa bears little resemblance to the concept as it was developed in pristine innocence of the realities of international power politics.

J. B. CONDLIFFE

Staff Scientist
Stanford Research Institute

JON B. MCLIN. *Canada's Changing Defense Policy, 1957–1963: The Problems of a Middle Power in Alliance.* Pp. xii, 251. Baltimore: Johns Hopkins Press, in co-operation with the Washington Center of Foreign Policy Research, School of Advanced International Studies, Johns Hopkins University, 1967. $8.50.

As Mr. McLin points out, Canada's defense policy has little to do with Canadian security. Canada's security is now rather a function of the strategic balance between the United States and the Soviet Union. Canadian defense forces, however, serve the purpose of supporting Canadian diplomacy, which Mr. McLin hints may have been a bit ambitious. The failure of Canadians, politicians, and public alike to comprehend the role of their defense forces explains in part the confusion and uncertainty of Canadian defense policy, especially during the period covered by this study.

The period 1957–1963 was one of agonizing, if unsystematic, reappraisal of defense policy. Major problems faced the incoming Diefenbaker government at the beginning of the period, some of which remained unsolved when this government was defeated six years later. A first problem boldly tackled, but without realizing all political implications, was that of establishing with the United States a unified air defense command for North America (NORAD). A second was that of re-equipping air defense forces with either the Canadian-developed and highly so-

phisticated "Arrow," but which was not in production, or American-built aircraft which were available and much less costly but perhaps less well suited to Canadian needs. After long equivocation, the "Arrow" was dropped, and the Canadian aircraft industry accordingly felt a severe blow.

Other problems which were handed to the successor government were whether Canadian defense forces should acquire nuclear weapons and whether the air divisions under the North Atlantic Treaty Organization (NATO) command should take on a nuclear role. Also there was the recurring problem of the obligations of partnership in North American defense, illustrated all too vividly in the Cuban missile crisis when the Canadian government was slow to indicate support for the senior partner. Inability to solve defense problems to the satisfaction of Parliament, and the particular inability to decide on nuclear weapons, ultimately brought down the government.

The book contains an interesting discussion of the problems of sharing in defense production between Canada and the United States. Although highly satisfactory arrangements had been in effect during World War II, the problem of achieving a mutually satisfactory scheme proved almost more intractable in peacetime. Mr. McLin gives full credit to Mr. Diefenbaker's government for the initial arrangement which has since been extended and improved.

Mr. McLin has made a major contribution to the literature of Canadian defense policy, which may be parallel to other studies in progress but which is unlikely to be superseded. His book is far from a mere monograph on a few years of policy; it is set in the larger problem of changing technology and of alliance problems in general. It is based on research in seemingly all of the available and significant sources, and it is clearly written with an absence of technical jargon.

The full story of the Diefenbaker years cannot, of course, be told until all the documentary evidence becomes available—under Canadian practice this means at least a third of a century hence. In the meantime, Mr. McLin's volume is a good stand-by.

R. A. MACKAY
Associate Director
School of International Affairs
Carleton University
Ottawa

FREDERICK MERK. *The Oregon Question: Essays in Anglo-American Diplomacy and Politics.* Pp. xiv, 427. Cambridge, Mass.: Harvard University Press, 1967. $7.95.

Developing the basic thesis that decisions of diplomacy and politics result from the interaction of forces at work in domestic and international society, Frederick Merk in these essays presents an illuminating account of the impact of such forces on the six negotiations between Britain and the United States to partition the disputed Oregon territory from 1818 to 1846.

Important to diplomatic historians, the essays also constitute an important segment of the frontier thesis of Frederick Jackson Turner, under whom Merk received his early training. The disturbing influence of the Oregon question on internal politics in both the United States and Britain is appropriately emphasized throughout, and especially in the essays on "British Party Politics and the Oregon Question" and "Presidential Fevers." New archival data are drawn upon to revise the previously accepted portrayal of an intransigent Polk and the concept that British concern over French naval ambitions was a dominant factor in the eventual settlement. Merk brings out the importance of the two "peace coalitions,' in the two countries. In Britain the Peelites and Russellites, seeking abolition of the Corn Laws, were able to defeat the Palmerston extremists; in the United States the Congressional coalition of Southern Democrats —concerned with Mexico, Texas, and Cuba —and peace-loving Whigs was able to dominate the "54° 40' or fight" jingoists.

A special word of appreciation is due to both the author and the Harvard University Press for their joint initiative in putting the book together. Professor Merk, emeritus since 1957, has collected nine of his articles on the Oregon question which have been published in various scholarly journals over a period of thirty years. To these and his 1950 monograph, *Albert Gallatin and the Oregon Problem*, are added four new essays and a lucid résumé of the entire series—altogether some ninety pages of new text. The result is a coherent and valuable contribution to American diplomatic history in particular and to the general study of the interplay of domestic and international relations.

OLIVER BENSON
Research Professor of Political Science
University of Oklahoma

AMERICAN GOVERNMENT AND HISTORY

HENRY J. ABRAHAM. *Freedom and the Court.* Pp. x, 335. New York: Oxford University Press, 1967. $7.50.

In *Freedom and the Court*, Professor Abraham has written a clear, interesting, and valuable book about the Supreme Court and its ongoing interpretations of the Bill of Rights. In particular, he discusses the extent to which the Court has extended the application of the Bill of Rights to the states; developed the notion of due process, substantively and procedurally; defined the limits of freedom of speech and press; refined the doctrine of a Wall of Separation between Church and State; and applied the notion of human equality in the Fourteenth Amendment, especially to the exploited Negroes.

Professor Abraham upholds three theses: (1) Since Congress and the States have generally failed to implement the Bill of Rights, the Supreme Court has been compelled to accept the responsibility of explaining the meaning of these rights and protecting them against persistent attempts to erode and destroy them. (2) The problem for the Court has usually been that of drawing a viable and useful line between the general welfare of the people of the United States and the rights of individuals. (3) The Court has, in general, arrived at judicial decisions which have, in the main, favored liberty and equality. While main-

taining these theses, he also maintains that the Court, as a whole, has reflected "even as it reveals the nature of American society."

While Professor Abraham seeks to give an appearance of uncommitted objectivity, of merely stating the facts, there are moments when his feelings get the better of him. At such moments, he becomes highly critical of the Court as in its interpretation of the nonestablishment clause respecting religion. At other moments, he becomes its fervent apologist. He admits that the clear and present danger doctrine raises "problems of great magnitude," yet he affirms both the Court's realism and common sense.

There are two intriguing aspects of this book. One aspect is Professor Abraham's emphasis upon the necessity that the Court find its way between the language of the Bill of Rights and the unavoidable needs of a rapidly changing society. This way he calls the "dividing line" between social welfare—which he identifies at times with the national interest and at other times with the poor, the oppressed, the many, and the underprivileged—and the welfare of the individual—usually conceived as nonconforming, often unpleasant, and even criminal—or the minority group. One would think, therefore, that the question of liberty of expression would be a question of the "dividing line." This is not so! It is a "philosophic" question: "Will the forbidding of freedom of expression further or hamper the realization of liberal democratic ideals?" (p. 271). Apparently, Professor Abraham considers the forbidding of freedom of expression a way of realizing "liberal democratic ideals." In this case, he seems to transform "liberal democratic ideals," whatever they are, into eternal absolutes unconditioned by the needs and social circumstances of a people.

The other aspect is Professor Abraham's indifference, as a whole, to the contradictory principles used by the members of the Supreme Court in arriving at their decisions, majority, minority, or unanimous. For example, he points to three conflicting criteria used in freedom of expression cases: (1) clear and present danger, (2) bad tendency, and (3) clear and present danger plus

imminence of evil. He does not mention Frankfurter's balancing of national security against individual rights. He also points to three conflicting principles in religious cases: (1) strict separation, (2) governmental neutrality, and (3) governmental accommodation. I should think that this would pose a pretty problem in juristic methodology: What legal and social purposes do such conflicting principles serve? Do they help in drawing the line?

RUBIN GOTESKY
Professor of Philosophy
Northern Illinois University

WILLIAM V. SHANNON. *The Heir Apparent: Robert Kennedy and the Struggle for Power.* Pp. 309. New York: The Macmillan Company, 1967. $5.95.

In the few short years since he began to manage his brother's 1960 campaign for the presidency, a library of books has grown up about Robert F. Kennedy. At first there were hasty biographies about tough, ruthless Bobby, the Kennedy "hatchet man." Then came books about Kennedy as "racketbuster" and singleminded pursuer of Jimmy Hoffa, followed soon by "inside" stories of the crusading young Attorney General and his fight for civil rights. When the President was killed at Dallas, a new spate of books dealt with Bobby as an ambitious stand-in. Then came a new run of biographies as Kennedy moved into New York politics and ran for the Senate. Finally, when the Senator was forty and drawing unprecedented crowds of the admiring and the curious wherever he went in the world, he began to be taken seriously as a major force in his own right. Now appears the first book about him to be taken seriously.

William V. Shannon, presently a member of the editorial board of *The New York Times,* is a veteran, skilled reporter, and commentator on Washington and New York politics. His book suffers to a disquieting degree from journalistic tricks—a tortured analogy between the Kennedys and the Bonapartes and excessive attention to the romantic "Bonnie Prince Charlie" nonsense about a Kennedy "Restoration." But in other respects *The Heir Apparent* is a perceptive, balanced, and always readable study of a phenomenon without precedent in American political history. Kennedy's anxious catering to youth, which Shannon criticizes, is more than matched by an unceasing effort to come to grips with the real issues of a troubled America: riots, poverty, Vietnam, and the credibility of elected officials. Bobby Kennedy has now become Robert Kennedy, and Shannon, like millions of other Americans, believes him destined for the White House, not as a replica of his brother but as a politician and statesman fully qualified in his own right and on his own record.

That record includes an immense achievement both as an executive and as a political leader: the great log of civil rights cases he instigated and fought as Attorney General; his work on the civil rights statute of 1964; his trouble-shooting missions in Indonesia, Latin America, and Europe; his successful campaign for the Senate; his quiet efforts to improve life in Bedford-Stuyvesant through nonprofit corporations; his program for dealing with the ghettos; and his moderate, incisive criticism of the Administration's Vietnam policy.

The same record also includes, as Shannon demonstrates with careful detail, a series of failures in dealing with the Democratic party politics of New York State and city and, of lesser consequence, a serious mishandling of the Manchester affair. The latter, Shannon believes, was owing more to fierce loyalty to Jacqueline Kennedy than to poor judgment. At any rate, Shannon is at his best in his study of New York politics and Kennedy's struggle to unite the Democratic party without making enemies of important factions. His successes have been only nominal, except for his dramatic intervention in a primary to defeat a candidate for surrogate who had been endorsed by both the Democratic and Republican organizations. His failures have come from uncertainty and inadequate attention, and, perhaps, from the inherent intractability of reformers and organization politicians when confronting each other. Kennedy has shown such immense popular drawing power that the Democrats of New York are his so long as

it is support for himself he seeks, but Shannon argues that it will have to be the national scene on which he can hope for organizational leadership.

Shannon's book inevitably loses something of its force when he comes to speculate on Robert Kennedy's future. He is the victim of the contemporaneity of the subject. In the few weeks since publication, for example, it has become evident that President Johnson will not dump Vice-President Humphrey in order to put Kennedy on the 1968 ticket, an eventuality Shannon thought possible if not likely. At the same time, the polls show Kennedy's popularity at a much greater peak (December 1967) than it was when Shannon's work went to press.

But *The Heir Apparent* deserves to be read as something more than a passing bit of popular journalism. Shannon has done a penetrating study of contemporary politics, useful both to the general reader and to students. And he has illuminated both the character and the potential of a man who is a good deal more than part of a legend floating in the nimbus of sentimentality. As Shannon says, "once he identifies an injustice, Kennedy loathes it with rare intensity and works relentlessly against it." Such a man, in the context of Kennedy's accidental advantages, will be a power in American life for years to come, whether or not he becomes President.

STUART GERRY BROWN
Professor of American Studies
University of Hawaii

JACK E. HOLMES. *Politics in New Mexico.* Pp. xi, 335. Albuquerque: University of New Mexico Press, 1967. $7.95.

Jack Holmes' book, *Politics in New Mexico,* is in the tradition of great Ph.D. theses. There are so few today that the story of how Holmes went about accomplishing his task is worth relating.

Holmes came to the University of New Mexico, as an instructor in government, after World War II. He had just completed his course work for his doctor's degree at the University of Chicago, but had not yet selected his thesis subject, which in time came to be the politics of New Mexico.

From the University of New Mexico, Holmes went to the state capital to head the newly revived Legislative Reference Service. Once before, the Reference Service had been started and abandoned, because it had been ineffective. Under Holmes it became a recognized asset by legislators, and it is now a permanent feature of the state's government.

On leaving the Legislative Reference Service, Holmes headed a brain trust for the Republican party of New Mexico, and the party scored an upset victory over the Democrats and elected a Republican governor. Holmes was appointed chief of the State Tax Commission, but after two years resigned and returned to the academic world, where he has been since.

Over a period of almost twenty years, Holmes continued to work persistently on his thesis. Fortunately, the University of Chicago did not impose on him a time limit. The Social Science Research Council helped him along with a grant-in-aid in support of his research. The result is, without doubt, the most significant book on New Mexico politics that has been written to date.

The volume represents an incredible amount of work over a long period of time and contains thousands of hard-won observations gained in daily contact with politicians and other operators in the New Mexico political scene. It is written in an urbane style and is enriched with salty good humor. It is also an optimistic book, because Holmes likes politicians, loves New Mexico, and believes that the state has the capacity to produce "a few new increments of social justice."

In planning his study, Holmes took as a model the works of V. O. Key, Jr., particularly *Southern Politics*. He takes a number of Key's theorems and tests them against the background of New Mexico politics to ascertain their applicability. Essentially, what Holmes does is to trace the history of New Mexico politics since statehood in 1912. However, instead of using a strictly historical approach, he traces the development of the legislature,

the executive branch, and the political parties, and depicts the interacting influence of each upon the others. Each state election gets a careful analysis, and the book is replete with enough tables, charts, and graphs to satisfy the most quantitative mind.

For the serious student of politics in New Mexico, the book is a gold mine of information. For the casual reader it will prove to be a bit tedious.

THOMAS C. DONNELLY
President
New Mexico Highlands University
Las Vegas

JAMES R. HOOKER. *Black Revolutionary: George Padmore's Path from Communism to Pan-Africanism.* Pp. 168. New York: Frederick A. Praeger, 1967. $5.50.

George Padmore (1902–1959) was an articulate, fervent, and tireless anticolonialist: He organized pressure groups and occasions of protest ceaselessly; a pamphleteer of energy, his tracts include book-length arguments of lasting importance; as a journalist, his outpouring—predominantly in the American Negro press—chronicled the growth of freedom movements in Africa and Asia long before such an interest was fashionable; finally, after directing his powers specifically to the liberation of Africa, Padmore spent the last two years of his life advising Kwame Nkrumah, a one-time protégé, in Ghana.

Padmore's kaleidoscopic life demanded a biographer. In Trinidad, where he was born, his secondary education and a brief career as a shipping news reporter left him with ambitions which were hardly satisfied by the opportunities then available to inhabitants of the island. After a conventional marriage, he abandoned his wife and child and, in time, his real name, and began first a medical and then a legal education at Fisk, and New York and Howard Universities in the United States. (At Howard he was well acquainted, among others, with Dr. Ralph Bunche and Benjamin Nnamdi Azikiwe.) By this time, he was a dedicated and obedient Communist, presumably having joined the Party because of its favorable racial posture. And for a time, particularly at Howard, Padmore demonstrated striking oratorical and agitational talents in the service of the Party.

In 1929 Padmore went to the Soviet Union and stayed. He became—for show purposes—a member of the Moscow City Soviet, and was often employed on international errands by members of the ruling echelon of the Communist party. (He wryly recalled fetching British razor blades for Molotov.) On behalf of the Comintern, he ran front groups and edited front publications in Vienna and Hamburg, resided briefly in Paris—where he began a long and productive friendship with Nancy Cunard—and then settled in London.

By this time (1932), Padmore had become a "petty bourgeois nationalist deviationist"—his formal denunciation by Communist-controlled publications took place in 1934—and an accomplished spokesman and publicizer of anticolonialism. His most influential writing and organizational work dates from the succeeding years—particularly the period of World War II. He was in touch with several leaders of African independence movements and maintained useful contacts among British radicals and members of the left-wing of the Labour party. He was largely responsible for calling the important Fifth Pan-African Congress in Manchester. At the end of World War II, he also knew and wrote about the aspirations of Ho Chi-Minh.

It is evident from Professor Hooker's account and from what is generally known about Padmore that he has a very real place in the recent history of the rise of self-assertion of dependent peoples. But it remains difficult to assess the precise extent or significance of his influence. Professor Hooker, who has otherwise managed with great industry to make a coherent whole of the confusing strands of Padmore's life, has unfortunately found it equally impossible to assess his subject's importance as a personality, an organizer, or a theoretician of anticolonialism.

ROBERT I. ROTBERG
Assistant Professor of History
Harvard University

JANE DEHART MATHEWS. *The Federal Theatre, 1935–1939: Plays, Relief, and Politics.* Pp. xii, 342. Princeton, N.J.: Princeton University Press, 1967. $8.50.

One of the paradoxes of American history is that this nation's only large-scale experiment with subsidized art came during the Depression of the 1930's. With the nation flat on its economic back, the New Deal, under the aegis of the Works Project Administration (WPA), financed four relief programs for unemployed professionals in music, writing, art, and the theater. While the major thrust of each was relief for the unemployed, each also conducted an extensive creative program that brought more culture to more people in a shorter period of time than anything the federal government has either done or contemplated in the years since.

Mrs. Mathews' excellent volume is a thorough recounting of the brief life of the Federal Theatre Project, the most exciting and undoubtedly the most controversial of these unique federal programs. In little more than three hundred pages of text, she succeeds in weaving together four major themes that are vital for an understanding of the program: first, the very considerable artistic accomplishments of the Project itself; second, the administrative complexities inherent in an unprecedented federal program and exacerbated by the unique requirements of the theater; third, the multiple conflicts among artists, bureaucrats, trade unionists, and politicians; fourth, the story of Hallie Flanagan, the remarkable professor of drama who left the campus to run the Theatre Project for the WPA and who seems to personify in herself all the glory and much of the agony that was the New Deal.

Well written and thoroughly researched, Mrs. Mathews' book is a veritable model for the kind of monographic study we need in much larger number before we can fully understand Franklin Roosevelt's New Deal. Of interest to all serious students of the Depression era, the volume should also be required reading for anyone currently interested in government subsidization of the arts. At the very least, a reading of Mrs. Mathews' book will indicate the range of problems which can reasonably be expected to recur, in fact, they have recurred if we consider the way in which Congress has treated the National Endowment for the Arts.

The book, unhappily, has its weaknesses. In her discussion of the Living Newspaper, the most controversial Federal Theatre unit, Mrs. Mathews is confused about the position of its director, Morris Watson. Watson was not the Vice-President of the American Newspaper Guild, but one of several engaged in organizing activities. He was available for full-time work with the Federal Theatre having just been fired by the Associated Press because of his union activities. This is hardly a minor point since it explains the radical, pro-labor militancy of *Injunction Granted,* one of the Living Newspaper productions, in a more realistic way than Mrs. Mathews' assertion that the radicalism of the play stemmed from an unnamed crew of "Young Turks." An important omission occurs in her restaging of the storm that raged around the production of the play for children, *The Revolt of the Beavers,* characterized at the time as "Marxism à la Mother Goose." There is no explanation for the attendance at the play's opening of such major New York theatrical critics as Brooks Atkinson or Robert Coleman. More important, the author does not even make an educated guess as to who paid for and distributed the copies of Atkinson's damaging review which showed up on the desk of "every congressman in Washington," and contributed to legislative bias against the Federal Theatre. Someone was obviously out to get the project; but who was he? I was surprised at the omission from the Bibliography of works such as Elmer Rice's autobiographical *Minority Report,* considering Rice's importance to the project in its earliest months, Mordecai Gorelik's *New Theatres for Old,* a brilliant piece of theater history, and Mary McCarthy's *Theatre Chronicles 1937–1962,* which contains a brief but brilliant analysis of the reasons for the Federal Theatre's ultimate demise.

Much more subjective is my feeling that the book lacks that quality of immediacy

and excitement generated by an earlier, undocumented history of the Federal Theatre, Mrs. Flanagan's *Arena.* Mrs. Mathews' book adds much to the information in that volume, but it does not supersede the earlier work. Both are necessary for a complete understanding of this important New Deal agency.

One final jarring note must be added. Considering the excellent job the author has done on the text, the notes, and the Bibliography, the Index is an insult to anyone trying to find items of interest after a first reading.

ALAN SCHAFFER
Associate Professor of History
Michigan State University

ROBERT F. WESSER. *Charles Evans Hughes: Politics and Reform in New York, 1905–1910.* Pp. xvi, 366. Ithaca, N.Y.: Cornell University Press, 1967. $8.50.

This painstaking biography of Charles Evans Hughes as Governor of New York contributes much to the historiography of the State from 1905 to 1910. With respect to depth and to objective analysis of the governorship, it is a better book than Pusey's Pulitzer Prize-winning biography of Hughes. Professor Wesser does not see leaders and factions in terms of black and white or "right" and "wrong." And, at last an observer of the period does not lump James W. Wadsworth, Jr., the powerful Speaker of the Assembly, with the other "bosses" of the Republican party, many of them admittedly "unduly partisan." Also, the author examined primary source material yet unused in the assessment of Hughes and the period in New York.

Professor Wesser concludes that although Governor Hughes was "an ineffective party leader and party reformer," his administration as Governor succeeded because of public support. At a time when the word "politics" was everywhere distasteful, Hughes' appeal to popular sentiment brought support for such legislation as the 1907 Public Service Commission bill, the 1908 banking laws, race-track regulation, and the 1910 Workmen's Compensation legislation. The author also notes much housing, health, sanitation, labor, and ever-important administrative reform in the Hughes era. It is hard to disbelieve the book's conclusion that Hughes was "one of those exceptional public servants who functioned as an agent for the reform of political, economic, and social disorders."

Charles Evans Hughes makes for exciting reading. His "David-like" struggle against the insurance and utility giants; his quick ascendency to high office; his independence of the party organization; his confrontation with inept administrators; his forthright appeals to the public; and his absolute commitment to his programs gave the author an edge in writing a good biography. Although Professor Wesser plans a trilogy with two additional works covering periods immediately following the Hughes era, one hopes that he will return to Hughes to give the rest of his life the same in-depth treatment this period of his governorship received. Author and reader alike must be curious to know what new materials might reveal to explain how this great reformer became one of the "nine old men" of the 1930's.

MARTIN L. FAUSOLD
Professor of American History
    and Government
State University College at Geneseo
New York

DAVID HERRESHOFF. *American Disciples of Marx: From the Age of Jackson to the Progressive Era.* Pp. 215. Detroit: Wayne State University Press, 1967. $7.95.

In recent years a number of historians have challenged what John Higham called the "Cult of the American Consensus," an interpretation prevailing in the 1950's which pretty much homogenized our past. David Herreshoff is among those who rightly discern in American history objective tension as well as subjective anxiety, fundamental conflict as well as shadow-boxing, bitter protest as well as empty reform rhetoric, and challenge and response that cannot properly be comprehended as a mere charade. As the title suggests, Mr. Herreshoff is concerned with American

disciples of Marx in the nineteenth century and more especially with their early attempts to imbue the American labor movement with the socialist vision. The focus is almost entirely on only four men: Brownson, Weydemeyer, Sorge, and De Leon. Alas, the author's reach so far exceeds his grasp as to render virtually valueless what might have been a very illuminating study.

For one thing, this is a sloppy book. Some misspellings are obviously typesetter slips, but perhaps the author is responsible for different spellings of the same name in the text, the Index, and the Bibliography. The Index is inaccurate. Some quotes are inexact, though carelessness rather than deliberate distortion is certainly the explanation. The use of periods to indicate omissions in the middle and at the end of quotes is haphazard. And is it no longer customary to italicize the name of a ship?

For a second thing, Mr. Herreshoff is billed as a professor of English and as a poet, yet the writing is uninspired. It is neither smooth and clear nor stabbing and arresting, but simply murky and leaden. The meaning of such terms as "progressive" and "left-liberal's," as used by the author, is obscure to this reviewer. Moreover, considering the contingency of the times, there is a hazard in such sentences as: "The assertion of constitutional rights through direct action, first proposed by Mrs. Woodhull, is *now* [reviewer's italics] part of the tactical arsenal of such militant organizations as the Student Nonviolent Coordinating Committee, the Congress of Racial Equality, and the Southern Christian Leadership Conference" (p. 88).

Thirdly, the footnoting is curious and ultimately exasperating. There seems to be no logical explanation why some quotes are documented and others are not. It is, therefore, often impossible to tell if the author is drawing on an original document or secondary work. Indeed, it is impossible to discern any source for some statements and quotes. Moreover, the citations are so abbreviated as to be difficult to use.

The mystery concerning Mr. Herreshoff's research is not cleared up by the Bibliography, a casual, incomplete listing of items, organized on no more logical principle than the alphabet. If it is unfair to characterize the research as shallow and excessively dependent on a few published studies, particularly those by Schlueter, Obermann, and Kuhn, then Mr. Herreshoff should have taken greater pains with his footnotes and bibliography.

The volume is dedicated to several individuals and to "my advisees of the Wayne State Afro-American Action Committee, Committee to End the War in Vietnam, Friends of the Student Nonviolent Coordinating Committee, Students for a Democratic Society, W.E.B. Du Bois Club, and Young Socialist Alliance." This dedication makes all the more inexplicable the fact that the book strikes this reviewer as being not only thin in substance, but also as being drained of tight analysis, intense passion, and bold interpretation.

ROBERT MOATS MILLER
Professor of History
University of North Carolina

WOODROW WILSON. *The Papers of Woodrow Wilson*, Vol. III: *1884–1885*. Edited by Arthur S. Link, in association with John Wells Davidson and David W. Hirst, in consultation with T. H. Vail Motter, and assisted by John E. Little. Pp. xviii, 648. Princeton, N.J.: Princeton University Press, 1967. $15.00.

This third volume of Wilson's unfolding collected papers is probably unique among the writings of any major political figure in our history. To some degree, its theme and partial contents have already been displayed in *The Priceless Gift: The Love Letters of Woodrow Wilson and Ellen Axson Wilson* (1962), which was edited by Wilson's daughter Eleanor Wilson McAdoo. Yet the editors have been well advised to reproduce them in full and to subject them to thorough scholarly implementation.

Wilson was almost unparalleled in his dependence on his loved ones, laying his uncertainties before them and responding sensitively to their real or imagined feelings. He can be, and has been, viewed as weak and temperamental, but such an interpretation would not explain how he became a famous academic figure and President of the United States. It seems more helpful to view him as the product of a firm and extraordinarily well-integrated society and academic community, and as one who forged a career out of his own profound intuitions and judgments. Wilson had turned from law as it was beyond him and unfruitful, though for others it was a road to the political influence he himself coveted. At Johns Hopkins he listened to the lectures of Herbert Baxter Adams, Richard T. Ely, and others. But though he hungered for status and longed for marriage—he was, after all, twenty-eight years old and still at school—he read almost randomly in literature, as well as in political theory and history. And his almost daily letters to his fiancée were as much concerned for his feelings as for his future.

Others of Wilson's papers include careful notes on bimetallism and reflections on the reality as well as the theory of constitutional government. Wilson joins the American Historical Association, but he also indites verses and discusses literature. Wilson considers himself a literary man, and here he feels free to despise Omar Khayyám's "miserable philosophy." He also patronizes George Washington Cable's negative attitude toward secession, which, as a loyal southerner, he feels free to defend.

His basic ideas he can express with high clarity, as in his contempt for "committee government," as compared with parliamentary government. The latter is "direct party government, Congressional government, indirect; in the one, responsibility rests upon a compact ministry all of one party, in the other, upon a disintegrate ministry of Committees which are made up of members of both parties and all factions, and which . . . do not come into direct contact with the practical affairs of administration" (p. 224).

In that year of 1884, however, Wilson was so excited about the presidential contest between James G. Blaine and Grover Cleveland that he was "desperately uneasy" and had little rest until he knew that "the right philosophy of practical politics" was in control. He expounds to his Ellen what he sees as the significance of Cleveland's triumph: "Overthrow is a much ruder task than achievement; and a party which became crystallized for the purpose of overthrow would not be fit for the execution of great comprehensive plans. We are fortunate in having overcome our enemies *before* we became organized *for that purpose*. Our *sympathy* is thereby established and we are free from the embarrassing necessity—the impossible task—of converting an army of conquest into a parliament of legislators" (pp. 410–411).

All this is apropos of Cleveland's victory. The idealist can ignore Tammany Hall and the Democratic trimmers and can see the Republican party as the "most unscrupulous political 'machine' that ever existed under free institutions." He can perceive himself as part of a progressive party "bound together by common opinions, common affections, and common interests." All of this would sound like mere rant did it not come from one who would later give voice to such a party and lead it into the New Freedom. Wilson was a spokesman for large social forces; so much, at least, is clear in retrospect. Here we see them being nurtured by hopes, victories, ideals, and, above all, preparations.

LOUIS FILLER
Professor of American Civilization
Antioch College
Yellow Springs
Ohio

REMBERT W. PATRICK. *The Reconstruction of the Nation*. Pp. xi, 324. New York: Oxford University Press, 1967. $7.50.

Reconstruction was national, with more of an era of good stealing outside the former Confederate States, where there was more to steal and where casualties of Indians, cowboys, sheepherders, miners, and strikers far outnumbered victims in the South. Any resemblance between a portrayal of the nation during Reconstruction and a volume which ventures beyond Washington, D.C. for only a few chapters remains coincidental.

Canonized carpetbaggers ride white horses, reversing the Dunning legend, as entrepreneurs "belatedly" discover their Republican party, which charges Democrats with corruption, orates aid to the overseas oppressed, and does not pack the Court when it coincidentally adds two justices who reverse the legal tender verdict, all behind the facade of a "bewildered general . . . without understanding . . . misled by scheming friends." Thaddeus Stevens, though "sincere, philanthropic, concerned," wants the president murdered, and "spotless, sincere" Charles Sumner becomes "vicious" when he attacks U. S. Grant, whose shiny halo is not tarnished by his virulent anti-Catholicism —that he and his vice-presidents had been Know Nothings is unmentioned. Andrew Johnson is held responsible for his own impeachment; if he had compromised, he "could . . . , would . . . , would" have succeeded.

But, were white-supremacy ideology, violence, and intimidation confined to the South? Or were incompetent instructors, elections as personality contests, public prayers, puritanism, orthodoxy, and failure to live up to professed faith found only in the South? Were only Reconstruction legislatures purchasable, or was this the only time that the curtain is pulled back? Were whites exempt from poll tax? Were not some Black Codes copied from New England apprenticeship statutes? Were Bible Belt Baptists believers in a flat world, and were not most Episcopal clergy educated? Were Indians "marauding," isolationists restricted to the West, and embezzlements errors of judgment? Were Republican victories overwhelming when changes in voting in salient states, from 1864 to 1880 of 32, 856, 28, 862, 89, 835, 116, and 10,518, a total of 162,196 votes, would have given Democrats five presidents?

As in Reconstruction, white is might, especially if Republican, and glittering generalities, armies of adjectives, pejorative or hagiological, irrelevant accessories, and antiquated inaccuracies keep the underprivileged under the Radical gravy train to graft and glory. To charge that "Booker T. Washington riveted the iron mask of caste on his people," while blurring the Republican retreat from the Negro, slurring slave fidelity, denigrating Negro religion, and regretting Haiti was not annexed, recalls the author's comment: "Fair evaluation was beyond the capabilities of nineteenth century Americans . . . the historian could not escape personal, racial and religious prejudice." But the volume is not dated 1877.

CHARLES G. HAMILTON

Editor
Crossroads
Aberdeen
Mississippi

ROBERT G. HARTJE. *Van Dorn: The Life and Times of a Confederate General.* Pp. xiii, 359. Nashville: Vanderbilt University Press, 1967. $8.95.

"I feel a greatness in my soul—and if I can make it take shape and walk forth, it *may* be seen and felt." These words were written by Earl Van Dorn—Mississippian, graduate of West Point, professional soldier, and soon-to-be Confederate general—early in 1861. Van Dorn burned for glory but never achieved it. He commanded armies on several fields during the war and at least twice seemed at the point of grasping victory, but on each occasion something intervened to swing the prize away from him. He was relegated finally to relatively minor commands, but he might have risen again had he not been killed in 1863. His death was ignominious—he was shot by a civilian doctor who thought that the general was too friendly with his wife. His career was one of the most unusual on either side during the war.

It is a career that Professor Robert Hartje thinks is worth recounting. Hartje argues that the generals who fail are as deserving of attention as those who succeed. The failing generals can tell us much about various areas—the culture of the society that produced them, that society's way of waging war, and the war in which the generals engaged and whose outcome they influenced. Accordingly, Hartje essayed to write the first biography of Van Dorn.

Showing a good sense of proportion, the author recites Van Dorn's career up to the Civil War in less than a hundred pages. In this short space, however, the influences that formed Van Dorn the soldier are cogently presented. Thus Hartje emphasizes that at West Point and in the regular army Van Dorn learned much, perhaps too much, about small-union tactics and relatively little about directing large-scale operations.

The bulk of the biography is devoted to the war. Hartje traces in detail Van Dorn's battle career: in his first command in Texas; in Arkansas, where at Pea Ridge or Elkhorn Tavern he almost won an important victory; at the defense of Corinth, where he served under Beauregard; in Mississippi in 1862, where he conducted the first defense of Vicksburg; and in the attack on Corinth late in 1862, where again he nearly won a victory. The Corinth operation was his last big command. His superiors, disillusioned with him, restricted him to commanding cavalry. He destroyed Grant's base at Holly Springs, Mississippi and delayed Grant's Vicksburg offensive. He was then shifted to Tennessee to command the gray cavalry under Bragg and seemed on the point of recouping his reputation when he met his death. Concerning the assassination, Hartje thinks there are some loose ends that cannot be tied up but is inclined to accept the traditional account.

Hartje is coldly critical in measuring Van Dorn's generalship. He thinks that his man was brave, daring, and imaginative but lacked some quality of character that prevented him from succeeding. Van Dorn usually overlooked an important detail in planning a battle, and this oversight caused him to fail. This shortcoming was inherent in Van Dorn's nature, the author argues convincingly, and was also, and here the argument is not so convincing, the product of something in Southern culture. Hartje was handicapped in analyzing Van Dorn because of a shortage of personal papers. He has, netherthless, written a commendable biography of a man who needed a biography.

T. HARRY WILLIAMS

Boyd Professor of History
Louisiana State University

ULYSSES S. GRANT. *The Papers of Ulysses S. Grant*, Vol. I: *1837–1861*. Edited by John Y. Simon. Pp. xxxix, 458. Carbondale and Edwardsville: Southern Illinois University Press, 1967. $15.00.

The reputation of Ulysses S. Grant—as a man, as a general, and perhaps even as a president—appears to be on the upswing. In the past he has often been pictured as a dull, plodding sort, who managed, with luck and superior forces, to succeed in war and who then failed ignominiously in politics. Recently, Kenneth P. Williams and other military historians have burnished his once-fading fame as a soldier, and the literary critic Edmund Wilson has reminded us of Mark Twain's judgment that Grant "possessed an admirable literary gift and style." Now the projected publication of *The Papers of Ulysses S. Grant*, which will run eventually to some fifteen volumes, including a new, annotated edition of the *Personal Memoirs*, promises to make him much better understood and increasingly admired.

The first volume, covering the years 1837–1861, presents a rather scanty record for so long a period. Nevertheless, the materials are more than sufficient to correct the image left by biographers who dismissed his antebellum life as merely "forty years of failure." Sketches, paintings, and water colors, done while he was a West Point cadet, and here reproduced, reveal an unexpected artistic talent in the young Grant. Personal letters, especially those to Julia Dent, his sweetheart and then his wife, show an eye for both scenery and humanity, as well as a heart capable of warm devotion. Reports of action in the Mexican War indicate an imperturbability that was later to characterize him in the Civil War. Of his very first battle experience he wrote: "There is no great sport in having bullets flying about one in ev[e]ry direction but I find they have less horror when among them than when in anticipation." Accounts of his prospects, after his resignation from the army, suggest that he never felt crushed by his misfortunes, even when, in 1860, he was reduced to clerking in his brother's Galena leather store.

All the items are reproduced, so far as possible, in their exact, original form—except for the excision of a few brief passages from some of the Mexican War letters reflecting on the Mexican people—an excision requested by representatives of the Grant family, who made the manuscripts available. The volume is handsomely designed, as well as excellently edited and copiously annotated. Historians interested in Grant and his times will look forward to the appearance of the volumes yet to come.

RICHARD N. CURRENT
Distinguished Professor of
  American History
University of North Carolina
Greensboro

JOHN C. CALHOUN. *The Papers of John C. Calhoun*, Vol. III: *1818–1819*. Edited by Edwin Hemphill. Pp. xxxiii, 772. Columbia: University of South Carolina Press, for the South Caroliniana Society, 1967. $10.00.

This third volume of the Calhoun Papers is meticulously edited. It is a large volume, including the papers of less than a year, most of which might now be considered insignificant, but the question of significance is a highly controversial one, and future historians may be grateful that the editor included such a mass of source material. Unfortunately, very few of the letters included were written by Calhoun himself. The editor has written an excellent introduction, and he has prefaced the letters for each month with a brief guide to their contents. He has pointed out what no biographer has noted that for a large part of the summer of 1818 when the President and Cabinet officers were away from Washington, the thirty-five-year-old Calhoun served as Acting President, and that in performing the duties both of Secretary of War and Secretary of Navy he anticipated the unification of the military forces under the Secretary of Defense.

Several events occurred in Calhoun's administration of the War Department during 1818–1819 that are relevant today. Calhoun sent out Major Stephen Long on a mission to explore the West that presaged the federal government's recent support of space exploration. Also, Calhoun had to deal with student protest, as the result of a petition from a committee of West Point cadets against the conduct of one of the professors. His decision that a group protest was against the maintenance of proper discipline caused the young cadets to reject the Secretary of War's ruling, preferring to sacrifice their interest for the sake of what they regarded as their honor. Calhoun was very modern in his ideas of reorganizing the General Staff and in ordering a generous supply of vegetables to be added to the diet of the soldiers, and in his advocacy of the federal government building national roads, to which Monroe and, surprisingly John Quincy Adams, opposed on constitutional grounds. Much of his attention was devoted to Indian treaties, the control of Indian trade, the establishment of schools by missionaries among them, and the supervision of the conduct of the Seminole War. In the exercise of this latter duty, he had to deal with the problem of Jackson's seizure of the Spanish forts. Calhoun's action in this crisis has been the subject of great historical controversy, to which this volume contributes valuable information in noting that at the height of the Congressional debate on censuring the general, Mrs. Calhoun invited him to dinner and wrote, "I am sorry Congress have abused him so much respecting the Seminole War, as I am confident that he acted to the best of his knowledge, and further, by censuring him, they must [also censure] my husband, as he directed him in one of his letters to act to the best of his knowledge."

CLEMENT EATON

Professor of History
University of Kentucky

MAURICE G. BAXTER. *Daniel Webster and the Supreme Court.* Pp. ix, 265. Amherst: University of Massachusetts Press, 1966. $6.75.

In 1901, Philadelphia lawyer Richard C. Dale declared: "In a sense, the lawyer receives the law from the bench, but in a larger sense, the law announced from the Bench is that which the bench has received from the bar." Daniel Webster, lawyer, politician, and legislator, furnishes an impressive illustration of Dale's dictum. During the first half-century of the Republic, when precedents were scarce, courts, including the United States Supreme Court, relied heavily upon arguments of counsel.

Professor Baxter's purpose is to examine the extent and nature of Webster's impact. The statistics of cases won and lost are in Webster's favor, but the author is disinclined to measure the lawyer's achievement in terms of "mere numbers." Quite rightly, he stresses more-subtle criteria. Sharing Chief Justice Marshall's primary values—national supremacy and property rights—Webster's influence seemed greater during the great Chief Justice's regime than in Taney's. In certain of his major opinions, Marshall unblushingly accepted Webster's arguments as his own. But there was such a mutuality of viewpoints as to make it difficult to determine who was influencing whom. In John Marshall's Court, arguments in support of national power and property rights suggest carrying coals to Newcastle.

"Esteem grew to veneration," Mr. Baxter comments, "and after Marshall's death, Webster could not mention the Virginian's name or decisions without recalling his pre-eminent judicial qualities. With the passage of time, Marshall seemed to symbolize for Webster the Constitution itself."

With the election of Andrew Jackson to the Presidency in 1828, and the appointment of Roger Brooke Taney as Marshall's successor, Webster despaired of the future. The Supreme Court was "gone." "Almost everything is gone," Webster grieved, "or seems rapidly going." But the nation survived, in part perhaps, because Webster was still carrying on.

One is naturally led to ponder the secret of Webster's power and influence. It has been customary to stress his forensic skill, and, surely, it was for his day unmatched. But there may be other contributing factors. From Mr. Baxter's pages, one gathers that Webster's training for the law was liberating. At a time when Blackstone and Coke were the highly revered texts, Webster made only a "half-hearted" perusal of them. "A 'student at law' I certainly was not," Webster confessed, "unless 'Allan Ramsay's Poems' and Female Quixotism will pass for law books."

"We learn the low recourse to attorney-ism," Webster went on, "when we should learn the conceptions, the reasonings and the opinions of Cicero and Murray."

One may query certain of Professor Baxter's judgments. He leaves the impression that Chief Justice Marshall's concept of judicial review was broad and Taney's relatively narrow. "Judicial review," he writes, "did not become so weak and useless as Taney's critics foresaw." The fact is that substitution of Marshall's concept of the Court, as an organ of the national government which is under obligation to maintain its supremacy, for Taney's notion that the Court serves as an umpire between two sovereignties expanded the Court's role. Taney substituted judicial supremacy for Marshall's doctrine of national supremacy. In cases involving conflict between the national government and the states, Marshall asked only one question: does Congress have the power? Taney asked two questions: does Congress have the power? do the States have any rights precluding Congressional action?

"As the Constitution itself does not draw the line," Chief Justice Taney observed, "the question is necessarily one for judicial decision, and depending altogether on the words of the Constitution." But the Constitution's words draw no line either. Supreme Court Justices, under Taney's leadership, assumed the responsibility for doing what the framers deliberately left undone, thus greatly expanding, rather than limiting, judicial power.

Though deeply absorbed in the living present, Webster had an uncanny vision of things to come. In the Massachusetts Convention of 1820, called to expand the base of popular power, he predicted: "The freest government . . . would not long be acceptable, if the tendency of the laws were to create a rapid accumulation of property in few hands, and to render the great mass of the population dependent and pennyless. In such case the popular power must break in upon property rights or else the influence of property must limit and control the exercise of popular."

By the end of the century, all aspects of this remarkable forecast had come to pass. Professor Webster's book, though somewhat lacking in literary grace and sophistication, is a worth-while contribution.

ALPHEUS T. MASON
Professor of Jurisprudence
Princeton University

ECONOMICS

ROBERT BARLOW, HARVEY E. BRAZER, and JAMES N. MORGAN. *Economic Behavior of the Affluent.* Pp. xiv, 285. Washington, D.C.: Brookings Institution, 1966. $6.75.

In this volume, the authors describe the saving, investment, and work habits of affluent Americans—those with incomes in excess of $10,000 per year in 1961. The analysis is based on a sample of roughly 1,000 individuals, selected so that the chance of inclusion is roughly proportional to income. The high-income "loading" of the sample design is further intensified by the fact that the basic unit in many of the tabulations is not an individual household but an "income-dollar." Hence, the statement "30 per cent of the sample does X" usually means that "households accounting for 30 per cent of the total income in the sample do X."

Respondents were questioned extensively about such topics as beneficial interest in trust funds, joint ownership of assets, general investment policies—importance of rate of return, safety, liquidity, and capital gains—purposes of saving, sources of information for investment decisions, portfolio composition and recent changes, inheritance and gifts received and given, experience with capital gains and losses, type of hours of work, retirement decisions, and work-experience of wives. All data were obtained from fixed-questions—free-response interviews, and quantitative information was limited to order-of-magnitude data only.

The survey was apparently designed in part to bring out any direct or indirect evidence linking saving, investment, or work-decisions with tax considerations; an un-prompted mention of taxes, in response to a "why did you do that?" question, was often taken as a measure of tax sensitiv-ity. If this approach is valid, the evidence suggests that tax considerations play a minor role in the economic decisions of the affluent.

Both the usefulness as well as the am-biguity of many of the findings are illus-trated by the treatment of that time-honored and much-disputed subject, the effect of taxes on the supply of effort. The survey indicates that the maximum disincentive effect shows up among house-holds located in the middle—50–59 per cent bracket—of a marginal tax-rate sched-ule that ranges from 14 to 91 per cent. A "familiarity threshold" hypothesis is of-fered as the likely explanation: when people reach the 50 per cent—or there-abouts—bracket, they become aware of the fact that the government is a major silent partner, and resentment arises. But after a while one gets accustomed to high brackets, and normal acquisitive instincts take over. This theory is plausible, though it cannot be the only reasonable explana-tion for the findings. The marginal tax rate is the amount paid on an extra dollar of fully taxable income. But untaxed or partially taxed income, for example, capital gains, is clearly much more important, relative to fully taxable income, the higher the taxable income level. Thus a person with an apparent marginal tax rate of 91 per cent would act as if the marginal rate were 25 per cent if effort is mainly directed to producing income in the form of long-term capital gains. Such a person will not work less because of taxes, but the fact that he may work at different things is highly relevant to an analysis of the economic effects of taxes.

Other findings need clarification. The discussion of savings motives is not very satisfactory, possibly because responses could not be pursued within the fixed-question framework of the questionnaire design. The savings motives offered by respondents seem to be largely "ex post" rationalization and do not provide much insight. Young people with young chil-dren say they save for education; people whose children are grown—or those who do not have children—say they save for retirement; and the aged—who are retired —say they save in order to make bequests. But the first two motives do not gen-erate any net saving unless there are con-sistent errors in individual forecasts, and the quantitative importance of bequests appears to be minimal based on other findings of the survey. Thus how do we explain the level of savings?

Gifts or inheritances are found to ac-count for a small fraction of total assets— probably less than one-fifth, or if one in-cludes appreciation on inherited assets. It is not clear what these data really show. For example, they do not measure the "typical" proportion of lifetime-wealth ac-cumulation due to an individual's own saving, nor the complementary proportion due to inheritance. At any point in time, the proportion of wealth represented by inheritance depends on whether one has already received all the inheritances that can be anticipated and on whether future saving will be positive or negative. Both factors evidently vary with age, as does the quality of the respondent's recall ability.

On the whole, this is a very useful volume both for social scientists and lay-men. The former will find the data in-valuable as a fertile source of behavior hypotheses. Some of these are suggested by the authors, although by and large they have concentrated on the difficult task of concise description. The latter will find a fascinating collection of information about the very affluent—what kind of people they are, and what kind of factors influence their economic decisions.

F. THOMAS JUSTER
Research Staff
National Bureau of Economic
    Research
New York City

E. C. STAKMAN, RICHARD BRADFIELD, and PAUL C. MANGELSDORF. *Campaigns Against Hunger.* Pp. xvi, 328. Cam-bridge, Mass.: Harvard University Press, 1967. **$7.50.**

They call themselves the "three ancients"; more accurately they are three men wise in the use of science and technology. In their book, Professors Stakman, Bradfield, and Mangelsdorf guide us through the conception, organization, and conduct of a quarter-century of co-operative Rockefeller Foundation international food product programs. From their direct involvement, we learn why the programs they describe are, among agricultural assistance efforts, uniquely great in their cumulative impact.

In 1941 Mexican scientific and political leaders requested Rockefeller Foundation assistance in food-crop production. The three authors, as Foundation consultants—roles they have continued since 1941—did a field survey of rural Mexico and recommended a favorable response. They suggested a co-operative science-based effort. Mexico and the Foundation entered into a scientific partnership in 1943. Today, in no small measure due to the accomplishments of that partnership, Mexico is a net exporter rather than an importer of wheat. New Mexican wheat varieties are known and grown throughout the world. The culture of corn, potatoes, beans, and other food crops in the subtropics and tropics has been materially advanced. Co-operative programs in the Mexican model have been established in Colombia (1950) and Chile (1955).

Programs of a different model operate in India. In the Philippines, the International Rice Research Institute, a direct beneficiary of Foundation experience, is well on its way to redesigning the architecture of the rice plant.

Program accomplishments are measured largely in terms of increased food-crop production per acre, changes in indigenous institutions, and advances in the quality and status of agricultural science. The authors attribute much of the program's success to "stable, persistent [Rockefeller Foundation] leadership, long-term commitment, competent long-term men [scientists]." They gloss over the reality that the biologically possible may not be economically feasible. Slow adoption of new technology is often attributed to inade-quate education and extension—not to research shortcomings. Almost uniformly, scientists involved are portrayed as good or excellent. Guidelines for the future emerge by implication through a summary of lessons learned (chapter 18).

The book is a descriptive tribute to the people, institutions, and nations involved rather than an analysis of costs, benefits, strategies, or tactics. Its thrust is technological, not political. The authors make no claim that all of the answers to development problems are to be found in technology. But in a period of dire forecasts concerning population-food supply imbalances, the "three ancients" offer solid evidence that if men put their minds to it, such forecasts need not become realities.

LOWELL S. HARDIN
Program Officer
Ford Foundation

DAVID GRANICK. *Soviet Metal-Fabricating and Economic Development: Practice Versus Policy.* Pp. xiv, 367. Madison and Milwaukee: University of Wisconsin Press, 1967. $8.50.

The author, David Granick, concentrates on the development of the Soviet metal-fabricating industries during the first two Five Year Plans of 1928–1937. In orientation, the author selected certain problems that are important for developing countries, particularly the choice of patterns of technology. He describes and evaluates Soviet solutions, with particular attention to the effectiveness of those methods that are under consideration by developing economies today.

In the first half of the book, Granick discusses positive investment in tangible capital, worker-training, and new technology. In Part II, he treats the organizational aspects of metal-fabricating development.

Professor Granick relishes controversy, and specialists in Soviet economics will find the book most stimulating. Others should read it as a warning not to accept without question the conventional "lessons" of Soviet economic development. The most important point that Granick makes is simply that no economic or technical policy, selected for the metal-fabricating industries, will succeed if, when the plants are built and the equipment is installed, there is not enough steel to operate them at anywhere near their designed capacity. If this point seems obvious to Western analysts of Soviet policy, it was, nevertheless, missed by the Chinese Communists, who at one time prided themselves on being careful students of Soviet economic development.

Granick's second most important point is that pressures in the Soviet system force metal-fabricating plant managers to assure their own supplies of raw materials, and this drives them toward vertical integration. They insist on making their own steel, their own castings, their own spare parts, and the like. This organizational imperative inherent in the system makes a shambles of the blueprints and dreams of central planners intent on realizing the economics of large-scale specialization.

The book is a gold mine of information about the insights into technology and organization of Soviet industry. The final chapter, "An Organizational Treatment of Soviet Industry," is no exception. In it, however, Granick develops and tests two conflicting models of Soviet industry of the type used in organizational theory. I read this chapter twice and concluded that the models add practically nothing to the valuable insights and interesting conclusions presented. On the contrary, the models make it more difficult and tedious to follow the argument, especially when Granick is trying to give reasons why the models fail to explain important points that could be easily understood without reference to the models in the first place.

M. GARDNER CLARK
Professor of Economics and
Industrial Relations
Cornell University

MARK J. FITZGERALD. *The Common Market's Labor Programs.* Pp. xii, 256. Notre Dame: University of Notre Dame Press, 1966. $6.95.

The present volume seeks to fill a gap in English-language reviews of the activities and studies in the labor field, conducted by the European Economic and the Coal and Steel Communities. The author contents himself with an enumeration of these programs and reports until the end of 1963, and the final chapter gives an over-all summary for the year 1964. The reader will not find a description of the setting into which these innovations have been introduced or an evalution of their significance and impact. Taken almost exclusively from publications and statements released by these agencies, it is difficult, on the one hand, to appreciate the deep sense of frustration prevailing in the trade union movement because of its slight influence upon the agencies and its over-all conviction that the social program has given way to the Commission's preoccupation with the construction of the economic community. On the other hand, the High Authority of the European Coal and Steel Community can report a large number of achievements. Those in the social field have, however, been unimpressive. Only at the end of 1966 did the Commission establish guidelines for its activities, and for the first time in 1967 did the Council of Ministers indicate some of the priorities in this field.

The author covers the structure of the two Communities: the European Social Fund, vocational training, retraining, conditions of employment, industrial health and safety, trends in wage-standards improvement, patterns for social security, workers' housing, regional development, and industrial relations. The outstanding innovation has been the European Social Fund, which now spends about 30 million dollars annually to cover up to half the cost of the programs for workers' retraining and mobility initiated by the member-countries on projects approved by the Community. The greatest criticism is that the funds are paid only after the expenditure has been incurred. The second outstanding accomplishment is the creation of the free labor market, which is to parallel the free economic market. But here again the actual contribution needs to be carefully defined. Other priorities have been social security for migrants, harmonization of programs on paid holidays, and equal pay for men and women. Much of the promise of harmonizing working conditions has still to be realized. Work in other fields has been primarily in the form of studies. The Coal and Steel Community has a more tangible record of achievements in the field of training, health and safety, housing, and regional development.

One regrets the inclusion of the author's short commentaries on the United States' activities in each of these areas. They are neither objective, balanced, nor related to the previous analysis of the Communities' efforts. The value of action as compared with studies is never underscored. The book could have benefited considerably from a clear focus on the supranational nature of the institutions, their precedent-making character, and the difficulties of operating such structures in the social field, particularly as the basic mandate is most limited. It is to be hoped that the trend of the future will fulfill the promise of those who envisaged a new day for the common man of Europe.

SOLOMON BARKIN
Deputy to the Director of
   Manpower and Social
   Affairs Directorate
Head of Social Affairs Division
O.E.C.D.
Paris

WILLIAM A. JOHNSON. *The Steel Industry of India.* Pp. xv, 340. Cambridge, Mass.: Harvard University Press, 1966. $7.50.

This book fulfills the need of a general and competent book dealing with India's steel industry. It first gives a short survey of the growth of the steel industry in India from the 1890's, when the steel industry, based on coke rather than charcoal, was started by the Indian house of Tatas. By 1939 their mill was one of the largest steel mills in the British Empire, and it was also one of the lowest cost producers in the world.

Johnson's analysis of factor endowments of India distinguishes that country for the growth of the steel industry. Not only does India possess 10 to 20 per cent of the world iron resources, but their iron content of 60 per cent is high by the world standard; though other resources like coal and limestone are comparately less abundant.

He further studies cost, demand, and the like to determine the best location and the likely returns on investment. He finds that the industry should yield a return in excess of 20 per cent if proper exchange rates $0.14 per rupee and international prices for products are used in the calculations. (Since his study, the rupee was devalued to $0.13.) According to these figures, the Bokaro project should get a return of 12 per cent during the initial stage and 24 per cent after the final one; this is contrasted with the United States Steel Corporation team's (1963) findings of losses until the final stage and then only earning 9 per cent.

Instead of integrating the steel industry into the total development process, Johnson feels that government policy and control are designed to scuttle the industry. The process of adoption of administrative machinery to a changing situation through public debate rather than by private secret decisions provides the data for Johnson's indictment.

Another major bias is in favor of foreign management. Success of the Tatas is attributed to foreign management and the failure of seventeen Tatas companies from 1825 to 1890 is attributed partly to its absence, forgetting that fifteen of them were British-owned-and-managed and that some advantages that Tatas derived from their English managers were negotiations with the British government.

Though the book is not an in-depth study, it is quite suitable for a general reader, who wants to get acquainted with the subject and who has little previous knowledge of the Indian conditions. However, its economic framework is only partial analysis, which is a very treacherous tool, indeed—especially for studying a capital goods industry in an economy made to develop by purposive action.

P. N. MATHUR
Gokhale Institute of Politics
   and Economics
Poona
India

SOCIOLOGY

NED POLSKY. *Hustlers, Beats, and Others.* Pp. 218. Chicago: Aldine, 1967. $5.95.

This book is a series of essays dealing with the subject of deviance in American society. Although each chapter delves into a different aspect of social behavior, the work is held together by its focus on the sociology of deviance and by the author's adherence to Albrecht Durer's statement to the artist to "pour out new things which had never before been in the mind of any other man." Durer's prodding, writes Polsky, "has always struck me as the only decent attitude to take toward one's intellectual endeavors" (p. 7). Consequently, the intellectual endeavors of the work range from pool players and poolrooms, hustlers, criminology and its research techniques, and the beats of Greenwich Village to the sociology of pornography in a fascinating and often witty attempt to analyze those areas too long neglected by social scientists. Utilizing historical, sociological, legal, and his individual approach, Professor Polsky begins each chapter with an overview of the contemporary knowledge and theories of each field of study. The opening chapter, "Of Pool Playing and Poolrooms," for example, contains perhaps the best historical analysis of the sport written by a social scientist. It will be argued that pool-playing and pool hustlers are not the proper domain for any social scientist, but Professor Polsky correctly places the sport into historical perspective and in its place within the social structure. The fact is that pool-playing or billiards has been, and to an extent continues to be, a sport of the upper classes. In recent years, commercial enterprises have attempted to eliminate the middle-class stigma attached to pool-playing by building family billiard establishments; but Polsky argues that "the heyday of the poolroom is over" (p. 40). Not incidental to his analysis is Polsky's own behavior; he plays pool for sport and for financial reward.

Other chapters in the book follow a similar format. Polsky establishes the perspective, notes his own involvement, and then proceeds to argue his thesis. He takes issue with the lack of field research in criminology: "every criminology textbook to discuss it is concerned above all to offer copouts for avoiding it" (p. 117); with the articles on beat life: "Paradoxically, nearly all articles on the beats neglect the thread that colors beat life: the overwhelming majority of beats are not exhibitionists or publicity-seekers but precisely the opposite" (p. 152); and with the "sociologizing" about pornography by many interested but confused persons (pp. 186–187). It would be unfortunate if Polsky's provocative insights, criticisms, and suggestions to social scientists regarding their postulates and research methods were to be ignored.

JOSEPH BOSKIN
Associate Professor of History
University of Southern California

MARVIN E. WOLFGANG and FRANCO FERRACUTI. *The Subculture of Violence: Towards an Integrated Theory in Criminology.* Pp. xxiii, 387. London: Tavistock (Distributed by Barnes & Noble, New York), 1967. $11.50.

Considering the antiquity of our concern about violence, the benefits gained from its study have been meager. Even in an age which surpasses all others in the infliction of bodily harm by man on his fellows and in a pervasive obsession with the topic, we do not understand the phenomenon. Some denounce it; some glorify it; and some declare it to be natural—"as American as cherry pie." But few study violence as a social problem. Those who do shed little light on those who commit it. We are as incapable as our ancestors to prevent violence, to predict it, to control it, or to change the behavior of those who resort to it.

The state of our understanding is demonstrated by the notion that frustration produces aggression. This formula does not account for those who are frustrated but subside into apathy. Nevertheless, it is the most promising hypothesis yet advanced, simple, obvious, and incomplete though it is. It has passed into the common sense of our culture, but we continue to increase repression and do little to relieve its consequences.

The beginning is late, but concepts and methods are becoming available to advance from the frustration-aggression equation. In *The Subculture of Violence*, a sociologist with a classic study of the taxonomy of homicide to his credit (Marvin E. Wolfgang, *Patterns in Criminal Homicide,* 1958) has collaborated with a clinician with a flair for empirical studies of the topic. Their work delivers more than the title promises. In addition to a heuristically auspicious theory, the authors provide a discourse on the nature of criminology as a discipline which almost convinced this reviewer of the autonomy of the study of crime. But for all their zeal, the authors do not manage to establish that a separate discipline can be claimed where only the subject matter can be bounded, but concepts and methods must be drawn from the basic social sciences. The argument is exhaustive, but the insistence of the authors is as puzzling as if ornithologists pressed for recognition of their independence among the biological scientists. Criminology is an indispensable forum for the exchange of knowledge about crime and the formulation of concerted strategies of research and action. Its claim for recognition should be aimed at inducing more social scientists to enter this market place of ideas.

But there is, indeed, a body of knowledge about crime. The authors demonstrate it with a diligence which simultaneously enlightens and astonishes the reader. The five chapters in the volume average 164 footnotes, ranging from a mere 31 in the introduction to 229 in the review of the literature on violence. Graceful respects are paid to all fellow toilers, from the nineteenth-century giants of Italian criminology to the eager young doctors emerging from contemporary graduate schools. As a survey, it is a model of its kind, beyond the stamina of most scholars.

It leads to a theory of violence which draws on the concept of the subculture. The difficulties in defining this neologism are recognized, but its usefulness in locating the sectors of society in which the ethos of violence prevails and in proposing remedial action compensate the authors for their labors. In their hands, a subculture is the vehicle which establishes and reinforces alternative norms to those which are legitimated by the dominant classes. The authors concede that they need empirical support for the propositions which compose their theory. They advance eight hypotheses which, if confirmed by social psychologists and sociologists, would firmly buttress their position.

Wolfgang and Ferracuti are optimists: "as the disparity in life style between the lower and middle classes is diminished, so too will be reduced the subculture of violence that views ready resort to violence as an expected form of masculine response." This is a long view in 1968. The daily news proclaims the distance which must be traversed before this subculture crumbles away in the most middle-class of nations.

Here is a theory for exploration by the social scientist and a program of action for the social planner. If the authors can make themselves heard amid the din of riot guns and molotov cocktails, their book will testify to the practical value of their great learning.

JOHN PHILLIPS CONRAD
Chief of Research
United States Bureau of Prisons
Washington, D.C.

HUBERT M. BLALOCK, JR. *Toward a Theory of Minority-Group Relations.* Pp. x, 227. New York: John Wiley & Sons, 1967. $6.95.

This slender volume makes a substantial contribution to theory-construction in the field of minority group relations. Blalock begins with his dissatisfaction with a mere propositional inventory, such as Robin Williams' *Reduction of Intergroup Tensions,* and with his conviction that the next step requires a set of deductively joined propositions of a systematic character. The ninety-seven propositions Blalock sets forth are not inferred from any overarching general theory, but from a number of special theories, each constructed to account for a limited class of events—like motivation theory, notions of choice behavior, frustration-aggression, or Nieboer's schematic statements on socioeconomic conditions facilitating slavery. From these special theories, Blalock deduces chains of singular propositions grouped around thematic or situational areas of major significance like "Frontier Contact Situations," "Middleman Minorities," "Power and Discrimination," and "Minority Percentage and Discrimination." His general approach is a sort of pluralistic parallel deduction, since his inferences are made from a plurality of special theories and are organized around multiple themes. It is evident throughout that Blalock regards power relationships as central for explanatory purposes, and that, in some obscure way, this is related to common assumptions about causality, as treated in the author's previous work on causal inference (1964).

The heavy reliance on deductive method has a tendency to narrow Blalock's results, particularly if they are to have cross-cultural relevance. Thus the use of historical data is meager, and when they are employed, the author leans too exclusively on a single source like Nieboer; the latter's emphasis on "open resources" as a precondition of slavery is plausible, but certainly not self-evident, and research has shown that fairly different preconditions existed in the slave societies of the Mediterranean during the fourteenth and fifteenth centuries (cf. D. B. Davis, *The Problem of Slavery in Western Culture*, chapter 2). Another limiting factor is in the range of data Blalock is trying to explain—most of these center in Negro-white relations in the United States, and whatever inferences take him farther afield focus on traditional race relations, such as would be found in Brazil, or Southeast Asia. However, the ninety-seven propositions have little relevance to ethnic minorities immigrating to the United States, or to the whole range of secessionist minorities in African countries today.

Since our knowledge of minority group relations on a comparative basis is so incomplete today, the main danger of a deductive approach, like that of Blalock, is simply premature closure; perhaps he himself recognizes this when he suggests that future theory-construction must be a team effort (p. 190). This, however, does not detract from the creative achievement that marks Blalock's work. It is an effort of consummate skill, logical rigor, and fidelity to evidence in a rare combination—in fact, one of the few indispensable works for all those who want to rethink the basic issues.

RICHARD A. SCHERMERHORN
Professor of Sociology
Case Western Reserve University
Cleveland

ALLAN H. SPEAR. *Black Chicago: The Making of a Negro Ghetto, 1890–1920.* Pp. xvii, 254. Chicago: University of Chicago Press, 1967. $7.50.

In recent years social historians have made significant contributions to research on the Negro's encounter with white America. One of the most important of these works is Spear's *Black Chicago*. This volume, which will particularly interest specialists in race relations and collective behavior, is a study of the rise of the Chicago ghetto, 1890–1920. Sociologists will recognize the author's indebtedness to Drake and Cayton's classic, *Black Metropolis*.

Spear studied the interrelationships between the Negro migration, white hostility, the ideology of Negro leaders, and the development of Negro institutions. Between 1890 and 1920, Chicago's Negro population grew from about 15,000 to 110,000. In the early period, many Negroes lived among whites or in little enclaves. Increasingly, mixed blocks became converted into all-Negro ones, and by the World War I era, a few Negro neighborhoods had expanded into sizable ghettos. In fact, this volume makes an important contribution by demonstrating that the process of "ghettoization," associated with the great migration of World War I and after, had actually begun by the turn of the century.

Chicago's tiny Negro elite around 1900 consisted largely of professional men having fairly close links with whites. These Negroes fervently embraced an integrationist ideology and opposed the creation of separatist Negro institutions. Thus, in 1889, they rejected a proposal to establish a Negro Young Men's Christian

Association (YMCA), and several years later at the Columbian Exposition they scorned a Colored American Day, even though various ethnic groups sponsored such celebrations at the fairgrounds.

In the two decades before World War I, as the Negro population grew, hostile whites demanded their rigid isolation. Restaurants and theaters increasingly excluded Negroes or Jim-Crowed them. The downtown YMCA barred them and applauded the creation of the all-Negro Wabash Avenue (YMCA), which opened in 1913. Nothing symbolized the growing polarization in Chicago more than the race riot of 1919, one of the most serious outbreaks of racial violence in the twentieth century.

As physical and social isolation widened, militant integrationism became somewhat irrelevant to a new generation of Negro leaders, who now dreamed about creating a Black Metropolis rather than an integrated city. This was a temporary expedient for some, but for others the dream was inspiring in and of itself, and they believed that a well-organized community supporting Black "captains of industry," professional men, financiers, and politicians was a satisfactory alternative to the destruction of segregation. The Depression of the 1930's was to reveal the flimsy foundation of Negro business in Chicago. While the Black political machine would grow in influence as the ghettos expanded, beyond the attainment of a few patronage plums and some lower-level jobs, the basic problems of the slums would remain untouched.

Black Chicago will deservedly attract a wide readership among social scientists, because it carefully delineates the ways in which Negroes coped with the increasing ghettoization of a major American city.

ELLIOTT RUDWICK

Professor of Sociology
Southern Illinois University
Edwardsville

LEONARD P. ULLMANN. *Institution and Outcome: A Comparative Study of Psychiatric Hospitals*. Pp. xvi, 197. New York: Pergamon Press, 1967. $7.50.

Leonard Ullmann, in a tightly organized, factual monograph, reports the results of a study of the effectiveness of the psychiatric hospital as a function of certain characteristics of the institution. Since the author regards returning the patient to the community to be the main function of the mental hospital, hospital effectiveness is measured by the rapidity with which the hospital accomplishes this. Appropriate data were collected on thirty Veterans Administration (VA) psychiatric hospitals during a full year. The general research strategy was to treat the various hospitals as subjects and to apply techniques commonly used by psychologists for studying individual differences.

The major findings of the study, that small hospital size and high staffing correlate positively with hospital effectiveness, are not surprising. However, the data permitted refinement of these general statements and additional correlations between hospital characteristics and effectiveness. For example, the percentages of the per diem expense per patient spent in various categories—food, shelter, and general administrative expenses—was associated with different degrees of hospital effectiveness.

In order to interpret the various findings of the study, the author makes extensive use of operant-reinforcement notions, which, in other recent research, have proved so useful in understanding the behavior and adjustment of hospitalized psychiatric patients. Here, the same model is applied to the behavior of hospital employees. Specifically, the author argues that at times, to maximize the effectiveness of the psychiatric institution, custodial aspects of patients care are encouraged rather than employee behaviors and practices.

From these considerations, the author makes some recommendations on the allocation of funds and resources in the psychiatric hospital to increase the effectiveness of the institution. It is rare, indeed, for such recommendations to be based on hard data subjected to a sophisticated analysis as is the case in the present study.

A limitation of the study is that the only criteria of hospital effectiveness was getting the patient out of the hospital for a minimum period of time. It would be valuable to know the relationship between these criteria and the quality of the patient's extrainstitutional adjustment. In any case, the book is a valuable contribution to the literature for several reasons: It provides a carefully developed and validated methodology for studying institutions as individual subjects; it yields some specific information on the relationship between institutional characteristics and hospital effectiveness; and the findings are meaningfully interpreted within a sociopsychological model of patient-staff interaction.

JOHN PAUL BRADY
Professor of Psychiatry
University of Pennsylvania

IRA L. REISS. *The Social Context of Premarital Sexual Permissiveness.* Pp. xiv, 256. New York: Holt, Rinehart and Winston, 1967. No price.

Although a fair amount of research has been done in the area of sex behavior, most of it has been done by biologists, psychologists, and anthropologists. Sociological contributions have been on the sparse side, and even today there are only a handful of sociologists actively engaged in sexual research. Ira Reiss is one of the handful, and the present volume represents a real contribution to our knowledge of sexual behavior and sexual attitudes.

The Social Context of Premarital Sexual Permissiveness is a report based on the "first probability sample of the nation that has been used for a sociological analysis of the sexual relationship, and it is the first book to fully focus on sexual attitudes and not just behavior." The total number of cases in the sample studied was 2,734. Reiss started with the assumption that groups which differed in their attitudes toward premarital sexual permissiveness would also differ in cultural characteristics; for example, social class, religion, family background, dating experience, and sexual behavior. Hypotheses were then formulated regarding the ways in which these independent variables would affect the dependent variable—premarital sexual permissiveness. The latter was measured by Guttman scales. Statistical findings were

then interwoven into a series of propositions, and the propositions were in turn integrated into a general theory of sexual permissiveness.

The result is a scholarly work of genuine sociological importance. Working with thousands of tables, and a staggering number of research referents, the author has performed a masterly analysis. The study was several years in the making, and the book is undoubtedly the definitive work on premarital sexual attitudes.

Reiss' findings contradict those of the Kinsey survey at several points. For example, the author found—somewhat unexpectedly—that premarital sex indulgence was accompanied by marked guilt feelings. Also, no statistical relationship was found between social class and premarital permissiveness.

Although space precludes reporting on the substantive findings, one of the author's main conclusions is as follows: "There are two basic institutions that are of key importance for the development of premarital sexual attitudes and behavior—courtship and the family. The fundamental orientation of the participant-run courtship institution is one of relatively high premarital sexual permissiveness. The orientation of the adult-run family institution is one of relatively low premarital permissiveness. Other social institutions have their effects primarily through these two institutions. As the individual matures in American society the relative strength of influence of these two institutions varies in accord with his role positions, and his premarital sexual attitudes vary accordingly. The female appears to break away slower and in more gradual stages than the male. The participation in the courtship institution leads to the breakthrough of the adult taboos on premarital sex. The later participation in the marital and family institution leads to at least a partial return to these adult taboos on premarital sexuality. The size of the "permissive gap" between the family and courtship institutions seems to be fairly similar for high- and low-permissive groups."

All in all, the Reiss volume is an invaluable addition to the literature. Sociologists specializing in the family, social class, personality, reference-group theory, race relations, and the sociology of religion will want to buy the book. The library copy will probably be in tatters.

WILLIAM M. KEPHART
Professor of Sociology
University of Pennsylvania

ALBERT MAYER. *The Urgent Future: People, Housing, City, Region.* Pp. xiii, 184. New York: McGraw-Hill, 1967. $16.50.

Albert Mayer has had a sense of urgency about improving man's environment for over forty years. He was a pioneer in putting the ideas of Geddes, Howard, and Unwin into practice in the United States; in the 1920's through the Regional Planning Association of America; in the 1930's through the Housing Study Guild, where the Works Project Administration (WPA) aided him and Henry Wright, young architects now holding senior posts in planning; and through the Greenbelt Towns of Tugwell's Resettlement Administration. As "planner of environment"—his self-characterization on the title-page—he has designed housing projects and whole communities, such as Kitimat, British Columbia, Chandigarh—before LeCorbusier—Bombay, and Ashdod, Israel. With his old friend Clarence Stein, he has been progagandist and a two-man pressure group for national legislation for New Towns, against the formidable opposition of the organizations of municipal officials unwilling to support federal aid to sewers in surburbs or in the central cities.

This rich lifetime of experience, world-wide observation, thought, and firm convictions is distilled in this folio book and is generously illustrated with photographs and plans from every apposite venture anywhere in the world. The great merit of the book is that it traverses the whole spectrum from urban public housing, urban renewal, central-city restructuring, and metropolitan planning to the regional city as few books have done, because few authors have had Mayer's scope. He never departs from his main concern: how can each of these devices enhance human living values?

Familiar obstacles in the path generate

sputters: "as long as land is a freely disposable private commodity, and speculative profit is a basic factor, large-scale logically related development is not going to take place." "The Wrong Way to Create New Towns" is his characterization of recent federal bills. Again and again he laments: "but in these matters a common sense of urgency is sadly lacking" (p. 148). This note of stridency pervades the book.

But this reviewer cannot share the romanticism of Mayer, Eliel Saarinen, and other masters. "We have to greatly struggle toward the birth of the total regional organism of which the great and small localities are to be living cellular parts" (p. 166). Cities are not organisms. They are artifacts whose shape is determined by decisions and acts of men: thousands of men singly and in groups clothed with public power. Does it help the understanding of difficult problems, technical, legal, and social to cloak them in poetry? Let us beware of being trapped in our metaphors.

CHARLES S. ASCHER
Professor of Political Science
Brooklyn College of the City
University of New York

HOPE JENSEN LEICHTER and WILLIAM E. MITCHELL, with the collaboration of CANDACE ROGERS and JUDITH LIEB. *Kinship and Casework.* Pp. xxi, 343. New York: Russell Sage Foundation, 1967. $7.50.

For quite a number of years the Russell Sage Foundation has been attempting to reintroduce the social science viewpoint into social work theory and practice. For many years social work was conceived—both by its practitioners and by social scientists—as applied social science. That conception was abandoned by both sides forty or more years ago. At that time social scientists began to eschew value notions, and social workers—social caseworkers, at least—began to draw their inspiration from Freud. Not that either of these new viewpoints became absolute, but they were dominant. They are still dominant, no doubt; but the Russell Sage Foundation's efforts have had a significant impact on at least the social work side of the situation.

The present study is an interesting and useful contribution to this cause. It is of particular importance because it challenges a favored theory of both social science and social work. On the social science side, it is widely held that, beyond the nuclear family, kinship ties are weak in American society, and the kinship system is of greatly diminished importance. On the social work side, the practical implications of the theory are illustrated in the lessened reliance on the younger generation for the economic support of elderly parents and relatives. The theory also—and this is the chief point of the study—affects casework practice, in that family caseworkers are apt to limit their consideration of kinship ties and influences to those that operate between wives and husbands—and their children—and between each of these and their own parents.

The study disturbs the complacency of this viewpoint by showing that in at least one ethnic group—American Jews whose parents were born in Eastern Europe—a much more extended family system prevails, even in New York City. True, the persons from whom this information was obtained were ones who were having difficulties in family relations, since they were clients of a family welfare agency. It seems likely, however, that the values they expressed—such as marrying within the religious group, living near but not with their parents, preference for the wife's over the husband's relatives, responsibility for aged parents, and pleasure in "cousins' clubs"—are widely shared.

From this finding, which is substantiated by a mass of material, the authors conclude that caseworkers should go beyond the immediate family in treating marital and parent-child relationship problems. Especially, they should give up their overweening reliance on Freudian theory for explanations of how family problems arise and how they should be dealt with. It may be, they say, that in dealing with this Jewish group the caseworkers are unwitting acculturation agents. Even so, they might be more helpful if they understood the kinship system better and were thereby more aware of sources of strength now overlooked.

Whether these are good and feasible suggestions cannot be discussed adequately in a brief statement. The question may be raised, however, as to whether we must be endlessly either-or about the use of sociological and psychiatric theory in social work. Cultural systems, the authors agree, induce strains in some individuals. To this reviewer, it seems a reasonable hypothesis that an important reason for such strains lies in psychological maladjustment—in the maladjusted person's inability to integrate his culture's requirements—and that dealing with the strain calls for knowledge of both culture and psychiatry on the caseworker's part.

HELEN L. WITMER

Research Division
Children's Bureau
Social and Rehabilitation Service
Department of Health, Education,
   and Welfare

JOHN P. KIRSCHT and RONALD C. DILLE-HAY. *Dimensions of Authoritarianism: A Review of Research and Theory.* Pp. xvi, 168. Lexington: University of Kentucky Press, 1967. $6.00.

The stimulus to do research provided by the monumental volume, *The Authoritarian Personality,* remains a vital force inspiring studies concerning social beliefs, attitudes, and behavior. By selectively reviewing work in the area of authoritarianism, Kirscht and Dillehay have contributed a useful, as opposed to merely encyclopedic, assessment of the progress of such research from 1956 to the present. Their conceptual framework is appropriately general to encompass the sea of studies which have inundated both the casual and the devoted connoisseur of the field. They assess authoritarianism as an antecedent factor causing other social behavioral manifestations, as a correlate of still other characteristics, and as a consequence of yet other factors, situational as well as personal. Though most effort is (understandably) devoted to describing uses of the F-scale itself, they very sensibly encompass other directly related research traditions, the prime example of which is

Rokeach's work in the areas of dogmatism and opinionation. The studies examined are presented in such detail that the reader may contrast his own conclusions with those of the authors'.

I quarrel with one major imbalance in emphasis. They relate exquisitely the response-bias problem in work with the F-scale as a measure of a personality predisposition. However, they relatively neglect a second methodological problem—that of experimenter-effect and situational demand characteristics in the evaluation of materials presented, particularly in their section on "Social Behavior and Authoritarianism." "Hard" experimental studies of authoritarian-like behavior—especially the work of Milgram—imply rather strongly that the percentage of variance in authoritarianism determined by personality is continually diminishing as that controlled by the situation in which a subject finds himself increases. More attention to this "artifact" would have improved an already excellent book.

I have one petty point to make: So that, at a glance, one could be aware of overwhelming, replicated findings as opposed to one-shot spectaculars, tables summarizing the essential features of groups of studies would have helped in understanding their assessment, as well as increased the usefulness of the volume as a reference.

I found the book informative, easy to read, and—in spite of the noted qualifications—a very judicious assessment of that disorderly, but important, area of research, authoritarianism.

HARRY A. SCARR
Assistant Professor of Sociology
University of Pennsylvania

BENJAMIN KAPLAN. *The Jew and His Family.* Pp. xv, 205. Baton Rouge: Louisiana State University Press, 1967. $5.95.

Despite the author's assertion in his preface that his account will not be "an emotional portrayal of the Jew and his family colored by sympathy," the book is just that. It consists primarily of a series of essays studded with quotations from the Bible, purporting to show that the roots of the Jewish people and their institutions may be traced back to Biblical times and to life in the East European village, or *shtetl.* Throughout, the writing is characterized by nostalgia and an idealization of life in the *shtetl,* in which the author was born and raised.

The culture of the Jewish people, according to the author, who is a professor of sociology at the University of Southern Louisiana, goes back to the time of Abraham, who, for some unexplained reason, is referred to throughout the book as Avrom—not Avram, as he is called briefly in the Bible before God changed his name to Abraham. The Jewish religion, the Jewish family, and the Jewish life-style in general can be understood and appreciated only through reading the Biblical accounts of events, as they are a continuation of the life of the ancient Hebrews. The author thinks that the Jewish people are not only unique but are more concerned with spiritual values than any other people.

The family, he points out, is central in all groups, but is especially so in the case of the Jews. The Jewish family is regarded by the author with a certain awe and is ascribed a mystical quality. It was a highly developed institution in the *shtetl.* There, he writes, the Jewish home was filled "with an indescribable charm, it covered family life with a genuine sanctity, it wove into a strong fabric the words of God, the legends of the past, the sayings of the sages, the preachments of the prophets, and the songs of the poets" (p. 110). In America, however, it no longer serves as a cementing force in Jewish life. The author is, therefore, filled with apprehension about the future of the American Jews. The Jewish family in America, he states, has degenerated. Jewish life in general has become estranged from its traditional values and is moving way from its former idealism and towards an ever greater materialism. The author realizes that minority groups inevitably adopt the values and attitudes of the dominant culture. Nevertheless, believing, as he does, that the Jews are a uniquely endowed people, he expects them to withstand the irresistable force to conform.

While the author believes that it is possible for the American Jews to return to the sources of their culture and institutions and to retain their identity, he is pessimisitic about it happening. The tragedy, he writes, is that the Jew is destined to remain and to be looked upon as a stranger in the countries in which he lives, including America. "Say what we will, to the Gentile he [the Jew] is not an American Jew but a Jew living in America" (p. 169). He sees little hope in the Jews surviving as a cultural group in America, unless a real effort is made by them. Of all the attempts made to counteract the forces of disintegration, the Reconstructionist Movement, founded by Dr. Mordecai Kaplan, holds the greatest promise, he maintains.

The author quite clearly is extremely subjective in his attitude towards the problem he discusses. He is too emotionally involved to analyze the issues scientifically. The book, therefore, could hardly be considered a sociological work. It is rather an emotional outpouring of a highly sensitive individual. It is beautifully written, poetically conceived, and rich in allusions. As such, it deserves high praise. As a scholarly work it is rather inadequate. It adds little to our understanding of the problem with which it deals.

SAMUEL KOENIG
Professor of Sociology
Brooklyn College of the
City University of New York

RAYMOND ARON. *Main Currents in Sociological Thought,* Vol. II: *Durkheim, Pareto, Weber.* Translated by Richard Howard and Helen Weaver. Pp. ix, 274. New York: Basic Books, 1967. $6.50.

In this, the second, volume of lectures at the University of Paris, Aron focuses his discussion on three figures—Durkheim, Pareto, and Max Weber—who are presumed to be symbols of a major theme in European sociology during the early decades of the twentieth century. For Aron, this theme is the confrontation of religion and science in complex society. Consequently, each thinker is analyzed in terms of this objective, rather than his contribu-

tions to the evolving character of sociological theory and its crucial repertory of distinctive problems.

If one accepts Aron's avowed objective in these lectures, then it is clear that he has provided a lucid, readable introduction to three theorists. His technique is understandably conversational and in general reliably casual, as he steers an intellectual course by reviewing each major work of Durkheim and Weber, and by confining his analyses of Pareto to the divisible portions of the overlong *Trattato,* which is so misleadingly titled in English as *Mind and Society.* Few writers or lecturers, to my knowledge, have Aron's analytical skill and literary felicity; consequently, this volume is eminently usable for students in the social sciences and the humanities, as well as for the intelligent layman, who occupies a convenient place in the penumbra of scholarship.

But I have several reservations about Aron's orientation to these theorists. For example, in the case of Durkheim, Aron's technique leaves little room for Durkheim's later work, particularly as this relates to socialization and personality—problems which Durkheim has been erroneously accused of ignoring. In addition, Aron tends to approach Durkheim's analysis of religion more from a philosophical than a sociological standpoint, concerned—irrelevantly—with the possibility of blasphemy or impiety in Durkheim's path-breaking discussion of the relationship between religion and social structure.

The choice of Pareto for extended discussion—instead of the more theoretically relevant George Simmel—seems to me unfortunate and generally unrewarding. Aron provides an overly extensive summary of Pareto's ideas, the most basic of which is the assertion that men are adequately identified by underlying and relatively unchanging interests (or residues), which inevitably prevent the dominance of rationality in social affairs.

In the case of Weber, Aron covers a considerable portion of that rich heritage, with particular emphases on methodology and the theoretical problems of legitimacy and religion. But too little attention is given to Weber's classic analysis of power and stratification; and the significant, highly detailed analysis in the sociology of law is barely mentioned.

In my opinion, the comparison of these three thinkers is more biographical and philosophical than sociological—understandably so in the case of discussions from the lecture platform, but not to be highly recommended in published form. The leisurely approach of the lecturer, even if well phrased, simply does not do justice to the caliber of ideas of a Durkheim or a Weber. Fortunately, rather good bibliographies are appended to the volume, so that the suggestive nature of these lectures may be further pursued by beneficent immersion in the sources themselves.

ALVIN BOSKOFF
Professor of Sociology
Emory University

CHARLES F. WESTOFF and RAYMOND H. POTVIN. *College Women and Fertility Values.* Pp. xx, 237. Princeton, N.J.: Princeton University Press, 1967. $7.50.

Since the mid-1950's, a number of major demographic investigations, including the Growth of American Families Studies and the Princeton Study, have focused on factors affecting the level of fertility in the United States. Although differing in research designs, comprehensiveness, and emphases, the studies agree in their findings that religious preference constituted the most important social determinant of the number of children born and expected. High fertility characterized Catholics; Jews had the fewest children; and Protestants were intermediary. Yet, in a further assessment of the high fertility of Catholics and their comparatively ineffective planning, the Princeton Study observed a significant differential between Catholics educated in nonsectarian schools and those educated in Catholic schools, especially Catholic colleges. Whereas the former closely paralleled Protestant women in their fertility-planning success and desired number of children, those with a Catholic education displayed an inverse relationship between planning success and education and a strong positive relation-

ship between education and family-size preferences. The authors of the Princeton Study could only speculate about the relative importance of educational experience per se or of the selective admission into Catholic institutions of women who already favored large families.

In order to examine the relative merits of the two alternative explanations for the observed differences, the senior author of the Princeton Study was joined by a Catholic sociologist in undertaking a study of freshmen and senior women in a stratified sample of forty-five American colleges and universities, selected on the basis of type of religious control—nonsectarian, Catholic, other denominational—coeducational status, region of country, and size. The over-all response rate of 72 per cent yielded about 15,000 usable questionnaires. Unfortunately, practical considerations led to basing the evaluation on comparison of the attitudes of freshmen and seniors enrolled during the 1963–1964 academic year. However, the authors fully alert the reader to the possible risks inherent in the use of such a synthetic cohort in lieu of a longitudinal study of the same cohort of women at the beginning and end of their college careers.

The volume is divided into two major parts. The first focuses on the effects of higher education on attitudes toward family size, family planning, marriage, and career. In these analyses, type of college, religion of students, and class status—freshman versus senior—are treated as key variables. The evidence clearly points to minimum differences, except for Catholics from Catholic high schools now in nonsectarian colleges. Whenever a differential was found between Catholics in different institutions, student selectivity provided the better explanation. Over-all, therefore, early socialization seems to provide the major mechanism through which fertility ideals are formulated, and college experience does little to alter them, at least during the span of college attendance.

The second part of the book assesses the influence of social factors and beliefs on fertility values. In this analysis, the data for freshmen and seniors are combined as are generally those of students in different types of institutions. Religious preference continues as a key variable but is used in conjunction with such other characteristics as nationality, socioeconomic status, number of siblings, and various aspects of religious attitudes, behavior, and influences. Several chapters employ more sophisticated approaches to summarize the earlier statistical comparisons of a multiplicity of subgroups. Measurement of the distance between items indicates that the Jewish and Protestant women are closer to those with no religious preference, and Mormons are closest to Catholics; but the more Catholics are educated in Catholic institutions, the more distant they become. Multiple-regression analysis shows that for the total sample combined, nine independent variables, including career plans, perception of family size, selected indices of religious behavior, and number of siblings, account for 38 per cent of the variance of the number of children desired. The number desired is more easily explained for Mormons and Catholics than for Protestants, Jews, and women with no religion, probably because the contents of Catholicism and Mormonism carry within them more substantive implications for fertility values.

The second part of the investigation, although more removed from the original purposes of the study, supports the argument that the early socialization process plays a key role in influencing fertility ideals and values. Justifiably, the authors conclude that full assessment of the validity of such an interpretation requires longitudinal research on a cohort of girls moving from early childhood through to adulthood. Hopefully, just as the Princeton Study inspired this well-designed, insightful, and well-reported study, so too this study will lead both to projects designed to overcome the risks involved in the synthetic cohort approach and to projects which will test the new ideas generated by this analysis.

SIDNEY GOLDSTEIN
Professor and Chairman
Department of Sociology
and Anthropology
Brown University

ROBIN F. BADGLEY and SAMUEL WOLFE. *Doctors' Strike: Medical Care and Conflict in Saskatchewan.* Pp. xiii, 201. New York: Atherton Press, 1967. $6.50.

In 1962 organized medicine in Saskatchewan staged an unsuccessful twenty-three-day strike against the new medicare program of a reformist Canadian Provincial government, which had been re-elected in 1960 in a campaign fought specifically on the medicare issue. The authors in Part I present an historical account of that epic confrontation. While attention is focused on the 1960's, the social background of Saskatchewan and the history of its medical services are also outlined. Some hitherto undisclosed aspects of the 1962 strike are revealed.

In Part II, the Saskatchewan experience is placed in an international perspective. British, American, and Canadian health-service developments over the last three generations are described and critically evaluated in very broad terms. These comparisons could well have been enlarged, and other countries might have been included. Finally, in the light of this overview, the authors attempt to estimate both the achievements and the deficiencies of Saskatchewan medicare.

Few recent professional publications have so effectively combined academically acceptable analysis with historical clarity and dramatic momentum. One author was a medical sociologist at the University of Saskatchewan; the other was a practicing doctor of medicine and public health, who supported the government medicare program. Although they are not neutral, they are objective. If that judgment seems paradoxical, let us remember that many of the best social analyses have dealt with large contemporary issues in both an evaluative and an insightful way.

Many weighty and disturbing problems are discussed in this book. Why has the technically admirable and socially prestigious North American medical profession become a social isolate? What is wrong with modern medical education? Why do social-reform movements like the Saskatchewan Co-operative Commonwealth Federation fall victim in their later phases to "hardening of the arteries?" How does the prevailing oligarchical and entrepreneurial organization of medical practice in North America militate against top-quality health services? Why did the Provincial university, long supported with pride by the people of Saskatchewan, so dismally fail in 1962 to provide disinterested leadership and counsel?

Some of these leading questions are tentatively answered in this book. The work is not definitive, but it is of lasting value: whatever it may lack in detail it makes up for by its sense of historical depth. To this reviewer, an eyewitness of the 1962 drama, *Doctors' Strike* so far as it goes is a true and moving record.

ARTHUR K. DAVIS
Professor of Sociology
University of Calgary
Calgary
Alberta
Canada

FREDERIC C. ENGELMAN and MILDRED A. SCHWARTZ. *Political Parties and the Canadian Social Structure.* Pp. 277. Englewood Cliffs, N.J.: Prentice-Hall, 1967. $5.95.

This little volume is offered, according to the Preface, as the first attempt "to present an account of Canadian parties as forces operating within Canada's political system." The two authors, a political scientist and a sociologist, abandon the standard institutional approach and proceed in a somewhat eclectic fashion to utilize the various methods and categories of contemporary political sociology. There is no pretense of inventing a new behavioral technique nor of offering a novel functional interpretation; the only innovation lies in applying to Canadian politics, in a comprehensive manner, the current methodology.

After a brief introduction on the role of parties, as analyzed by Duverger, Almond, Easton, and others, they turn to the "shaping of political parties" in Canada. This second section of six chapters occupies half of the book and deals successively with the historic, regional, and cultural settings, the role of interest

groups, mass media, and the influence of the internal system of government and of the external factors—to illuminate several tables of statistics which are provided. In the third section, "The Effects of Political Parties," the authors proceed to analyze the party role in the electoral process, leadership, decision-making, public opinion, and consensus-making. In the final brief chapter of "Conclusions" the authors mainly summarize their findings.

It is clear that the authors did not have the general reader in mind when they adopted the current terminology of political sociology and paraded new methodology. It is also evident that they did not intend to impress the expert by new techniques or interpretations. The readership that will profit most will be the students who have some knowledge of Canadian affairs but have not been exposed to such a careful exposition of the forces that operate in Canadian politics or have not had access to such an extensive bibliography. It is only fair to add that the authors are fully aware that their mode of treatment may not suit all readers and suggest resort to the Index for the purpose of drawing together materials dispersed by their method throughout the book. The severe critic may be inclined to note that even the use of the Index does not leave one with any differentiation between the several parties and their professions or policies or between the rival "nationalisms" that keep "Confederation" in crisis.

H. McD. CLOKIE
Department of Political Science
University of California
Berkeley

PHILOSOPHY AND EDUCATION

ERNEST BECKER. *Beyond Alienation: A Philosophy of Education for the Crisis of Democracy.* Pp. xiv, 305. New York: George Braziller, 1967. $6.95.

This book, like so many, asks the proverbial question: What is the purpose of knowledge? The role of values in social research will be hashed over for years to come with little thought of its over-all purpose. Becker insists that we are facing a crisis concerning knowledge; that is to say, we have a situation in which there is much available knowledge with little tying it together and with no ultimate purpose in mind. Our educational institutions are part and parcel of this trend—they typify an "aimless drift," as he calls it.

His solution is to create an integrated body of knowledge about man, embodied in a university curriculum which is oriented to the "anthropodocy"—that is, Becker's coinage for a concept explaining the "evil" in the world resulting from man-made arrangements—of alienation. Alienation is a conceptualization which, while not always contained by the term itself, has a historicity reflected in thinkers such as Plato, Augustine, Calvin, Rousseau, and Marx. The idea, in spite of and because of its ambiguity, is, suggests Becker, the central theme of our age. It defines, and intrinsically poses the antidote to, modern man's powerlessness and the stifling of his creative energies in the three dimensions of his existence: the individual, the social and historical, and the theological.

The last dimension, along with the others, is included in his proposal for a "New Moral View of the World," a secular "reasoned creed," which retains man's unique subjectivity as essential to any philosophical anthropology. Roughly within the tradition of John Dewey, Becker's "theological" dimension entails an integration of aesthetics, ethics, and theology. Some may find this idiosyncratic usage somewhat tedious. But it can be plausible if we accept his view of aesthetics as the free and creative merging of the person and society with the cosmic process—a kind of *élan vital*. "Good" ethics then becomes anything furthering this glorious process and vice versa. The answer then seems to lie in substituting a "good" scientific myth for bad ideology.

Becker seems confident in the illusion that once his scheme becomes the guiding principle of a university curriculum—designed to produce self-critical men for a self-critical society—there will be "no need for any State to fear an education that will fashion whole men, and direct their loyalty to the highest principle of all."

Hence, an autonomous university, linking education to the community, automatically produces the ideal society. Like the utopianists before him, Becker is obviously fixing the odds in advance. His wide-eyed optimism neglects the gloomy fact that knowledge may after all be ethically neutral; and that the lions and foxes who peopled Machiavelli's intriguing drama will continue to be the enterprisers they must be, producing the bitter-sweet things States are.

Perhaps the most unique aspect of this book is the way in which the author has cast developments in sociology, anthropology, psychology, and psychiatry into a refreshing perspective on man. It falls into line with the symbolic interactionist tradition in sociology, but lacks much of its trivial preoccupation with superficial detail. The style of the writing, however, often belabors the points he makes. He seems to be entertaining himself with a myriad of rhetorical questions and playful answers.

The pervasiveness of alienation in society still remains an open question, especially with respect to its political overtones. Intellectuals, perhaps one of the most distinguishable alienated groups in our society, should beware lest they project their own unhappy kind onto the world.

GLENN JACOBS

Marathon County Center
University of Wisconsin
Wausau

WILLIAM E. CONNOLLY. *Political Science & Ideology.* Pp. viii, 179. New York: Atherton Press, 1967. $5.95.

This little volume is a healthy reaction to the widespread belief in the political science profession that ideology is not, and cannot be, a proper and legitimate object of useful scientific analysis, except in a purely historical or descriptive manner. The author defines ideology rather broadly as an "integrated set of beliefs about the social and political environment. It purports to tell us how the system is organized, which desired goals can be promoted, what agencies and channels can most effectively be employed to forward the goals in the given setting, and what the required action will cost vigorous groups in the short and long run in terms of status, power, happiness, wealth, and so on" (p. 2). Ideology thus contains not only normative elements and criteria by which political reality can be judged, but it embraces also "empirical claims not fully tested" (p. 49). The function of such incompletely tested empirical claims is to guide political activity and to protect higher-level values from attack or destruction. The author applies this hypothesis in his confrontation of various theories of power, with special emphasis on the elitist concepts of Charles Wright Mills and the pluralist approach of writers such as Robert Dahl. In chapters 3 and 4, the author examines the problem of sociology of knowledge and the concept of "perspective." His analysis of sociology of knowledge is largely an exposition of Karl Mannheim and George Herbert Mead, leaning much more heavily, however, on Mannheim. While Professor Connolly does not claim that Mannheim has said the last word on the subject, it is difficult to see in what manner he significantly modifies Mannheim. The author's emphasis on the concept of perspective is hardly a major step forward. He defines perspective as a "social emergent selectively derived from structured communication networks" (p. 114).

The last chapter, "Toward Responsible Ideology," is the most interesting in the book. The author rejects the notion that the view of value preferences as "emotive expressions" settles the problem of the role of the social scientist in dealing with values or ideologies. Just as the social scientist often finds himself in a position in which he has to make judgments and propositions in the presence of factual uncertainty and incompleteness, he may also have to make value judgments "though he cannot advance his recommendations with intuitive or metaphysical certainty" (p. 129). Responsibility in this context means being "deliberately responsive" to all factors that impinge on a given situation or problem.

On the whole, Professor Connolly's book is a worth-while effort in a difficult area.

A question of this importance cannot be brushed aside by any fiat of doctrinal purists and censors. His contribution would perhaps have been more effective if the author had made less use of sociologuese and if he had adduced more empirical illustrations in making his points. However, in conclusion, any author who has the courage to deal with an important subject and who takes a clear stand on highly controversial matters is to be commended. And though he is at times wrong, it is better to be wrong in wrestling with important issues than being right in trivial matters.

WILLIAM EBENSTEIN
Professor of Political Science
University of California
Santa Barbara

JOHN RAPHAEL STAUDE. *Max Scheler, 1874–1928: An Intellectual Portrait.* Pp. xv, 298. New York: Free Press, 1967. $6.95.

Max Scheler has had a considerable influence on European thought, both in sociology and philosophy. We are, therefore, indebted to Professor Staude for explaining this influence and for illuminating the dynamics of an enigmatic personality. The author has had the advantage of extensive conversations with Scheler's second wife and with a number of surviving friends and colleagues; he also shows a wide-ranging knowledge of intellectual and political currents in Germany during the first part of this century.

Professor Staude has sensibly concentrated on Scheler's social and political philosophy, discussing his contributions to phenomenology, metaphysics, and educational theory only so far as these are relevant to his sociology. Scheler's leading ideas seem to have been (1) a deep feeling for community, (2) a belief in elites, (3) a conviction that the scientific world view has prevailed, not because it is "true," but because it serves the interests of the dominant classes in contemporary society, and (4) a commitment to the propostion that values are objective, not relative.

The interplay between this set of fundamental convictions, on the one hand, and

Scheler's changing personal circumstances on the other hand, resulted in the development of a succession of ingenious but contradictory theories. As long as Scheler was a Catholic—his father was Protestant and his mother Jewish, but he was converted to Catholicism at an early age—he attacked positivism and argued in favor of a "solidarity" modeled on an ideal Christian community. When he broke with Catholicism—because the Church refused to sanction his divorce—he rejected Christianity and replaced it with a highly personal version of pantheism. Before and during World War I, he glorified militarism and Prussian aristocracy. After Germany's defeat and the establishment of the Weimar republic, he supported liberalism and those bourgeois values which, earlier, he had condemned.

That Scheler lacked "intellectual integrity" seems clear. As Professor Staude writes, "he always managed to switch parties in time to be speaking for the group that was on top." But Scheler may not have been merely an opportunist. He was a very complex person; given his views about the nature of knowledge, he probably conceived his social function to be that of supplying a plausible ideology to fit the needs—as he saw them—of his countrymen. Thus, in all of Scheler's many shifts, one constant was his conviction that Germany's greatest problems stemmed from the lack of any unified world view. Indeed, it seems that Scheler was led to develop his sociology of knowledge chiefly in order to provide unity at what we would now call a meta-level. But, being granted this motive, was the undertaking successful? Is it possible to reconcile sociology of knowledge with Scheler's belief in an objective hierarchy of values? Professor Staude hardly tackles this fascinating problem; to have done so would have taken him deeper into Scheler's phenomenology than he wished to go. Instead, he reminds us that this is not merely an abstract, theoretical question; it is reflected in the deepest way in Scheler's own personal tragedy: "In a relativistic age he taught a theory of absolute values; yet he not only failed to live by the values he taught, but freely adopted his philosophical theories to the endless changes in his personal life."

W. T. JONES
Professor of Philosophy
Pomona College
Claremont
California

RICHARD A. HUMPHREY (Ed.). *Universities and Development Assistance Abroad.* Pp. 196. Washington, D.C.: American Council on Education, 1967. $3.00.

In the continuing debate concerning the intent, nature, and efficacy of United States development assistance to modernizing nations, this volume has some notable significance. Its focus is upon the nation's universities as key resources of experts for United States overseas development programs, particularly with regard to contractual arrangements for managing overseas development projects. In the decade and a half since the initiation of this partnership with universities, the number of contracts has increased markedly. Presently, under the Agency for International Development (AID), contract personnel have come to replace a high proportion of direct-hire professionals, who now are assigned more to over-all planning with the host country than to specific development projects.

University personnel at times have found themselves at loggerheads with the various administrations of United States technical assistance because of their quite different perspectives. John Gardner's report, *AID and the Universities* (1964) and its acceptance by the Agency for International Development marked a promising turning point, at least in the Washington offices. Essentially, this volume of essays is a cogent recapitulation of the Gardner Report. There are, however, some further important suggestions for colleges and universities aspiring toward continuing involvement in the overseas development arena.

For example, it is suggested that, while in the past universities have responded to the requests of the government, the time has come for universities to exercise initiative. A fundamental basis for this new leadership must be the adoption of a point of view that transcends *ad hoc,* fire-brigade, short-term, and crash-project piddling. Instead, the development process must be aimed at conceptualizing tasks in more comprehensive terms than the conventionally delimited economic, political, or technological designations; propagating new talents and leadership here and abroad; effecting needed and co-operatively determined social changes—the comments of one contributor against co-operative determination notwithstanding; creating new knowledge relevant to overseas situations; and conducting research, experimentation, and evaluation procedures that probe the far-reaching effects of efforts expended.

The dialogue between government and universities must reach new levels of intellectual and educational sophistication. American scholars sent abroad must graduate from the status of "expatriates," as they are described in one essay to key faculty in their universities. Universities must see themselves as part of a new world-wide intellectual community and must give total commitment to the challenge. By the same token, the government must be prepared to give "reasonable autonomy" to our major sources of the intellectual capital upon which success overseas will depend.

There is repeated comment that much still must be learned about the development process; and, several of the authors outline in broad strokes the aspects which still demand study and in which universities must develop their capabilities. One is forced, however, to wonder what has been learned in the substantial period of apprenticeship in technical assistance, spanning a decade and one half. Why is there a paucity of case studies and analyses of past and current activities overseas? At this point in the International Development Decade, declared for the 1960's, analyses of the development process and of the role of the university, as sketched in this provocative publication, is, indeed, urgent.

EUNICE S. MATTHEW
Associate Professor of Education
Brooklyn College of the
City University of New York

HENRY ALLEN BULLOCK. *A History of Negro Education in the South: From 1619 to the Present.* Pp. xi, 339. Cambridge, Mass.: Harvard University Press, 1967. $7.95.

For its many useful insights, this is a work that invites reflection from its opening pages. Professor Bullock begins by asserting that slavery, however unintentional, opened a "hidden passage" to educational opportunity inasmuch as a trained bondman brought a good price on the market. The Civil War and Reconstruction periods gave rise to public schools in the South, some of them racially mixed and all based on the principle of an undifferentiated curriculum for whites and Blacks alike. But this interlude soon gave way to an insistence by white people on vocational education for Negroes, a development which Bullock styles the "great detour." However, this too bore the seeds of its own dissolution. In spite of itself, the Southern school system bred a large number of Negroes who were unwilling to settle for unequal educational opportunity. A corps of college-trained leaders, aided by Negro protest organizations and the Negro press, began to step up their demands, culminating in the movement to desegregate the schools.

Bullock takes a broad view as to what is encompassed by the term education, not confining himself to such stand-by's as the work of philanthropic agencies, like the Rosenwald Fund, or the statistical tables showing the racial differentials in per capita pupil expenditure. Reflecting the viewpoint that the influence of the schools is pervasive, Bullock ranges from the portrayal of a literary movement, such as the Harlem Renaissance, to a description of the social mechanisms employed to make the Negro think of himself as a lesser being. But on whatever he touches, Bullock has his materials well in hand. Indeed, it would be hard to find a clearer description of the aftermath of the 1954 Supreme Court decision, as it affected both public school desegregation and the social order. Reflecting his skills as a sociologist, Bullock's final chapter describes a process which he labels "withdrawal to resegregation," and to which he relates the Black-power dissidents.

Bullock incorrectly identifies the abolitionist Lydia Maria Child; he inexplicably omits John Hope Franklin from the list of Negro historians who received their undergraduate training in the South; he does not indicate the larger, nation-wide impact of vocational education, or that Negroes outside the South had been protesting against Jim Crow education since the 1840's. But putting these caveats aside, Bullock has produced a stimulating work that would richly repay reading by students and teachers in education, race relations, social history, and American thought.

BENJAMIN QUARLES
Professor of History
Morgan State College
Baltimore

LETTERS TO THE EDITOR

Professor Wayne A. Wilcox' challenging analysis of "The Influence of Small States in a Changing World," in the July 1967 issue of THE ANNALS, demonstrates that despite their lack of military or economic power, the small states retain a remarkable degree of influence over world affairs. Unfortunately, Professor Wilcox does not deal with the question of how well the small states have used this influence, or how they might be encouraged to use it more constructively.

He does not mention that the nonaligned eight in the Geneva disarmament talks prodded and shamed the Soviet Union and the United States into agreeing to the 1963 nuclear-test-ban treaty. Certainly, this must be rated as a use of the influence of the small powers that benefited the people of the entire world. Is not the whole pressure of the small states for the diversion of funds from gigantic armament to economic development a constructive thing that should be put in the balance when the role of the small nations is being evaluated?

Professor Wilcox states that very few small states "have found in the United Nations an adequate forum for their pro-jection." Is this the fault of the small states, of the concept of nonalignment, or of the world—and particularly the United States—press? Adlai Stevenson said in a Harvard lecture in 1955 that what he thought the United States needed most was "a good hearing aid."

There are many members of the United States academic community who are critical of the "arrogance of power" in Washington. Why should they not make common cause with the smaller nations who are also challenging the "arrogance of power," but at the level of international diplomacy?

WILLIAM B. LLOYD, JR.
Editor
TOWARD FREEDOM, A Newsletter on New Nations

OTHER BOOKS

ABSHIRE, DAVID M. *The South Rejects a Prophet: The Life of Senator D. M. Key, 1824–1900.* Pp. xii, 250. New York: Frederick A. Praeger, 1967. $5.95.

ADAM, THOMAS R. *Western Interests in the Pacific Realm.* Pp. vi, 246. Paper-bound edition. New York: Random House, 1967. $2.95.

AGARWALA, S. N. *Corrected Age Data on the 1931 Indian Census.* Pp. 104. New York: Asia Publishing House, 1967. $4.75.

AGINSKY, BURT W., and ETHEL G. AGINSKY. *Deep Valley.* Pp. 224. New York: Stein and Day, 1967. $5.95.

ARCHER, PETER, and LORD REAY. *Freedom at Stake.* Pp. 111. Chester Springs, Pa.: Dufour Editions, 1967. $3.50.

ARON, RAYMOND. *Peace and War: A Theory of International Relations.* Translated from the French by Richard Howard and Annette Baker Fox. Pp. xviii, 820. Paper-bound edition. New York: Frederick A. Praeger, 1967. $4.95.

ASHBY, JOE C. *Organized Labor and the Mexican Revolution under Lázaro Cárdenas.* Pp. x, 350. Chapel Hill: University of North Carolina Press, 1967. $7.50.

BARTOS, OTOMAR J. *Simple Models of Group Behavior.* Pp. xii, 345. New York: Columbia University Press, 1967. $8.00.

BELOFF, MAX. *The Balance of Power.* Pp. vii, 73. Montreal: McGill University Press, 1967. $2.95.

BERRY, BRIAN, J. L. BERRY, and JACK MELTZER (Eds.). *Goals for Urban America.*

Pp. vi, 152. Englewood Cliffs, N.J.: Prentice-Hall, 1967. $4.95.

BEYER, GLENN H. *The Urban Explosion in Latin America: A Continent in Process of Modernization.* Pp. xx, 360. Ithaca, N.Y.: Cornell University Press, 1967. $9.95.

BIRD, RICHARD M., and OLIVER OLDMAN (Eds.). *Readings on Taxation in Developing Countries.* Pp. xii, 547. Baltimore: Johns Hopkins Press, 1967. $10.00.

BLAINE, GRAHAM B., JR. *Youth and the Hazards of Affluence: The High School and College Years.* Pp. xi, 144. Paper-bound edition. New York: Harper & Row, 1967. $1.45.

BOMBWALL, K. R. *The Foundations of Indian Federalism.* Pp. xiii, 348. New York: Asia Publishing House, 1967. $6.50.

BOWEN, WILLIAM G., and FREDERICK H. HARBISON (Eds.). *Unemployment in a Prosperous Economy: A Report of the Princeton Manpower Symposium, May 13–14, 1965.* Pp. vii, 173. Paper-bound edition. Princeton, N.J.: Industrial Relations Section, Woodrow Wilson School of Public and International Affairs, and the Princeton University Conference, 1967. $3.00.

BUCK, SOLON J. *Illinois in 1818.* Pp. xiii, 356. Second (Revised) Edition. Chicago: University of Chicago Press, 1967. $7.50.

BUNN, RONALD F., and WILLIAM G. ANDREWS (Eds.). *Politics and Civil Liberties in Europe: Four Case Studies.* Pp. ix, 222. Paper-bound edition. Princeton, N.J.: D. Van Nostrand, 1967. $2.55.

BUSIA, K. A. *Africa in Search of Democracy.* Pp. 189. New York: Frederick A. Praeger, 1967. $4.25.

CADY, JOHN F. *The Roots of French Imperialism in Eastern Asia.* Pp. xiv, 321. Reprint Edition. Ithaca, N.Y.: Cornell University Press, 1967. No price.

CARLSON, PHILLIP G. *Quantitative Methods for Managers.* Pp. viii, 181. Paper-bound edition. New York: Harper & Row, 1967. No price.

CARROLL, FAYE. *South West Africa & the United Nations.* Pp. vii, 123. Lexington: University of Kentucky Press, 1967. $5.00.

CARY, FRANCINE CURRO. *The Influence of War on Walter Lippmann, 1914–1944.* Pp. ix, 184. Madison: State Historical Society of Wisconsin, for the Department of History, University of Wisconsin, 1967. $3.25.

CHIANG CHUNG-CHENG. *Soviet Russia in China: A Summing-up at Seventy.* Translated under the direction of Madame Chiang Kai-shek. Pp. xiv, 218. Second (Revised) Edition. New York: Farrar, Straus and Giroux, 1967. $4.50.

The China White Paper: August 1949, Vols. I and II. Pp. xli, 1,079. Paper-bound edition. Stanford, Calif.: Stanford University Press, 1967. $5.95.

COHAN, AVERY B. *Yields on Corporate Debt.* Pp. xxii, 180. New York: National Bureau of Economic Research (Distributed by Columbia University Press), 1967. $7.50.

Congress and the President: Readings in Executive-Legislative Relations. Selected by Walter Earl Travis. Pp. vi, 179. New York: Teachers College Press, 1967. $5.75.

CONQUEST, ROBERT (Ed.). *Industrial Workers in the U.S.S.R.* Pp. 203. New York: Frederick A. Praeger, 1967. $6.25.

———. *The Politics of Ideas in the U.S.S.R.* Pp. 175. New York: Frederick A. Praeger, 1967. $5.25.

COX, DONALD F. (Ed.). *Risk Taking and Information Handling in Consumer Behavior.* Pp. xiii, 667. Boston: Division of Research, Graduate School of Business Administration, Harvard University, 1967. $10.00.

CRICK, BERNARD (Ed.). *Essays on Reform, 1967: A Century Tribute.* Pp. vii, 222. New York: Oxford University Press, 1967. $4.80.

DANDEKAR, KUMUDINI. *Communication in Family Planning: Report on an Experiment.* Pp. xii, 109. New York: Asia Publishing House, 1967. $3.25.

DEMERATH, N. J., III, and RICHARD A. PETERSON (Eds.). *System, Change, and Conflict: A Reader on Contemporary Sociological Theory and the Debate over Functionalism.* Pp. viii, 533. New York: Free Press, 1967. $9.95.

DEMPSTER, PRUE. *Japan Advances: A Geographical Study.* Pp. xviii, 329. New York: Barnes & Noble, 1967. $12.00.

DENISON, MERRILL. *Canada's First Bank,* Vols. I and II: *A History of the Bank of Montreal.* Pp. xxxii, 923. New York: Dodd, Mead, 1967. $15.00.

DEY, S. K. *Sahakari Samaj: The Co-operative Commonwealth.* Pp. 138. New York: Asia Publishing House, 1967. $4.00.

DORE, R. P. (Ed.). *Aspects of Social Change in Modern Japan.* Pp. x, 474. Princeton, N.J.: Princeton University Press, 1967. $9.50.

DUBOIS, W. E. B. *The Philadelphia Negro: A Social Study.* Pp. xliv, 520. Paper-bound edition. New York: Schocken Books, 1967. $2.95.

EDINGER, LEWIS J. (Ed.). *Political Leadership in Industrialized Societies: Studies in Comparative Analysis.* Pp. vii, 376. New York: John Wiley & Sons, 1967. $8.95.

THE AAPSS

THE CHANGING AMERICAN PEOPLE: ARE WE DETERIORATING OR IMPROVING?

THE OFFICERS AND DIRECTORS ANNOUNCE
THE SEVENTY-SECOND ANNUAL MEETING OF
THE AMERICAN ACADEMY OF POLITICAL AND
SOCIAL SCIENCE

APRIL 5 AND 6, 1968
THE BENJAMIN FRANKLIN HOTEL
PHILADELPHIA, PENNSYLVANIA

The Annual Meeting, which will be addressed at each session by prominent scholars and officials, will be devoted to a qualitative appraisal of the changing American, and will attempt to provide an answer to the question whether he is deteriorating or improving. Approximately 1,000 persons will be in attendance sometime during the two days of sessions, who will represent cultural, civic and scientific organizations in the western world.

Proceedings of this 72nd Annual Meeting will be published as the July issue of THE ANNALS.

MEMBERS ARE CORDIALLY INVITED TO ATTEND AND WILL AUTOMATICALLY RECEIVE FULL INFORMATION · FOR DETAILS, WRITE TO: THE AMERICAN ACADEMY OF POLITICAL AND SOCIAL SCIENCE · BUSINESS OFFICE · 3937 CHESTNUT STREET, PHILADELPHIA, PENNSYLVANIA 19104

ELDREDGE, H. WENTWORTH (Ed.). *Taming Megalopolis*, Vol. I: *What Is and What Could Be*; Vol. II: *How to Manage an Urbanized World*. Pp. xxii, 1,166. New York: Frederick A. Praeger, 1967. $18.50.

FEIWEL, GEORGE R. *The Soviet Quest for Economic Efficiency: Issues, Controversies and Reforms*. Pp. xx, 420. New York: Frederick A. Praeger, 1967. $15.00.

FISHER, BERNICE M. *Industrial Education: American Ideals and Institution*. Pp. xiii, 267. Madison and Milwaukee: University of Wisconsin Press, 1967. $6.50.

FISHER, PAUL L., and RALPH L. LOWENSTEIN (Eds.). *Race and the News Media*. Pp. x, 158. New York: Frederick A. Praeger, 1967. $4.95.

FRANKE, WOLFGANG. *China and the West*. Translated by R. A. Wilson. Pp. viii, 165. Columbia: University of South Carolina Press, 1967. $5.95.

FRAZIER, E. FRANKLIN. *Negro Youth at the Crossways: Their Personality Development in the Middle States*. Pp. xxxv, 299. Paper-bound edition. New York: Schocken Books, 1967. $2.45.

FREUND, PAUL A. *On Law and Justice*. Pp. vi, 259. Cambridge, Mass.: Harvard University Press, 1967. $4.95.

FRIEDMANN, W. *Legal Theory*. Pp. xx, 607. Fifth Edition. New York: Columbia University Press, 1967. $12.00.

GALTUNG, JOHAN. *Theory and Methods of Social Research*. Pp. 534. New York: Columbia University Press, 1967. $10.00.

GETZ, ROBERT S. *Congressional Ethics: The Conflict of Interest Issue*. Pp. vi, 202. Paper-bound edition. Princeton, N.J.: D. Van Nostrand, 1967. $1.95.

GOLDMAN, THOMAS A. (Ed.). *Cost-Effectiveness Analysis: New Approaches in Decision-Making*. Pp. xvi, 231. New York: Frederick A. Praeger, 1967. $13.50.

GOLDSCHMIDT, WALTER. *Sebei Law*. Pp. xiii, 303. Berkeley and Los Angeles: University of California Press, 1967. $7.50.

GOLLIN, GILLIAN LINDT. *Moravians in Two Worlds: A Study of Changing Communities*. Pp. viii, 302. New York: Columbia University Press, 1967. $8.75.

GOODMAN, JAY S. *The Democrats and Labor in Rhode Island, 1952–1962: Changes in the Old Alliance*. Pp. xi, 154. Providence: Brown University Press, 1967. $5.00.

GRAHAM, HUGH DAVIS. *Crisis in Print: Desegregation and the Press in Tennessee*. Pp. viii, 338. Nashville: Vanderbilt University Press, 1967. $7.50.

GRUBER, JACOB W. (Ed.). *The Philadelphia Anthropological Society: Papers Presented on Its Golden Anniversary*. Pp. ix, 162. Philadelphia: Temple University Publications (Distributed by Columbia University Press), 1967. $7.50.

HANNAH, H. W., and ROBERT R. CAUGHEY. *The Legal Base for Universities in Developing Countries*. Pp. xix, 455. Urbana: University of Illinois Press, 1967. $10.00.

HANSLOWE, KURT L. *The Emerging Law of Labor Relations in Public Employment*. Pp. vi, 117. Paper-bound edition. Ithaca: New York State School of Industrial and Labor Relations, Cornell University, 1967. $2.50.

HAN SUYIN. *China in the Year 2001*. Pp. vii, 268. New York: Basic Books, 1967. $5.95.

HARDIN, CHARLES M. *Food and Fiber in the Nation's Politics*, Vol. III. Pp. xi, 236. Paper-bound edition. Washington, D.C.: U.S. Government Printing Office, 1967. No price.

HARRIS, LEON. *Only to God: The Extraordinary Life of Godfrey Lowell Cabot*. Pp. xiv, 361. New York: Atheneum, 1967. $8.95.

HARTER, LAFAYETTE G., JR., and JOHN KELTNER (Eds.). *Labor in America: The Union and Employer Responses to the Challenges of Our Changing Society*. Pp. 144. Paper-bound edition. Corvallis: Oregon State University Press, 1967. $2.95.

HAYEK, F. A. *Studies in Philosophy, Politics and Economics*. Pp. x, 356. Chicago: University of Chicago Press, 1967. $6.50.

HENDEL, SAMUEL (Ed.). *The Soviet Crucible: The Soviet System in Theory and Practice*. Pp. xiii, 451. Third Edition. Princeton, N.J.: D. Van Nostrand, 1967. No price.

———, and RANDOLPH L. BRAHAM (Eds.). *The U.S.S.R. after 50 Years: Promise and Reality*. Pp. viii, 299. Paper-bound edition. New York: Alfred A. Knopf, 1967. $3.95.

HINSHAW, RANDALL (Ed.). *The Price of Gold: Monetary Reform and Alternative Approaches*. Pp. x, 180. Baltimore: Johns Hopkins Press, 1967. $6.95.

HODDER, B. W., and D. R. HARRIS (Eds.). *Africa in Transition*. Pp. xii, 378. New York: Barnes & Noble, 1967. $8.00.

HOGAN, WILLIAM T. *Depreciation Policies and Resultant Problems*. Pp. x, 130. New York: Fordham University Press, 1967. $4.50.

HOLCOMBE, ARTHUR N. *A Strategy of Peace in a Changing World*. Pp. 332. Cambridge, Mass.: Harvard University Press, 1967. $7.95.

HOUN, FRANKLIN W. *A Short History of Chinese Communism.* Pp. viii, 245. Paperbound edition. Englewood Cliffs, N.J.: Prentice-Hall, 1967. $2.45.

HOWES, ROBERT CRAIG (Eds.). *The Testaments of the Grand Princes of Moscow.* Translated by Robert Craig Howes. Pp. xvii, 445. Ithaca, N.Y.: Cornell University Press, 1967. $10.00.

HULL, ROGER H., and JOHN C. NOVOGROD. *Law and Vietnam.* Pp. xi, 211. Dobbs Ferry, N.Y.: Oceana, 1968. $7.50.

JECCHINIS, CHRISTOS. *Trade Unionism in Greece: A Study of Political Paternalism.* Pp. 205. Paper-bound edition. Chicago: Labor Education Division, Roosevelt University, 1967. No price.

JEFFRIES, SIR CHARLES. *Illiteracy: A World Problem.* Pp. xi, 204. New York: Frederick A. Praeger, 1967. $5.00.

JOUGHIN, LOUIS (Ed.). *Academic Freedom and Tenure: A Handbook of the American Association of University Professors.* Pp. xiv, 343. Madison and Milwaukee: University of Wisconsin Press, 1967. $7.50.

KAPLAN, JACOB J. *The Challenge of Foreign Aid: Policies, Problems, and Possibilities.* Pp. xxviii, 405. Paper-bound edition. New York: Frederick A. Praeger, 1967. $2.95.

KAPLAN, MORDECAI M. *Judaism as a Civilization: Toward a Reconstruction of American-Jewish Life.* Pp. xvi, 601. Paper-bound edition. New York: Schocken Books, 1967. $3.45.

KAYNOR, RICHARD S., and KONRAD F. SCHULTZ. *A Practical Guide to Industrial Development.* Pp. xvii, 336. New York: Frederick A. Praeger, 1967. $15.00.

KIRBY, E. STUART. *Economic Development in East Asia.* Pp. 253. New York: Frederick A. Praeger, 1967. $10.00.

KIRKENDALL, RICHARD S. (Ed.). *The Truman Period as a Research Field.* Pp. v, 284. Columbia: University of Missouri Press, 1967. $6.00.

KITAGAWA, DAISUKE. *Issei and Nisei: The Internment Years.* Pp. viii, 174. New York: Seabury Press, 1967. $5.95.

KITTY, DANIEL R. *Planning for Development in Peru.* Pp. xvi, 196. New York: Frederick A. Praeger, 1966. $12.50.

LAMB, BEATRICE PITNEY. *The Nehrus of India: Three Generations of Leadership.* Pp. vii, 276. New York: The Macmillan Company, 1967. $5.95.

LASLETT, PETER, and W. G. RUNCIMAN (Eds.). *Philosophy, Politics and Society.* Pp. 232. New York: Barnes & Noble, 1967. $5.75.

LAWSON, JOHN. *A New Voyage to Carolina.* Edited by Hugh Talmage Lefler. Pp. liv, 305. Chapel Hill: University of North Carolina Press, 1967. $10.00.

LEIBY, JAMES. *Charity and Correction in New Jersey: A History of State Welfare Institutions.* Pp. xii, 500. New Brunswick, N.J.: Rutgers University Press, 1967. $17.50.

LIPSET, SEYMOUR M., and STEIN ROKKAN (Eds.). *Party Systems and Voter Alignments: Cross-National Perspectives.* Pp. xvi, 554. New York: Free Press, 1967. $9.95.

LLOYD, P. C. *Africa in Social Change.* Pp. 362. Paper-bound edition. Baltimore: Penguin Books, 1967. $1.65.

LOCKHART, R. H. BRUCE. *The Two Revolutions: An Eye-Witness Study of Russia 1917.* Pp. 144. Chester Springs, Pa.: Dufour Editions, 1967. $3.50.

LUBIN, BERNARD, and EUGENE E. LEVITT (Eds.). *The Clinical Psychologist: Background, Roles, and Functions.* Pp. xii, 370. Chicago: Aldine, 1967. $11.75.

LYONS, EUGENE. *Workers' Paradise Lost: Fifty Years of Soviet Communism: A Balance Sheet.* Pp. 387. New York: Funk & Wagnalls, 1967. $6.95.

MACMILLAN, HAROLD. *The Blast of War, 1939–1945.* Pp. xiii, 623. New York: Harper & Row, 1967. $11.95.

MADISON, JAMES. *The Papers of James Madison,* Vol. V: *1 August 1782–31–December 1782.* Edited by William T. Hutchinson and William M. E. Rachal, with the assistance of Jean Schneider and Robert L. Scribner. Pp. xxx, 520. Chicago: University of Chicago Press, 1967. $12.50.

MARTIN, PAUL. *Canada and the Quest for Peace.* Pp. xi, 93. New York: Columbia University Press, 1967. $3.95.

MEAD, DONALD C. *Growth and Structural Change in the Egyptian Economy.* Pp. xv, 414. Homewood, Ill.: Richard D. Irwin, 1967. $8.50.

MELADY, THOMAS PATRICK. *Western Policy and the Third World.* Pp. 199. New York: Hawthorn Books, 1967. $6.95.

MERRIAM, ALAN P. *Ethnomusicology of the Flathead Indians.* Pp. xvi, 403. Chicago: Aldine, 1967. $8.95.

MILLER, RICHARD S., and ROLAND J. STANGER (Eds.). *Essays on Expropriations.* Pp. ix, 165. Columbus: Ohio State University Press, 1967. $5.00.

MILLIKAN, MAX F., and DAVID HAPGOOD. *No Easy Harvest: The Dilemma of Agriculture in Underdeveloped Countries.* Pp. xiv, 178. Paper-bound edition. Boston: Little, Brown, 1967. No price.

INDEX

INDEX

Abortion, U.S., 3, 72, 109, 121, 136–147, 149, 150
 present policies' social dysfunctions, 136, 141–143
 criminalization and guilt, 136, 143
 dangers of illegal abortion, 136, 141
 socioeconomic differentials, 136, 138, 139, 141–143
 present status delineated, 136, 137–141, 142–143
 illegal, 136, 139–141, 142–143
 therapeutic, 136, 138–139, 141–142
 social change and, 136, 137, 143–147
 moral considerations, 136, 146–147
 prospects, 136, 147
 social sources of change, 136, 145–146
 trend toward liberalization, 136, 143–145
 social structure and, 136, 137, 141–143
ABORTION, Edwin M. Schur, 136–147
Acquitaine, 62
Actors Equity, U.S., 23
Adler, Alfred, 100
Adolescence and adolescents, U.S.
 sex and, 5, 18, 19, 20, 25, 27, 28, 29, 34–35, 53–60 passim, 76, 80, 83, 92, 93, 99, 110, 111, 117, 127, 128, 131, 133–134, 150, 153
 sex education and
 church and school, 53–60
 family, 25, 27, 34–35
 sexuality
 depolarization of sex roles, 18, 19–20
 masturbation, 5, 28, 29, 80, 99, 110, 111–112
 social class, 61–75 passim, 76, 80, 83, 110, 111, 117
 See also Juvenile delinquency and delinquents, U.S.
Adultery, 3, 13, 38, 74, 126, 149, 150
Advertising, U.S.
 sexual standards and, 14, 16, 107
Affluence, U.S.
 sexual standards and, 11, 16–17, 84–85, 109, 113
Africa, 75
Agape, 62, 63
Age
 first-marriage statistics, 15–16
 sexuality and, 5, 86–95, 153
 See also Adolescence and adolescents, U.S., Aged and aging, U.S., Children, U.S.
Aged and aging, U.S.
 stereotype of "sexless older years"

factors responsible for declining sex activity, 86, 93–94
 great need for research, 86, 94–95
 growing body of research data, 86, 89–91
 harmful influence of the myth, 86, 88–89
 no automatic cutoff date, 86, 91–93
 self-fulfilling prophecy, 86, 87–88
 unmarried, the, 86, 94
Alabama, 64
Alaska, 56
Alcoholic beverages
 sex and, 22, 66–67, 74, 93, 124, 125, 140, 151, 152, 153
Alcoholism, 149, 153
Alpert, Richard, 97
American Civil Liberties Union, 149
American Dream, An, 38–41, 43
American Law Institute (ALI)
 Model Penal Code
 recommendations on abortion, 144–145, 147, 149
American Medical Association (AMA)
 House of Delegates, 144
American Male, The, 56
Anal intercourse, 39, 133, 149
Andrews, Julie, 23
Anthropology and anthropologists, 11, 71
Apocalypticism, sexual
 in literature of United States "high culture," 36–52 passim
Appalachians
 poor white subculture in Chicago
 sexual patterns, 61, 64–67, 68, 69–74, 75
Archaeology and archaeologists, 22
Architecture, U.S., 18, 22–23
Aristophanes, 88
Aristotle, 62
Arizona, 138
Armed services, U.S., 10
Arnold, Magda, 101
Arson
 pathological, 150, 152, 153–154
Arts, U.S., 18, 23–24, 56
 performing
 depolarization of sex roles and, 18, 23–24
 See also specific arts
Asceticism and eroticism, 62, 77, 84, 87, 99, 114, 117, 130–131
Assault, see Violence, U.S.
Association for the Study of Abortion, 144
Athens, Greece (ancient), 62
Attitudes, U.S.